Teaching Physical Education

Related Benjamin Cummings Kinesiology Titles

Austin/Crawford, *Therapeutic Recreation: An Introduction*, 3e (2001)

Bishop, *Fitness Through Aerobics*, 5e (2002)

Darst/Pangrazi, *Dynamic Physical Education for Secondary School Students*, 4e (2002)

Darst/Pangrazi, *Lesson Plans for Dynamic Physical Education for Secondary School Students*, 4e (2002)

Freeman, *Physical Education and Sport in a Changing Society*, 6e (2001)

Fronske, *Teaching Cues for Basic Sports Skills for Elementary and Middle School Children* (2002)

Fronske, *Teaching Cues for Sport Skills*, 2e (2001)

Powers/Dodd, *Total Fitness: Exercise, Nutrition, and Wellness*, 2e (1999)

McGown/Fronske/Moser, *Coaching Volleyball* (2001)

Metzler, *Badminton* (2001)

Metzler, *Golf* (2001)

Metzler, *Racquetball* (2001)

Carr/Metzler, *Soccer* (2001)

Metzler, *Tennis* (2001)

Poole/Metzler, *Volleyball* (2001)

Pangrazi, *Dynamic Physical Education for Elementary School Children*, 13e (2001)

Pangrazi, *Lesson Plans for Dynamic Physical Education for Elementary School Children*, 13e (2001)

Plowman/Smith, *Exercise Physiology for Health, Fitness and Performance*, 2e (2003)

Schmottlach, *Physical Education Activity Handbook*, 10e (2002)

Silva/Stevens, *Psychological Foundations of Sport* (2002)

Check out these and other Benjamin Cummings Kinesiology titles at:
www.aw.com/bc.

Teaching Physical Education

FIFTH EDITION

Muska Mosston

Sara Ashworth

Benjamin Cummings

San Francisco   Boston   New York
Cape Town   Hong Kong   London   Madrid   Mexico City
Montreal   Munich   Paris   Singapore   Sidney   Tokyo   Toronto

Publisher: Daryl Fox
Acquisitions Editor: Deirdre McGill
Publishing Assistant: Michelle Cadden
Managing Editor: Wendy Earl
Production Editor: Janet Vail
Copy Editor: Anne Friedman
Proofreader: Martha Ghent
Cover and Text Designer: Brad Greene
Compositor: Greene Design
Manufacturing Buyer: Stacey Weinberger
Marketing Manager: Sandra Lindelof

Library of Congress Cataloging-in-Publication Data

Mosston, Muska.
   Teaching physical education / Muska Mosston, Sara Ashworth.-- 5th ed.
     p. cm.
   Includes bibliographical references and index.
   ISBN 0-205-34093-8
   1. Physical education and training--Study and teaching. I. Ashworth, Sara. II Title.

GV361 .M75 2002
613.7'07'1--dc21

                                           2001052816

ISBN 0-205-34093-8

6 7 8 9 10 OPM 08 07 06

www.aw.com/bc

Muska Mosston

1925–1994

This book is dedicated to Muska Mosston.

Born in Israel to Russian immigrants, Muska grew up surrounded by idealism and a sense of purpose. Life focused on realizing dreams, creating new opportunities, and participating in all the aspects of life required for establishing a nation. Muska was a man with myriad interests; he was a concert violist, a gymnast, a soccer player, a paratrooper, a champion decathlon athlete, a horseman, a mountain climber. He participated in what are now termed outward-bound challenge experiences. He played the harmonica, and he was always a flamboyant personality—rejoicing in life and its opportunities. He graduated with the first class at the Wingate Institute in Israel; he earned degrees from City College of New York, a doctorate from Temple University, and an Honorary Doctorate from the University of Jyvaskyla in Finland. He began teaching physical education in the small farming community of Kfar Witkin Israel in the fall of 1945, with sand dunes for his gymnasium and eucalyptus trees for his equipment! After coming to the United States, he taught physics, geometry, math, Hebrew, and physical education. He directed summer camps: one for brain-injured children, another for the blind. He chaired the department of physical education at Rutgers University and was the first to change the name of a physical education department to the Department of Kinesiology & Human Movement. He trained Peace Corps volunteers. He designed playground and physical education equipment that invited inclusion. He had a television program, *Shape-Up,* on CBS in New York City for seven years.

He loved physical education and the opportunities it offered for physical, social, cognitive, ethical, and emotional development. When he saw children being denied opportunities *to think and to move*, he became outraged, and was exasperated by colleagues who seemingly could not expand

MUSKA MOSSTON

1925-1994

their views of what physical education could be. He was magical with children—from top athletes to the most disabled—he would observe children, identify their strengths, their weaknesses, and then create a *spectrum* of *developmental* opportunities for them to discover themselves and rejoice in the process of learning. If success was not forthcoming, he would become engrossed, if not obsessed, in analysis until he could find the missing connection—the conceptual gap that prevented the child from succeeding. Muska was dedicated to the process of *becoming*.

He could not think in a haphazard or random fashion—he needed to know the logical and sequential connections among ideas. This scientific orientation led him to seek fundamental and universal concepts like those that form the basis for *Developmental Movement* and *The Spectrum of Teaching Styles*.

Developmental Movement identifies the fundamental attributes that link all physical movements, while *The Spectrum of Teaching Styles* identifies the underlying structure of the teaching-learning process—*decision making*. It is paradoxical that Muska, a person of great energy, charisma, and drama, would discover two theoretical structures that operate independently of a teacher's idiosyncrasies. His concepts expand the base of professional knowledge, and frequently expand the personal boundaries of those who learn the non-versus paradigm.

Both concepts invite deliberation. Although this emphasis on deliberate, conscious teaching sometimes resulted in unfounded attacks. It was repeatedly observed by Mosston and this author that the more teachers demonstrate *with fidelity* the knowledge of the Spectrum, the more capable and spontaneous they become in designing beneficial learning experiences.

Muska Mosston fought to advance the theory and practices of physical education. He was often excluded from active membership in professional organizations by those who disagreed with his strong opinions on *how to improve* physical education. This exclusion did not dissuade him—he merely shifted his energies to general education and continued to scrutinize the validity of the *Spectrum theory* in the total school arena. Years later, invitations from around the world brought Muska back to his first professional love—physical education. The *Spectrum of Teaching Styles* has been implemented at all grade levels and in all subject matters. The fact that *decision making* is the underlying element that shapes teaching-learning events is no longer debated.

Muska Mosston was a pioneer who discovered a new paradigm about teaching and learning. I feel honored and grateful to have been Muska's colleague and friend for 25 years. In the last years of his life, he considered himself an educational ambassador, spreading the humanitarian message of the Spectrum and the ideas of the universal concepts of *developmental movement* across cultural boundaries and political agendas. He profoundly touched people's lives. He was an inspiration, undaunted by rejection, faithful to his mission, and dedicated to improving the practices in teaching and learning.

May his legacy be that he is remembered as the *Discoverer of The Spectrum of Teaching Styles: From Command to Discovery.*

Sara Ashworth
Tequesta, Florida

Forewords

The gap between what we say we want to do and what we are doing in practice has been and still is the main problem in physical education, as it is in many branches of education. I have read numerous curriculum books with their goal taxonomies and subject matter lists, and cookbook style methodology books, which list different kinds of teaching methods. Although excellent analyses of goals of physical education can be found in those books, as well as detailed instructions on how to teach different kinds of activities, the most important issue is lacking: a clear bridge between goals and actions. When I first read Muska Mosston's book in the 1960's I was charmed by his systematic and clear approach to bridging the gap between intention and action.

There is substantial consensus among physical education experts that the field's most important goals are to promote life-long physical activity and to support the physical, psychological and social development of school-aged youth. In more concrete terms, these goals mean, among other things, development of intrinsic motivation for physical activity, strengthening the self-concept, learning to take personal responsibility and adopting cooperative skills. When these kinds of objectives are provided, students learn to be independent, to make decisions concerning their learning process, and to feel responsibility for themselves and for others. This is precisely one of the basic ideas of the Spectrum, namely to shift decision making and responsibility, little by little, from teacher to student.

For many years I had the privilege and pleasure of following the fruitful collaboration between Muska Mosston and Sara Ashworth. I learned how the professional dialogue between these two authors developed the Spectrum. From the very beginning the Spectrum was for me a strong cognitive, as well as an aesthetic, experience. Just as mathematicians refer to solutions as beautiful or elegant because of their internal logic, the Spectrum is a logically beautiful system. Its logic makes it universal.

That this opinion is not only my personal idea is evidenced by the fact that the Spectrum has been used in all continents and has been translated to many languages. This also indicates that Spectrum is not only an American system but it really is universal. After the fourth edition, Sara Ashworth very successfully continued developing the beauty and cleanness of the Spectrum. With the amendments to the fifth edition, *Teaching Physical Education* is a book which should belong to and be used by every teacher trainer and teacher of physical education.

Risto Telama, Professor Emeritus
University of Jyvaskyla
Department of Physical Education
Jyvaskyla, Finland

Teaching Physical Education can change your life as a teacher. It has mine. It is a book that I've held close through nearly forty years of teaching. Many ideas about effective teaching can be found within its covers but, most importantly, it will enable you to better translate your intent as a teacher into purposeful action.

This book is about The Spectrum of Teaching Styles—a unified theory of teaching. Any theory attempts to explain a phenomenon based on a set of principles. In this case, the phenomenon is teaching, and the organizing principle is that teaching can be defined in terms of decision-making. Other theories about teaching exist, but none is as intuitive or as elegant as the Spectrum. You will learn about a continuum, a spectrum, of teaching styles, each of which is defined by who, teacher or learner, makes which decisions. Each style is unique in terms of the learning conditions it engenders; yet each is connected to an integrated whole—a spectrum. You will learn about the relationship of each style to the three essential elements of any teaching transaction: teacher, learner and content.

In introducing the Spectrum I've used the word elegant advisedly. This adjective implies richness, grace, and refinement. It implies, simultaneously, simplicity and complexity. A spider's web and a snowflake are elegant structures. As you will see, the Spectrum is indeed elegant. Yet it is also practical, intuitive, and fundamentally humane. Intuitive in the sense that it is user-friendly. Humane in the sense that it clarifies and amplifies that essential human-to-human interaction we call teaching.

As you go through the chapters of this book, each new set of ideas will fit together to illuminate an emerging vision about effective teaching. As you complete your initial Spectrum study, you will experience a sense of understanding and challenge. Try out these ideas in your own teaching and, as you do, you will feel more and more comfortable with them. Do not be distracted by the new terminology—these words are explained within Spectrum theory. Learn them and use them. As you begin this journey, set aside your assumptions and postpone judgment. Be open to new ideas.

It is important that you understand that teaching style, in Spectrum terms, has nothing to do with either your interpersonal style or your personal philosophy. We each can learn to competently utilize each style along the Spectrum. The concept of "mobility ability" is about the ability of a teacher to comfortably shift from one teaching style to another to match changing learner objectives. You should aim to learn and practice all the styles so you can achieve mobility ability. This mixing and matching of teaching styles is not only acceptable, it is the hallmark of an effective Spectrum teacher.

The Spectrum is a "universal" theory about teaching—it applies to teaching events. Although written for physical education, the theory is applicable to all content areas. Indeed, on numerous occasions we have observed the collegiality of Spectrum teachers from different disciplines, as they clearly share plans, experiences and triumphs. In my own experience, whenever I've read or heard about a "new" teaching approach, I've analyzed it through the Spectrum rubric of "who makes which decisions" and found that this new approach falls somewhere along the Spectrum. The Spectrum is universal!

It is also a useful conceptual framework for research on teaching. It can serve both to organize results and to frame relevant research questions. In 1973, eminent teaching scholars John Nixon and Larry Locke described the Spectrum as "the most significant advance in the theory of physical education pedagogy in recent history" (p. 1227). They called for a full program of empirical testing. It has been over a quarter century since that encyclopedia article was written, and dozens of research studies focusing on the Spectrum have been completed. Dr. Mark Byra, an accomplished scholar, provides within this book a wonderful review and critique of Spectrum research to date. Suffice it to say, the Spectrum has undergone extensive verification and, without equivocation, there is no question of its validity. Furthermore, these research results have enriched our practice of teaching physical education and have provided new insights about effective teaching.

Many of you reading this book are physical education students about to take your first teaching methods class. Some resist the new terminology and the amount of time that must be devoted to this class. Most people are not used to thinking about their behavior in analytical terms. They think of their behavior as occurring naturally. It is perhaps something they take for granted. But I can assure you that effective teachers spend more hours planning than in front of a class. The Spectrum will provide you with a way of organizing your planning. After using the Spectrum in my teacher education classes for twenty-five years, I can assure you that learning this material will serve you well. If all teachers were Spectrum teachers, education would be much further advanced today and we would be closer to meeting the needs of 21st century children.

As you learn about the Spectrum you are invited to visit the Spectrum website at www.esu.edu/Spectrum. There you will find up-to-date information, examples of episodes, a research page, a chat room, and the names and addresses of Spectrum veterans who would be happy to communicate with you.

Teaching Physical Education by Dr. Muska Mosston was first published in 1966. Mosston didn't invent the elements that make up the Spectrum. Rather, through his extraordinary insight and instinct, he systematically "uncovered" the Spectrum. Just as a physicist or chemist works to reveal the secrets of the natural sciences, so did Mosston work to reveal the underlying structure of teaching and learning. Over the years many of Mosston's colleagues have contributed to the information. After his untimely passing in 1994, Mosston's long-time colleague Dr. Sara Ashworth continued the quest to further delineate the Spectrum theory. Ashworth's numerous insights about the connections among the teaching behaviors have contributed significantly to the Spectrum's refinement. This latest edition will continue Mosston's legacy.

Michael Goldberger, Ph.D.
Professor and Director
School of Kinesiology and Recreation Studies
James Madison University
Harrisonburg, VA

Contents

Preface

Muska Mosston formulated *The Spectrum of Teaching Styles* and presented it to the field of physical education over thirty years ago. His theory continues to influence pedagogy because it offers a universal, comprehensive body of knowledge about teaching and learning. The Spectrum's theory, which is based on decision-making, delineates landmark teaching and learning options (styles/behaviors). Each successive behavior is derived from the systematic, cumulative shifting of decisions from teacher to learner. The cluster of decisions shifted in each style creates a distinctive set of learning objectives; consequently, each teaching style is a *landmark* decision-relationship that leads both teacher and learners to a specific set of learning objectives and outcomes.

The theoretical progression from one landmark style to another shows the relationships and connections among the styles, and the contributions of each style to various educational ideas and programs. The Spectrum does not designate any single behavior as superior to the others, nor does it prescribe a linear implementation order; rather it offers a range of styles to draw upon according to the objectives that are the focal point of the learning experience. The educational value and contributions of the Spectrum to learners can only be achieved when the full range of teaching-learning styles are used appropriately.

Several major changes in the Spectrum theory have occurred over the last thirty years. Perhaps the most significant change has been the shift in the schematic representation of the Spectrum. The cone-shaped diagram in

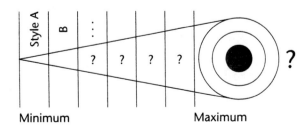

Figure 0.1. Diagram of the Spectrum—1966

Mosston's first edition represented his preferences at the time. He wanted to move the profession from its predominant teaching style (the Command Style) to discovery teaching-learning experiences.

But this cone-shaped diagram was inconsistent with the non-versus premise of the Spectrum—that all behaviors contribute to educational objectives, and that no one behavior is more important than any other. When a student at Rutgers University brought this conflict between theoretical intention and schematic representation to Mosston's attention, he changed the diagram. The schematic representation of the Spectrum is now a continuum with equal spaces and dotted lines representing the incremental, yet cumulative, shift of decisions and the design variations that exist between landmark styles.

Figure 0.2. Current Diagram of the Spectrum

Another change from the first to this fifth edition is the precision with which decisions are analyzed to distinguish one behavior from another. Each landmark style is defined by its decisions, which inherently produce specific objectives. This precision in analyzing decisions led to the addition of several new landmark teaching-learning behaviors (and to eliminating one—*the small group style*). The more Mosston and this author observed actual classroom events to research the assumptions of the Spectrum, the more we realized that decisions are the pivotal element in the chain of events that form the teaching-learning relationship.

This fifth edition incorporates many theoretical and practical changes made since the fourth edition. For example, (1) because of their importance and applicability to all teaching-learning styles, separate chapters are provided on feedback, cognition, and designing subject matter. (2) All classroom implementation shares a sequence; therefore, a chart has been designed, which offers greater ease when designing the *sequence of events* in each episode. Awareness of this shared sequence allows teachers to re-think the way they deliver expectations and how to incorporate alternative behavior expectations in episodes. (3) The *Anatomy of Any Style* identifies and defines the decisions that are intrinsic to all teaching episodes. Although this is the key to understanding the decision shifts that define each new teaching-learning behavior, it is frequently misunderstood. This text provides expanded information about the importance and use of the Anatomy. (4) This edition clarifies the important role the Developmental Channels play in providing increased opportunities for teachers to create new design variations within and between each style. The attributes along the Developmental Channels add vitality, variation, and diversity to all teaching-learning styles.

In the Preface to the first edition of *Teaching Physical Education*, (1966), Mosston stated that "The identification of each style, its premise, its operational design, and its implications strengthen the teaching process and elevate it to the level of consciousness and deliberation." This goal *to achieve an elevated level of consciousness and deliberation* remains the primary goal of this revised edition of the Spectrum of Teaching Styles.

The Spectrum has transcended cultural and national boundaries. It has been used with children and adults and has been applied to many subject matter contents. Mosston and this author gave hundreds of workshops together on four continents. During the years with the Center on Teaching in New Jersey, we gave over 250 presentations. In 1984-85 a lecture in Scotland turned into an eleven-month lecture tour during which we gave 87 presentations in eleven European countries. Mosston's itinerary for 1994 included presentations in Greece and Crete, Venezuela, Israel, Sweden, and Colorado and Virginia in the USA. Unfortunately, he passed away in July 1994, before his scheduled presentations in Puerto Rico, The Netherlands, and Taiwan.

The Spectrum continues to offer teachers an expanded view of pedagogy—a teaching repertoire that offers learners opportunities to develop a broad range of educational objectives. Anyone who desires to reach for a non-versus pedagogical approach, rich in alternatives, can benefit from learning the Spectrum from Command to Discovery.

Acknowledgments

The magnitude of the Spectrum's influence in the field of physical education is due to our many colleagues around the world. They are responsible for establishing the Spectrum as a recognized theory. Muska and I were always grateful for those colleagues who implemented the ideas, conducted research, and offered insights that helped clarify and refine the theory. Friends made through the Spectrum now share the loss of Muska, however, each of us remains committed to continuing the development and implementation of the Spectrum. For those of us who knew Muska, we continue to be energized and inspired by his memories.

For fear of leaving out a colleague's name, I choose to omit listing the many names of dear Spectrum colleagues, from around the world, who have been involved in the Spectrum. To each of you, I thank you very much.

Several colleagues provided their classroom Spectrum materials for this book. They were so generous with their lessons that there are enough materials for another book of just Spectrum examples! Thank you, Dr. Mark Byra of University of Wyoming, WY, Dr. Joanne Dusel of Towson University, MD, and Dr. Phil Gerney of Newtown, PA.

I also wish to thank the reviewers of this edition: Mark Byra, University of Wyoming; Carol Alberts, Hofstra University; Betty Block, Georgia College and State University; and Christopher Malone, SUNY Cortland.

It is necessary to thank several editors who helped shape this text. I am grateful to Susan Cumins for her continued assistance, over several years, to see this project to completion. She began this project as an editor but in the process has become a Spectrum colleague. My thanks to Constance Earl, whose role as a mentor shaped my first years as a teacher. Because of her I attended a conference in Memphis, Tennessee, in 1969, where I met Muska when he presented the *slanted rope concept*. Attending that conference presentation changed my life. To Emily Grace, a physical educator at the University of Mississippi for twenty-five years, your editorial comments from the perspective of a novice to the Spectrum, were invaluable and very much appreciated. A special thanks to both Shawn Pennell for her talented graphic art contributions, and to Elissa Rudolph for providing the final touches of layout consistency.

And finally, I wish to express my gratitude to Larry Tabat, my husband, who taught me to understand the concept that this is now and that was then. Thanks for your humor, which sustained us during this process, and for honoring my commitment to the Spectrum. You are my dream-maker. You always showed me how to create paths to my dreams.

Sara Ashworth
Tequesta, Florida

CHAPTER 1

Key Factors That Shape All Teaching

In 1966 Muska Mosston introduced the Spectrum of Teaching Styles to the field of Physical Education.[1] Since that time, his theory about teaching, which identifies a unifying framework that delineates alternative teaching–learning styles, has permeated the literature. The Spectrum theory has been referenced continuously in most physical education method textbooks for three decades (Metzler, 2000; Graham, Holt, & Parker, 1998; Pangrazi, 1998; Rink, 1993; Siedentop, 1991; Hellison, 1985; Mitchell & Wright, 1977). In spite of this sustained recognition, many facets of the Spectrum remain unused.

Over the years, readers have requested that specific issues be addressed about and within the Spectrum. This book attempts to address those issues and to present the latest details, refinements, and discoveries of the Spectrum theory. For the new reader, this chapter offers the necessary background information for understanding the overall contributions of the Spectrum theory to teaching and to learning. How did the Spectrum evolve and why is it such a unique theory?

---

[1] The phrase *Spectrum of Teaching Styles* was coined in the mid-1960s to designate this particular framework for teaching. The term *teaching style* was selected to differentiate the descriptions of specific teaching behaviors from contemporary terms of that time. Terms like *methods, models, approaches, strategies,* and *techniques* were used and are still being used in many different ways by different writers. Recently, the term *style* has been used to mean personal qualities. In publications on the Spectrum, the term *teaching style* refers to a structure that is independent of one's idiosyncrasies. To avoid possible confusion, the term *teaching behavior* will be alternated with Mosston's term *teaching style*. In this text the terms—style, behavior, method, approach—carry the same meaning: decision patterns that define *the teacher's and the learners' actions so that a prescribed set of objectives can be accomplished.*

A Paradigm Shift

The gradual discovery of the Spectrum came about as Mosston thoroughly studied every facet of education. His study led to the identification of three primary issues that shaped the direction of thought about teaching and learning. Understanding these three issues provides the foundation from which Mosston's new paradigm emerged:

1. The versus approach
2. The role of idiosyncrasies
3. The inconsistent use of terminology

The Versus Approach

Mosston discovered that ideas in education are generally presented *in opposition to* the status quo. For example, in pedagogy, individualization is pitted against socialization, the cognitive movement against the affective movement, direct vs. indirect instruction, the humanists vs. the behaviorists, etc. The versus approach extends to content areas. In physical education, it is action vs. motor approach, games vs. fitness, sports vs. recreation, etc. Often these ideas, proposed to redirect and reshape education, emerge from crisis situations, individual preferences, fads, political interventions, or short-lived movements. This educational "tug-o-war" has created fragmentation and separation. It has prevented the profession from systematically approaching teaching and learning from a broad structure that would both embrace and connect ideas.

Because of the versus approach, educators are constantly asked to abandon existing theories for the sake of new ones. Each teacher has experienced the various fads and movements that have directed the profession, from emphasis on socialization, character education, multiple intelligences, and currently, to content standards, etc. Since each of these programs, as worthwhile as they might be, represent only a portion of what teaching–learning can embrace, the programs are eventually replaced with a different emphasis. In time, programs reappear under new names. Historically, ideas in education have been introduced using the versus and the cyclical approach.

Because the versus approach rejects ideas, it limits educational practices. Mosston's discovery of the limitations of a versus approach led him to seek a unifying framework, one that would invite, absorb, and link new ideas into a system. Such a non-versus system honors the full range of educational ideas, thus rejecting none.

The Role of Idiosyncrasies

Both the versus and the cyclical approaches continually ask teachers to *abandon* ideas. This perpetual shifting and refocusing prevents teachers from accumulating knowledge, from seeing the larger pedagogical picture, from relying on any set of ideas for too long. Consequently, teachers must be strong, resilient, and resourceful. They must not only give meaning to, and breathe life into educational terminology, but they also must learn to flow from one fad or movement to another. Without the benefit of a broad professional system and/or a reliable theoretical foundation, they approach this daunting task of daily teaching from an idiosyncratic approach. That is, each teacher, according to his or her personal understanding and previous experiences, decodes theory into daily practice. As a result, today's classrooms are characterized by an idiosyncratic approach to the implementation of pedagogical theories.

Because an idiosyncratic approach represents personal interpretations and biases, it limits educational practices. Mosston's discovery that one's idiosyncrasies represent only a portion of what teaching can be led him to search for a body of knowledge about teaching that was beyond his idiosyncratic preferences and behavior. Such an approach honors the full range of educational ideas, without injecting personal interpretations or biases.

The Inconsistent Use of Terminology

As Mosston investigated pedagogical approaches, he observed that commonly-used terms often had little consistency or uniformity. He found that a lack of conceptual agreement, variability in meanings, and contradictory results in the educational literature were more often the norm than the exception.

Without professional consistency in terminology, reliable communication, accurate implementation, and assessment of ideas is difficult, if not impossible. Imprecise terminology allows teachers, supervisors, and researchers to interpret events differently. They then make assumptions about what they do in the classroom or make research conclusions that are unreliable and at times inaccurate. Fundamental professional terminology requires consensus. An understanding of the fundamental knowledge in a profession is the *minimum* level of quality management that a profession can have. Without it, each individual in the organization defines his or her specific standards and establishes the quality of events.

Because inconsistent use of terminology creates confusion and leads to misinterpretation of events, it limits educational practices. Mosston's realization that inconsistent terminology was a major reason for inconsistent learning led him to search for a systematic approach to teaching that precisely delineates events, terms, definitions, and implementation procedures. Mosston's framework embraces a non-versus approach to teaching; it logically and sequentially presents this body of knowledge, providing any teacher with the opportunity to learn the structure and options in teaching—a Spectrum from Command to Discovery. Such an approach honors, with reliability, the full range of educational ideas.

The identification of these three issues served as the foundation for Mosston's paradigm shift—the versus approach, the role of idiosyncrasies, and inconsistent terminology. These issues caused him to think differently about teaching and learning.

The Spectrum

The three issues identified above forced Mosston to examine the act of teaching and learning from the structural approach rather than from preference or situational need. *What is the body of knowledge about teaching that is beyond idiosyncratic behavior?* That inquiry led Mosston to the discovery that *teaching behavior is a chain of decision making.* The literature on teaching no longer contests that assumption, rather it supports Mosston's axiom about teaching. Good & Brophy (1997, p. 358) state, "Once again we see that teacher decision making, guided by clear goals, is the key to effective instruction." Westerman's summary of the literature on teaching concluded that "decision making is involved in every aspect of a teacher's professional life" and that a "teacher's thinking and decision making organize and direct a teacher's behavior and form the context for both teaching and learning" (Wilen, et al, 2000, p. 2).

What remains unacknowledged and absent from current statements about teaching is the delineation of the specific decisions that are inherent to teaching. Mosston stated "… neither teacher nor student can make decisions in a vacuum. Decisions are always made about something. This 'something' is the subject matter of teaching and learning" (Mosston, 1966a, p. 3). (See Chapter 3 *The Anatomy of Any Teaching Style* for the specific decisions).

These decisions *are always made* (deliberately or by default) in every teaching–learning event, independent of the teacher's emphasis in the decision making process. Mosston's identification of specific decisions that comprise *any* teaching–learning behavior is the critical and pivotal discovery that led to a systematic and universal approach to teaching—the Spectrum from Command to Discovery. When the specific decisions were arranged according to *who makes which decisions about what and when*, Mosston observed that mutually exclusive learning objectives resulted.

The Spectrum delineates teaching–learning options. It equips teachers with the fundamental knowledge for developing a repertoire of professional behaviors that embrace all the objectives needed to connect with and to educate students. Fundamental to the structure of the Spectrum is that all teaching styles are beneficial for what they *can* accomplish; none is more important, or more valuable, than another. Rather than directing one's teaching toward any one behavior, the goal of the Spectrum for teachers is to demonstrate *mobility ability*. Proficient Spectrum teachers have the ability to shift among the behaviors, as needed, to accommodate learners' needs, content focus, time constraints, and the myriad goals of education.

It is the configuration of selected decisions that determines specific behaviors that deliberately draws teaching closer to learning. Without knowledge about decisions and the ability to manipulate them, the versus and idiosyncratic approaches to teaching and learning will remain prevalent. Names, labels, and projections of objectives and outcomes alone do not define alternative teaching–learning behaviors—*decisions do*. Teaching intentions, learning objectives, and outcomes are the expressed results of the teacher's and learners' patterns in decision making

The teaching–learning behaviors within the Spectrum are tools for accomplishing the various functions of education. A hammer is a tool. It is only one tool among many. This tool satisfies a particular *kind* of need. Although hammer designs may vary, all hammers share the same primary function. Sometimes a shoe can be used to perform the function of a hammer and sometimes a hand is used. In teaching, because of the possibilities in shifting the decisions, there is a myriad of teaching–learning behaviors. Each has a unique educational function in all design variations, and each can be configured appropriately or inappropriately. Tools are not *the process* but, as in any profession, tools are invaluable for reaching the overall intended purpose. A repertoire of teaching–learning behaviors is the tool that all teachers rely on for creating worthwhile and challenging learning experiences.

How the teacher plans, selects, and sequences the content, feels about students, and envisions successful classroom learning experiences is not accidental; it primarily reflects the teacher's knowledge. The teacher's professional and personal knowledge and beliefs are sources from which the teacher makes decisions (deliberately or by default) to create classroom events.

The Spectrum is offered to teachers who wish to examine the tools they have, and to see if there may be others they can learn to use in the teaching–learning process. Learners rely on teachers to offer them the full range of educational ideas; therefore, a repertoire of teaching–learning behaviors is fundamental for both teachers and learners.

The Spectrum's framework proposes a paradigm shift in the ways we look at teaching. This book presents that framework. Mosston's Spectrum is a *system* that:

1. Delineates the range of options that exist within teaching and learning
2. Identifies the unique objectives of each option
3. Identifies the specific set of decisions that must be made by the teacher and learner in each option for the objectives to be reached
4. Identifies the placement of one teaching style relative to the others, based on the incremental and cumulative shifting of decisions
5. Acknowledges the design variations that exist within each style
6. Provides a variety of options for examining subject matter
7. Predicts events
8. Shows the relationship among scattered and seemingly random ideas
9. Integrates disparate research findings to support the larger system rather than promote any single idea
10. Serves as a model that can assist in determining the congruence between intent and action

Most significantly, the Spectrum provides teachers with the fundamental theoretical knowledge necessary for building a learning environment that offers learners the full range of educational opportunities.

The Benefits of a Universal Theory

Good and Brophy observed, "We have discussed behaviors that teachers engage in without full awareness and noted that even when teachers are aware of their behavior they may not realize its effects. We believe that teachers' lack of awareness about their behavior or its effects lessens their classroom effectiveness" (1997, p. 35). A universal model of teaching would equip teachers with the knowledge needed to be deliberate when designing and assessing teaching–learning events. Universal theories explain events and reliability shows the connections and relationships among events. Therefore, universal models provide information that is consistent and dependable. Reliable information forms the template on which events are planned, predicted, and assessed. Such information does not restrict ideas; rather, it provides a steady foundation from which new ideas and investigations can emerge. The universal model delineated in this book empowers teachers by giving them the knowledge they need to become fully aware of, and to understand the effects of, their behaviors.

CHAPTER 2

An Overview

A Framework About Teaching and Learning

W hy is a framework necessary for the understanding of alternative teaching approaches? Why did Mosston search for an underlying structure in teaching and learning? What was the genesis of this idea that motivated Mosston to construct a framework that offers a new paradigm for the theory and practice of teaching? Mosston stated:

> At the time the ideas of the Spectrum came about, I was teaching at Rutgers University presenting my students with ideas, notions, techniques, and experiences in teaching.
>
> One day a student approached me and said: "I want to talk to you about the things you are teaching us." "Certainly," I replied. "What is it?" After a slight pause, the student uttered: "I can't be you!" "Thank you," I responded—and began to walk away. "Furthermore," the student said, "I don't want to be like you." I was quite stunned. I was upset. It took me some time to recover, but that statement kept gnawing at my mind. Is that what I was doing to my students? Did I impose my ideas on them? Did I demand replication of "me"? It was, indeed, a moment of revelation. I realized that my experiences, my idiosyncrasies were mine—solely mine. I realized that they were only a part of the story of teaching. But, what is the other part? Or perhaps other parts? I kept asking myself: What is the body of knowledge about teaching that is beyond my idioysyncractic behavior? Is there such a possibility? Is it possible to identify a framework, a model, a theory that will embrace the options that exist in teaching, or a framework that might embrace future options?
>
> It became clear to me that arbitrary teaching, scattered notions, fragmented ideas, and isolated techniques—successful as they might be—do not constitute a cohesive framework that can serve as a broad, integrated guide for teaching future teachers. The search for a universal structure of teaching had begun.

It has been a search for a "unified theory" that will show and explain the relationship between deliberate teaching behavior and learning behavior, a theory that will identify with consistency the structure of the options in teaching and learning behavior. The search was for a single, unifying principle that governs all teaching—hence the identification of the axiom: Teaching behavior is a chain of decision making. (Mosston & Ashworth, 1994, pp. vii–viii)

In 1966 the search for a theory beyond personal idiosyncrasies resulted in Mosston's Spectrum of Teaching Styles. Since that time, adjustments in various aspects of the styles have been made; however, the theoretical framework that follows has remained constant. The Spectrum is referred to as a universal and unifying framework. A framework is defined as "a structure composed of parts fitted and joined together" [Random House, (1987)), p. 760]. Universal refers to something that is "applicable everywhere or in all cases" (p. 2078), and unifying means "to make or become a single unit, as to *unify conflicting theories*" (p. 2071).

An Overview of the Spectrum

The Spectrum is a theory that is constructed from a single unifying statement.

The fundamental proposition of the Spectrum is that *teaching is governed by a single unifying process: decision making*. Every act of deliberate teaching is a consequence of a prior decision. Decision making is the central or primary behavior that governs all behaviors that follow: how we organize students; how we organize the subject matter; how we manage time, space, and equipment; how we interact with students; how we choose our verbal behavior; how we construct the social-affective climate in the classroom; and how we create and conduct all cognitive connections with the learners. All these concerns are secondary behaviors that emanate from, and are governed by, prior decisions.

Identifying the primary decisions and understanding the possible combinations of decisions opens a wide vista for looking at teacher–learner relationships. Each landmark teacher–learner relationship in the Spectrum has a particular structure of decisions that defines the specific roles of the teacher and the learner and the objectives most predictably reached by each option.

This theory delineates possible teaching–learning decision structures; it presents an axiom that encompasses all teaching–learning approaches; it presents a rationale that explains why each option is sequenced as it is; and it presents the learning focus of each option. This framework is independent of age, content, gender, grade, and ability levels. It is a unifying theory about the structure of teaching and learning.

Six Premises of the Spectrum

Figure 2.1 is the schematic overview of the structure of the Spectrum. This structure is based on six underlying premises, each of which is described as follows:

The Axiom   The entire structure of the Spectrum stems from the initial premise that teaching behavior is a chain of decision making. Every deliberate act of teaching is a result of a previous decision.

The Anatomy of Any Style   The anatomy is composed of the conceivable categories of decisions that must be made (deliberately or by default) in any teaching–learning transaction. These decision categories (which are described in detail in Chapter 3) are grouped into three sets: the pre-impact set, the impact set, and the post-impact set. The pre-impact set includes all decisions that must be made prior to the teaching–learning transaction; the impact set includes decisions related to the actual teaching–learning transaction; and the post-impact set identifies decisions concerning evaluation of the teacher–learner transaction. The anatomy delineates *which* decisions must be made in each set.

The Decision Makers   Both teacher and learner can make decisions in any of the decision categories delineated in the anatomy. When most or all of the decisions in a category are the responsibility of one decision maker (e.g., the teacher), that person's decision-making responsibility is at "maximum" and the other person's (the student's) is at "minimum."

The Spectrum   By establishing who makes which decisions, about what and when, it is possible to identify the structure of eleven landmark teaching–learning approaches as well as alternative approaches that lie between them on the Spectrum.

   In the first style (Style A), which has as its overriding objective precise replication on cue, the teacher makes all the decisions; the learner responds by adhering to all the teacher's decisions. In the second style (Style B), nine specific decisions are shifted from the teacher to the learner and, thus, a new set of objectives can be reached. In every subsequent style, specific decisions are systematically shifted from teacher to learner—thereby allowing new objectives to be reached—until the full Spectrum of teaching–learning approaches is delineated.

The Clusters   Two basic human capacities are reflected within the structure of the Spectrum: the capacity for reproduction and the capacity for production. All human beings have, in varying degrees, the capacity to reproduce known knowledge, replicate models, and practice skills. All human beings have the capacity to produce a range of ideas; all have the

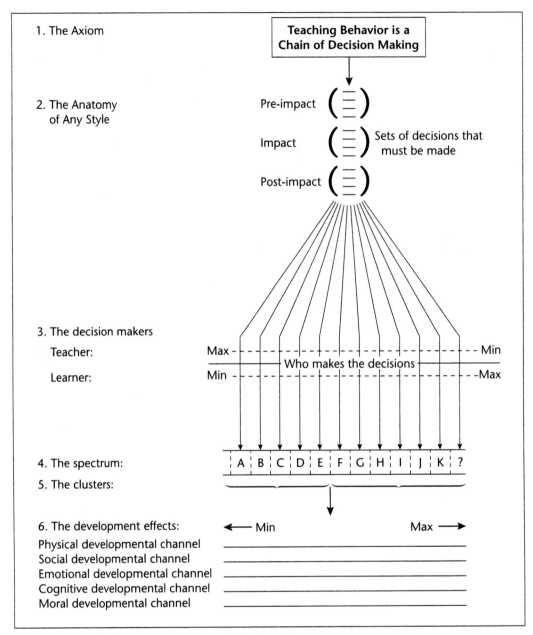

Figure 2.1. The structure of the Spectrum

capacity to venture into the new, thus providing the opportunity to tap the yet unknown.

The cluster of styles A–E represents teaching options that foster reproduction of past knowledge; the cluster of styles F–K represents options that invite production of new knowledge—that is, knowledge that is new to the learner, new to the teacher and, at times, new to society. The line of demarcation between these two clusters is called the *discovery threshold* (Figure 2.2). The threshold identifies the boundaries of each cluster.

Styles A–E are designed for the acquisition of basic skills, the replication of models and procedures, and the maintenance of cultural traditions. Activities in styles A–E engage the learner primarily in cognitive operations such as memory and recall, identification, and sorting—all operations that deal with past and present knowledge. This knowledge includes factual data, names, rules, sequences, procedures, events, dates, computation, and the use of tools and equipment. It also includes the knowledge that is required to perform in music, dance, and sports.

The cluster of styles F–G represents the teaching options that promote the discovery of single correct concepts. The cluster of styles H–K is designed for discovery of divergent responses, alternative designs, and engagement in new concepts. Cognitively, styles F–K invite the learners to go beyond facts and memory—to experience the discovery processes.

The clusters and each of the styles within them are integral parts of our humanity. Each approach contributes to our development, and none seeks (nor merits) supremacy over the others. For both teacher and student, the Spectrum serves as a guide for selecting the style appropriate for a particular purpose, and for each to develop deliberate mobility in moving from one style to another.

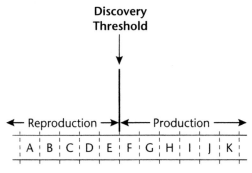

Figure 2.2. The clusters of styles

The Developmental Effects   Perhaps the ultimate question in education and teaching is: What really happens to people when they participate in one kind of an experience or another? The questions *why* and *what for* are paramount in education. The structure of the decisions in each landmark style affects the developing learner in unique ways by creating conditions for diverse experiences. Each set of decisions in the landmark styles emphasizes distinct objectives that learners can develop. Objectives, aside from the content expectations, are always related to human attributes along the cognitive, social, physical, emotion, and ethical Developmental Channels (Figure 2.3). The ability to identify the attributes makes it possible for the teacher to assess the quality and focus of each educational experience. Every teaching event provides opportunities for learners to participate in, and develop, specific human attributes along one or more of the Developmental Channels. Although one channel may, at times, be more strongly in focus than others, all channels function concurrently; it is virtually impossible to isolate experiences to only one channel. Teaching physical activities is unique in that its developmental focus always activates as primary goals the physical and the cognitive channels.

**The Goal of Education is to
Provide Opportunities for Participation and Development Along . . .**

The Developmental Channels

	minimum	maximum

Cognitive _____

Social _____

Emotional _____

Physical _____

Moral/Ethical _____

Figure 2.3. The Developmental Channels

Each Developmental Channel comprises a variety of human attributes—characteristics associated with humanity. For example, attributes primarily emphasized along the social channel include cooperation, communication skills, sharing, being courteous to others, etc. Comparing, sorting, categorizing, interpreting, and imagining are capacities and attributes along the cognitive channel. The above-mentioned attributes are primarily exclusive to one channel; however, other attributes are shared among all channels. All channels can promote and provide experiences that emphasize the attributes of respect, empathy, perseverance, patience, tolerance, self-control, resilience, etc. The manner in which subject matter is designed always emphasizes (overtly or covertly) attributes along the channels. Each channel has an array of attributes that can be selected and joined with the specific content expectations to create the episode's teaching–learning focus.

Perhaps the most important discovery related to the Spectrum has been the influence of the Developmental Channels on *design variations* within and between each teaching–learning behavior. In addition to accomplishing specific content goals, the focus of education is to emphasize the development of people; this development always correlates to specific attributes along the channels. The infinite number and combinations of attributes on the various channels creates the diverse opportunities that can occur in teaching, learning, and curriculum design; consequently, many alternatives within and between each landmark style can be designed.[1] The landmark styles are distinct points that create significantly different learning opportunities. However, variations—shades of the behaviors between the distinct landmark styles—do exist. For example, in the Command style the teacher makes all decisions, while in the Practice style, the learner makes nine specific decisions. If the teacher doesn't make all decisions, is it still the Command style? Likewise, if the learner doesn't make all nine decisions, is it still the Practice style? The Spectrum is a continuum that identifies the landmark behaviors that create significantly different learning experiences; it does not ignore or reject the existence of design variations within or between the landmark styles. In fact it is this multiplicity of design variations, within and between the landmark styles, that produces diverse and creative learning experiences. By identifying landmark behaviors, teachers can readily see the affiliation and the influence of the many design variations that contribute to teaching and learning.

The Spectrum, with its emphasis on the Developmental Channels, provides a framework for studying the influence of each teaching–learning behavior on the learner's developmental experiences.

The O–T–L–O Relationships

The previous section presented an overview of the Spectrum and offered the large picture of the entire structure. This section describes the inseparable relationships among its elements and how they constitute any given episode.

The *interaction* between teacher and learner always reflects a particular teaching behavior, a particular learning behavior, and particular sets of objectives that are reached. The bond among teaching behavior (T), learning behavior (L), and objectives (O) is inextricable. The T-L-O always exists as a unit. This relationship is diagrammed in Figure 2.4.

[1] This notion of design variations within and between each style is also referred to as the *Canopy*.

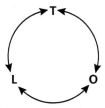

Figure 2.4. The T–L–O relationship

Since each style is defined by the particular behavior of the teacher (the decisions made by the teacher), the particular behavior of the learner (the decisions made by the learner), and the objectives that the relationship reaches, each style has its own distinct T–L–O.

There are always two sets of objectives in any teacher–learner interaction: subject matter objectives and behavior objectives (Figure 2.5). The first set contains specific objectives that pertain to the particular content of the episode (e.g., performing the folk dance, executing the tennis serve, maneuvering the obstacle course, dribbling the basketball, creating new defensive strategies, etc.). The second set contains specific objectives of human behavior (e.g., attributes representing cooperation, self-assessment, honesty, accuracy of performance, self-control, etc.).

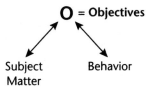

Figure 2.5. The two sets of objectives

Separate objectives for subject matter and behavior always exist in teaching. The T–L decision relationship determines the kinds of objectives that can be reached in the subject matter and in behavior. Conversely, the identification of particular objectives (both in subject matter and in behavior), in advance of the actual T–L interaction, determines which teaching–learning behaviors are more likely to achieve them.

One more aspect of the T–L–O relationship needs to be considered in this context. Objectives are an a priori statement of what is to be achieved in a given episode. At the end of an episode, however, there are always outcomes in both subject matter and behavior. The intended objectives of the episode guide the selection of the particular behaviors (decisions) of the teacher and learners; this interaction always produces *outcomes* in subject matter and behavior. Therefore, the smallest pedagogical unit that embraces the entire process of any single episode constitutes a flow and an interac-

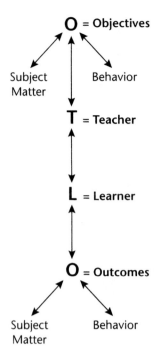

Figure 2.6. The Pedagogical Unit—O–T–L–O

tion of objectives, teaching behavior, learning behavior, and outcomes (O–T–L–O). This flow is diagrammed in Figure 2.6.

Stated differently, the objectives of an episode (O_B) affect the teaching behavior (T), which in turn influences the interaction with the learning behavior (L). This interaction culminates in the particular outcomes (O_U), outcomes in subject matter and in behavior. Then, logically in a successful teaching–learning episode, the outcomes are congruent with the objectives ($O_B = O_U$). In a successful episode, the intent and the action are congruent:

Intent $\cong$ Action

The Need for a Spectrum

There are at least four compelling reasons for developing and using a Spectrum teaching framework. Portions of this section are from Mosston's JOPHER (1992) article:

1. Personal
2. The diversity of the student population
3. The multiple objectives of education

4. The need for a coherent, comprehensive, integrated infrastructure for teaching.

Personal

Sooner or later, every one of us evolves a favorite way of teaching, a personal style that has been successful in our teaching behavior. Our personal style reflects a unique combination of who we are, how we do things, and what we believe about our relationship with students. One might call this unique amalgamation our "idiosyncratic style." With this personal style, each teacher travels through the vicissitudes of his or her career, succeeding in some lessons, failing in others, but generally staying within the parameters of the personal style.

This realization often evokes two points of view. One, that this is what teaching is all about—"I teach my way." The other suggests that being anchored in one's idiosyncrasies (successful as they may be) limits the teacher's options and potential contributions to the students' learning. This point of view raises the question: Is there more to teaching beyond my own experience, my values, my successes? The birth and development of the Spectrum were motivated by this question.

If you have asked yourself this question, then you may add a few more: How many styles do I use in my teaching? Where am I on the Spectrum? Do I know the impact of each style on my students? Am I anchored in a particular style? Am I willing to expand?

Diversity of the Student Population

Students are unique individuals. They learn in different ways and have different needs and aspirations. They come from diverse cultural backgrounds. Our classes mirror this human diversity. In fact, this diversity is the hallmark of our schools. We know it and experience it. We acknowledge it and, at times, we honor it.

Where, then, is the point of entry in teaching diverse students? Assuming for a moment the predominance of personal styles, how can a teacher connect with and reach students who do not respond to his or her personal style? Is it possible that this condition invites exclusion of some students? In our teaching is it possible to create conditions that promote inclusion? Any teacher who wishes to reach more students must learn additional points of entry, and to do so, the teacher must learn additional options in teaching styles.

Multiple Objectives

School curricula are rich in goals and objectives: objectives that span a wide range of human abilities. Physical education encompasses objectives that range from uniformity and synchronization of performance in rowing or precise replication of models in gymnastics, to individualized forms of freestyle swimming and modern dance performance. Objectives range from aesthetics in springboard diving to appreciation of nature during hiking, or from individual skills and tactics in fencing to group cooperation and strategy in team ball games.

This wide range of objectives requires a range of teaching styles, each with its own structure of teaching behavior that invites a particular learning behavior. When the two successfully interact, the specific objective (or set of objectives) can be achieved. Teachers who are willing to expand their teaching repertoire beyond their personal styles and who also wish to reach more objectives and more students are ready to learn additional teaching styles, experiment with them, and then integrate them.

Need for an Integrated Framework

Teaching styles in the Spectrum represent two basic human thinking capacities: the capacity for reproduction and the capacity for production. *Reproduction* thinking seeks replication of ideas, movements, known models, and procedures whereas *production* thinking relies on the discovery of principles, rules, laws, new knowledge, new movements, or the creation of new models.

All humans—in varying degrees of depth and speed—possess these thinking capacities. All subject-matter areas emanate and develop from these capacities. All activities reflect these capacities.

Every activity, every sport, every subject contain aspects that can, and sometimes should, be taught using styles that invite reproduction (replication) and aspects that can and should be taught using styles that invite production (discovery and creativity). The fundamental issue in teaching is not which style is better or best, but rather which style is appropriate for reaching the objectives of a given episode. Every style has a place in the multiple realities of teaching and learning!

For example, in teaching basketball skills, the styles in the reproduction part of the Spectrum are most appropriate. If the episodes focus on developing the psychomotor skills of passing or shooting, the command and practice styles are appropriate. Practice, repetition, and replication of the correct form of the skills, in addition to frequent feedback from the teacher, will improve and sharpen the performance. If the social skill of cooperating with a partner is added as an objective of learning, the reciprocal style is most appropriate. When independence and assessment in practice are to be enhanced, episodes in the self-check style are introduced. When a task can be designed using the principle of the "slanting rope" (a range of degree of difficulty within the same task), inclusion of all participants becomes the objective.

In physical education tasks, many of the objectives in the physical domain can be reached (by many students, but not all) by implementing the first two styles on the Spectrum (Command and Practice styles). However, when other Developmental Channels, attributes, and educational objectives enter the picture, by definition, these two styles alone cannot accomplish them. The other styles on the reproduction side of the Spectrum need to be called on. Relying on this teaching–learning variety is necessary for accomplishing the overall objectives in all activities in physical education from skateboarding, ball games, gymnastics, swimming, skiing, to scuba diving.

Every activity has opportunities for discovering the unknown. There is always a possibility of designing a new strategy in ball games, discovering a new combination of movements in gymnastics, or creating new dances. When these learning behaviors become the objectives of an episode, the teaching styles on the production side of the Spectrum must be recruited. The teacher who aspires to reach the objectives of reproduction and production will inevitably learn by experimenting with the array of styles and will become mobile along the Spectrum. This repertoire will greatly enrich the experiences of the students. This enrichment includes a wide variety of cognitive involvements that are not possible when only the reproduction styles are activated. The discovery and the creative processes require special conditions that are only possible when the production styles are employed in episodes specifically designed for these objectives. Moreover, specific episodes must be designed for specific cognitive operation such as comparing, contrasting, extrapolating, problem solving, and designing.

The structure of the Spectrum is based on the existence of two clusters of styles: one contains the styles that can be used for reproduction (replication), the other contains the styles that invite production (discovery or creativity). Each style in each cluster has a specific purpose. Each style has an active part in the rich variety of teaching–learning objectives; hence, a non-versus view of classroom realities is created, in which no single style is better or best. Each style is best for the objectives it can reach. Teachers no longer must struggle with the "tug-o-war" of selecting the teaching style best suited for their needs and the needs of the students.

The teacher's role in using the Spectrum is to understand the structure of each style, to learn how to incorporate it into a repertoire of teaching behaviors, to experiment with it when teaching different students different tasks, and to refine its operation. It takes time to learn and internalize a new style. It is awkward in the beginning. When trying anything new, one must persist, identify the discrepancies, correct them, and try it again. There is ample evidence that attests to the value of each style. The main challenge is to learn how to use each style for its own unique purpose.

CHAPTER 3

The Anatomy of Any Teaching Style[1]

The anatomy comprises the conceivable categories of decisions that must be made in any teaching–learning transaction. Once Mosston identified the axiom which unified all teaching–learning experiences, he searched to answer: *What are the specific decisions that must be made, or that are being made, in all teaching events?*

After considerable study, Mosston organized the randomly identified decisions that are always being made in all teaching events into three sets. The identification of the unique characteristics of the three sets permitted the clustering of the specific decisions according to their overall purpose (Figure 3.1):

Decision Clusters (Three Sets)	Overall Purpose
Pre-impact	Intent—Objectives
Impact	Action—Implementation
Post-impact	Assessment—Feedback

Figure 3.1. The decisions in any style, clustered according to purpose

1. The pre-impact set defines the intent—planning and preparation decisions.
2. The impact set defines the action—the face-to-face implementation of the pre-impact decisions (the transaction, task engagement, or performance).

[1] Adapted from Mosston, M. and Ashworth, S. *The Spectrum of Teaching Styles.* Copyright 1992 by Sara Ashworth.

3. The post-impact set defines the assessment—including feedback about the performance during the impact and overall evaluation of the congruence between the intent and the action of the learning experience

The ubiquitous decisions within the three sets represent The Anatomy of Any Style (Figure 3.2). All styles function from all the decisions; what makes one style different from another is *who makes which decisions about what and when*. Before identifying who makes which decisions, it is necessary to understand the individual decisions. The three sets cluster the decisions by purpose, not time.

It is incorrect to suggest that the three sets refer to decisions made before, during, and after class. Time is not the factor that conceptually defines or distinguishes the three sets; it is the *purpose* of the decision—either planning, implementation, or assessment. Conceptually, the three sets are a unit, which, when viewed as a whole, delineates a "decision map" (the O–T–L–O) that indicates a specific teaching style.

Because pre-impact decisions take time to prepare in most episodes, these planning decisions are most often made outside the actual face-to-face situation. However, there are situations during the actual transactions or performance (impact set) when additional or alternative planning decisions (pre-impact) must be made. Consequently, planning decisions (pre-impact set) are not restricted to outside the class. The post-impact set embraces decisions about evaluation and feedback. Feedback is not restricted to "after" class—it can and must be offered to students while they are practicing the task (impact set). Therefore, impact and post-impact decisions can occur concurrently. For example, while some learners perform a task (impact), it is possible for the teacher, peers, surrogate authority figure (coach, judge, referee, etc.), to observe these students' performances and offer feedback (post-impact).

It is also possible for evaluation decisions to be made about the overall quality and effectiveness of the teaching–learning experience; these evaluation decisions are made outside the teacher-student time frame.

The order and time frame for making these three decisions may vary, but the category each decision represents remains constant. An accurate conceptual and practical understanding of the Anatomy of Any Style is crucial for proper planning, implementation, and evaluation of the teaching–learning experience.

Understanding the specific decisions, who makes them, how they are made, and for what purpose they are made, leads to insights into the *structure* of the possible relationships between teacher and learner and the consequences of these relationships.

What are specific decision categories in each set that are (deliberately or by default) always present in each teaching episode?

Decisions Sets	Decision Categories

Pre-impact (**Content: preparation**)	1. Objective of the episode
	2. Selection of a teaching style
	3. Anticipated learning style
	4. Whom to teach
	5. Subject matter
	6. Time (when):
	    a. Starting time d. Stopping time
	    b. Pace and rhythm e. Interval
	    c. Duration f. Termination
	7. Modes of communication
	8. Treatment of questions
	9. Organizational arrangements
	10. Where to teach (location)
	11. Posture
	12. Attire and appearance
	13. Parameters
	14. Class climate
	15. Evaluative procedures and materials
	16. Other

Impact (**Content: execution and performance**)	1. Implementing and adhering to the preimpact decisions (1–14) 2. Adjustment decisions 3. Other

Post-impact (**Content: assessment and feedback**)	1. Gathering information about the performance in the impact set
	    (by observing, listening, touching, smelling, etc.)
	2. Assessing the information against criteria
	    (instrumentation, procedures, materials, norms, values, etc.)
	3. Providing feedback to the learner:
	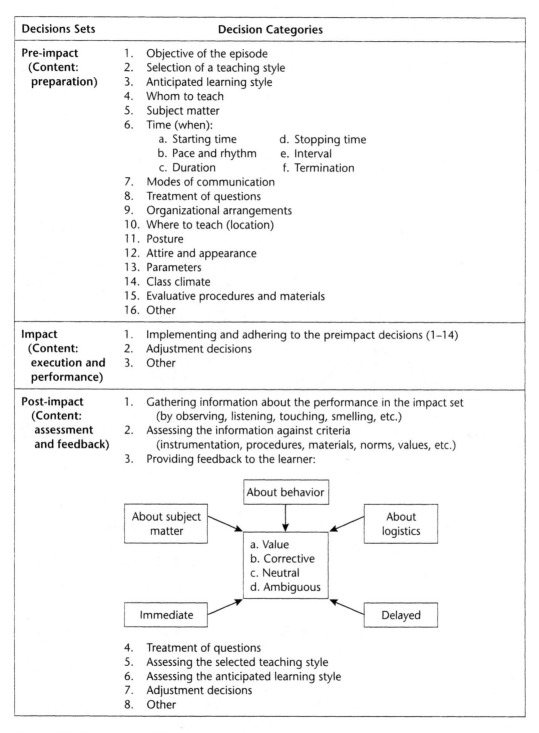
	4. Treatment of questions
	5. Assessing the selected teaching style
	6. Assessing the anticipated learning style
	7. Adjustment decisions
	8. Other

Figure 3.2. The decisions of the Anatomy of Any Style

The Pre-Impact Set

1. *Objective of the episode.* This decision identifies the intent, goal, or purpose of the episode. It answers the teacher's questions: *What do I want to accomplish? What are the learners expected to learn from this episode? What are the specific expectations for this episode? (O–T–L–O)*

2. *Selection of a teaching style.* This category identifies the specific decision patterns—the plan of action—for both the teacher and the learner that will lead to the objectives of the episode (O–T–L–O).

3. *Anticipated learning style.* This decision can be approached in two ways:
    a. If the selection of a teaching style serves as an entry point for the conduct of the episode, then the learning style anticipated is a reflection of the selected teaching style.
    b. If the needs of the learner at a given time serve as an entry point, these needs determine the selection of the teaching style. (L–T–O)

    This dual approach means that, at times, the learner is invited to behave in correspondence to the teaching style. This approach is based on the "non-versus" foundation of the Spectrum—that is, no style is in competition with any other style as the best or most effective teaching–learning style. Each style has its own assets and liabilities; the goal is for teachers and learners to be able to move from one style to another in accordance with the objectives of each episode. The assumption here is that every learner should have the opportunity to participate in a variety of behaviors. In the context of the Spectrum, a learning style is conceived in terms of the learner's ability to make decisions. Therefore, in a given episode, when the teacher is in style X, the learner is also in style X. At other times, the learning style of the student invites the teacher to select the teaching style that corresponds to "where the learner is." The interplay between these two approaches, each possible as entry point to an episode, represents the most crucial decision determining the success of an episode. (For a detailed discussion of this issue, see "Selecting a Style" in Chapter 18.)

4. *Whom to teach.* A decision must be made about the participants in a given episode. In any given class a teacher can address the entire class, part of the class, or individuals. (This decision is separate from the institutional decision concerning who shall attend school, how many will enroll in a given class, etc.)

5. *Subject matter.* This category involves decisions about what to teach and what not to teach. It involves decisions about the knowledge and presentation of the subject matter:
    a. *Subject matter topic/content focus.* This decision takes into account the

reasons—philosophical or practical—for selecting a given learning focus. It answers the questions: *Is this subject matter appropriate for the learners? Relevant? Congruent with the objective?*

b. *Quantity of task(s).* There is no human activity devoid of quantity; therefore, a quantity decision must be made that answers the questions: *How much? How many?*

c. *Quality of performance.* This decision answers the question: *How well? What is expected in the performance of the given task?* (See Chapter 5 for a detailed discussion of quantity and quality of subject matter.)

d. *Order of performance.* This decision answers the question: *In what order (sequential or random) will tasks or parts of tasks be performed?*

6. *Time decisions.* This decision answers questions about when: *at what moment, at what speed,* and *for how long.*

a. Starting time of each specific task

b. Pace and rhythm of the activity—the speed at which the task is performed

c. Duration—the length of time per task

d. Stopping time per task

e. Interval—the time between any two tasks, parts of a task, and/or the time between episodes (Figure 3.3)

f. Termination of the entire episode or lesson

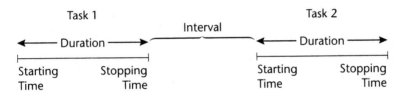

Figure 3.3. The interval decision

7. *Modes of communication.* These decisions concern the modes of communication that will be used in the teaching episode (audio, visual, tactile).

8. *Treatment of questions.* In varying situations, people ask different kinds of questions, and questions can be dealt with in multiple ways. Decisions, therefore, must be made about how to treat questions.

9. *Organizational arrangements.* These are the decisions about various logistical and management needs—materials, space, and time.

10. *Where to teach.* This decision identifies the exact spot—the location—of the teacher and learners.

11. *Posture.* This decision refers to the positioning and carriage of the body during the performance of the task.

12. *Attire and appearance.* A decision must be made about clothing, safety apparel, arrangements of hair, makeup, accessories, etc. that accentuate the content or conduct of the teacher or learners.

13. *Parameters.* These decisions refer to limits, particularly in conjunction with the categories of management of quantity, time, location, interval, posture, and attire and appearance.[2]

14. *Class climate.* Class climate refers to the affective and social conditions that evolve in the physical education setting. These conditions result from the sum total of the decisions referred to in categories 1–13.

15. *Assessment procedures and materials.* Decisions must be made about the assessment that will take place in the post-impact set. *What kind of assessment? What assessment materials and criteria will be used? How to assess the accomplishment of the objectives? What performance quality will and will not be accepted? Which forms of feedback will be used?*

16. *Other.* The Anatomy is an open-ended structure. If another exclusive category is identified, it can be included here.

The Impact Set

This set includes decisions related to the actual face-to-face transaction and performance of the tasks. These decisions define the action—*the implementation.*

1. *Implementing and adhering to the pre-impact decisions.* This category includes decisions about how to execute the decisions in categories 1–14 above during the face-to-face interaction.

2. *Adjustment decisions.* Since planning and performance are not always perfect, and since we learn from our learners during the impact phase, mishaps do occur. When this happens, adjustment decisions must be made. There are two options:
   a. Identify the decision that caused the mishap, correct it, and continue the teaching episode.
   b. If the problem is severe and the decision cannot be immediately identified to remedy the situation, terminate the episode and move on to another activity.

3. *Other.* The model is open-ended.

---

2 We are fully aware that a *parameter* is "a constant whose value may vary." However, in this context the more common meaning of "limits" will be used. For discussion on the uses of this word, see William Safire's column *On Language.*

The Post-Impact Set

The post-impact set includes decisions that deal with *assessing* learner performance of the task(s) and selecting the appropriate feedback offered to the learner during the impact set. This set also includes decisions about assessing the congruence between the pre-impact and the impact sets (intent ≅ action). This assessment determines whether adjustments are needed in subsequent episodes. These decisions are made in the following sequence, a sequence that is intrinsic to any evaluative procedure.

1. *Gathering information about the performance in the impact set.* This can be done by observing, listening, touching, and/or smelling.

2. *Assessing the information against criteria.* Decisions are made in the course of comparing, contrasting, and making conclusions about the performance against the criteria, the standard, or the model.

3. *Providing feedback to the learner.* Decisions must be made about how to provide feedback, how to give information and/or judgment to the learner about the performance of the task, and also about their decision-making role. Feedback can represent any one or a combination of the *four forms of feedback* (see Chapter 4 for specifics about the *four forms of feedback*). Additionally, feedback can be either immediate or delayed, it can be offered by gesture, symbol, or verbal behavior; it can be given publicly or privately, etc.

4. *Treatment of questions.* Decisions about how to treat questions are made: how to acknowledge the response, which feedback form to use, etc.

5. *Assessing the selected teaching style.* Decisions are made about the effectiveness of the teaching style used in the completed episode and its impact on the learner.

6. *Assessing the anticipated learning style.* In connection with the decisions made in the previous category (5), a decision is made as to whether or not the learner has reached the objectives of the episode. Together, categories 5 and 6 provide the information concerning the congruity between intent and action (O–T–L–O).

7. *Adjustments.* Based on the assessments of the episode, decisions are made about whether adjustments are immediately needed in any particular decision or in subsequent episodes.

8. *Other.* The model is open-ended.

To summarize, these three sets of decisions—the pre-impact, impact, and post-impact—comprise the Anatomy of Any Style. At times these decisions are made deliberately; at other times they seem to represent habits; at still other times some of the decisions are overlooked or are made by default.[3] Regardless of the situation, the primary behavior in teaching is the act of making decisions in the sequential three sets of the anatomy. The Anatomy of Any Style, therefore, is a universal model that is at the foundation of all teaching. It describes the decisions that must be made in any teaching–learning interaction, model, strategy, or educational game.

Before addressing fundamental questions about the anatomy and how it is manipulated to identify and differentiate specific styles, two topics that affect all styles will be examined. Feedback and cognition have such profound implications within teaching and learning that an entire chapter is dedicated to each topic.

---

[3] Even when a decision is not made, a decision still occurs: which is, the decision *not* to make a decision! The teacher's lack of awareness does not alter the reality of the decision-making process within every teaching–learning interaction.

Chapter 4

Feedback[1]

Feedback (assessment[2]) is ubiquitous; its presence and power pervade every aspect of life. Everybody knows about it, gives it, and receives it. At times, everyone has relied on it or avoided it.

Less well known is the fact that there are different *forms of feedback*, each of which has characteristics and implications for the learning process.

Feedback's scope and content are independent of any specific teaching style, yet fundamental to all. Feedback is generally defined as "telling people how they are doing." Such a simplistic definition ignores the magnitude and hypnotic power of feedback to affect performance and shape perceptions. Feedback is fundamental to the learning process for two primary reasons.

All feedback (all assessment) serves to:

1. Reinforce or change subject matter, behavior, or logistics

2. Shape self-concept

Feedback can be delivered to the learner via several *modes of communication*: symbols, gestures, and verbal behavior. *Symbols* are represented by letter grading (A, B, C, etc.), by numbers (1–10), by percentages (0–100%), by awards (first place, second place, etc.) or by pictures (☺, ☹). These symbols represent scales on which individual learners' actions are assessed. *Gestures* (also called *body language*) are represented by head movements, facial expressions, hand movements, and finger configurations. *Verbal behavior* is represented by written or spoken words and phrases, which project meanings and connotations that can change when spiced with different intona-

---

[1] This chapter is adapted from a forthcoming book on Spectrum Teaching by Sara Ashworth.

[2] The primary function of the post-impact set of decisions is assessment. The verbal comments and expressions used in the classroom reveal the degree of understanding a teacher has of the scope, options, and implications of assessment.

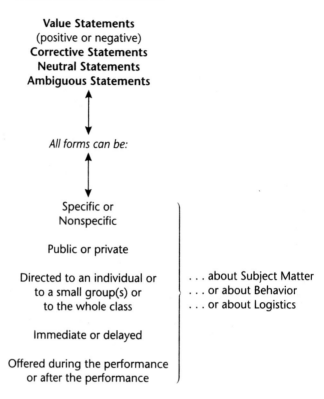

Figure 4.1. Feedback overview

tions or cultural interpretations. Regardless of the above modes of communication, there are four forms of feedback:

1. Value statements (positive or negative)
2. Corrective statements
3. Neutral statements
4. Ambiguous statements

Each of these forms has its own criteria, purpose, focus, and implications. No one form is the best, and each form is necessary and essential for reinforcing or changing subject matter, behavior, or logistics, and in shaping self-concept. All forms, however, can:

- Affect behavior
- Affect learning results
- Motivate, challenge, inspire, or reject, frustrate, confuse
- Reinforce or change standards

- Show respect or disrespect
- Encourage or discourage
- Exhilarate or humiliate
- Expand or destroy emotional connections
- Others

Figure 4.1 provides a general overview of feedback.

Four Feedback Categories

Value Statements

The single criterion for value feedback is the presence of a judgment (value) word, either positive or negative. If no judgment word is present, then the statement belongs to a different form of feedback. Value statements (both positive and negative) carry the power to declare judgments about others (see Table 4.1). This power can either benefit or damage relationships, inspire or impede the learning process.

The following are value feedback examples:

- "Good job maintaining a fist and keeping your palm up for the volleyball underhand serve."
- "Great shot."
- "You did an excellent job remembering all the steps and arm movements of the folk dance routine."
- "You displayed outstanding restraint in the game when the other team member tried to get you angry. Well done."
- "Michael, excellent remembering where to put the equipment."
- "Terrific job remembering to spread the fingers and balance the ball like a waiter's tray."
- "It is wrong to throw the baseball bat after a hit."
- "Very good. All right, way to go!"

Table 4.1 Characteristics of Value Feedback

Form	Criterion	Purpose	Focus
Value statement	• Judgment word(s) stated (either positive or negative)	• Projects judgment—a degree of satisfaction, an evaluation • Inculcates a set of values, standards • Expresses feelings + / - *Caution:* excessive use develops dependency	• The giver of the value statement

Table 4.2 Specific and Nonspecific Feedback Analysis

Nonspecific	Specific
• Great shot.	• Good job maintaining a fist and keeping your palm up for the volleyball underhand serve.
• Very good. All right, way to go!	
additional examples:	• You did an excellent job remembering all the steps and arm movements of the folk dance routine.
• You're not good enough to be on the team.	• You displayed outstanding restraint in the game when the other team member tried to get you angry. Well done.
• That's pretty good.	
• Not bad.	• Michael, excellent remembering where to put the equipment.
• Good try.	
• This is much better.	• It is wrong to throw the baseball bat after a hit.
• Wrong.	
• That was wonderful!	• Terrific job remembering to spread the fingers and balance the ball like a waiter's tray.
• You make me sick.	

Value statements can deliver general or specific messages. Table 4.2 sorts the feedback statements according to specific and nonspecific value feedback. Notice that the focus of the value examples is on subject matter, behavior, and logistics.

The above nonspecific statements are generalities; they do not indicate *what* was good/bad, wonderful/terrible; however, they do convey an overall message of approval or disapproval. A general message about standards or feelings is sufficient when addressing a total experience without attempting to reinforce, replicate, or change any particular part. "That was wonderful!" or "Great shot!" provides a satisfying overall assessment; nothing is singled out as being particularly worthy of notice or repetition.

These comments are pleasing to hear (Hayakawa, 1939, p. 45). The converse is also true: "That was terrible"—an overall assessment of dissatisfaction is conveyed; the message is not pleasing to hear. Nonspecific statements, which do not specify exactly what was *wonderful/terrible*, leave room for misinterpretation. Although nonspecific statements are appropriate at times, misinterpretation of these comments often leads to unintended task performance, behaviors, and feelings.

Specific value statements are preferable when replication, change, or special attention to details, processes, or procedures are sought. Specificity activates cognitive and/or emotional processes that allow learners to grasp and focus on the statement's intention. The more specific the statement, the more precise and powerful the message.

Note: the examples "You make me sick" and "You're not good enough" are harsh statements that are not appropriate for teachers to use under any

Table 4.3 Feedback and Developmental Channels Focus

Specific Value Feedback	Developmental Channel Focus
• Good job maintaining a fist and keeping your palm up for the volleyball underhand serve.	Cognitive—applying knowledge Physical—coordination, strength, skill accuracy
• You did an excellent job remembering all the steps and arm movements of the folk dance routine.	Cognitive—precision in remembering subject matter sequence and movement expectations Emotional—evoking the feelings of success and recognition Physical—coordination, endurance demands of the dance routine
• You displayed outstanding restraint in the game when the other team member tried to get you angry. Well done.	Emotional—self-control Ethical—physical restraint and judgment Physical—restraint
• Michael, excellent remembering where to put the equipment.	Cognitive—subject matter/logistical procedures
• It is wrong to throw the baseball bat after a hit.	Ethical—social, physical respect, and safety
• Terrific job.	Emotional—this nonspecific statement projects strong approval and enhances "feelings."
• Terrific job remembering to spread the fingers and balance the ball like a waiter's tray.	Cognitive–Emotional–Physical—positively reinforces the "thinking" process and its effect on performing. By adding a specific focus to "terrific job," learners receive concrete information about their performance and that produces focused good feelings.

circumstances. Statements—specific or nonspecific—that violate the learner's integrity are unacceptable.[3]

Specific Feedback and the Developmental Channels

Feedback in the gymnasium can be related to each of the Developmental Channels. Physical education is more than the skills, rules of the games, or the freedom to discover movement. Since specific feedback acknowledges a particular reference point, it is possible to identify the developmental intentions of each statement. The statements in Table 4.3 permit the receivers to obtain information about themselves on different Developmental Channels.

Appropriate, supportive, specific feedback on a variety of Developmental Channels shapes one's overall self-concept. Such variety in feedback teaches learners that all channels are important in the educational process.

The nonspecific feedback statements in Table 4.4 do not indicate the

---

[3] Although professional behavior avoids abusive language, learners can benefit from *episodes* in learning how to "handle" abusive statements. Handling abusive statements can involve episodes designed to teach physical restraint, emotional disconnection, social adjustment, or ethical assessment. The ability to handle unpleasant situations is necessary for survival.

Table 4.4 Value Nonspecific Feedback Analysis

Nonspecific	Developmental Channel Focus
• Great shot. • Very good. All right, way to go!	Each statement leaves room for the question: at what?
additional examples: • You're not good enough to be on the team. • That's pretty good. • Not bad. • Good try. • This is much better. • Wrong. • That was wonderful! • You make me sick.	Learners have an option to interpret the specific point of reference, the ultimate meaning, and select the Developmental Channel to be in focus. The teacher's intended learning focus may, or may not, have been accurately interpreted by the learner.

learning focus, leaving learners to interpret (or misinterpret) the intended meanings and implications.

The Focus of Value Feedback Differences among feedback forms emerge when the question is posed: Who or what is in *focus* when each feedback form is in use? When value feedback is in use, the teacher—the one making the value statement—is in focus. The feedback emanates from the teacher's (the authority's) value system and although the learner is the receiver and the one who is affected by the feedback, it is the authority's judgments that are projected and that prevail.

Drawback: Reciprocal Dependency Can Develop When one feedback form is used exclusively, intrinsic liabilities emerge. Dependency can develop when exclusively positive or exclusively negative feedback is excessively offered. A condition of *reciprocal dependence* develops: the teacher becomes dependent on feeling the power of dispensing judgments and having them gratefully or fearfully received. The learners become dependent on the authority figure who is the source of constant approving or disapproving statements. In the gymnasium, excessive positive value feedback lowers standards and, rather than nurturing positive self-esteem, this warped perspective of value curtails feelings of self-worth.

Value Feedback and I Statements The focus now is to understand what happens when value statements and *I* statements are combined. The younger the child, the more *I value* statements influence development. This power to influence can be beneficial or detrimental. Literature is filled with accounts of children with exceptional talents, capable of performing at levels far beyond their ages. Most of these stories acknowledge the influence and direction of an adult. The driving force *to please, to be good, to make you proud of me* can produce extraordinary feats. Conversely, there are instances in which adults have used the power and influence of I value statements to control and abuse children. The need to feel emotionally connected (*you are loved and valued*) is so strong a human desire that actions themselves can become secondary to a child's need to feel a sense of belonging. Maintaining a proper and healthy balance when dispensing I value statements and not overusing or abusing this form of feedback requires constant introspection and self-discipline.

Two verbal behavior options exist for making I value statements: One verbal option teaches that others make decisions about you; others tell you how right or wrong, how good or bad, how ugly or beautiful, how smart or stupid you are. "I think you are..." "I said to..." "I know what is best for you..." "I will tell you...," the values of the giver are projected upon others. In this option, others' opinions and feelings shape one's self-concept, and a sense of self is acquired through the judgments of outside sources. The list of verbal examples of this dependence-reinforcing option is long: "Tell me what you think." "How did I do?" "Tell me how to do it." "Show me." "Don't leave me, I won't know what to do." "Are you sure I was okay?" Dependency can be confined to one Developmental Channel or it can include them all.

The second verbal option acknowledges the adult's degree of satisfaction but attempts to shift the value onto the learner. See Table 4.5 for examples.

Table 4.5 Verbal Options That Shift the Value to the Learner

Avoid Repeatedly Saying	Alternative Verbal Behavior
I am very proud of you.[4]	You must be very proud of yourself.
I like the way Josh is keeping his arm, eye, arm, eye, and hand lined up with the basket.	Excellent remembering, Josh, to keep your and hand lined up with the basket.
You're mean.	Your behavior is mean.

Learning to restate I value statements requires examination of one's need for power and control over others.

Appropriate value feedback statements are absolutely essential in our lives; they establish personal attachments and set standards that form individual value systems. Value feedback statements serve as the models from

---

[4] The frequency of this comment is the issue. When learners hear this comment from teachers/adults, it lets them know others value and care about them. But used too frequently, the phrase can develop dependence on others for approval.

which we each design our personal code of behavior and create our view of humanity, but other forms of feedback also contribute to development and acquisition of content.

Corrective Statements

There are two criteria (Table 4.6) for identifying corrective statements:

1. The feedback refers to an error. Examples: "Don't breathe from both sides when using the crawl stroke." "Keep your glove in front of your body." "That's not the correct position." "This is incorrect."

2. The feedback includes the identification of the error and the correction. Example: "You lifted your head. Keep your chin down." "Next time maintain eye contact with the ball and follow through with the club." Sometimes only the correction is offered and identification of the error is implied. Example: "Straighten your left leg during the cartwheel." This statement not only gives the correct posture, but also implies that the posture practiced by the learner was incorrect.

Table 4.6 Characteristics of Corrective Feedback

Form	Criteria	Purpose	Focus
Corrective	• Refers to error(s) • Identifies the error and provides the correction • Identifies only the correction	• Identifies the error, point of deviation, problem • Invites redoing the task • Focuses on performance accuracy—reduces errors • Clarifies standards and details of the performance in subject matter, behavior and/or procedure expectations *Caution:* excessive use develops a preoccupation with errors	• The error—in either subject matter, behavior or logistics

Table 4.7 provides examples of corrective statements.

Ambiguous Corrective Feedback "Stop! Don't!" "That's enough." "That's not the way to do it." These nonspecific corrective statements leave room for learners to misinterpret or perhaps manipulate; therefore, these expressions can also be categorized under *ambiguous feedback*. There are times when a single and impulsive nonspecific *stop, no, don't* is appropriate for correcting, but when the circumstances require precise follow-through, specific, clarifying, corrective statements are required.

"How many times do I have to tell you not to...?" Although this statement addresses the error and supplies the correction, the selected verbal

Table 4.7 Corrective Feedback Examples

Refers to an Error	Identification of the Error and the Correction
• The step sequence is not slide, slide, turn.	• Next time, when scuba diving, breathe out continuously as you surface.
• Keep your eye on the ball.	• No. Your wrist collapsed when the tennis ball hit the racket. Be ready for the force of the ball by keeping a firm wrist and firm grip.
• Move faster.	• This is not socializing time.
• Incorrect.	• You produced four movement sequences; the task asked for six.
• No.	• The task is to practice a controlled hit of the ball to your partner; not to hit the ball as hard as you can.
• Stop!	
• Don't.	• That's incorrect. The volleyballs go in the green basket.
• That's enough.	• How many times do I have to tell you not to....? (This is an inappropriate statement; see explanation below.)
See section on Ambiguous Feedback	

behavior inappropriately overshadows the intended focus. The "How many times do I have to..." provides an escape for learners in terms of follow-through. Defiant learners will say under their breath, "A hundred more times, teacher!" The relationship becomes one of personal power rather than error correction.

The Focus of Corrective Feedback Incorrect performance invites the use of this form. The focus is on errors, without value judgments. Errors can occur in any of the three expectations: subject matter, behavior, or logistics.

Drawback: Overemphasis on Errors Excessive use of this form leads to a preoccupation with errors.[5] Identification of the error becomes more important than consideration of the individual who made the error. Overuse of corrective feedback can cause individuals to stop trying: *Why bother, since I already know there will be errors?* A sense of giving up and, in extreme cases, when the identification of the errors spans many attributes on several Developmental Channels, a serious detachment from society can result.

Some errors deserve correction without the emotional dimension of judgment. Many errors are not related to good or bad, right or wrong; adding judgment only blurs the error focus.

The next category avoids judgment and error identification.

---

[5] For some learners who have a pattern of failing, the term *error* is laden with negative value implications. Therefore, alternative terms may need to be selected. One possibility is the word *miscue(s)*. Teachers explain they are trying to locate the point where the *miscue* occurred, where the understanding of the content went off track. For some learners this different verbal interaction is less threatening and permits a more sustained interaction between teacher, learner, and subject matter.

Neutral Statements

All neutral feedback statements share the following criteria: they factually acknowledge or describe the action; they neither judge nor correct. Note, however, that tone of voice can alter the perceived meanings of any feedback statements (particularly neutral statements), moving them to one of the other forms of feedback.

Table 4.8 Characteristics of Neutral Feedback

Form	Criteria	Purpose	Focus
Neutral	Acknowledge without judgment • Factual • Descriptive • Nonjudgmental	• Projects a sense of objectivity • Acknowledges events • Identifies what happened—factual description • Establishes nonjudgmental interaction • Permits continued conversation • Avoids escalating tense, awkward, and controversial moments • Provides face saving opportunities (in moments of embarrassment or tension, prevents flare-ups) • Supports negotiation skills—diplomacy • Projects personal attentiveness, recognition, and attitude of listening *Caution:* excessive use develops feelings of detachment and isolation	• Receiver of the statement (Neutral statements allow the receiver to select, to determine the meaning of the statement.)

Notice how the examples in Table 4.9 avoid value words or reference to an error.

Table 4.9 Examples of Neutral Feedback

Neutral	
• Each of your defense strategies protects one shooter for a possible clear shot. • You included many extensions in your routine. • True. / Yes. / Nodding. • I see you are very angry. • You completed all the station tasks. • Yes, that is a possible movement design. • Take your time, I'm listening. • A soft grunt, "mmm." • Correct. • Repeating the learner's response.	These statements acknowledge. They are free of judgment. They are factual.

Neutral feedback is often considered meaningless and impractical in our society. Americans are so accustomed to relying on value judgments and corrections that other kinds of comments are difficult to comprehend. Neutral statements acknowledge acceptance of the learner. Neutral feedback does not project absolutes or conclusions, so learners are invited to remain active cognitively and emotionally in the physical activity, conversation, or dialogue, so the final conclusion (meaning) of neutral interaction comes from the learner, not the teacher. In this form of feedback, the opportunity to make the final assessment decision is deliberately shifted to the learner. Therefore, the focus of this feedback form is the *learner*. In value and corrective feedback, the learners are subject to the authority and the content; they must accept the feedback and act on it. Neutral statements focus on the receiver's ability to initiate and develop assessment skills. In some teaching styles, neutral feedback is needed to deal with conflict situations, emotional traumas, or discussions of controversial issues. Neutral feedback permits individual cognitive and emotional development and is essential if citizens are to monitor their own behaviors as they function in society.

Drawbacks: Can Cause Sense of Detachment   Exclusive use of neutral feedback can lead the receiver to experience feelings of personal detachment; isolation and aloneness emerge in the absence of approval, disapproval, or corrective feedback. "Tell me how you feel about me!" "Don't you care about what or how I do things?" "Don't my actions mean anything to you?" "Haven't you an opinion about what I am doing or want to do?" "Say something to me!" "Doesn't somebody see me?"[6] are comments that reflect overexposure to neutral feedback. Praise, reprimands, corrections, and neutral conversations are all needed for individuals to develop their own value systems that correspond with society's boundaries.

Appropriate neutral feedback teaches tolerance, acceptance of diverse responses and actions, independence, self-reliance, and confidence in developing assessment skills. Neutral feedback is essential if learners are to develop a sense of identity.

"Correct/Incorrect" versus "Right/Wrong" Feedback   Two word pairs commonly used in feedback are often used interchangeably: *correct / incorrect* and *right / wrong*. Yet their meanings are significantly different. *Right*

---

[6] Very young children are good at requesting *see me*. They have two techniques: When they feel the adult is not focusing on their conversation, they literally place their little hands on the adult's face and turn the head! They also verbally request that you notice them by repeatedly saying, "Watch me, Watch me!" "Look at me!" "Did you see me?" Veciana-Suarez quoted her son's expression, "Listen to me with your eyes!" (1989). Children need to know that "somebody sees them." Using any one form of feedback exclusively produces liabilities.

and *wrong* is the most frequently used pair of words. These terms are meant to attribute moral value, yet they are often used inappropriately with unfortunate results.

The dictionary's primary definition of right and wrong connects these words with morality and ethics (subsequent entries suggest colloquial meanings and uses). Thus, it is inappropriate to say to a child who kicked a ball with the toe rather than the side: "This is wrong" or "You are wrong." The placement of the soccer kick has nothing to do with morality, but rather with the correctness of the foot's position as it makes contact with the ball. The appropriate feedback is: "Kick with the instep, not the toe, for a more controlled pass."

Every subject matter has tasks that are factual and deserving of feedback that focuses on correct and incorrect responses, without interjecting morality. Only when the responses are within the domain of morality (and the moral standards have been clearly specified) could the right / wrong pair be considered appropriate feedback.

The connotation of being right or wrong has a powerful affective implication for the learner. Consider what it means to a learner who repeatedly hears "You're wrong" when dribbling, spelling, adding, drawing, mixing chemicals, or pronouncing new words in another language. The distinction between the person and the content becomes blurred and the feelings toward self are negatively formed on several developmental channels.

Ambiguous Statements

The characteristic common to all *ambiguous* feedback is the opportunity for the statement to be interpreted or misinterpreted. Ambiguous statements do not project a specific value, they do not identify an error or make a clear correction, nor do they factually acknowledge events. They are statements that require the receiver to make a conclusion about (interpret) the meaning of the comment. In some situations, this lack of precision can be desirable and does not lead to conflict or differences of interpretation. However, when ambiguous feedback statements are misinterpreted and lead to misunderstandings or conflicts, they are inappropriate.

When used appropriately, ambiguous feedback deliberately avoids taking a position and permits the receiver to interpret the meaning of the statement. "My position on this issue is in line with yours," says the administrator, teacher, parent, or politician! Deliberate and appropriate use does not lead to conflict or confrontation; in fact, it sidesteps them.

Ambiguous feedback can hinder learning and cause misunderstandings when specific data or a precise expectation is desired. Frequent use of ambiguous feedback during content interactions suggests to learners that the teacher lacks knowledge of the task, lacks clarity about the evaluation criteria, or is not sure how to make the corrections.

Of all the forms, probably more confusion, mixed messages, misunderstandings, and conflict result from nondeliberate or inappropriate use of ambiguous feedback. Usually neither the giver nor the receiver of the statement is aware of the discrepancy in interpretation until a conflict occurs. See Table 4.10 for the characteristics of ambiguous statements.

Table 4.10 Characteristics of Ambiguous Feedback

Form	Criteria	Purpose	Focus
Ambiguous	• Statements that leave room for interpretation or misinterpretation	• Creates a safe climate—on all the Developmental Channels • Projects a feeling of acceptance • Allows others to interpret statements • Assumes a noncommittal position • Avoids precise information • Hinders efficient learning • Generates opportunities that lead to conflict and misunderstanding *Caution:* a false sense of trust and inappropriate ownership of the misunderstandings can develop	• Uncertain • Since statements can be interpreted or misinterpreted, the exact focus is uncertain • When used deliberately, the giver of the statement is in focus

Table 4.11 illustrates possible interpretations or misinterpretations of ambiguous feedback statements. These statements have been observed to interfere with efficient learning.

Connection Between Nonspecific Value and Ambiguous Feedback
Ambiguous statements avoid stating a specific position or judgment. Note that many nonspecific value feedback statements are *ambiguous comments.* These statements leave room for interpretation and therefore possible misinterpretation. They may convey satisfaction or dissatisfaction, but their specific intent is ambiguous; therefore the outcomes produced by these statements are unpredictable and their use unreliable. (See section on value nonspecific analysis.)

Pretty Good, Not Bad
Perhaps the most prevalent pair of nonspecific value statements is *pretty good / not bad.* Neither statement reflects a definite position on the part of the teacher; neither offers concrete information about how the task was performed. These linguistic modifiers establish a safety zone for the teacher, but leave the learner in a state of ambiguity. How does a learner interpret "Pretty good, but this isn't right...?" or "Not bad for a first practice" or "Pretty good for someone your age"?

Table 4.11 Examples of Ambiguous Feedback

Ambiguous	Interpretation or Misinterpretation
• Do it again. • Let's try again.	• Why? These statements do not provide the *reason* for repeating the experience. This omission prevents learners from recruiting the deliberate developmental channel that is in focus. Why are learners repeating the experience? Was the task correctly done and the teacher wanted to reinforce it? If so, the specific verbal behavior could have been: "Class, that was perfectly performed; let's repeat the sequence again." The emotional and cognitive channels are in focus. Perhaps there was an error: "No, class, the turn movement looks like ___. Let's repeat it again." Now, the cognitive developmental channel is in focus. Did the teacher not see the response? "Class, I didn't see the last segment, please repeat it." Ambiguous comments do not emphasize the learning focus.
• Perhaps. • Close.	• Do these responses mean approval or correction? Cognitively, the learner is left guessing at their meaning.
• Excuse me.	• "Excuse me" is often used as a corrective comment to stop behavior. "Excuse me" is an ethical / emotional statement seeking an apology, a pardon. Teachers who inaccurately use this statement confuse the learning situation. Offering corrective feedback is different from teaching good manners. Avoid using this comment to stop behavior.
• That's original, even I couldn't have come up with that.	• This statement is both a compliment and a put-down. Different students will hear this statement very differently. This comparative *I* statement really focuses on the teacher.
• Interesting.	• This frequently used expression is noncommittal. It does not state why or in what way something is interesting. This word acknowledges without stating a position. For content clarification purposes, it is inappropriate.
• That's okay, but you could have done it differently.	• Is the final product acceptable or not? Specifically how could it have been performed differently? This comment invites learners to dismiss the alternative suggestion; after all, if it's okay, why bother to do differently?
• You have an error in the way you dribble the ball.	• This corrective statement is appropriate and challenging only for learners who are skilled enough to assess the task to find the error. But for learners who are not skilled in the task and who would be overwhelmed trying to find the error, this statement is not appropriate.
• Are you sure it's correct? • Did you look at this carefully? • You're not using your potential • Try harder next time	• These statements cause learners to doubt their performance, although students who are skilled can accept these challenges. These statements do not cognitively or emotionally benefit students who have experienced success less frequently. These students activate their emotions and either defend themselves or put themselves down more. Self-doubt is the outcome for them. "Well, I thought it was correct, I thought I was careful." "I thought I was using my potential..." "I am working as hard as I can..." "I couldn't have tried harder." "I really am a failure." Approaching content errors from the cognitive channel generally produces better results.
• That's enough. Stop! • Don't...	• These comments seek to correct, however, they are nonspecific and allow the learners to determine the focus of the correction. Discrepancies are possible.
• Did you hurry on this task?	• The teacher has implied that the quality of the work is flawed, yet the supposed reason for less-than-satisfactory work is based on an assumption. If the learner worked diligently on this task, the teacher's comment is both insulting and deflating. Focus on the observed error, avoid assumptions.

Learners' feelings about themselves will determine the precise meaning of *pretty good* and *not bad*. Learners with positive self-concepts will interpret these expressions favorably. However, those who have experienced relentless correcting and critical perfectionism and who are self-doubting, timid, and emotionally fragile will perceive negative connotations in these expressions. These learners cannot afford to receive more nonspecific value and ambiguous feedback, since they frequently distort these statements into negative feedback.

The Focus of Ambiguous Feedback   This feedback form reflects a lack of clarity and causes the learner to interpret or guess at the teacher's meaning; therefore, the focus is not specific—it is *uncertain*. Since an assumption cannot be made about the degree of common understanding, ambiguous feedback is unreliable. These comments are, however, feasible, if not desirable, in many social situations where projecting values or corrections would be inappropriate.

Drawback: Ambiguity Leads to False Sense of Trust   Learners who experience frequent ambiguous feedback begin to assume responsibility for failing to understand the content. Learners begin to doubt their own capacities to understand, to think, to interpret. Excessive ambiguous feedback increases feelings of disappointment and detachment.

Excessive use of any feedback forms can lead to abuse and detachment. Some adults provide neutral and ambiguous statements toward their children's school cognitive (grades) results, but explosively deliver value-negative and corrective statements about sports participation and physical development. Others shower value superlatives on the child's every endeavor, but this excess of praise often makes it difficult for a child to accept corrective or value-negative feedback. Extremes and feedback omissions generally result in emotional distortions. Since each feedback form has its particular focus and influence on the learner, no one kind of feedback is universally desirable. The desirable form of feedback depends on the subject matter and behavior expectations, the overall learning objectives, the learners' participation, and the selected teaching style. Providing all forms of feedback requires reflection, perhaps an adjustment in the teacher's verbal behavior, and a view of the teacher-learner relationship.

Feedback Combinations

At times feedback comments remain within one category; at other times, combining forms may be more appropriate. Teachers who know the feedback forms are able to deliberately combine the four forms in an infinite number of ways. No single pattern can be prescribed for all feedback—to do so would deny the variety of human relationships and learning opportunities that can and do exist in the classroom. The possible connections among teacher, learner, and content are so diverse that limiting interactions to any single pattern would reduce the value and use of this feedback framework.

When combinations become a fixed pattern and are continuously used, such as the *feedback sandwich*[7] (Docheff, 1990, p. 18), negative implications develop. Corrective feedback constantly surrounded by positive feedback teaches that praise is a camouflage for identifying errors (Farson, 1997). Learners soon realize the positive value statements are not the focus, but simply cushions that surround the essence of interaction pointing out errors. Reliance on a single form or fixed pattern/combination will eventually evoke the liabilities rather than the assets of the feedback. Feedback always has a purpose: it always reinforces or changes subject matter, behavior, or logistics and it always contributes to shaping self-concept. Feedback must reflect the intended learning expectation.

Ignoring Behavior

Ignoring is an example of ambiguous feedback. This form of feedback can be face-saving and highly desirable in certain situations, but used to an extreme, ignoring is the most severe expression of abandonment. To be shunned, particularly by people we want to value us, is the harshest feedback. Continuous and excessive ignoring is humiliating. Schools need to be safe environments where opportunities for attachments, development, and participation are guaranteed, not places that compound children's traumas. Schools cannot remedy neglect and abuse by family and society, but the schools can serve as safe and trusted places.

Some Current Issues

Current research has isolated "states specific academic praise" as a factor that improves learning. This finding led to the narrow and restricted mandate that this feedback option be primarily, if not solely, implemented. Other forms or expressions often resulted in demerits and their use was discouraged. This limited conception for viewing all feedback in the classroom ignores knowledge, violates the notion of providing alternatives, and suppresses other possibilities for relating to and motivating learners.

This mandate was the result of classroom research that indicated teachers gave negative value feedback more than any other form (Bellon, Bellon,

---

[7]Docheff's approach suggests that feedback should begin with a positive value comment, followed by the identification of what was performed correctly or indicating what needed to be corrected, then finished with a positive statement. "Good job, Bob. With your elbow in like that you will always have good alignment when shooting the basketball. Keep up the good work."

& Blank, 1992, p. 100; Brophy, 1981, p. 16). Positive and specific content feedback was far less frequently stated. Various programs have attempted to present alternatives. Although each program provides excellent examples and insights, none offers a comprehensive framework that embraces the multiple options in feedback.

The lack of variety and appropriateness in classroom feedback is not corrected by mandating one feedback form over all others. Rather, teachers need to understand the knowledge and options, the verbal behavior precision and impact, the magnitude and power of feedback, before deliberate change can occur in classroom feedback.

Although current attempts to focus on assessment are desirable and worthwhile, they have led to misleading and ambiguous terminology. The *authentic assessment* movement overlooks the fact that when any kind of assessment (feedback) is given, it is authentic to that learner, regardless of its content accuracy, degree of dignity, or emotional expression. The effects of feedback are too powerful to imply that some feedback can be dismissed as not authentic. The ambiguous terminology of this movement is at issue, not the program's intentions.

Subject Matter Note

In some situations, any of the feedback forms would be uncomfortable, awkward, or inappropriate. In these moments, what do you say to a learner? In most cases, it is desirable to bypass feedback and immediately shift into a review of content, moving directly to content clarification. This approach is face-saving and focuses on the existing need: review, clarification, and an effort to identify the student's point of content deviation and misunderstanding. A variety of teaching–learning styles can be used when clarification of content is deemed necessary for a student.

Degree of Privacy During Feedback

All feedback is directed to a particular audience. In the classroom, possible receivers of feedback are:

- An individual
- One or more small groups
- The whole class

Classroom research indicates that regardless of the intended receiver, teachers primarily give *public* feedback. *Private* (soft-spoken, individual, eye-level) feedback is rarely given, and dialogue feedback (sustained interaction) is infrequent. Classroom feedback primarily (Ashworth, 1983):

1. Is value nonspecific and refers to correctness of the subject matter or discipline

2. Is projected in a volume that allows all learners in the area to hear the comment, regardless of the intended receiver

3. Is not modulated: the volume remains public even when a side-by-side, private interaction is possible

4. Is given from a hovering position: teacher stands over and offers feedback from behind students

5. Is frequently withheld from students who give correct answers

6. Is passive. While circulating, teachers often look at students' work without offering any of the communication modes (verbal, visual, tactile, gesture, or picture comments such as happy face drawings for elementary children).

7. Demonstrates less "withitness" skills (Kounin, 1970). While the teacher's attention is directed to the individual student receiving feedback, the focus and awareness of the whole class action fades.

8. Is principally verbal rather than written. Circulating with a marker in hand can be useful to: randomly acknowledge performance (which saves time later); indicate quantity of work completed per time; reinforce accountability; indicate teacher presence; serve as a content reminder; reinforce personal connections; set a base for the next interaction in terms of quantity or quality expectations; encourage the student.

Used appropriately, private rather than public feedback changes class climate and offers opportunities for personal and individual connections between learner and teacher.

Private feedback requires that teachers modulate their voice volume. Respecting differences, accepting all, and maintaining dignity is often violated in the classroom when public value negative or corrective feedback is directed to one person. In most cases, learners have the right to be reprimanded, corrected, or praised in private. Not all comments are appropriate for public disclosure.

When to give feedback is another variable to consider: Will the feedback be most beneficial during or after the performance or behavior? The lesson's purpose and the need for variety will direct this decision. At what point in time will the feedback most benefit the performance, behavior, or emotions? The number of variables that influence and affect feedback are many. It takes both knowledge and skill to know how to use these variables when giving feedback.

Summary of the Assets and Liabilities of Different Forms of Feedback

In analyzing the possible assets and liabilities of each feedback form, the questions to consider are: What are the purposes of each form of verbal behavior? What does it do *for* the learner? What does it do *against* the learner? Tables 4.12–4.15 summarize the feedback forms.

Table 4.12 Value: Conveys Judgment

Value	Assets	Liabilities
Positive	1. It is pleasing to hear praise. 2. It is rewarding and reinforcing. 3. It ensures willingness to repeat performance. 4. It lets the learners know how the teacher feels about them.	1. Continuous and lavish positive feedback loses effectiveness. Students quickly learn that any attempt, any performance, will be met with rewarding feedback. Some teachers habitually bestow superlatives on every action. These words soon lose their meaning and learners gradually lower their performance quality. 2. The learner may become emotionally dependent on value feedback. This may enhance the need always to be the best, which is difficult to sustain. 3. Reciprocal dependency develops.
Negative	1. It informs the learner about the teacher's value system. 2. It may temporarily stop unwanted behavior. 3. It reminds the learner that negative value words are a part of reality.	1. It is not pleasing to hear. 2. It can become oppressive to hear repeatedly how bad one is, how poorly one reads, how terrible one's handwriting is, etc. 3. The learner may perceive this feedback as personal rather than a reference to the errors.

Table 4.13 Corrective: Attention Is Directed to the Error

Corrective	Assets	Liabilities
Error referred to	1. Learner is invited to redo. 2. Learner is aware that an error exists.	1. If the learner cannot correct the error, frustration may set in. 2. The learner may stay on the problem too long.
Error identified, correction offered	1. The correct information is available. 2. The learner can focus on the area where the error is identified. 3. There is no guesswork. 4. Correct performance is more likely to occur.	1. The learner does not or may be unable to come up with the correction.

Table 4.14 Neutral: Factual, Descriptive, Nonjudgmental

Assets	Liabilities
1. It indicates that the teacher acknowledges the performance.	1. It may be awkward for both teacher and learner when first used.
2. It opens the door for more communication between the teacher and some learners. (An initial neutral statement is less threatening to some learners.)	2. Initially it may be confusing to the learner who is accustomed to receiving corrective and / or value feedback
3. It decreases the learner's dependency.	
4. It can serve as a face-saving technique during tension or conflict.	3. It may cause some learners to prod the teachers for their opinions— for value statements. They will say: "Yes, but how do you like it?"
5. It delays the need for immediate resolution of a situation.	
6. It weans learners from expecting value or corrective statements all the time.	4. It may give some learners a feeling that the teacher does not care.
7. It can promote the development of self-evaluation.	
8. It permits the learners the option of assessing their own work, independent of the teacher's view.	

Table 4.15 Ambiguous: Statements That Leave Room for Interpretation or Misinterpretation

Ambiguous	Assets	Liabilities
	1. It creates a safe climate in some social situations.	1. It interferes with efficient learning and precise performance of task.
	2. Others?	2. Others?

To summarize, feedback shapes perceptions, personality, and one's view of humanity. Since each form of feedback acknowledges events from a particular point of reference, expanding the use of all the forms of feedback can expand our perceptions of the teaching–learning process. Implementing the knowledge about feedback, rather than relying on personal preferences, is a worthwhile pursuit for all teachers.

CHAPTER 5

Cognition[1]

Physical education has the inherent capacity to facilitate development on all the channels. Mosston was intrigued and captivated by the educational possibilities that existed in physical education—no other field could so deliberately contribute such a wide set of developmental opportunities in every individual lesson. Deliberately designed decision-making experiences in physical education have the capacity to actively invite students to think (cognitive channel) while moving (physical channel), and to interact with others (social channel) while practicing fair play (ethical channel) and self-control (emotional channel). Mosston's experimentation with the relationship between *thinking* and *moving*[2] in the different teaching–learning behaviors led to the development of a framework that explained and described the various thinking processes. Mosston sought to bridge the gap that existed between the notion of *academic* and *nonacademic* content areas in school curriculum. Mosston rallied to alter the versus perception that pitted mind against body; the Spectrum theory shows the inseparable connection among the various Developmental Channels and the power of physical education to accomplish educational goals and objectives. Every activity—in any subject matter field—enlists a cognitive focus. The following framework delineates the cogitative possibilities that exist during the teaching–learning process.

It is imperative that physical education teachers realize they teach *thinking* (cognitive) skills. It is also important to realize that the structure that governs cognitive development is the same in all fields. What is unique about physical education is the physical (visible) expression of the cognitive process. Few fields give teachers the opportunity to observe their students as they partake in the cognitive process. Although motor skill development is accomplished only through active participation on the physical channel, the tasks for motor learning always highlight a cognitive process. Before

---

[1] This chapter is adapted from a forthcoming book on Spectrum Teaching by Sara Ashworth.

[2] *Thinking and Moving* is the title of an unfinished manuscript by Muska Mosston.

motor skills become patterned demonstrating physical development, they are first a cognitive process. Every motor skill in the beginning phase requires deliberate cognitive attention. Learning movement patterns that are kinesiologically effective and physically accurate requires thinking. When motor skills become correctly patterned and automatically wired (using anatomy, physiology, and kinesiology principles), the cognitive attention to motor skill development moves to a supportive role for the physical demands of the new activity.

The vast professional literature contains treatises on the nature of thinking, research on specific aspects of thinking, and proposals for the teaching of thinking. The proliferation of ideas has, inevitably, produced a rich array of terms that often conflict in meaning and in usage. This chapter presents a formulation of the processes and operations of the complex phenomenon of human thinking. This formulation is an attempt to identify a framework to show the relationship among the various thinking processes and cognitive operations that characterize teaching–learning experiences. Several terms that were coined in conjunction with the formulation are used consistently throughout this book.

Cognition: The Premise

The formulation presented here identifies three basic processes of conscious thinking: *memory, discovery,* and *creativity.*

The *memory* process enables the reproduction aspect of learning by recalling and replicating past knowledge. This knowledge may include facts, dates, names, events, routines, procedures, rules, previous models, etc. Replicating information or a physical movement in any sport or activity relies on the *memory* process.

The *discovery* process, unlike memory, engages learners in production of information that was previously unknown to them. This knowledge can include concepts, relationships between or among entities, principles, and theorems. Designing physical movements, games, strategies, choreography patterns, or interpreting movements all rely on *discovery.*

The *creative* process refers to responses that are perceived as *unique* or *original*—something that is new, different, beyond commonly known or anticipated responses. It is suggested here that the word *creative* is a value word that bestows an attribution of uniqueness and originality. Therefore, it may be said that responses that are considered creative can be produced in any of the cognitive operations (See: Creativity: A Different Viewpoint, pp. 68–70).

The line of demarcation between discovery and creativity is often subtle, and even blurred. The interaction of these three processes, however, is fundamental to the very structure of thinking (Figure 5.1).

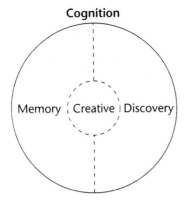

Figure 5.1. Three basic processes of thinking

A General Model for the Flow of Conscious Thinking

Thinking occurs when something triggers the brain to engage in memory, discovery, or creativity. The trigger is always a particular *stimulus* (S) that induces a state of unrest or irritation that evokes the need to know.[3] The stimulus moves the person into a state of *cognitive dissonance* (D) (Festinger, 1957). The need to know motivates the individual to start a search for an answer, a solution or a response that will reduce the dissonance. The search may engage the memory process, the discovery process, the creative process, or all three. This phase in the flow of thinking is designated as *mediation* (M). When the search, regardless of how long it takes, is completed, a *response* (R) is produced in the form of an answer, a solution, a new idea, or a new movement pattern. In summary, the phases and sequence in the flow of conscious thinking are

> S = The stimulus (the trigger)
>
> D = The state of cognitive dissonance (the need to know)
>
> M = Mediation (the search)
>
> R = The response (the answer or solution)

This flow is inherent to conscious thinking. These phases are not sequences that are imposed or externally applied to thinking, rather they are what the brain does when thinking. Awareness of this inherent process offers greater understanding of the complexities involved in thinking.

---

[3] The stimulus could be triggered by a question, an emotion, a sunset, a song, a movement, a comment, a bird gliding in the wind—anything that triggers the brain. The word *stimulus* is not referring to any conditioned responses or Skinnerian principles.

Schematically, the model inherent to the flow of conscious thinking looks like this:

$$S \rightarrow D \rightarrow M \rightarrow R$$

The Stimulus (S)

Many kinds of stimuli trigger thinking: a task to be done, a social situation, an emotional problem, a game, a creative endeavor. In fact, any life event can serve as a stimulus. Regardless of the event, the stimulus always raises a *question* in the mind of the person; a question induces cognitive dissonance and thereby arouses the need to search for an answer. All questions, whether they are asked by others or by oneself, can be assigned to one of three categories that correspond to the three basic thinking processes used in searching or mediating. Some questions trigger the memory, some questions trigger discovery, and other questions invite creativity. The stimulus actually invites engagement by producing the next phase: cognitive dissonance.

Cognitive Dissonance (D)

Dissonance is a state of unrest, a state of an irritation, or a condition manifested by the need to find an answer. Learners enter the state of cognitive dissonance when the stimulus (the question) is relevant to their interest, need, and level of knowledge. The dissonance motivates learners to act on the need to know, and then moves them to the next phase: mediation. Dissonance varies in intensity: it can be subtle, the response so automatic that the dissonance is unnoticed, or it can be cognitively and emotionally so disturbing that it compulsively drives and motivates the mediation phase.

If the stimulus is not relevant, the learners will ignore the question and will not enter the state of cognitive dissonance. This disengagement is manifested by an absence of the need to know and the need to search.

Mediation (M)—The Search for a Specific Cognitive Operation

Human thinking capacities span a variety of cognitive operations. For example, all humans can engage, with varying degrees of proficiency and speed, in specific cognitive operations. Some examples include:

- Naming
- Modeling
- Comparing
- Contrasting
- Categorizing
- Analyzing
- Designing
- Hypothesizing
- Others

Mediation activates the search for the specific cognitive operation that is triggered by the specificity of the stimulus (the question). One will engage, for example, in comparing only if a stimulus calls for this operation; otherwise, there is no need to compare. The need to compare may arise from different sources: a question that arises in one's mind, a question presented by another person, the need to choose between or among options, and so on. Only when the question is specifically directed at comparing will this cognitive operation be activated. Otherwise, it will lie dormant, waiting to be called on. The same is true for all other cognitive operations. The learner will engage in modeling, contrasting, categorizing, etc., only when there is a need to do so, and that need is triggered by a specific stimulus.

Now, each one of the cognitive operations can be activated by any of the three basic thinking processes: memory, discovery, or creativity. It is possible, for example, to remember how to categorize a set of objects (or a set of movements or events, etc.) based on previous experience. It is also possible to discover previously unknown options for categorizing the same set of objects (movements or events). It is also possible to create entirely new/unique categories (movements or events). The activation of the particular cognitive operation and its use—via memory, discovery, or creativity—during the mediation period depends on the nature of the stimulus or the question. It is as if the cognitive operations stand poised waiting to be recruited to bring to fruition any of the three thinking processes (Figure 5.1).

Dominant and Supportive Cognitive Operations

During the mediation period (S → D → M→ R), the specific cognitive operations can serve one of two functions:

1. A dominant function
2. A supportive function

Every stimulus/question has a dominant cognitive focus. However, most, if not all, cognitive operations require support from other cognitive operations in order to properly function. It is important to provide learners with experiences that develop different cognitive operations so more complex operations can be tackled. When a task or question asks the learners to compare one movement to another, a series of cognitive operations are assembled in a particular sequence to guide the thinking process to the desired outcome—*comparing*. Comparing relies on observing each movement, recognizing the sequence of each movement, identifying patterns in the movements, and then matching similarities. In this way, dominant cognitive operations rely on their supporting cognitive operations.

The Temporary Hierarchy

In the previous example, the interacting cognitive operations formed a temporary bond—a hierarchy—for the purpose of answering the question that governed the episode: How are these two movements alike? The supporting operations (observing, naming, sequencing, matching, comparing,) that interacted to lead to a response functioned in sequence or in reciprocation—the cognitive interaction moved back and forth between any two operations when additional information was needed (memory ←→ matching; matching ←→ comparing). The supporting cognitive operations did not function simultaneously. The gathering of information, however, always flowed in the direction of the dominant operation; in this case, comparing.

The temporary hierarchy formed during the mediation phase acts as a bridge between the question (stimulus) and the solution (response). The temporary hierarchy serves to provide the information needed at that time, and is sustained only as long as the learner remains in the state of cognitive dissonance.

When a solution is found, the temporary hierarchy is dissolved, the learner returns to a state of cognitive consonance, and engagement in the episode ends. The temporary hierarchy is a formation of temporary relationships. When another stimulus is aimed at another dominant cognitive operation, a different temporary hierarchy will be formed. Other supportive operations will be recruited as needed during the mediation time, in order to serve the purpose of the new episode. The sequence and interplay between the S → D → M → R and the dominant and supportive operations continuously move the thinking process to the final response.

Dominant cognitive operations do not work in isolation; they selectively recruit supporting cognitive operations to assist in generating the response. The stimulus (question) indicates the dominant cognitive operation, but the supporting operations are essential in reaching the desired response. Learners unable to produce responses frequently have not developed, or are confused about, one or more of the supporting cognitive operations. Without competence in the supporting cognitive operations, learners are unable to successfully resolve the stimulus. Rather than badgering them to produce the dominant cognitive operation, adjust the question, identify the weak supporting operation, clarify misconceptions and meanings, and practice using the cognitive operations that are unfamiliar to the learners. Since each dominant operation is dependent on the learner's competence in executing supportive operations, it is necessary for teachers to become knowledgeable in the operations, skilled in manipulating the tasks to highlight different dominant cognitive operations, and astute in detecting the specific operations in which learners "get stuck."

The Response

The interplay between the dominant and supporting cognitive operations sooner or later results in a response. The mediation phase, regardless of the length of time it requires, terminates when a response is available. The response can be a consequence of memory, discovery, or creativity, but it is always within the domain of the dominant cognitive operation, if answered correctly. The speed, the quantity, and the quality of the response depend on the learners' experience in the given cognitive operation, their prior knowledge of the particular subject matter area, and perhaps on their unique abilities or talents.

Convergent and Divergent Thinking

The flow of thinking in the three basic processes and in the specific cognitive operations can follow one of two possible paths:

1. Convergent thinking
2. Divergent thinking

It is possible to engage in memory via a convergent path that requires the learner to remember a single correct answer to a question. Examples of this process are: "Name the location of the next Summer Olympics." "Locate the path of the major muscle that extends the arm at the elbow joint." "Recall the first cue for the volleyball overhand server." "In the freestyle stroke, recall when you are supposed to breathe." In order to answer these questions, the learner's search during mediation converges on a correct answer. Practicing the modeled movement involves reproducing a series of movements to accomplish *the* demonstrated movement (the cartwheel, the tennis over-hand serve, the basketball free-throw shot, etc.). Although there are multiple parts within the movement, the cognitive path is divergent memory—recalling the parts to reproduce the indicated movement.

It is also possible to engage a divergent path in memory that requires the learner to recall several correct answers to a single stimulus/question.[4] For example:

• Recall the names of five team sports that are in the Olympics.
• Perform three basketball passes.

---

[4] In the educational literature, convergent thinking refers to reproduction thinking and divergent thinking to production thinking (McIntyre & O'Hair 1996, p. 184; Louisell & Descamps 1992, p. 87). Beyer even suggests that "whereas creative thinking is divergent, critical thinking is convergent" (1987, p. 35). The cognitive formulation presented in this text, however, suggests that it is possible to think in memory (reproduction), discovery (production), and the creative process following either a convergent or divergent path.

- Name five strokes that can be used in badminton.
- Provide examples of the movements we have practiced in gymnastics that incorporate agility.
- Recall four strategies used in the game when the defenders were in …
- State three reasons for keeping your center of gravity low when performing this move in basketball.

In order to answer these questions, during mediation a learner's search diverges and seeks to remember multiple answers/parts to the question/stimulus.[5]

When engaging in the discovery process, it is possible to follow a convergent path that leads the learner to discover a single solution or a single concept. (See Guided Discovery and Convergent Discovery chapters for more details).

It is also possible to take a divergent path, in which the learner discovers multiple solutions to the same problem. (See chapters Divergent Discovery and Learner-Designed Individual Program). Similarly, the attribution of creativity can be associated with convergent responses resulting in a single response, or it can flow in divergent paths to produce a variety of new responses.

All the options—convergent and divergent memory, discovery, and creativity—adhere to the sequence described in the general model for the flow of conscious thinking:

$$S \rightarrow D \rightarrow M \rightarrow R$$

Two Paths for Thinking

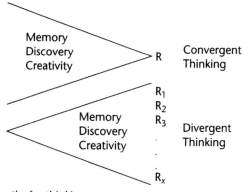

Figure 5.2. Two paths for thinking

---

[5]Divergent-memory stimulus/questions provide choices among many possibilities. Each learner's responses can vary and still be correct. For example: Using the definition just stated, provide four examples of a third class lever.

The stimulus triggers the dissonance that, in turn, determines the path that will be taken during mediation—will it be a convergent or a divergent path (Figure 5.2)? At the end of mediation, the result emerges in a form of a single response (R) or multiple responses (R*x*)—emanating from memory, discovery, or creativity.

The Discovery Threshold

The teaching–learning options within the Spectrum are clustered by their cognitive focus. The cluster of styles A through E serve the human capacity for reproduction (memory) and the cluster of styles F through K serve the human capacity for production (*discovery*) (Figure 5.3). Between the cluster of behaviors that trigger memory and those that evoke discovery, there is a theoretical, invisible line called the *discovery threshold* (Figure 5.3).

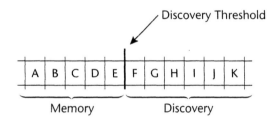

Figure 5.3. The discovery threshold

In the memory cluster of teaching behaviors (A–E), teachers may be actively engaged in various cognitive operations, but their role is to deliver acquired knowledge or skills. The role of the learners is to be receivers who reproduce the knowledge or skills in the designated memory cognitive operations.[6] Throughout the cluster of teaching behaviors A–E, the learners remain in a relative state of cognitive acquiescence with regard to active production in cognitive operations other than memory. Staying in this state ensures the success of episodes designed for engagement in memory and reproduction. Any engagement by the learner in comparing, sequencing, applying and solving, etc., is done by remembering the comparison, recalling the sequence, accurately applying and solving; the learner performs by replicating the content model.

When the intent of an episode shifts to discovery (styles F–K), both teachers and learners must cross the discovery threshold by changing their

---

[6] *Deliver* and *receive* do not imply lecture and passive sitting. There are many techniques for delivering and receiving information.

behaviors. The teaching–learning behaviors shift when the teacher introduces different stimuli/questions that move learners across the threshold and engage them in the discovery process. The learners behavior shifts to active production in discovering—by designing movements, by sequencing information, by actively discovering in the intended cognitive operation.

In order to cross the creativity threshold, both teacher and learner must change their behaviors once again. The teaching–learning behaviors shift with the introduction of different stimuli/questions that move learners to engage in the creative process, or the learners themselves ask questions that stimulate the creative process in any of the teaching behaviors.

The Role of Cognitive Operations

During the mediation phase, a search begins among the known cognitive capacities to select the cognitive operation that will satisfy the response. These cognitive words, inviting each of the three thinking processes, can be specific or ambiguous. Specific cognitive operation questions are appropriate when:

1. Introducing new cognitive operations and experiences
2. A predetermined thinking expectation is anticipated by the teacher
3. Learners repeatedly fail to provide anticipated responses
4. Competition exists among learners
5. Answers are to be graded
6. Time is limited and answers require a predicted response or desired thinking process
7. Producing random responses would not assist the learning objectives or content acquisition

Ambiguous cognitive questions are appropriate when:

1. The answer is independent/free of a specific correct response or thinking process
2. Learners' predominant cognitive preferences are sought
3. The teacher is seeking opinions
4. Interaction is casual, short term (often appropriate in social situations)
5. Searching for a new direction to answer a question, problem, or issue
6. Stalling or regrouping techniques are necessary
7. The learning objectives support exposure to random, often unrelated, responses

Specific Cognitive Words

Many words can trigger cognition. Knowing which words trigger specific thinking processes permits teachers to deliberately construct questions that lead to the intended subject matter goals. As illustrated in Figure 5.4, words can be clustered according to the thinking processes they activate.

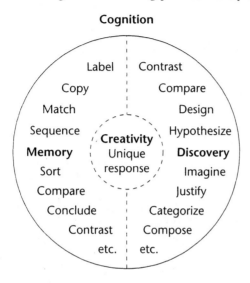

Figure 5.4. Different cognitive operations trigger different thinking processes

Figure 5.5 suggests that it is possible to identify and cluster words that represent specific cognitive expectations according to their predominant thinking process—memory or discovery. Because the creative process is an attribution of uniqueness to responses, there are no specific words that exclusively represent the creative process. It is possible for all the cognitive operations—in either memory or discovery—to produce responses that are considered creative. This figure is only a guide to acknowledge the elaborate network and possibilities that exist in the language to trigger cognition. Note that it is possible for the same cognitive words to appear in each process. Although the words are the same, the thinking processes and the final responses are very different. In order for the desired mediation (search) to occur, the verbal behavior used in the stimulus/question must specify the cognitive process.[7]

---

[7] It is not suggested here that the learner's brain does not think unless a teacher or others provide a stimulus. The brain's function is to be engaged in thought. Thought always highlights a process and specific cognitive operation(s). The brain, with its involuntary continuous activation, jumps from one cognitive operation and topic to another. Relentlessly it performs its function—it thinks! Understanding the functions and structure of the brain is indeed the new frontier. So much remains unknown.

Memory

Observe	trace track	Browse Scan	Decode	Repeat Spell	Copy Emulate	Tell, State Restate	Sketch Diagram
label name	define	Match Assemble	Locate	Select Estimate	Sequence		Sort Cluster
mapping associate	provide examples	Locate	Summarize Paraphrase	Calculate Manipulate	Prove		Translate Convert
cause	effect	Compare	Contrast	Conclude	Reasons for...	Etc.	"Opinion"

........."Creative" *

The following words do not identify a clear cognitive intent. As stated, these words are cognitively ambiguous. Each needs a specific cognitive operation word to clarify the inteded thinking process, ...identify, organize, discuss, examine, show, memorize, list, recognize, describe, explain. The specific cognitive word selected will determine which thinking process is engaged: explain by restating the sequence or explain by justifying the actions; organize by sorting or organize by categorizing.

Discovery
Cognitive Operations Beyond Memory

sequence	select manipulate	Compare	Contrast	Distinguish Differentiate	Conclude, Prove Draw Conclusions
categorize	mapping	Classify Systematize	Compile Build	Analyze, Dissect Simplify	Debate Defend
refute	Infer Deduce	Propose, Reason Rationale	Imagine, Dream Wonder	Hypothesize Speculate	Forecast Suppose
Produce Implications Consequences	Interpret Dramatize	Propose	Compose	Formulate Predict	Construct Devise, Plan
Design Model	Invent Conceive	Problem Solve	Verify	Prioritize Rank	Rate	Criticize
Argue, Induce Persuade	Justify	Evaluate Judge	Assess	Value...	ETC...

........."Creative" *

Figure 5.5. Cognitive operations—A possible clustering. NOTE: The word *creative* is an attribution about the "uniqueness" of an idea(s). Creative ideas stem from or are anchored in one or more cognitive operations from either memory or discovery.

Scan Figure 5.5 and review your classroom language, marking the cognitive words you use. Chart those you use primarily, infrequently, and never. Physical education has as many opportunities to emphasize a variety of cognitive operations as other fields.

Figure 5.5 presents only a few of the possible words in the English language that refer to and invite thinking.[8] Cognitive words within the question/stimulus can either point learners in the desired direction or lead them on unnecessary cognitive tangents. Omitting the cognitive intent also disrupts interacting in the task. Every task in physical education activates a cognitive process.

The complexity and richness of the cognitive process is rooted in the variety and quantity of individual operations, and the visible quality in physical education makes the process even more intriguing. This variety provides human beings with uniquely unlimited possibilities and capacities, but cognitive proficiency requires practice.

Ambiguous Cognitive Words

Ambiguous cognitive words require clarification to convey their intent. Identify, organize, discuss, examine, describe, explain—these familiar classroom directives fail to clearly convey a cognitive expectation. Using these words increases the chances for error, confusion, and misconceptions. Cognitive ambiguity can be removed by indicating the specific cognitive operation expected. Note that either memory or discovery operations can be used to clarify the intent of these words. Using the word *identify* by itself is ambiguous; however, indicating a specific operation clarifies the intent. For example:

> *Identify by:*
> matching, or
> copying—(in physical education, performing)
> contrasting
> providing examples
> justifying
> imagining alternatives
> constructing a model
> others...

---

[8] F. Smith (1990), p. 2, suggests that approximately 77 words in the English language refer to thinking.

Clarity of cognitive intent is efficient, saves time, and reduces frustrations. Perhaps the most commonly used ambiguous cognitive words in the classroom are: what, why, when, where.

The What, Why, When, Where, and How Misconceptions

None of the above W-words appear in the cognitive figure. After much study and many classroom observations, the author concluded that, generally speaking, *What, Why, When, Where,* and *How* are words that:

1. May represent either memory, discovery, or creativity

2. Do not project a specific cognitive operation

3. Require another word in the question or statement to indicate the specific cognitive intent

4. Let students select the specific cognitive operation to answer the question. (When particular responses are not sought, this latitude carries minimal liabilities. However, when responses are intended to match anticipated answers, this option often leads to errors, misunderstandings, and confusion.)

5. Can provide insight into an individual's cognitive preferences

6. Require flexibility and latitude when teachers are evaluating responses, because no specific cognitive operation is stated

7. Permit, even encourage, opinions or position statements. (Interview questions and conversation interactions primarily rely on these words.)

8. Others

There are times in the gymnasium/classroom when it is cognitively appropriate to ask questions that begin with *what, why, when,* and *where.* For example, these words are essential when a person is seeking opinions, determining cognitive preferences, obtaining information from the expert, or exploring new topics.

The process of inquiry into the unknown often begins with a general question: *What is...? What would it be like to...? What if...?* Individuals who ask such questions a priori are anchored in discovery; they are not seeking to remember or reproduce; for them, these words do not project memory or ambiguity. For these individuals the W-words invite and activate the discovery/creative thinking processes. During the mediation phase, the search

---

[9] E. DeBono's work also acknowledges the cognitive confusion in the classroom caused by asking *What.* He designed a program that used different colored hats that the teacher would wear to indicate one of several cognitive operations. One hat color meant that factual answers were sought from the WHAT question, another colored hat indicated that the learners were supposed to answer that WHAT question with an interpretative answer, etc.

process explores (tries out) many cognitive operations in both memory and discovery, trying to assemble a solution, design or invention – trying to discover the product or response that expands current boundaries.

However, in the classroom, the W-words are frequently used inappropriately.[9] Indicating the cognitive path the teacher wants the learners to travel reduces the liabilities of these ambiguous W-words. A common movement task is: How would an elephant move? Now, move like an alligator would move. Both examples imply reproduction—remembering, then copying the movement. However, in many cases the teacher is seeking imaginative movements. By not clarifying the cognitive intent, the teacher leaves the decision to the learners as to which process—memory or discovery—will guide their movements.

Analyze, Explore, Problem Solve: Terms That Indicate a Cluster of Cognitive Operations

Some cognitive operations represent a cluster of supportive cognitive operations rather than one dominant operation. The reciprocal nature of the supportive operations leads to production of a response that is then labeled *analyze, explore, problem solve.* Unlike the operation of, say, comparing, which is precisely defined as *identifying that which is the same, alike, similar,* there is no precise single definition for these words. Rather than leading to a dominant cognitive operation, these words are represented by a series or cluster of supporting operations. Therefore, it is imperative for the teacher to determine the task's cognitive focus and to clearly describe to the learners which supportive operations are to be emphasized.

Discussion

This word is often used to indicate a cognitive process. "Discuss the..." "Let's talk about..." "We are going to have a discussion...." The word *discuss* implies that a conversation, an interaction, a sharing of thoughts and ideas, will occur. Although many teachers refer to this word as though it were a distinct teaching behavior and a particular thinking process, the word does not inherently indicate either one. Conversations, expressions of one's thoughts, can stem from reproduction-memory or production-discovery. Unless discussion questions specify another cognitive operation, the primary operation activated generally is an opinion. "Let's discuss the story...." Since this conversation will be guided by each student's opinion, the content discussion typically jumps from one point of reference to another. When a specific cognitive operation is included, the discussion begins with a common point of reference and a specific learning intent: "Discuss the differences between the two formulas ... the differences among the main characters..., the differences in forms of feedback, etc." In these examples, the content discussion will center around the primary cognitive operation of memory contrasting. However, discussions that evoke discovery and the production of alternative thoughts, center around the specific cognitive operation included in the question: "Discuss the possible implications to individual freedom if a new law was established that...."

Beginning a conversation with: "Let's discuss this situation" can be controversial. This ambiguous statement can lead to misunderstanding and conflict as the participants do not know whether the discussion will stem from memory or is intended to produce new reactions, solutions, or interpretations. Arguments, disappointments, feelings of confusion, and even betrayal can result when individuals approach a conversation from different cognitive entry points. Knowing the cognitive intent in advance makes selecting the appropriate verbal behavior easier. Errors and random cognitive development occur when teachers predominately select ambiguous cognitive words. Think of other words that teachers use to stimulate discussion.

Cognitive Operations and Verbal Behavior

Although learners in any given classroom do not perform equally, they have a more equal opportunity to "enter" the task if ambiguous stimuli/questions, which cause unnecessary searching for the intended cognitive operation, are reduced. In order to achieve cognitive clarity, teachers must be familiar with various cognitive operations, operational definitions, and suggested verbal behaviors.

Operational Definitions

Each cognitive operation has its own image and invites its unique cognitive request.

Familiarity with the various operations and their definitions is necessary in order to formulate questions that:

1. Deliberately develop cognition
2. Correctly select the appropriate cognitive function to obtain the intended content experiences or objectives
3. Diagnose cognitive proficiencies and identify specific deficiencies
4. Offer developmental cognitive opportunities

Table 5.1 presents operational definitions for a variety of cognitive operations and suggested verbal behaviors that trigger each operation. The concept presented is that only a limited range of verbal behaviors triggers each operation and that it is not possible to say "What do you think?" or

Table 5.1   Cognitive Operations and Verbal Behavior

Operation	Operational Definition	Suggested Verbal Behavior
Memory:		
Copying, Emulating	Replicating, reproducing a model exactly: identical, similar representation	1. Copy exactly the.... 2. Reproduce the skill sequence, the movement pattern, the drill exercise.... 3. Emulate each action, movement, sound 4. Mimic my actions, movements, follow exactly
Comparing	Examining and identifying specific characteristics that are the same about various items (x,y,z)	1. What is *alike* about...? 2. What is the *same* about *x, y, z*? 3. Compare items *x,y,z*
Contrasting	Examining and identifying specific characteristics that are different about various items (x,y,z)	1. How do these items *differ*? 2. What is *different about*...? 3. Contrast items *x,y,z*
Sequencing (memory)	Arranging in a series according to a point of reference, a designated criterion (in a,b,c order, largest to smallest, which affects you most, etc....)	1. Place these ... in order from .... 2. Arrange these ... items from tallest to shortest. 3. Chronologically sequence the ... historical events
Sorting, Clustering	Arranging together or grouping items by a shared criterion or category (functions, strength, speed, agility, etc.)	1. Place each ... into the group that matches its.. 2. Cluster the movements, items, facts, events into the group that identifies its.... 3. Sort by.... 4. Sort the type of movement according to physiological ....
Opinion	Expressions of individual preferences, thoughts, likes, and dislikes	1. What do you think about...? 2. What's your opinion about...? 3. Move the way you want to 4. How do you think the ... moves?
Discovery:		
Sequencing (discovery)	Producing a point of reference, a criterion that determines the order items or movements are arranged in a series	1. Produce a point of reference ... (movement, skills, factor, characteristic, criteria, etc.) that can link these... (movements, items, ideas, dates, events, etc.) in an order. 2. Produce a possible criterion by which these movements, skills, items can be sequenced (placed in an order, a series.) 3. Identify a pattern that could be used to link these items (movements, skills) together. Pattern implies an order.
Categorizing	Arranging items or movements into different groups, where each group shares a common attribute.	1. Arrange these activities, actions, moves, skills, objects in two groups so that one group will share a common element not present in the other group. 2. Categorize these items.

(continues)

Table 5.1   Cognitive Operations and Verbal Behavior *(continued)*

Operation	Operational Definition	Suggested Verbal Behavior
Discovery:		
Imagining	Forming a mental image of something; producing something that goes beyond the boundaries of what is known	1. What are possible movements that could express this sound... 2. Conjure up another... movement, picture, story, solution, that is different from what has already been produced.
Pretending	In order to pretend, imagining is evoked. Pretend generally emphasizes *fantasy* and *imagination*	3. Imagine that.... 4. Pretend that....
Designing	In order to design, a mental image about the product in focus must be imagined	5. Design four strategies for passing when ... includes three players... 6. Design three different routines for interpreting....
Interpreting	Attribute possible meaning to something (in any form—moving, performing, speaking, writing, drawing, etc.). Note that interpreting relies on imagination to produce something that goes beyond what is known	1. Produce three different interpretations that suggest.... 2. Interpret the possible feelings the folk dance projects 3. Produce an interpretative dance routine to the music....
Problem solving	Designing a solution to resolve an obstacle, an issue, a situation, irritant; overcoming a problem. Note that many problem solving situations rely on imagining	1. Produce three possible solutions to.... 2. Design an alternative game that incorporates.... 3. Given the limitations of the situation, produce three possible solutions to the problem. 4. Using the materials provided, design a new ... that is able to.... 6. Link different skills in ... to form new movement patterns. Produce three different patterns.
Hypothesizing	Making assumptions about movements, events, issues or happenings, then designing an active investigation to verify the accuracy of the assumption	1. What might be the possible relationship between item x and item y? 2. What would be the possible results if ... happened? 3. What if ... happened and produced ..., could the cause be...?
Justify	To produce supportive evidence to defend a position, act, situation, or decision and providing evidence that legitimizes the actions	1. Produce possible reasons/evidence to support the actions taken. 2. Justify your decision/position. 3. Substantiate your position with evidence.
Others		

"What's your opinion?" and elicit a preselected cognitive operation other than opinion. Before a cognitive operation can be deliberately activated, it is necessary to use the verbal behavior that will accurately recruit it.

Acquiring content from limited cognitive experiences (one or two cognitive operations) produces a shallow knowledge-base. Becoming skilled, competent, and confident in content requires tackling it from a variety of cognitive approaches. When minimal cognitive operations are experienced in class, learners develop a *cognitive economy* and they try to repeat only what was experienced in class. Many do not know how to tackle the content from a variety of cognitive approaches. Movement acquisition must be accompanied with a cognitive emphasis. Movement development is not isolated to the physical channel; it, like all learning, emerges from the cognition Developmental Channel.

Examine the tasks and activities in physical education classrooms for their cognitive requests. What portion of the tasks requires the students to practice the demonstrated task by trying to physically copy, imitate, or reproduce? What portion of all the tasks that learners are engaged in represents reproduction or production? Implementing a variety of cognitive operations for each topic can expand the learners' understanding of, and motivation in, the content.

Verbal Behavior and Ambiguous Cognitive Statements

Ambiguous cognitive statements leave room for cognitive interpretations or misinterpretations and should be used sparingly. The following examples let learners choose to either engage or disengage in the cognitive process; they permit selection of the specific thinking operations.

Can you...? This ambiguous statement and the following variations produce two unwanted responses.[10]

1. They invite the response *no*.
2. They cognitively permit the learner not to engage.
    * "Can you...?"
    * "Who would like to...?"
    * "Would you like to try?"
    * "Can anybody...?"
    * "Would someone like to...?"

---

[10]Ambiguous statements are appropriate when used deliberately. There are times in the classroom when the teacher may want to offer students the opportunity to say *no*. However, when these statements are used with reluctant or defiant learners, they provide opportunities for these learners to cognitively disconnect—by saying no.

- "Can anybody think...?"
- "Can you give an example...?"
- "Does anybody remember...?"
- "Who wants to help out...?"
- "Could you put that another way?"
- "Could you explain your reason to us?"
- "Can you give me...?"

There are no alternatives for these verbal statements when cognitive engagement is the goal. Simply avoid statements that permit learners to say *no* to cognition. Classroom observations documented that after these statements were made, additional comments followed that occupied air time but did not enhance content time-on-task. Generally these statements are nonproductive and time-consuming in the classroom.

Questions that evoke either a *yes* or *no* response typically stop or short-circuit engagement and bypass the teacher's cognitive intent,[11] because the S → D → M → R is completed when learners respond yes or no. Additional cognitive engagement depends on the teacher or the learners asking themselves another stimulus/question to continue cognitive participation. A yes/no question permits the learner to take a position (both cognitive and emotional) before engaging in the content; therefore, restoring cognitive engagement may be difficult. Stopping and starting cognitive engagement is taxing.

Do as many as you can... How many can you do? Actually, these statements permit learners to do one or none, then stop and feel fine about not producing more. Stating quantity is important for sustained cognitive engagement and for appropriate feedback.

Including the pronoun you in the question The pronoun *you* in the question permits cognitive limits based on what is desirable and best for each student. Stating *you* in the question permits learners to personalize, censor, justify, and contour responses according to their past experiences. "What would you...?" "How would you...?" "If you were...?" "Can you think of...?" When the cognitive intent is to divergently examine possibilities beyond an already established position or opinion, inclusion of the pronoun "you" in the question is counterproductive.

---

[11] Asking *yes/no* questions that are a part of a series of questions designed to lead the student to a content focus is a different cognitive experience from asking single or random questions that evoke yes or no.

These questions invite answers that reflect a personal position; therefore, defending one's position, opinion, or response becomes more important than engaging in the content and the development of the specific cognitive operation. Altering the verbal behavior from "How would you pass the soccer ball in this play?" to "Design three possible passes that move the soccer ball beyond..." invites the learners to go beyond their personal preferences. It allows the same learner to produce divergent responses, even seemingly contradictory responses, and it permits acknowledging others' ideas as possible solutions. Inclusion of *you* invites protective and competitive behaviors with winners and losers.

When questions a priori seek exposure of personal beliefs and persuasions, then inclusion of the pronoun *you* is appropriate and necessary. Although therapy, trust-building exercises, and developing friendships rely on the expression of thoughts and feelings that stem from *you*, the majority of classroom content questions are hampered by the inclusion of *you*.

Incorrect responses   When learners lack information and give incorrect responses to questions, teachers generally move on to other students, thus leaving behind the learner who answered incorrectly. An alternative approach is to return to the student who did not know, *after* the correct response has been given, and ask this learner to repeat the correct answer. "Repeat the correct answer, Brenda..." If the learner did not hear or see (most of the time learners will "tune out" after answering incorrectly), have the correct answer repeated. Then ask again, "Brenda, repeat the correct answer?" This technique lets learners know that both participation and accuracy are expected, and that the teacher is committed even to learners who need more time.

Saying, hearing, and seeing the correct answer is an important reinforcement. In a class of 30 learners, generally only one learner states or models the correct answer (which is usually a one-, two-, or three-word response). In some situations, an alternative could be, once the correct response has been given, to call on another learner to repeat the same answer, then another learner, and yet another. The same answer is repeated three or four times. Including learners in active participation in the subject matter not only assists content acquisition, but it also enhances class climate. Frequently learners hear far more incorrect responses than they do correct responses (Ornstein, 1988).

Parameters for answering questions   Knowing when to apply which logistical parameter is another skill that affects the question and answer process. In some situations it is necessary to request order: "one person, one voice at a time." When ordered responses are sought, a preparatory phrase is necessary before stating the question, *With a raised hand...* (then ask the question) or *One voice at a time...* These parameter statements set in-advance expectations. There are other situations where raising the hand interferes with the cognitive and behavior intent (Chinn, 1998). Stating the procedures for expressing questions and answers sets clearer expectations.

Questions/situations that avoid stating, or that confuse, the cognitive intent... Asking questions/designing situations is a major part of any teacher's behavior. Although there are many reasons for asking questions, obtaining a remembered answer and/or inviting a discovered answer on any of the Developmental Channels are two primary classroom objectives. Designing questions/situations requires:

1. Identification of the teacher's overall *reason* for asking the question
2. Awareness of the desired response
3. Identification of the specific (or ambiguous) cognitive operation
4. Ability to determine whether that desired response and cognitive operation would be best served by memory, discovery, or the creative process
5. Ability to precisely select the verbal behavior in the stimulus/question to match the intent!

Questions are asked so that learners can be guided to develop cognitively within a content. Among other professional requirements, teachers must be professional question askers. This skill does not develop automatically; it is learned. The ability to formulate questions and design situations that develop cognition is a skill with profound implications.

Questions that confuse need to be redesigned.

Creativity—A Different Viewpoint

The creative process invites the unexpected, the unusual, a deviation from the norm. It is the uniqueness of the response that merits the distinction *creative*. Unlike the reproductive and productive processes, creativity does not have a mutually exclusive list of cognitive operations that trigger uniqueness. Creative responses are always anchored in a specific cognitive operation from either memory or discovery. This notion of creative-memory and creative-discovery is perhaps new to many readers; however, in reality, creativity is possible in all memory and discovery cognitive operations. It is possible to produce unique responses in all cognitive operations. For example, some dancers conceive of their original routines from imagination, while others flawlessly and with exact perfection, copy the routines and patterns of the masters. In some artistic circles, both are regarded as creative. One is creative-copying, the other creative-imagining. Each cognitive operation can be analyzed in the same manner. Designing is a discovery cognitive operation; when the design is given the attributions of unique, original, or beyond the known or anticipated, it can be considered creative-designing. We have all seen competitive routines in synchronized swimming or ice skating that were unusual (discovery-designing). All the designs were different, but there is always that one routine which added elements meriting the attribution of creative-design.

People generally have preferences among cognitive operations, and it is possible for each person to develop a way of thinking that results in creativity, if only in one cognitive operation. This view of creativity suggests that all people can be encouraged to practice creative responses. Exceptionally talented individuals, who are designated as creative, can generally produce unique responses in an array of cognitive operations.

In the gymnasium/classroom, introductions to creative tasks are often general and unrelated to previous cognitive experiences. Typical class introductions are: "Produce a creative move." "Come up with a creative idea for...." "Be creative in the game. Creativity counts!" "Go for it; let your mind go! Be original."

The words used to indicate the specific cognitive operation are ambiguous and they do not direct the learners' cognitive search, nor do they teach a learner how to initiate the creative process. In fact, the word "creative" often evokes emotions rather than inviting cognitive freedom, exploration, or expression.

Learners who are anchored in memory, and accustomed to giving responses that are correct/incorrect, "freeze" or "get stuck" when teachers select this verbal behavior to introduce the creative expectations. They become emotionally preoccupied with the value implications, and are paralyzed trying to search for *what is uniqueness? What is creative?* On the other hand, learners who are comfortable in divergent discovery are eager to enter creative cognitive dissonance. This emotional and cognitive difference represents an initial cognitive inequality among the learners.

Entering tasks with some degree of cognitive equality is more likely to occur when the question (stimulus) invites and directs learners to the specific thinking operations. Although there may be times when ambiguous and nonspecific questions are appropriate, specific questions are generally more productive to learning in the classroom.

The creative process can be an exhilarating cognitive experience; but for some, feelings of satisfaction occur only after the fear of failure, of being wrong, of being judged by peers and teachers, have passed. Students who are secure in their thinking capacities immediately begin the search for cognitive operations that project their creativity; their cognitive freedom and pride emerge as they experience their own thinking powers. For other learners, this process is frightening and painful; feelings of frustration, embarrassment, inadequacy, and a host of other emotions come forth when creative expressions do not materialize.

The creative process is possible for each of us within our predominant and preferred cognitive realms. Encouraging each individual to produce responses that are unique and unpredictable within cognitive preferences can trigger new creative opportunities and possibilities.

Honoring the Creative Learner

Learners who enjoy engaging in the creative process often shift themselves into a state of creative cognitive activation. Many of these learners, when confronted with memory questions, prefer to go beyond the expected answer and produce creative responses—yet they correctly answer the question! These students' personalities often remain in a constant state of creative cognitive dissonance. Their thinking predominantly views the world from outside the norm and they deliberately avoid the predictable! These learners constantly activate creative responses and are not satisfied with just remembering or discovering. They must produce beyond the known or expected—even when situations and time are not appropriate. They seek air-time, recognition, and approval (feedback) just as the learners do who prefer to function within the established boundaries. In some schools, creative learners often suffer judgment and intolerance for their creativity—for stepping beyond the boundaries.

Although some teachers attempt to subdue or discipline learners whose expressions are constantly unpredictable, many professions require these traits. Computer program designers, advertising agencies, design engineers, improvisational performers, graphic and set designers, etc. seek individuals who are able to go beyond the known. Designing gymnasium episodes that encourage creativity in different cognitive operations invites learners to expand their cognitive, emotional, social, ethical, and physical limits and boundaries.

Cognition and Wait Time

Teacher *wait time* varies with each cluster of teaching behaviors. In general, memory questions require a shorter pause period than do discovery questions. Within the temporary hierarchy, the more supportive cognitive operations that are needed to activate the dominant cognitive operation, the longer the wait time must be before the teacher intervenes. No single time frame is appropriate for all situations/questions or all teaching behaviors. Many immediate memory responses are best practiced with a minimal pause (wait time), whereas producing responses to discovery questions requires longer teacher wait time. When learners are skilled in the thinking process and the cognitive operations, less wait time is possible. The objectives of the content and the teaching behavior selected affect the amount of wait time that is desirable. That issue will be addressed in each teaching behavior.

Designing the Subject Matter

Each cluster of teaching behaviors approaches the design of content with different criteria. In the reproductive teaching styles (styles A–E), tasks share the following characteristics:

1. Reflects a single standard in design and performance. There is only one correct factual response, representing either divergent or convergent memory.

2. Elicits only the cognitive operations included within the memory and recall process.

3. Contains specific descriptions of what to do.

4. Contains specific descriptions of how to do it (performance standard). This prescribes the quality of the task, and includes an example of the process or the procedures to follow.

5. Conforms to and facilitates the decision structure of the selected teaching behavior.

6. Prescribes the quantity.

Although each *reproductive* behavior (A–E) adheres to these criteria, each teaching behavior invites a different task focus; these specific differences are delineated in each teaching behavior chapter.

In the *productive* behaviors (F–K), task design is approached according to the kind of discovery each behavior emphasizes: guided, convergent, or divergent discovery.

Task Sheets

Even in the physical education gymnasium/classroom, one of the most useful aids for accommodating the learner's engagement in a task (or series of tasks) is the *task sheet* (sometimes called a work sheet or a ditto). The presence of these papers does not inherently indicate one behavior or another—the task description, the cognitive emphasis, and the learner's expectation in the task (decision structure) do. The purposes of task sheets are:

1. To begin to reduce the learners' dependency on the teacher and provide an opportunity for them to engage in the task on their own.

2. To present the task and assist the learner in remembering the task (what to do)

3. To increase the efficiency of time-on-task and teacher–learner communication.

4. To reduce the number of repeated explanations by the teacher.

5. To teach learners to listen to the initial set of expectations.

6. To teach the learners to follow specific written instructions.

7. To record the learners' progress (optional).

Whether the learners are asked to listen and observe the explanation/demonstration, or whether the task sheet actually delivers the task, the task sheet becomes the source of information. The learner is responsible for following through and completing the task on the sheet.

The use of task sheets has several implications to content involvement and teacher–learner interaction. It reduces the learner's manipulation of the teacher (in any behavior). Students who have learned to manipulate ignore the teacher during the initial delivery of expectations, then, while the class is engaged in doing the task, they call the teacher for another explanation, a private one thus dominating the teacher's time. When this behavior occurs, it reverses the control in the class and reduces the teacher's available time to move about, observe, and offer feedback. For example, the manipulative learner may say: "I forgot what you said." The teacher cannot ignore the request to repeat the expectations, nor can the teacher hold the learner accountable for the initial explanation. The teacher may feel frustrated, but compelled to repeat the directions.

When task sheets are used and when learners do request clarification, the interaction between teacher and learner is different. They can be asked, "What does the description on the task sheet say?" The teacher thereby initiates a different relationship with the learner, who now must refer to information available on the task sheet. The teacher continues: "Is the description clear?" (The teacher has initiated a second interaction.) The learner must focus on the description of the task, and now has only two options. One is to say, "Yes, it is clear." The teacher could then say: "Now, you are ready to begin." The teacher may or may not stay to offer feedback before moving on to the next learner.

The learner's second option is to answer "No." The teacher then can say: "Which *specific* phrase or word is not clear?" (Again, the teacher initiates.) This question invites the learner to either focus on the description of the task and to be specific about the unclear phrase or word or to begin engagement and be accountable to practicing the task. Pending the learner's action, the teacher provides the appropriate response (offering clarification or acknowledging the learner's understanding) and then moves on.

The relationships when using task sheets are different from those where no task sheets are used, because the interactions are based on verbal behaviors that decrease manipulation by learners. The interactions where task sheets are used reestablishes the teacher in the appropriate role of assessing and inviting the learner to participate in understanding and performing the task according to the decisions of the selected teaching behavior.

Well-designed task sheets in all the reproductive behaviors include the six characteristics for task design. The productive behaviors task sheets also include the specific discovery structure of the selected teaching behavior. (See the individual teaching behavior for examples.)

Cognitive Format Designs

Although physical educators use format designs less frequently than classroom teachers, it is important to present this concept so that more experiences using a variety of cognitive operations can occur in the gymnasium. Some cognitive operations have a distinctive look, shape, or form that can be visually sketched. These visual representations of specific cognitive operations assist the learner's thinking in his or her search (during mediation) to locate the corresponding cognitive function. Visual cognitive formats do not replace the need for introductions and explanations of cognitive operations; however, they do help learners visualize the new abstract cognitive functions. The educational movements called advanced organizers and graphic organizers reinforce this concept of producing materials that use visual formats to complement cognitive functions.

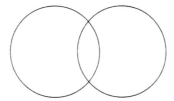

Figure 5.6. Venn diagram

Although cognition always occurs within content, each cognitive operation's function and definition can be understood independent of any specific content area. Comparing in any context means searching for the specific characteristics that are the same. Contrasting in any context refers to those characteristics that are not alike. Venn's diagram (Figure 5.6) visually reinforces these two cognitive operations; it visually presents two spaces for responses that represent contrasting and a different space for those that represent comparing. The overlapping circle permits learners to see that different items can share common features or characteristics. Although this diagram is a powerful visual tool for introducing comparing and contrasting, an introduction to the cognitive processes is still necessary. Note that the Venn diagram asks the brain to function in a reciprocal manner between two cognitive operations. Separate experiences in each operation are needed first in order to verify the learners' understanding and proficiency.

Figure 5.7 presents *comparing* and *contrasting* in another visual format. It, too, provides separate spaces for responses in each cognitive operation. The design, with its boxes, arrows, and key words, visually guides cognition and directs learners to search for the requested cognitive operation. As with all notions in this text, constant use of visual organizers produces liabilities: Visual designs can lull the brain, and some learners who successfully follow the organizer do not actively forge the new cognitive pathways on their own. For these learners, later recruitment of these cognitive operations without the organizers is difficult. At a given point, learners must produce their own cognitive designs, rather than filling in the spaces on prepared

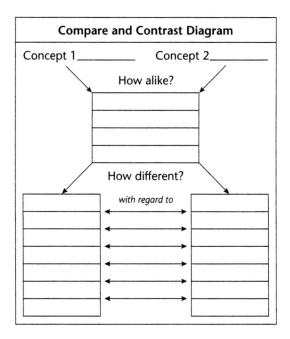

Figure 5.7. Compare and contrast diagram[12]

pages. Cognitive format designs can introduce material, reinforce, and motivate thinking in different operations.

There are many cognitive format design examples. Examine other examples and experiment with them in the gymnasium. They can be fun while teaching learners deliberate cognitive skills.

The notion of the non-versus approach is the cornerstone of the ideas presented in this text. Within the educational arena there is no single idea or notion so uniquely powerful in human development that it stands alone as *the* important issue! The non-versus approach of the Spectrum acknowledges and values the importance of all the developmental channels, each of the components of teaching, each of the three basic processes of thinking, and, as we will see, all teaching behaviors. It is the reciprocation and supportive relationship among these functions that contribute to human growth and development—to the process of educating.

In summary, the Spectrum describes two clusters of behaviors: A–E, which serves the human capacity for reproduction, and F–K, which serves the human capacity for production. Cognitive development is not a haphazard process; it requires knowledge about the thinking processes, specific cognitive operations, and precise verbal behavior. A challenge to teachers to increase awareness and introspection was extended in the verbal behavior and feedback sections; that same challenge for awareness of cognition is extended now. What teachers say and how they say it influences learning. The cognitive channel is always activated whether the content is science or expressing feelings, math or self-control, reading or practicing kind and caring techniques. Cognition directs our actions in all the Developmental Channels. Thinking is what people do; reinforcing the possibilities in thinking is what teachers are asked to do.

CHAPTER 6

The Command Style—A

Pre-impact (T)
Impact   (T)
Post-impact (T)[1]

The defining characteristic of the Command style is precision performance—reproducing a predicted response or performance on cue. In the anatomy of the Command style the role of the teacher is to make all the decisions, and the role of the learner is to follow these decisions on cue. When this behavior is achieved, the following objectives are reached in subject matter and in behavior.

The Objectives

Subject Matter Objectives	Behavior Objectives
To reproduce a model by immediate performance	To socialize the individual into the norms of the group
To achieve accuracy and precision of performance	To achieve conformity
	To achieve uniformity
To achieve immediate results	To build group identity and pride—a sense of belonging
To achieve a synchronized performance	To enhance esprit de corps
To adhere to a predetermined model	To follow directions on cue
To master subject matter skills	To achieve specific aesthetic standards
To perpetuate cultural traditions and rituals	To develop habits and routines
	To perpetuate cultural traditions, ceremonies, and rituals
To use time efficiently	To control groups or individuals
To cover more material	To instill safety procedures
Others	To adhere to a particular kind of discipline (Command style discipline; each behavior has its own form of discipline)
	Others

The O–T–L–O is the fundamental unit of relationships. The particular roles (decisions) of the teacher and learner in the Command style produce

[1] This diagram represents the anatomy of the Command style.

a particular set of outcomes. The outcomes can be compared to the anticipated set of objectives that this decision relationship produces to determine the degree of congruence (agreement) that occurred between the intended set of objectives and the actual classroom action. When any of the above objectives arise, the decision structure of the Command Style will lead to them.

Some of the many examples that represent the decision structure of the Command style include:

- Synchronized swimming
- Classical ballet dancing
- School figures in ice skating
- Crew (rowing)
- Group calisthenics
- Performing in an orchestra
- Square, folk, line dancing
- Singing in a choir
- Pronouncing new words or words in another language
- Landing a plane on an aircraft carrier
- Acting in theater productions
- Participating in martial arts
- Trapeze performances
- Cheerleading
- Performing in a drill team
- Marching in a band
- Marching in military parades
- Dancing with the Radio City Rockettes
- Precision flying with the Blue Angels
- Taking part in formal ceremonies—weddings, inaugural celebrations, funerals, etc.
- Precision parachuting
- Others

Few fields are as rich in examples of the Command style as physical education. Precision physical performances are represented in all aspects of the society. Some examples maintain traditions, while others challenge them. Some examples are necessary for an orderly society, while others are intended as entertainment. Regardless of the content, all share the same decision structure: the teacher (leader, or authority figure) makes all the decisions, while the participants/learners/performers execute the performance decisions on cue. The decisions are the defining factor that establishes the teaching– learning relationship and the ensuing objectives.

Although Mosston deliberately selected the name Command style because it captured the essence of this style's decision relationship, the name is arbitrary. Mosston could have named this first behavior any of the following: Precision Practice, Cued Response, Imitation Practice, Follow the Leader Practice, Choral Responding Practice, Immediate Response Practice, Boot-Camp Practice, etc. What is unwavering is the decision structure that defines the relationship. When the behavior of the teacher and the learner adheres to the anatomy of the Command style, that behavior, independent of its arbitrary name, leads to the objectives of this relationship. For some, the name Command style produced a negative emotion that prevented them from acknowledging the validity of this teaching–learning behavior. The purpose of establishing landmark names for different teaching–learning behaviors is to establish a common language, a frame of reference, that "enables us to converse about teaching in a clear, efficient manner and to claim this jargon as our own—different from other teaching fields" (Metzler, 1983, p. 146). The importance of any teaching–learning relationship is not its name, but the set of decisions that lead to the educational objectives.

The Anatomy of the Command Style

All teaching styles evolve from the Anatomy of Any Style (Figure 6.1). From this Anatomy how can we derive the specific structures of different teaching styles? How many teaching–learning styles are there? What *differentiates* one from the other?

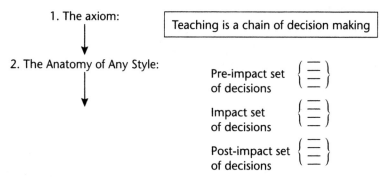

Figure 6.1. The Anatomy of Any Style

The specific styles and the differentiation among the styles are identified by who makes which decisions, when. In any teaching–learning relationship, there are two decision makers: the teacher and the learner. Each can make the minimum to the maximum number of decisions as delineated in the Anatomy (see Chapter 3). This minimum-to-maximum continuum in decision making constitutes the theoretical limits that can be applied to the Anatomy of Any Style (Figure 6.1). Thus, each option in the teacher–learner relationship can be expressed by a precise identification of who makes which decisions, about what and when.

The landmark Command style emerges when the teacher makes the maximum, and the learner makes the minimum, number of decisions in the Anatomy (see Chapter 3). This kind of teaching–learning relationship (style) is in effect for the experiences (episodes) described at the beginning of this chapter.

The schematic representation (Figure 6.2) describes the flow from the axiom to the emergence of the specific structure of the Command style.

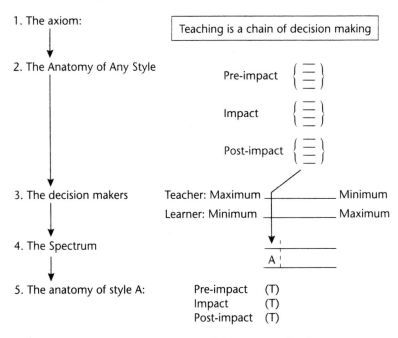

Figure 6.2. The emergence and anatomy of the Command style—A

- *Step 1:* Identifies the axiom.
- *Step 2:* Identifies the Anatomy of Any Style. It describes *what* decisions must be made.
- *Step 3:* Identifies the first condition on the Spectrum, in which the teacher makes the maximum number of decisions and the learner makes the minimum number.
- *Step 4:* Identifies the relationship between the teacher and the learner that is designated style A, the beginning of the Spectrum.

- *Step 5:* Identifies the role of the teacher as one who, in the specific anatomy of this style, makes *all* the decisions in the pre-impact, impact, and post-impact sets, designated as:

  (T)

  (T)

  (T)

  The role of the learner is to perform—that is, to follow the decisions made by the teacher in the given episode.

The designation (L), therefore, does not appear in the anatomy of the Command style—A. It will appear in later styles when the learner actually makes decisions in specific sets. In the Command style, the only decision the learner makes is the choice between "yes, I'll do it" or "no, I will not do it." Once a *yes* decision is made, the learner proceeds to follow every decision made by the teacher. If the learner makes a *no* decision, there is no transaction between the teacher and learner as anticipated in the pre-impact set.

The essence of the Command style is the direct and immediate relationship between the teacher's stimulus and the learner's response. The stimulus (the command signal) by the teacher precedes every movement of the learner, who performs according to the model presented by the teacher. Hence, all the decisions listed in the Anatomy of Any Style—subject matter selection, location, posture, starting time, pace and rhythm, stopping time, duration, and interval, feedback, etc.—are made by the teacher. The schematic representation of the beginning of the Spectrum and the anatomy of the Command style appear in Figure 6.2.

The Implementation of the Command Style

The focal questions for the teacher who wishes to implement an episode (or a series of episodes) in the Command style are: What is the "picture" of this kind of a relationship between a teacher and students? How does one translate the theoretical model (intent) into actual teaching–learning behaviors (actions)? How does the teacher determine if the objectives of this style are reached? Let us start with a general description of an episode and then identify the steps needed to implement it.

Description of an Episode

An episode in the Command style must reflect the essence of this relationship: the teacher makes all the decisions and the learner responds to each decision. In this episode, correspondence between the learner's behavior and the teacher's behavior is continuous for each and every performed movement; the teacher gives the command signal for each movement and the learner performs accordingly. Examples of this relationship can be observed in classes of karate, ballet, aerobics, and folk dances. Sometimes the command signal and the rhythm-support techniques are relegated to other people or to instruments such as the beat of the music in aerobics, the drums in some folk dances, the coxswain in rowing, the student leading a class in warm-up exercises, and so on. The essence of the relationship is the same—one person (or surrogate) is making all the decisions for the others. When this relationship exists, the objectives for the Command style are reached.

A teacher who wishes to use this style needs to be fully aware of the decision structure (the anatomy of this style), the sequence of the decisions, the possible relationships between command signals and expected responses, the appropriateness of the task, and the present level of ability of the learners (their ability to perform the movements with reasonable accuracy and adhere to the demonstrated model).

How to Implement the Command Style

The following steps describe how to use the anatomy of the Command style as guidelines for implementation. This process involves the pre-impact, impact, and post-impact decisions.

The Pre-Impact Set   The purpose of the pre-impact set of decisions is to plan. During the planning set, all the decisions in the anatomy are made in accordance with the selected teaching–learning behavior. Deciding which specific teaching–learning behavior to select is determined by making decisions about the objectives for the task and the behavior. The planning will eventually result in a lesson plan (see Chapter 11).

The Impact Set   The impact set is the actual face-to-face implementation time. The purpose of the impact set of decisions is to engage the learners in active participation and to execute—follow through with—the decisions made during the pre-impact. It is the time to put the intent into action.

It is imperative (in all styles) that the expectations be sequenced during delivery in the episode. The learners must know the expectations of the task performance and the expected teacher–learner relationship (roles/decisions of the teacher and learner). Therefore, the teacher is responsible for setting the scene by presenting the expectations during every episode.

Setting the scene, in any style, always includes delivering three sets of expectations:

1. Subject matter—the content
2. Behavior—the roles/decisions of the teacher and the learners
3. Logistical procedures—equipment, time, location, and other considerations

These three expectations can be delivered in the order that best leads to the anticipated objectives. Expectations about subject matter establish what is to be done; behavior focuses on how the teacher and learners are expected to look while engaging in the task (behavior image); the logistical procedures indicate the supporting details and parameters for the environment and task. Logistical examples include distribution of equipment, organization of learners, location boundaries, movement patterns from one station to another, time limits, attire and appearance requests, and other task or environment parameters. It is important to deliver the three expectations in separate statements/segments rather than mixing them. It is easier for learners to grasp the expectations when they are presented individually.

In the initial stages of using the Spectrum (or any new style) the students will need an introduction to the idea of different teaching–learning styles/behaviors. For the first two or three episodes in this style, the teacher could present something similar to the following to prepare the learners for an expanded classroom reality.

Initial Introduction—Roles/Behavior Expectations

1. The teacher explains to the students that when a teacher and student are in a face-to-face situation, a variety of decisions can be made by the teacher or the learner.

2. These decisions can be distributed between the teacher and the learners in a variety of ways depending on the relationship's purpose at the particular time and the particular episode.

3. One of these particular arrangements is a relationship where the teacher's role is to make all the decisions and the learner's role is to follow, perform, and respond to each decision—each command (stimulus).

4. The purpose of such a relationship (called the Command style or Precision Practice) is to elicit an immediate response so that certain tasks can be learned accurately and in a short period of time.

5. A series of episodes in this style facilitates the accomplishment of objectives such as replication of a model, precision and accuracy of performance, and synchronized performance. (See the list of objectives cited earlier in this chapter).

Experience with the Spectrum styles indicates that most students can internalize the structure and operation of the styles within two or three episodes when the introduction to the styles covers points 1 through 5. Therefore, to set the expectations in subsequent episodes, the teacher announces the name of the style and moves on to the delivery of the subject matter.

Initial Introduction—Subject Matter Expectations

1. The teacher demonstrates the whole task, its parts, and its terminology (the order here may vary according to purpose). This establishes the model for the performance.

2. The demonstration may be relegated to videotape, pictures, task sheets, or to a student who can perform the task according to the model.

3. The teacher explains the movement sequence or details necessary for efficiently or safely understanding the task.

4. Varying time ratios of demonstration and explanation may be necessary for different tasks.

Initial Introduction—Logistical Procedures Expectations

1. The teacher establishes the preparatory and command signals for the episode. These may change during the episode to accommodate different aspects of the subject matter.

2. Most episodes require parameters regarding: time, location, interval, where to get and return equipment, attire, and appearance.

3. Other procedures may be identified, depending on the subject matter or behavior expectations.

At this point, the teacher and the learners are ready to begin the activity, which is the essence of the impact set. The learners respond according to the command signals and the rhythm support procedures conducted by the teacher.

The Post-Impact Set   The post-impact set of decisions offers feedback to the learner about the performance of the task and about the learner's role in following the teacher's decisions. (See the section on feedback forms in Chapter 4).

The Command style experience is one of action. The repeated movement in performing each task and replicating the model brings about the contribution of this style to physical development. Passivity is incongruent with this style. In any given episode, the learners use a maximum amount of time in active participation. A minimum amount of time is used by the teacher for delivery of the three expectations—subject matter, behavior/role, logistics. Active time-on-task in this style is very high. Schematically, the time distribution looks like Figure 6.3.

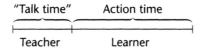

Figure 6.3. Time distributions in the Command style

Figure 6.4 presents the flow of events that occur in each episode. The first three expectations can appear in any order to best facilitate the objectives of the episode.

Episode #: _____ Content _____ Objective _____		
Expectations	**Sequence of Events**	**Time**
Subject Matter Presentation	Expectations:	
Behavior Presentation	Expectations:	
Logistics Presentation	Expectations:	
Questions for Clarification	Verify Understanding of Expectations before the Action:	
Action, Task Engagement, Performance		
Feedback		
Closure	Reinforce the Stated Expectations:	

Figure 6.4. Events per episode

The Implications of the Command Style

Each style on the Spectrum differently affects learners, subject matter selection, and task design.

Each style suggests a set of implications. Whenever a Command style behavior is used in an episode, it implies that:

- The teacher can design experiences for group synchronization and success.
- The teacher can design a stimulus-response experience that produces developmental benefits.
- The teacher is aware of the need for conformity to certain principles for safety, or movement proficiency, or for accuracy in performance.
- The teacher is able to develop group cohesiveness.
- The learners can function and develop physical skills within a stimulus-response relationship.
- The learners are willing to acknowledge their roles and partnerships within the group.
- The learners acknowledge the teacher's expertise and are willing to accept the teacher's decisions.

Subject Matter Considerations

The overriding purpose of the Command style is to develop automaticity of responses or movements; therefore, content that is performed by what appears to be "wired reflexes" or "instinct" requires precision practice of the Command style (Mechling, 1990, pp. 49–65). Aspects of many activities or sports require accuracy and precision in body positions and movements. Fencing, archery, swimming, baseball, proper holding of racquets, clubs, balls, hoops, repetition of basic steps or routine performances—all require frequent experiences in precision practice.

A common assumption in the command–precision practice is that "overlearning" needs to occur to produce automaticity. The following suggestions relate to using the command–precision practice. When learners are inexperienced and new to the content, the task should deal with one stimulus at a time (a moving ball, but in a stationary position).

However, when learners are skilled in the task, focusing their attention on the individual parts of what is already an automatic "learned" response will disrupt the wired reflex and skill proficiency. When errors are observed in an "automatic" or "wired reflex" performance, the performance must be rewired by interrupting the automatic flow of the action by focusing on the flawed section. Relearning is difficult because it emphasizes multiple Developmental Channels—first the emotional channel to accept that a "known" skill must be altered, then the cognitive channel to understand the differences, and finally the physical channel to alter a movement pattern.

The following guidelines summarize subject matter selection for the Command–Precision style:

- The subject matter is fixed. It represents a single standard.
- The subject matter is best learned by immediate recall and through repeated performance.
- The subject matter can be divided into separate elements that can be replicated by a stimulus-response procedure and can be learned in a short period of time.
- The greater the speed of recall, the more proficient the learner will be in moving on to other aspects of the subject matter.
- Individual differences are not invited; instead, replication of the selected subject matter is sought.
- Through frequent replication, the group can perform the task in unison.

Style-Specific Comments

Since each behavior represents a different teacher–learner decision relationship, a different reality emerges with the use of a given style. Each behavior has its own dos and don'ts, its own occurrences, and its own potential difficulties. Awareness of these reality aspects helps to develop insights into the style's essence and contributions, as well as preventing mishaps that might reduce the possibility of reaching the objectives. The following section offers some style-specific comments regarding episodes in the Command style.

The teacher must be aware of the sensitive nature of the Command style. This relationship of one person making all the decisions for others must be used with full consideration of the emotional state of the learner, the learner's capacity to respond, and the nature and purpose of the task. Young children, for example, enjoy many Command style activities, such as Simon says, mirroring actions, and follow the leader. All represent imitating behaviors. Emulating, repeating, copying, and responding to directions are necessary activities for young children. Learning to do a task is a part of growing and of becoming socialized into a group. Responding to directions is an important behavior for young children. Feeling a sense of accomplishment, rather than just the act of responding, is the primary motivator for learners of any age group in the Command style.

Adults participate in Command style activities for two primary reasons: personal development and/or participation in a subculture's activities or rituals. An example of such an experience is step or dance aerobic sessions. These illustrate all the components and objectives of the Command style— high time-on-task, repetition, high degree of uniformity, precision, and safety. It is reasonable to assume that the primary purpose for participating in step or dance aerobics is not these components, but the sense of development (fitness, being in shape, losing weight) conveyed to participants. Command style experiences will best accomplish this goal. An equally powerful reason for participating in an aerobics class is the sense of participation in a socially accepted environment and activity. Another example of a Command style experience is karate, primarily the training aspect. Many of the participants in these activities accept not only the Command style behaviors, but the manners and rituals that may not have been part of their culture or personal conduct. A third type of experience includes high-risk sports. Acquiring some of the necessary skills requires Command style relationships and discipline. When safety is paramount, Command style behavior relationship is mandatory during training and often during the experience itself. In activities such as parachuting, mountaineering, and scuba diving, Command style episodes focus on the particular physical responses and the appropriate, precise use of equipment and accessories. In addition, controlled episodes are designed to teach deliberate management of stress and panic. Only when these aspects are learned and integrated (mostly by Command style experiences) can participants move on to the real experience of participating in and enjoying the sport.

Cultural/aesthetic experiences represent a fourth type of Command style activity. The Command style is often used to teach dance techniques. Examples can be found in ballet, certain aspects of modern dance, and in folk dance. In these diverse forms of dance, precise performance and adherence to a predetermined model are both important. The dance forms themselves project aesthetic values and the continuity of cultural standards.

The fifth type represents some of the competitive experiences in sports. Synchronized swimming may represent the epitome of the Command style because of its high-level precision, synchronization, and projection of a particular set of aesthetic values. The compulsory part of competitive gymnastics is another example, and rowing cannot be successful without maximum synchronization and precision.

It is fascinating to realize that activities so diverse in structure and purpose share the same teaching–learning process or teaching behavior—the Command style.

The teacher must be aware that the Command style is only one of the options in human interaction; to realize the maximum benefits of this style, an integration of several elements must be present when this behavior is in process. Some of these elements are: selection of the subject matter, time-on-task, logistical accommodations, appropriate feedback, and an appropriate affective relationship with the learner. Style A must not be perceived as the "time-efficient style," or the "strict" style. Style A is a combination of all the dimensions just cited. The skilled teacher who also cares for the learners can elevate this relationship to a level of mutual respect and emotional comfort.

The teacher must be aware of the emotional context of this behavior. There are at least two possibilities that can develop. One is the abuse of power by the teacher, who may use this behavior for control and reprimand purposes. (When we reprimand someone, we usually take away decisions.) When this kind of teaching behavior prevails, negative feelings often result and the learner will reject the teaching style, the teacher, and the subject matter. The second possibility is that the teacher will use the Command style with affection, charm, and care. The Command style does not mean "being mean"; this behavior can be used to motivate learners, elevate their self-concept, and develop esprit de corps.

Common Pitfalls to Avoid

When an episode in the Command style is not reaching its objectives, it may be due to one or more of the following:

1. Excessive amount of teacher-talk and too little time for the learners' active participation.

2. The class is not synchronized in the performance of the movements. The teacher needs to examine the pace and rhythm speed (too fast or too slow).

3. The teacher is giving annoying or overlapping command signals. Loud or continuous repetition of a signal, or a signal inappropriate to the task can be counterproductive and even cause discomfort. Overlapping or unclear signals confuse time decisions—starting, pace and rhythm, and stopping. The teacher should consider alternative signals.

4. Excessive repetition of the same task may cause boredom, fatigue, or both. Learners need to feel challenged and satisfied that they have learned something from this behavior.

5. Stopping the action of the entire class because one or two learners are having difficulty stops the flow of the activity and diverts the class's attention to the inadequacies of the individuals.

6. The teacher stays only in one spot. In this behavior, the teacher does not have to stay in one fixed position when conducting the episode. Moving about (using rhythm-support techniques other than counting) provides the teacher an opportunity for individual and private feedback without stopping the action.

7. Unclear introduction of the expectations causes tangents. Displaying a classroom chart reminds the learners that multiple behaviors will be in use in the gymnasium (Figure 6.5).

There may be other pitfalls, but when something goes awry, it can always be traced to a particular decision. The role of the teacher is to examine that decision and make the proper adjustment.

Figure 6.5. Visual classroom chart

The Developmental Channels

The importance of the Developmental Channels must not be overlooked. They are the source from which teaching–learning derives its meaning, and the tools from which diversity and variability are created. Each landmark style is defined by decisions that focus on specific objectives (attributes along the Developmental Channels). Each learner has the opportunity to make the decisions and develop the attributes (objectives) of the landmark styles.

It is possible to alter the developmental emphasis (the attributes), without changing the decision distribution of the landmark style. When the emphasis shifts, a *design variation* is created that offers learning experiences in attributes that expand the landmark style. *Design variations* are created when attributes on the different Developmental Channels are emphasized and the decision distribution remains consistent with the specific style.[2] The possible design variations within each landmark style are infinite. For example, using the criterion of social involvement, the examples provided to illustrate the landmark Command style have not focused on the social

[2] The concept of design variations is also referred to as *canopy*: Design variations exist under the canopy of each teaching–learning style.

channel or on any of the attributes within this channel; therefore, learners are minimally involved in any specific social involvement attributes (Figure 6.6). However, it is possible to emphasize specific social attributes while participating in the Command style. As long as the decision distribution remains that of the Command style, task variations that emphasize social interplay still represent this style. Choreographed teamed dance routines—ballroom, folk, modern dancing—are examples. Movements in calisthenics that require synchronization and teamwork in a "cued" performance also represent the Command style with a social emphasis. Review the list of examples at the beginning of the chapter for the ones that emphasize social responsibility and respect, while highlighting individual precision performance. The tasks and the developmental channel selected for Command style episodes can reinforce an individual experience, or a group experience that does not emphasize social interplay, or it can elicit a highly dependent social structure. The developmental channel emphasis within the decision structure pinpoints the focus of the learning experience as it relates to the subject matter.

Social Emphasis
The Developmental Channels
minimum   maximum
Cognitive _____
Social _____
Emotional _____
Physical _____
Moral/Ethical _____

Figure 6.6. Social emphasis and the Command style

Likewise, design variations that emphasize attributes along the emotional, ethical, or cognitive channels can be designed using the Command style decision distribution. The idea of design variations within a style provides an expanded view of each style and it offers more possibilities for creating a variety of learning experiences within each style.

Notice that when attributes on the social channel are emphasized, attributes along the emotional, cognitive, and ethical channels are activated. These attributes are reinforced within the decision distribution of the Command style. This social, emotional, cognitive, and ethical learning focus is different from a social experience that uses a different teaching style. The learning focus is the result of the interplay between the teaching style and the attributes that are emphasized on the Developmental Channels and their influence on the task expectations.

Design Variations

Each landmark behavior identifies a set of objectives that learners can accomplish in a specific decision configuration. That statement does not imply that there is a single desired image to each style. When a teaching style becomes fixed in its implementation image, it means that the attributes emphasized on the various Developmental Channels are the same in all or most episodes. Expectations about the kind of tasks selected and the performance/practice involvement are predictable and fixed. In some specific situations this single image may be desirable; however, in the gymnasium/classroom such experiences limit accomplishing a wide set of educational objectives. When teachers design variations within the same teaching style, by emphasizing various attributes on the Developmental Channels, they offer their students a variety of learning opportunities. Learning to design variations using the same teaching style requires making a decision about the focus/the objectives (the attributes on the Developmental Channel) that will complement the task, while retaining the decision distribution of the landmark style.

Design variations within the Command style can emphasize any current issue. For example, if character education is the developmental criterion, how could a teaching–learning episode in physical education be designed in the Command style to emphasize attributes in character education? To design episodes with this focus, decisions would need to be made about the physical task, the specific attributes in character education, and about the Developmental Channels to be emphasized in the task. Indeed, the possibilities for learners to experience various attributes in character education while performing physical tasks and participating in the objectives of the Command style are plentiful.[3]

---

[3] It is suggested here that current issues, such as character education, be integrated into physical education tasks and reinforced in a variety of behaviors by using different teaching styles, rather than taught as separate lessons. Many tasks in physical education can be selected and designed to acknowledge attributes associated with the character education movement. Isolated lessons that wish to shape behavior are ineffective. Shaping behavior must be integrated into, and reinforced as a part of, the content of the lessons.

Designing a task from a specific developmental emphasis, rather than just selecting a physical activity, moves episodes, lessons, and unit designs to a different developmental level. Such learning experiences emphasize human attributes; they become associated with human qualities rather than just the content or the specific task.

Let's use the parachute in a classroom example. Many of the tasks using the parachute in physical education require the Command style. Learners, working as a group, are expected to physically move in a synchronized behavior (often to the signals of the teacher or music). Some physical activities include:

- Lifting and lowering the parachute
- Shaking the chute
- Having a designated learner run under or around the chute
- Running to the center, then back
- Practicing curls

All of these activities focus completely on the physical channel with no connection to any other attributes on other developmental channels.

It is possible to make generalized assumptions about the effect of the first set of tasks on the development of the learners in each channel. However, it would be incorrect to say that because the learners were in a group, socialization was being developed. Nor that, because the learners had to be aware of those beside them, they were developing ethical consideration for others. Such objectives are neither substantiated nor emphasized in the task directions; therefore, it is presumptuous to assume that they are being experienced or developed.

Let's add a different learning focus to the task "Run to the center then back." Calling out the task—run to the center then back—generally leads to a collision. Because the task emphasis is on physical participation, without mention of any attributes, the learners have the choice to bombard one another. It's fun! It's physical. It's active. However, if the teacher wanted to add a specific human attribute (self-control) to this task, the teacher could say, "Without invading the space of others, now, let's run to the center and maintain our own self-space." Give the concrete example of skydiving. "When skydivers jump, they have to be very careful not to get too close to other divers to avoid entangling the parachutes. This time, as you run to the center, maintain self-space." This task can be made more challenging, in the same attribute of physical self-control. Have the learners move in a circle and on signal move to the center while continuing to walk, skip, run forward—all without touching. Using the parachute as a tool and movement as the form, human attributes among the Developmental Channels can be emphasized in tasks.

This example emphasizes the human attribute of physical restraint (not colliding with others). This same task could be modified to incorporate specific social, emotional, or ethical attributes.[4]

When tasks are designed with a deliberate link to attributes on the Developmental Channels, a new vista is opened in teaching and learning.

Figure 6.7. Images representing the Command style

The decision distribution of the Command style, the first landmark teacher–learner relationship, creates a set of learning objectives that is essential for all students to experience. When teachers design experiences that emphasize a variety of attributes along the Developmental Channels, they create enriching experiences that can foster goals in both physical education and character development. The Command relationship is only one of the ways in which teachers and learners can interact and relate to subject matter. The next landmark behavior shifts specific decisions to create a different landmark learning experience.

[4] Refer to Chapter 18 for additional information on designing subject matter.

CHAPTER 7

The Practice Style—B

Pre-impact (T)
Impact → (T)
Post-impact (T)[1]

The defining characteristic of the Practice style is individual and private practice of a memory/reproductive task with feedback. In the anatomy of the Practice style the role of the teacher is to make all subject matter and logistical decisions and to provide private feedback to the learners. The role of the learner is to individually and privately practice a memory/reproductive task while making nine specific decisions (presented next). When this behavior is achieved, the objectives described below are reached in subject matter and in behavior.

The Objectives

Subject Matter Objectives	Behavior Objectives
To practice by oneself reproducing the model	To experience the beginning of independence by making the nine decisions
To activate memory cognitive operations necessary for the task	To develop initiating skills in the nine decisions
	To realize that decision making accommodates learning the task
To acquire and internalize content from private practice	To learn to be accountable for the consequences of each decision, for example: • relationship between time and tasks • regulation of one's pace and rhythm • consequences of use of time
To realize that proficient performance is related to task repetition	
To realize that proficient performance is related to knowledge of results-feedback	To learn to respect others' rights to make decisions in the nine categories
	To initiate an individual and private relationship between the teacher and learner
	To develop trust in shifting and making the nine decisions

[1] This diagram represents the anatomy of the Practice style.

The Practice style establishes a new reality, offers new conditions for learning, and reaches a different set of objectives than the Command style. The landmark O–T–L–O relationship of the Practice style occurs because certain decisions are shifted from the teacher to the learner. This shift, in who makes decisions about what, when, creates new relationships between the teacher and learner, between the learner and the tasks, and among the learners themselves.

In every field, the Practice style is a predominant behavior—people individually practice tasks and receive feedback. This landmark teaching–learning behavior can emphasize any of the attributes along the Developmental Channels. Consequently, the classroom image of this behavior is not singular. Although there are more variations in the class-room image of this style than most styles, the decision distribution for these variations represents the anatomy of the Practice style. To determine the developmental focus of any teaching–learning event it is necessary to iden-tify the specific decisions made by the teacher and the learner as they par-ticipate in the content.

The Anatomy of the Practice Style

To design episodes in the second style on the Spectrum, a change in the decision distribution—who makes which decisions, when—must take place; specific decisions are shifted from the teacher to the learner. In this new landmark style, which has significantly different objectives from the Command style, the following nine specific decisions are shifted from the teacher to the learners in the impact set:

1. Location
2. Order of tasks
3. Starting time per task
4. Pace and rhythm
5. Stopping time per task
6. Interval
7. Initiating questions for clarification
8. Attire and appearance
9. Posture

The decisions in the pre-impact and post-impact sets remain unchanged—the teacher makes those decisions (Figure 7.1).

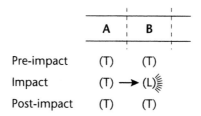

Figure 7.1. The decision shift from the Command style to the Practice style

In the anatomy of this style, the teacher's role is to make all the decisions in the pre-impact and post-impact sets. In the impact set, the teacher shifts the nine decisions to the learner; therefore, the learner's role is to make the nine decisions while performing the task(s) designed by the teacher.

In the post-impact set of decisions, the teacher observes the performance and offers individual and private feedback to learners about both their tasks and their decision making in the nine categories.

This shift of the nine decisions marks the beginning of the individualization process—inviting different behaviors from both teacher and learner. The teacher must begin to see the learners as individual performers who are responsible for decision making in nine categories. The teacher must learn to shift time decisions and refrain from giving commands for every movement, task, or activity. The learner has the opportunity to initiate practice, to initiate interaction with the task on his or her own, and to initiate and learn to make the nine decisions within the logistical parameters determined by the teacher. The learner learns to make time decisions as they relate to practicing the task.

The original name for style B was the Task style (Mosston, 1966a); however, this name was changed because all styles have a task. Mosston realized that task style was too ambiguous and too nonspecific a name to identify the essence of this landmark decision relationship. In the 1970s we discovered that whenever one individually practiced a task, the nine decisions of this landmark behavior were intrinsically made. Although Practice style correctly identified the essence of this relationship, it also was observed that styles A–E are all practice styles. Perhaps the most accurate name for this landmark decision relationship is Individual Practice style. Despite the variety of names used to describe this behavior, it is vital to focus on the distribution of the decisions that determine the learning objectives.

The Implementation of the Practice Style

Style B—the Practice style—is the first style on the Spectrum that involves the learner in making some decisions during the episode. A new reality evolves in style B episodes where learners actually practice not only the task, but also the deliberate process of making decisions in the nine categories. In this style, a new interaction and a new relationship unfold between the teacher and learner. The teacher learns to trust the learner to make appropriate decisions while practicing the task and the learner learns deliberate and independent decision making in conjunction with performing the task.

Description of an Episode

An episode in style B must reflect the essence of this new teacher–learner relationship. Initially, the teacher will describe to the class the concept of shifting decisions to produce different learning objectives, the nine decisions of the Practice style, and the meaning of the nine decisions. This explanation establishes the behavior expectations for the ensuing episode. The teacher continues with the subject matter explanation/demonstration and the logistical expectations. (The order of these three expectations changes according to the objectives of the episode.) Once the three expectations have been delivered, the learners begin while the teacher observes the learners making the nine decisions. The learners will pick up the necessary materials, establish their locations, and within a reasonably short time, will settle into the performance of the task. The teacher begins to individually and privately contact each learner.

The manner in which time is used marks a major contrast between the realities of the Command behavior and the Practice style. Signaled or cued performance is the essence of all variations of the Command behavior. Learners respond when they are cued or signaled (time decisions) to achieve a precision performance. The essence of all variations of the Practice behavior is the availability of a unit of time (within the stated parameters) allotted for learners to make the decisions while practicing the task(s). The primary learning focus in the Practice style is to develop awareness in making decisions about time, and also to realize the importance of time in task acquisition for oneself and for others.

The essence of the classroom image of this style is a particular cycle of relationships between the teacher and the learner. The teacher presents the expectations for the task, the behavior/decisions, and the logistics; the learner performs the task making the nine decisions for a period of time; the teacher observes the performance and offers feedback.

How to Implement the Practice Style

The following steps describe how to implement the Practice style.

The Pre-Impact Set   As in the Command behavior, the teacher's role is to make all the decisions in the pre-impact set. Two major differences are the teacher's awareness of the deliberate shift of decisions that will occur in the impact set, and the selection of tasks conducive to this style.

The Impact Set   During the face-to-face interaction, events in the episode unfold. The categories that comprise all episodes are identified in the following table. The need or focus of the experience will determine the order of the first three expectations. There is no set order for presentation of the first three expectations—subject matter, behavior, logistics.

Table 7.1 shows the events in the episode:

Table 7.1 Events—The Practice Style

Episode Events		Feedback	Time
Behavior-decision presentation	1. The teacher sets the scene by introducing the learners to the idea of new expectations (Figure 7.2).		
	2. The teacher states the style's expectations and objectives: a. To offer time for each learner to work individually and privately b. To provide time for the teacher to offer individual and private feedback to everyone		
	3. The teacher describes the role of the learner and the shift in decision making. Initially, the teacher actually names the nine decisions (or points to a chart, Figure 7.3, p. 101). This procedure clearly identifies the specific decisions shifted to the learner.		
	4. The teacher describes his or her role: a. To observe the performances and offer individual and private feedback b. To be available to answer questions from the learner		
Subject-matter presentation	5. The teacher presents the task(s). The teacher must be aware of the following Components of Communication (see Chapter 11) and the options within each component: a. Content: Each task has particular expectations of what is accomplished. b. Mode: Each task can be presented through different modes: audio, visual, audiovisual, and tactile. The teacher decides which mode is best for a given task. c. Action: Each mode has its own form of action; the teacher has a choice of speaking about the task, demonstrating it, or using a combination of both. Each choice depends on the task, on the situation at hand, and on the purpose of the communication. At times, a demonstration of the task conveys a clear image of what is to be practiced; at other times, a few words are needed to clarify the task. d. Medium: Various media can deliver the task: the teacher, a film, a video, or a task sheet. A decision must be made about which option to choose.		

Table 7.1 Events—The Practice Style

Episode Events		Feedback	Time
Logistics presentation	6. The teacher announces the logistics and parameters that are necessary for the task and/or behavior, which include: a. The number of repetitions per task, or the length of time that the task is to be performed b. The order of the tasks (sequence or random) c. Location parameters for the tasks d. Equipment information and details e. Interval activities f. Attire and appearance parameters		
Questions for clarification	7. At this point, the learners have been introduced to the three expectations. Before asking the learners to begin, the teacher asks for clarification questions to check for understanding. a. The teacher is available for clarification questions, or the teacher initiates questions to verify the degree of understanding of the new expectations. b. The learners are then asked to begin practicing individually and privately on the task when you—each of you—is ready.		
Feedback **Post-impact set of decisions**	8. The teacher moves from learner to learner, observing both the performance of the task and the decision-making process, then offers feedback and moves on to the next learner. During this process, the teacher will: a. Identify, as quickly as possible, the learners who are making errors in either the performance of the task, or the decision-making process, or both b. Offer corrective feedback to the individual learner c. Stay with the learner to verify the corrected behavior (in many cases, a few seconds are sufficient for this step) d. Move on to the next learner e. Visit, observe, and offer feedback to those who perform correctly and who do make the nine decisions appropriately. These students also need the teacher's time (often teachers offer feedback only to those who make errors). f. In the beginning episodes, circulate to all students. For some tasks, it may take two or three episodes to observe every learner in the class. Learners usually develop the patience needed for such cycles. g. Develop awareness of the feedback forms used. Corrective, value, neutral, and ambiguous feedback are always available. (Review the section on feedback forms in Chapter 4, and consider the impact of each on the learner in a given instance.) h. Develop awareness in seeing the overall performance and behavior of the learners. When a significant number of learners are incorrectly performing, call the class together and provide group corrective feedback.		

(continues)

Table 7.1 Events—The Practice Style *(continued)*

Episode Events	Sequence of Events	Feedback	Time
Closure—reinforces the stated expectations	9. When the time parameter for the practice is up, the teacher brings closure to the experience (a sense of completion) by offering overall feedback to the learners.		
	10. The teacher assembles the class for a one-minute "ceremony" to end the lesson. This can take many forms such as:		
	a. a quick review of the learned content		
	b. general feedback to the class		
	c. a statement about the next lesson		
	11. Closure acknowledges the degree to which the stated expectations were accomplished. The teacher offers feedback to the learners about their participation in the task and/or their decision making.		
	A moment of closure provides the teacher and students with a sense of completion.		

THE PRACTICE STYLE—B

The purposes of this teaching style are to offer the learner time to work individually and privately and to provide the teacher with time to offer the learner individual and private feedback.

Role of the learner

- To perform the task
- To make the nine decisions
  - Order of the task(s)
  - Starting time
  - Pace and rhythm
- Stopping time
- Interval
- Location
- Posture
- Attire and appearance
- Questions for clarification

Role of the teacher

- To be available to answer the learner's questions
- To gather information about the learner's performance and offer individual and private feedback

Figure 7.2. The Practice style classroom chart

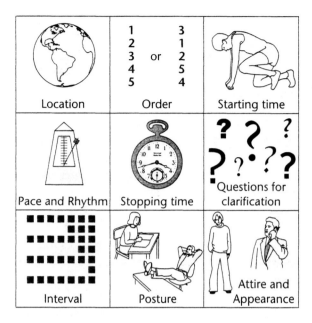

Figure 7.3. Decisions classroom chart

Additional post-impact decisions will likely be made after the face-to-face interaction has ended. Reviewing and assessing the events of a class are necessary for reflective teaching and to prepare for the next class interaction.

When one episode ends, another begins as soon as the expectations for the next event are stated. The next episode could be in the same style, reinforcing the same set of objectives, or it could be in the same style but with a different developmental channel emphasis, or it could be an entirely different teaching–learning behavior with another set of decision-making expectations and outcomes.

The Implications of the Practice Style

Each event, each decision in the classroom, has consequences. Because learners enter the classroom from different philosophical, psychological, social, and cognitive points of view, it is imperative to know the network of implications that each teaching–learning behavior implies. Episodes in the Practice style imply that:

- The teacher values the development of deliberate decision making.
- The teacher trusts the learners to make the nine decisions.
- The teacher accepts the notion that both teacher and learner can expand beyond the values of one style.

- Learners can make the nine decisions while practicing the task(s).
- Learners can be held accountable for the consequences of their decisions as they participate in the process of individualization.
- Learners can experience the beginning of independence.

Although there are numerous examples of teaching strategies in the literature, each is associated more closely with one landmark behavior than another. Because all models, strategies, or methods suggest a decision distribution between the teacher and the learner in reference to the subject matter, it is possible to identify which landmark styles (set of objectives) different behaviors represent.

In the literature, the term "guided practice" has been described as a unique teaching behavior. However, in the literature, the "actions" of the teacher and learners are not consistently described; at times the behavior suggests the Command style, at other times the description supports the Practice style. When guided practice is described as a cued practice—in which each part is demonstrated and students are "guided" step by step and told what to do and when to do it—the decision distribution represents style A. When guided practice describes an individual practice "on your own," the decision distribution represents style B. In both situations, frequent feedback is offered to "guide" the practice. Although the name *guided practice* suggests something different from Command or Practice styles, the underlying decision distribution is the same. When teachers know the implications—the primary focus and value of the learning experience—of various teaching terms that are used in the literature, they are able to more accurately implement the approach and succeed in reaching the anticipated goals and objectives. Philosophical intention about teaching and learning must be followed by the decision distribution for the teacher and learner; that is, if the benefits of the idea are to be reached.

Selecting and Designing the Subject Matter

This section deals with two questions that the teacher must answer while planning episodes in the Practice style: What kinds of tasks are appropriate for this style? How does one design and organize a cluster of tasks to accommodate the process of this style?

Kinds of Tasks

The characteristics of a task appropriate for an episode in the Practice style are:

1. That it is fixed, and must be performed according to a specific model; no alternatives are sought.

2. That the movement or responses can be identified as correct or incorrect.

Many activities in physical education consist of fixed tasks. In many cases they form the basis of the activity by defining its structure. For example:

- When a teacher demonstrates the position at the starting blocks for a short dash, that demonstration becomes the model, the fixed standard. In the Practice style, all learners are expected to practice and perform that position as demonstrated without individual variations and adjustments. (Perhaps later, if a variation proves to be beneficial to one runner or another, it will be adopted.)

- When a forehand stroke in tennis is demonstrated, all the learners are expected to practice the stroke as demonstrated, with the same motion and same foot position.

- When a "one-and-a-half, front somersault in tucked position" is the description of the task, all learners are expected to practice the dive according to the accepted standards.

By delivering and demonstrating these tasks, the teacher has the capacity to offer feedback about the "correctness" of the performance. The teacher compares the performance with the demonstrated model.[2]

At least three sources determine the need for fixed tasks:

1. Kinesiological and biomechanical principles
2. Past experience of teachers and coaches
3. Aesthetic standard

Kinesiological principles establish the correctness of postures and movement combinations based on scientific analyses. These analyses tell us precisely which posture and which movement is most appropriate for attaining given objectives. Laws of physics, for example, help determine the degree of difficulty for various exercises (Mosston, 1965). It is futile to produce alternatives when a specific posture or movement works best.

One cannot ignore the knowledge provided by teachers' and coaches' observations. Over the years, they have developed special and subtle insights into the activity and designed appropriate movement sequences that lead to attaining the task. Their knowledge serves as a powerful basis for establishing correctness for performance.

---

[2]This discussion does not intend to promote fixed tasks, nor is it a statement against alternatives. It is merely emphasizing the importance of precise performance when tasks call for it— it is fixed for this task and this episode. Another style on the Spectrum develops insights into the process used to invite alternatives.

Aesthetic standards generally evolve from cultural agreements and are transmitted and preserved by ceremonies and rituals. Certain postures, movements, and movement combinations are considered attractive, beautiful, and symbolic. They are used to maintain and project a tradition. In this sense, these movements are correct for this purpose. The actions of cheerleaders, drill teams, marching bands, gymnastics demonstrations, and traditional dance performances all represent this category of adhering to a particular standard or of attaining the predetermined standard by performing the correct movements. Performing these standards is represented by the Command style; practicing them is often represented by the Practice style.

The Design of the Task Sheet

The Purposes of Task Sheets/Task Cards As mentioned in the chapter on cognition, the purpose of the task sheets is to increase the efficiency of time-on-task and teacher–learner communication. The task sheet is the most useful aid for any of the four organizational formats in any style. (See "Organizational Options" in Chapter 11.)

Although the purposes of the task sheet were presented in the chapter on cognition, the following reviews these goals:

1 To assist the learner in remembering the task; what to do and how to do it

2. To cut down on the number of repeated explanations by the teacher

3. To teach the learner to concentrate when listening to the explanation the first time

4. To teach the learner to follow specific written instructions and enhance precise performance

5. To record the learner's progress

It is quite common to see learners in the gymnasium who do not know some details of the task to be performed. This high visibility factor is an advantage in physical education—one can see from a considerable distance whether a learner knows how to perform a task. Often, this lack of precise performance is not related to the physical capabilities, but rather to the learner's inability to remember, for a variety of reasons, the details that were previously demonstrated or explained.

Using a task sheet makes clear to learners that part of schooling is listening and observing. It is the learner's role to listen to the explanation and observe the demonstration. Then, during practice time, the task sheet becomes the source of information. This puts the focus on the learner, who becomes responsible for following up by using the information on the task sheet.

In the gymnasium or the playing field, there is the question of physical distance. Task sheets make it possible for the teacher to direct learners without physically moving to widely scattered locations. When task sheets are used, however, the interaction between the teacher and learners can focus on the understanding of the task description, the learner's understanding of the specific parts. The teacher is able to refer to the task sheet and ask questions that lead the learner to understanding.

This climate is psychologically effective, because it rapidly teaches learners about the assets of the Practice style—its contributions to their performance improvement and their responsibility for making the nine impact decisions.

The Design of the Task Sheet

- An effective task sheet contains the necessary information about what to do and how to do it. It always focuses on the task or tasks to be performed during the given episode.
- It describes the specifics of the task.
- It identifies the quantity of the task (number of repetitions, distance, length of time for the particular exercise, etc.)
- It uses one of two verbal behavior forms:
  a. "Your task is to perform three consecutive forward rolls in tuck position and to finish in squat position." (infinitive)
  b. "Place your left hand on the lower part of the bat and keep your right hand..." (imperative)
- It has space for notations concerning the learner's progress, feedback comments, and other pertinent information.

This design (Figure 7.4) serves as a general format for a task sheet. Its parts include:

1. Identifying information (i.e., name, class, date)
2. Designation of the behavior/style used in the task sheet. In this example it is style B. The same task sheet may also be used for styles A, C, and D.
3. Task sheet sequence number. This helps keep the sheets organized for future use.
4. The general subject matter refers to the name of the activity or sport (i.e., volleyball, gymnastics, swimming).
5. The specific topic indicates the particular aspect of the sport that will be practiced (i.e., serve, handstand, backstroke).

Name _____   Style A <u>B</u> C D
Class _____   Task Sheet # ____
Date _____

The general subject matter—the specific topic

To the student:

_____
_____
_____
_____

Task description (and illustrations)	Quantity of the task	Progress notation; other information	Feedback by:

1. _____
    a. _____
    b. _____
2. _____
    a. _____
    b. _____
3. _____
    a. _____
    b. _____
    c. _____			

Figure 7.4. A general sample of a task sheet

6. To the student. This space is to describe the purpose of the activity and any logistical or other relevant information.

7. Task description. This space is available for describing the tasks and their parts. When necessary, the description should also include an illustration of the tasks and their parts. These can be drawings or photographs of the desired positions. Videos can be used to illustrate the task in motion in conjunction with the task sheet.[3]

8. Quantity is indicated using units that are relevant to the prescribed task (i.e., the number of repetitions, the length of time for doing the particu-

[3]The task description, using line drawings, printed illustrations, or media demonstrations, establishes the quality of the performance. It presents the model to be attained. It is always bound, however, with the quantity of performance. There is always a relationship between quantity and quality and the ratio varies with individual learners. The decision about the quantity of repetitions, length of practice time, and so on, is often arbitrary. Only with the availability of instrumentation and measurements from the sports sciences has it become easier to establish quantitative goals for individuals.

lar task, the number of successful trials out of total number of attempts).

9. Progress notation. This column can be used by the student and teacher to mark the completed task, to indicate incompletion, or to comment on the next session, etc.

10. Feedback. Space is available for feedback comments, which may be provided by different people, depending on the style. In this Style B example, the feedback is provided by the teacher.

To design tasks with reasonable accuracy and usefulness, teachers must frequently gather the information from the sports sciences; otherwise, the design of these task sheets is left to anyone's guesses or hunches.[4]

Style-Specific Comments

Observing the Practice style in operation has revealed several style-specific insights. Awareness of these issues can positively influence planning and implementation.

1. The theoretical structure of the Practice style calls for shifting nine decisions from the teacher to the learner; however, there are two decisions that need some commentary, particularly in physical education: (1) posture and (2) attire and appearance. In all other classroom or laboratory subjects, posture is an accommodating feature of the learning situation. In physical education, however, posture is a part of the subject matter. The description of a task includes the posture to be attained and sustained during the performance; therefore, posture decision is not shifted during the practice for fixed tasks in physical education.

   The second decision that may not be shifted to the learner concerns attire and appearance. This is often an institutional decision—the school authority makes the decision concerning uniforms. Other institutional decisions concern safety procedures for a particular sport (protective gear, safety gear) or what attire is appropriate for the rules and procedures of a given sport (particular uniforms for wrestling, judo, modern dance, or track and field).

2. If a considerable number of learners make the same error when performing the task and/or making the decisions (role error), then an adjustment decision by the teacher is needed. Stop the action of the class, call them around you, repeat the demonstration and explanation, and send the students back to continue. This technique of recalling the learners for group feedback has several advantages:

---

[4] Refer to Chapter 18 for additional information on designing subject matter.

    a. It is time-efficient to give feedback simultaneously to all those who made the same error.

    b. The physical proximity of the teacher and class members can create a particular climate of ease, different from the climate created when the teacher broadcasts the feedback by shouting or using a P.A. system.

    c. During this time, learners can ask questions and the teacher can ascertain whether most or all learners understood the correction.

    d. It may reinforce those who have performed correctly.

3. Since Style B is designed for individual and private practice, communication among or between students must be kept to a minimum. When a student talks to a peer, he or she interferes with the other person's decisions. This must not be perceived as the "no talking" style, but rather as a style that provides for private practice.

4. On the elementary school level, two phenomena may occur in the initial stages of the Practice style. First, individual learners often follow the teacher around to show what they have learned and to seek feedback. Second, learners will stop after one performance and then wait for the teacher to get to them for feedback.

In both situations, the quickest and most neutral way to handle the learner's behavior is to review with the learner the teacher's role. Reassure your learner that you will get to him or her, just as you will get to all other learners in the class.

5. Task selection must be appropriate for the behavior requests of this style. Because the learners are working individually and privately on a task while the teacher circulates among the class members, learners must have a degree of proficiency in the task. If the learners cannot sustain engagement in the task, if they constantly need assistance or their work is primarily incorrect, or if the teacher–learner ratio prohibits frequent individual contact—then the task selected is not conducive to this landmark Practice style. Unless learners can be relatively successful in the task, time-off-task increases, discipline problems develop, and the objectives of the experience are not met. (See Design Variations for additional comments.)

6. When learners' performance levels vary, the teacher can assign tasks to individuals or small groups according to ability. This adjustment in the assignment keeps the learners actively on-task. In Style B, the teacher makes this decision to accommodate differences in performance (Graham, Holt/Hale, & Parker, M, 1998, Intratask Variation, p. 158).

When teachers are preoccupied with other students and cannot circulate to offer feedback for extended time intervals, it is mandatory that the learners be independent enough in the task to maintain active time-on-task.

7. Another situation may call on the learner to select, for example, three out of five available tasks. The teacher has made the subject matter decision about the task design, but the learner makes the decision about which tasks to select for the present episode (Graham, et al., Teaching by Invitation, p. 158)

8. Avoid hovering behavior. At times teachers will observe learners for a sustained period of time and then walk away without saying anything. The learners must guess at the meaning of the teacher's actions. This interaction is ambiguous and doesn't enhance the task performance or the emotions. At other times, teachers will observe and stay for an extended period of time, offering continuous feedback. Be aware that constant scrutiny inhibits decision making and the essence of this behavior—individual practice.

9. At times, learners finish before the allotted time (time parameters). This may occur in all styles except the Command style. This interval time (also referred to as transition time) must be planned for because this interval invites learners to engage in decisions that may not be appropriate for the episode. A choice of two or three interval activities could always be available—during a certain number of lessons, weeks, or the entire semester—for those who finish their tasks early.

10. A useful aid in style B (and in other styles) is the wall chart. A wall chart is a reminder of the series of tasks to be performed, the tasks to be practiced in each station, or a list of decisions in the style. These charts, the task sheets, and transparencies serve as sources of information for the learners about the tasks and their own role in decision making. The wall chart relieves the teacher of being the only source, allowing time to provide feedback.

11. By identifying the specific roles of the teacher and the learner, and by making a decision analysis of various programs, procedures, strategies, and models of teaching, this makes it possible for teachers to include those proposals in the Spectrum. For example, "Mastery Learning" is an excellent example of style B in operation—the teacher makes decisions about feedback and the necessary adjustment of the tasks for various learners.

The intent of this section is to bring attention to the often subtle actions that can cause an episode to go astray. It is frustrating to experience mishaps when implementing episodes; however, the slightest adjustments often can lead to significant improvement. Mishaps occur because decisions (in the task, with the logistics, by the teacher or learner) are not made appropriately. The key is to reflect on the events and identify the decision(s) that caused the learning experience to go off course.

The Developmental Channels

Design Variations

The influence of the Developmental Channels on task design in style B is powerful. Few teaching–learning behaviors can match the number of variations that the Practice style offers for emphasizing different attributes and combinations of attributes along the Developmental Channels.

The nine decisions in the Practice style relate principally to the physical domain—where (location), when (time), speed (pace and rhythm), posture, attire, etc. The learners make these decisions to accommodate their individual practice of the task. These decisions are the first steps in the process toward independence; therefore, the landmark style is an individual practice. However, as with all landmark styles, design variations that emphasize various attributes and Developmental Channels are possible.

Teaching by Invitation is a design variation of the Practice style with emphasis on the emotional Developmental Channel. This idea offers learners a choice between two (or more) tasks to practice.

You may want to continue dribbling in self-space, or you may want to begin dribbling and walking in general space.

You may want to continue striking a ball with your paddle, or you may want to try striking a shuttlecock. (Graham, et al., 1998, p. 158).

Making a choice feels good emotionally. The assumption here is that if learners select the task they want to practice, they will be more cognitively engaged. The underlying decisions of this variation conform to the Practice style—the teacher identifies the tasks from which the learners will choose, the teacher sets the logistics, and gives the feedback. The learners decide which of the tasks to practice.

The intratask variation approach (Graham, et al., 1998) matches the decision distribution of the Practice style with emphasis on the emotional and cognitive channels by having the teacher make individual adjustments in task assignments. The teacher, in private one-on-one interactions, "makes the task easier or harder to better match the skill level" for an individual child. "Todd, why don't you try striking a balloon instead of a ball?" (Graham, et al., 1998, p. 158). This variation on the Practice style supports the fact that the teacher is aware of different children's needs and that one task standard is not always appropriate for all students. This task adjustment for some students can increase successful time-on-task and avoid unnecessary emotional frustrations. The underlying decision distribution between the teacher and the learners conforms to the Practice style. In any episode, if learners cannot perform the task, adjustments need to be made.

Active teaching (Siedentop, 1991), interactive teaching (Rink, 1993), and mastery learning, to name just a few, are examples of approaches whose decision distributions conform to the Practice style while emphasizing a particular learning focus.

Episodes in cooperative learning (groups working together) are frequent experiences in the gymnasium/classroom. Which decisions and teaching style are they more akin to? Although the intent of this arrangement promotes social and cognitive cooperative interaction, the reality is that the decisions shifted in most cooperative learning experiences represent only the nine decisions of the Practice style. Although the learners are given license to interact, decisions that develop social skills are not shifted. If interaction occurs, it is generally the learner who knows how to do the task telling or showing the others how to do it. In this case the learner who knows is acting as the surrogate teacher—the one who gives others the feedback (Polvi and Telama, 2000).

The label "cooperative learning" does not carry a fixed decision structure; therefore, the decisions within the group situations must be determined before learning conclusions can be made. In some groups the specific tasks for each learner actually separate the learners; therefore, rather than cooperative interaction, a parallel learning experience occurs.

Although the decisions of group situations are more akin to a canopy under the Practice style, these arrangements do not lead to the primary objectives of the landmark Practice style—that of being trusted to work independently and responsibly.[5]

Examples of Task Sheets for the Practice style   This task sheet (Figure 7.5) incorporates Fronske's content descriptions and cues into the task design. This vital information serves as a review of the overall movement, specific body positions, and cues that guide independent practice. The teacher circulates offering content feedback.

---

[5]Refer to the next chapter for additional comments about cooperative learning.

Name _____   Style A Ⓑ C D E
Class _____   Task Sheet # _____
Date _____

Basketball—Shooting and Dribbling

To the student:
Perform each task as described in the program below, indicate results, and
place a check next to the completed task.

Set Shot Criteria and			
Task Description	Skill	Cue	Common Error
Palm up; balance a waiter's tray	**Set-Up** *Shooting hand*	Spread fingers Palm up; balance a waiter's tray	Ball held in palm
	Nonshooting hand	Hand faces side wall; fingers only touch ball	
	Alignment	Arm, eye, and hand lined up with basket, like throwing a dart	Push ball sideways Arm at 45° angle Elbow points to side
	Sight	Focus on back edge of rim Basket looks like a big bin	
Elbow points at basket, like throwing a dart	*Legs*	Slightly bend knees and buttocks out	Insufficient force from no use of legs
Set Shot—Set-up	*Balance* **Shooting Action**	Body square to basket	
	Fingers	Spin ball off middle and index finger: fast spin, lines on ball not visible	Ball is thrown
	Wrist	Flip wrist, wave good-bye to	Inadequate wrist action

Task	Quantity	Results completed	Dates	Teacher's feedback
A. 1. Set shots—foul line	25 shots			
2. Set shots—45° angle left of basket	25 shots			
3. Set shots—45° angle right of basket	25 shots			
4. One-hand shot—foul line	25 shots			
5. One-hand shot—right side of basket	15 shots			
6. One-hand shot—left side of basket	15 shots			

Figure 7.5. Basketball—shooting and dribbling (Task description from Fronske, H., p. 43.
Permission for adaptation granted by Allyn & Bacon Publishing Co., Boston, MA.)

The next task sheet (Figure 7.6) asks learners to record their results.

Name _____   Style A Ⓑ C D
Class _____   Task Sheet # ____
Date _____

Archery—Shooting

To the student:
Perform the tasks as presented in the program below. After all 6 arrows are shot, score from highest to lowest value (points) and record the number of hits and your total score. For example:

						Hits	Score
9	6	6	3	0	0	4	24

Tasks
A. From 10 yards:

						Hits	Score

B. From 20 yards:

						Hits	Score

C. From 30 yards:

						Hits	Score

D. From 40 yards:

						Hits	Score

Figure 7.6. Archery—shooting (Task example contributed by Dr. Joanne Dusel, Towson University, MD)

The next task sheet (Figure 7.7) provides concurrent tasks (see Chapter 11 for details). Tasks at each station represent the Practice style.

Name _____   Style A Ⓑ C D

Class _____   Task Sheet # _____

Date _____

Archery—Stations

To the student:

Today there are 6 stations, each with a task. Stations 1, 2, 5 and 6 need to be performed with a partner. Stations 3 and 4 can be performed by yourself. The equipment needed is at each station. You may do the tasks in any order. No more than 4 people per station. I will be available for questions and clarifications and to give feedback to each of you.

Station 1: Tic-Tac-Toe

There are 8 arrows per person at this station. Take turns with your partner shooting at the tic-tac-toe board for three in a row (diagonally, vertically, or horizontally). You will be standing 15 yards from the tic-tac-toe target.

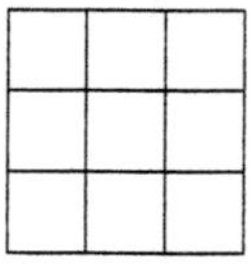

Station 2: Wand Shooting

There are 4 arrows per person at this station. Take turns trying to hit the 3-inch strip of masking tape placed on the target from 15 yards. Score one point for hitting the tape.

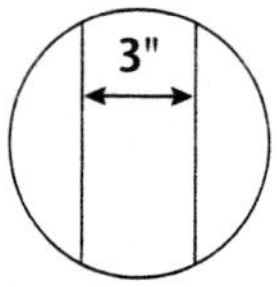

Station 3: Accuracy

There are 3 arrows per person at this station. Work on your accuracy from the positions below, shooting from 15 yards. Shoot all three arrows before moving to the next position.
a. kneeling
b. standing

Station 4: Balloon Shooting

There are 4 arrows, a lot of balloons, and many thumb tacks for each person at this station. Blow up 4 balloons. Use the thumb tacks to pin the balloons on the target 15 yards away. Shoot the arrows at the balloon targets.

Station 5: Novelty Shooting

There are 4 arrows per person at this station. Shoot 4 arrows each from 15 yards away at the target. Total individual scores after all the arrows have been shot.

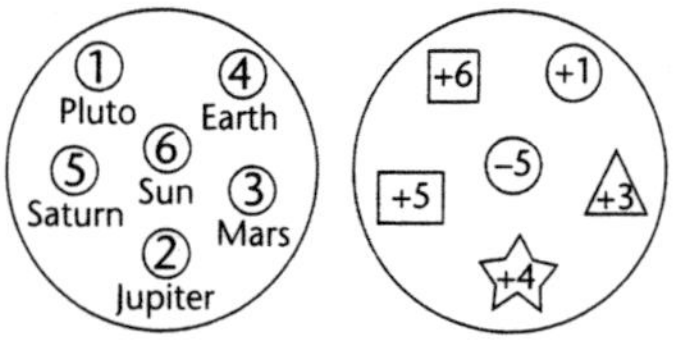

Station 6: Four Round Elimination

There are 4 arrows per person and a dark quarter of a circle for each partner group, at this station. On the first round, place the dark quarter circle over "A" (see diagram). Aim for sections "B," "C," "D," while attempting to bypass the darkend area. Arrows landing inside noncovered sections count as one point. Arrows in the covered zone count as minus 3. On the second round, section "B" is eliminated, third round "C" is eliminated etc.

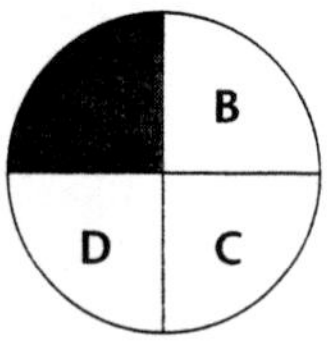

Figure 7.7. Archery stations (Task example contributed by Dr. Joanne Dusel, Towson University, MD)

The task design in Figure 7.8 is not appropriate as a task sheet for the Practice style because:

- No specific descriptions, pictures, or parts of the tasks are provided
- No quantity is indicated
- Assessment decisions (can do/cannot do) are shifted to the learner. In the Practice style the teacher makes post-impact decisions.

Jump Rope Task Sheet					
	Can	Cannot		Can	Cannot
Single rope skills Double bounce Single bounce Jogging step Side swing Side straddle Double unders Skier Bell Rocker			*Long rope skills* Run in front door Run in back door Jump Run out Bounce B-ball 10x Frisbee catch Pogoball		

Figure 7.8. Inappropriate task design

The Practice style is perhaps the most pervasive in the classroom because of the unlimited variations that can be incorporated into this decision structure. The Practice style is a teacher–learner relationship that invites the learner to participate in the responsibilities and the independence offered by shifting nine decisions.

The next teaching–learning relationship offers learners more decisions and more opportunities to develop human attributes that emphasize significantly different learning objectives, which leads to increased responsibilities and independence.

CHAPTER 8

The Reciprocal Style—C

(T)
(d)
→ *(o)* [1]

The defining characteristics of the Reciprocal style are social interactions, reciprocation, and giving feedback (guided by specific criteria). In the anatomy of the Reciprocal style, the role of the teacher is to make all subject matter, criteria, and logistical decisions and to provide feedback to the observer. The role of the learners is to work in partnership relationships. One learner is the *doer* who performs the task, making the nine decisions of the Practice style, while the other learner is the observer who offers immediate and on-going feedback to the doer, using a criteria sheet designed by the teacher. At the end of the first practice, the doer and the observer switch roles—hence the name for this landmark behavior—The Reciprocal style. Doer 1 becomes observer 2 and observer 1 becomes doer 2. When this behavior is achieved, the following objectives are reached in subject matter and in behavior:

The Objectives

Subject Matter Objectives	Behavior Objectives
To internalize the specifics of the subject matter by having repeated chances to practice with a designated observer	To expand socialization and interaction skills
	To practice communication skills (verbal behavior) that enhance a reciprocal relationship
To visualize the steps, sequence, or details involved in a given task	To learn to give and receive feedback from peers
To learn to use subject matter criteria to compare, contrast, and assess performance	To develop patience, tolerance, and acceptance of others' differences in performance
	To develop empathy
	To learn social manners
To practice identifying and correcting errors immediately	To develop social bonds that go beyond the task
	To trust interacting/socializing with others
To practice a task without the teacher	To experience the rewards (feelings) of seeing one's peer succeed

[1]This diagram represents the anatomy of the Reciprocal style.

The structure of the Reciprocal style creates a reality that reaches a new O–T–L–O. The new objectives in this landmark behavior emphasize two dimensions—the social relationships between peers and the conditions for immediate feedback.

The Anatomy of the Reciprocal Style

To create a new reality in the gymnasium that provides for new relationships between the teacher and the learner, more decisions are shifted to the learner. These decisions are shifted in the post-impact set to heed the principle of immediate feedback. The sooner learners know how they have performed, the greater their chances of performing correctly. Therefore, the optimum ratio providing for immediate feedback is one teacher to one learner. How, then, can the teacher accommodate this goal in physical education classes? Style C, the Reciprocal style, calls for a class organization that offers this condition. The learners are organized in pairs with each member assigned a specific role. One member is designated as the doer (d), and the other as the observer (o). When the teacher (T) gets involved with a given pair according to role expectations, a triad relationship forms for that period of time. The triad is designated as shown in Figure 8.1.

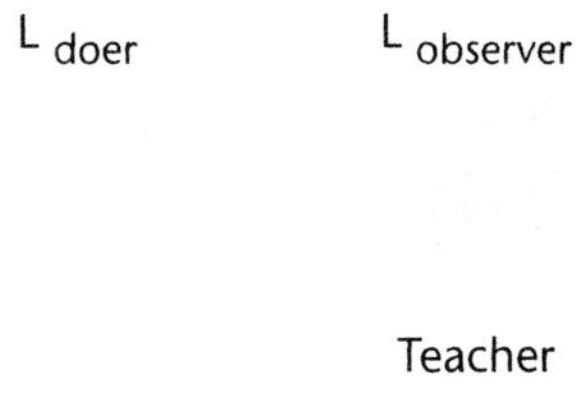

^L doer   ^L observer

Teacher

Figure 8.1. The triad

In this triad, each member makes specific decisions within his/her specific role. The role of the doer is the same as in the Practice style, including communicating only with the observer. The role of the observer is to offer ongoing feedback to the doer and to communicate with the teacher, if necessary. The role of the teacher is to observe the doer and observer, but to communicate only with the observer. Thus, the lines of communication are as shown in Figure 8.2.

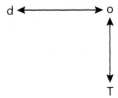

Figure 8.2. Desirable directions of communication in style C

The teacher, then, is making all the decisions in the pre-impact set; the doer is making the nine decisions in the impact set; the shift of decision making takes place in the post-impact set, when the observer makes the feedback decisions. The teacher does not communicate with the doer to avoid usurping the observer's role. Initially it is difficult for the teacher to be in the proximity of the doer and see either a correct or incorrect performance without offering feedback; however, it is important to stay within the structure of the style. The teacher must not interfere with the observer's role and the decisions shifted to the observer in the post-impact set. (Schematically, Figure 8.3 represents the shift of decisions in Reciprocal style).

	A	B	C
Pre-impact	(T)	(T)	(T)
Impact	(T) → (L)		(L_d)
Post-impact	(T)	(T) → (L_o)	

Figure 8.3. The anatomy of the Reciprocal style and the shift from Practice style-B to Reciprocal style-C

The new decisions, made by the observers in the post-impact set, detail the process intrinsic to giving feedback. Offering feedback involves:

1. Knowing the criteria—the task expectations
2. Observing the doer's performance
3. Comparing and contrasting the doer's performance against the task criteria
4. Drawing conclusions about what is the same and what is different
5. Communicating results

These five steps are not only imperative for anyone in the role of assessing performance, but they are intrinsic to the feedback process. Before any performance assessment can be done, one must have clear criteria or a model of the expected performance. In this style, the teacher provides information on a criteria card. Once the criteria are known, observing the performance and gathering data is necessary before comparing and contrasting the performance with the criteria. This step provides the observer with information about the correctness of the doer's performance. The observer is now ready to communicate results to the doer and offer the appropriate feedback. (These five steps are essential when the teacher offers feedback, as well. In fact, if one step is out of sequence, the feedback cannot be accurate.)

The Implementation of the Reciprocal Style

Although the Command and Practice styles are familiar to everyone in one form or another, the Reciprocal style is new to many. The new reality and roles create new social and psychological demands on both the teacher and the learners; considerable adjustments and changes of behavior must be made. This is the first time in the teaching–learning process that the teacher deliberately shifts the decision of feedback to the learner. The implicit power of feedback that has always belonged to the teacher is now shifted to the learner. The learners, therefore, must learn to use this power responsibly when they give and receive feedback with peers. Both teacher and learners need to experience this new reality with trust and comfort; all must understand the value of this behavior in the growth of the individual learners. Just as the teacher had to refrain in the Practice style from making the decisions of the Command behavior, so the teacher in the Reciprocal style must refrain from offering performance feedback to the doers.

The following section combines the description of an episode with the steps used for implementation. These steps and explanations are needed only during the first two or three episodes. Once the teacher and the learners experience the behaviors and benefits of this behavior, they can shift into it swiftly when the teacher announces the name of the style at the beginning of a lesson or episode.

Description and Implementation of an Episode

As in the previous two styles, it is the decision configuration in the anatomy of the Reciprocal style that guides the implementation and leads to the specific objectives.

The Pre-Impact Set   In addition to the decisions made by the teacher in the Practice style, the teacher pays special attention to:

1. Selecting and designing the subject matter.
2. Designing the criteria sheet/card for the observers.
3. Determining logistics appropriate for the episode.

The Impact Set   The major task for the teacher is to set the scene for the new roles and the new relationships. In beginning introductions, teachers explain the need for a reciprocal relationship. Some teachers have used the following: "At times in a private practice I am unable to circulate to all students and offer feedback when it is needed. Therefore, this new practice is designed to eliminate that waiting period. Each student will have a partner who has the answers, which I have prepared, and who will provide information to you while you are practicing. There's no waiting in this style."

When the reason for a new relationship is clear, learners are more willing to participate in the roles. Continue with the introduction as presented below. Table 8.1 shows the events in the episode:

Table 8.1 Events—The Reciprocal Style

Episode Events		Feedback	Time
Behavior presentation[2]	The teacher:		
	1. States the reason for using this style and the new objectives		
	a. To work with a partner[3]		
	b. To offer feedback to the partner		
	2. Explains the social arrangement		
	a. Identify the triad (Figure 8.1)		
	b. Explain that each person in the triad has a specific role and that each learner will be both doer and observer		
	3. Explains the role of the doer:		
	a. To do the task		
	b. To make the nine decisions as in style B[4]		
	c. To initiate questions and communicate only with the observer		
	4. Describes the role of the observer:		
	a. To refer to the performance criteria (prepared by the teacher) for content information		
	b. To observe and/or listen to the performance of the doer		
	c. To compare and to contrast the doer's performance against the criteria		
	d. To draw conclusions about the accuracy of the performance		
	e. To offer feedback to the doer		
	f. To initiate, if necessary, communication with the teacher		

[2] The age of the learners will determine the amount of detail that is provided. This introduction is an example of a delivery that includes all information about each expectation within the episode.

[3] In elementary classrooms when teachers mention that learners will work with a partner, learners often get very excited, begin talking, moving, and actually start to select a partner. Expect this reaction. Do not tell them who their partner will be at this point—if you do, they will shift their attention to their partner selection and not listen to the new roles. Bring them back to focus, "You don't know who your partner is going to be yet, first focus on what each partner will do."

[4] At this point the nine decisions of style B are not repeated; the learners are already familiar with them. Introducing these decisions makes the episode too long and distracts the focus from the decisions of style C. Referring to a wall chart which lists the nine decisions is all that is necessary.

Table 8.1 Events—The Reciprocal Style *(continued)*

Episode Events		Feedback	Time
	5. Introduces the role of the teacher: a. To offer feedback to the observer b. To answer questions by the observer		
Subject matter presentation	Subject Matter: 1. The teacher delivers/demonstrates the subject matter presenting the model. 2. The teacher explains the criteria sheet. a. Presents how to use the criteria. If the students have not had the experience of using specific criteria as a source of feedback, it is important in the beginning to take the time for detailed explanation of how to use the criteria. b. Explain how to offer feedback.[5] 3. The teacher makes necessary subject matter logistical decisions.		
Logistics presentation	Logistical expectations: The teacher establishes only those parameters necessary for the episode. • location • time • equipment/material pick up location(s) for task sheets—doer • equipment/material pick up location (s) for criteria/observer sheets • equipment/material return location(s) • interval • posture • attire and appearance		

(continues)

---

[5]Offering appropriate feedback is critical for achieving the objectives of this style. Some learners are comfortable offering the various feedback forms, but for others these skills are new. Therefore, before introducing the Reciprocal style, conduct a separate episode to review or acquaint the students with the four feedback forms and their purposes. Additionally, provide practice exercises for students to experience using appropriate verbal behavior. If necessary, short exercises in error detection can also be designed. This is a necessary skill for the observer.

Table 8.1 Events—The Reciprocal Style *(continued)*

Episode Events		Feedback	Time
Questions for clarification	Verify understanding of expectations before action: Are there any questions for clarification? In most situations, it is necessary for the teacher to establish that the learners understand the essence of the new behavior before shifting into the action. When the learners are clear, the teacher shifts them into action. There are two approaches.[6] After the appropriate technique for selecting partners is completed, the teacher may say, *Select a partner and decide who will be the doer and who will be the observer first. Then continue*		
Action, task, engagement, performance	The students begin by selecting partners, picking up the equipment/materials, and criteria sheets, and settling down to the performance of their roles. The doers start making decisions appropriate to their role of performing the task and the observers follow through with their decisions while the doer is practicing. Initially this process may take a few minutes, but after two or three episodes in this style, students go through the logistical aspects rapidly and begin the task performance in a minimum amount of time.		

(continues)

[6] The learners' ability to make independent decisions—the nine decisions of style B—determines the approach the teacher selects for *how to shift* learners into the action in Style C. Two techniques exist:

1. If learners are not skilled at physically moving about the room to find a partner, the teacher says, "With your eyes only, select a partner." The learners remain in their spots, but looking among the class members, search for the person they want to gesture to and ask to be their partner. With young learners, heads will nod or shake as they search for a partner. This procedure reduces physical movement and negotiation time. After teaching style learners engage in a few minutes of distant negotiation, the teacher says, "Once you have a partner, you may begin" or "This group of learners may go to their partner and begin. Now this group…" As students move, it becomes clear to the teacher who is without a partner. The teacher moves in immediately to offer guiding statements to these students, and assist them in making a decision.

2. If the learners have developed physical independence and can move about the gymnasium to select partners, the parameter statement can be, "Select a partner and decide who will be the doer and who will be the observer first. Then continue."

Table 8.1 Events—The Reciprocal Style *(continued)*

Episode Events		Feedback	Time
Feedback **(post-impact)**	The observers engage in their role and offer continuous feedback to the doers.		
	The teacher waits, observes the partners settling down, and then moves from one observer to another. The teacher stays with each observer just long enough to hear the interaction, acknowledge the observer, and then move to the next observer.[7]		
Closure	At the end of the episode the teacher offers closure/feedback to the entire class, addressing the role of the observers. The specific verbal behavior (either positive-value or corrective statements):[8]		
	"The feedback offered by the observers was specific and continuous. Well done."		
	"While circulating, I noticed that the observers referred to the criteria and offered specific details to the doers."		
	"The observers need more time to practice giving feedback privately."		

Note: When describing the role of the observer, it is desirable to use charts when first introducing the behavior expectations. Figure 8.4 is an example for learners in the elementary grades. Older learners need only the diagram with words.

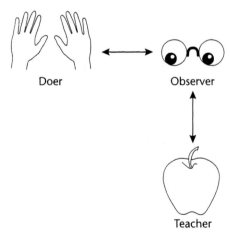

Figure 8.4. Classroom chart

[7]Avoid asking, "How is the doer doing?" This question elicits a one word ambiguous response okay or fine. Ask a question that requires conversation, "What is your doer able to do?" If the response is still ambiguous, ask the observer to comment about the points mentioned on the criteria sheet. Then ask the observer, "What didn't the doer do well?" Conversations about content are the focus of the teacher-observer interaction.

[8]Note that the feedback offered by the teacher at the end of the episode does not include comments about the performance of the task. The observers deliver this information during the episode. The purpose of giving feedback to the entire class at the end of the episode is to enhance the new role expectations of the observer.

Style C invites learners of all ages to develop positive social attributes and feedback skills while acquiring a specific task. Both are critical dimensions in all aspects of life.

In a well-functioning class in the Reciprocal style one can actually see the relationships budding and developing. New dimensions evolve that go beyond the mere performance of the physical tasks, such as social interaction, giving, receiving, trying out ideas, correcting, and succeeding.

The Implications of the Reciprocal Style

Just as the previous two styles have implications affecting the teacher and the learner, so does this style. The implications unique to the Reciprocal style are:

- The teacher accepts the socializing process between observer and doer as a desirable goal in education.
- The teacher recognizes the importance of teaching learners to give accurate and objective feedback to each other.
- The teacher is able to shift the power of giving feedback to the learner for the duration of Reciprocal style episodes.
- The teacher learns a new behavior that requires refraining from direct communication with the performer of the task (the doer).
- The teacher is willing to expand his or her behavior beyond those of the Command and Practice styles and takes the needed time for learners to learn these new roles in making additional decisions.
- The teacher trusts the students to make the additional decisions shifted to them.
- The teacher accepts a new reality where he or she is not the only source of information, assessment, and feedback.
- The learners can engage in reciprocal roles and make additional decisions.
- The learners can expand their active roles in the learning process.
- The learners can see and accept the teacher in a role other than those intrinsic to Command and Practice styles.
- Learners can spend time learning (by use of the criteria sheet) in a reciprocal relationship without the constant presence of the teacher.

Selecting and Designing the Subject Matter and Criteria Sheet

When selecting and designing the task(s), follow the same procedures described in the Practice style. The teacher's additional task in this style is designing the criteria sheet (Figure 8.5).

The Criteria Sheet

The single factor that can determine the success or failure of an episode in the Reciprocal style is the criteria sheet (or criteria card). It determines the parameters for the observer's behaviors; it keeps the doer accurately informed about the performance; it provides the teacher with a concrete basis for interacting with the observer. In subject matter other than physical education, each doer practices a different set of problems/questions in the same subject matter topic and each observer has a corresponding criteria sheet. However, in physical activities, both doer and observer perform the same task(s). In physical activities the task sheet and the criteria sheet are essentially the same. Observing the performance and offering feedback to the doer who performs a cartwheel or throws a softball will not guarantee that the observer will be able to perform the same task. When a task requires physical precision and dexterity, only one task/criteria sheet is needed for both learners. The task/criteria card/sheet must present an explicit overall image and detail the body/equipment sequence that is essential for correct performance.

A criteria sheet includes five parts:

1. Specific description of the task—this includes breaking down the task into its sequential parts.
2. Specific points to look for during the performance—these are potential trouble spots in performance that the teacher recognizes from previous experiences.
3. Pictures or sketches to illustrate the task.
4. Samples of verbal behavior to be used as feedback. This is useful in the early experiences of style C.
5. Reminder of the observer's role—this is useful in the first few episodes. Once the learner demonstrates the appropriate behaviors, it is no longer necessary to include the reminder in the criteria sheet.

Name _____   Style A B ©D E
Class _____   Task Sheet # _____
Date _____

To the doer: **Tennis**

Practice the shot 10 times, receive feedback from your observer after each shot
Observer:

1. Observe the performance, use the criteria (below) to analyze the performance, and offer feedback to the doer.
2. Offer feedback after each shot. Practice 10 shots.
3. At the completion of the task, switch roles.
   Sample verbal behavior for the observer: First , acknowledge what was done well, and then offer corrective feedback about the errors.
1. Your racquet swing went from low to high, well done.
2. Although you cut through the ball, your racquet is not tilted back.
3. Your feet are together, move left foot in front.

Spin and Smash Shots				
Task Description	Skill	Cue	Alternate Cue	Common Error
Racquet swings high to low Racquet is tilted back Cut through ball **Backspin**	Topspin	Racquet swings low to high Candy cane swing Racquet starts knee high and finishes nose high	Racquet head perpendicular J swing Shake hands with a friend, and finish shaking hands with a giant	Swinging level
	Backspin (slice)	Racquet swings high to low Cut through ball	Racquet is tilted back	Swinging level
	Overhead smash	Hit like the serve Racquet back to neck Left foot in front—power with left foot Point elbow to ball with left hand	Refer to serve action	Power comes from both feet or back foot Misjudging ball by losing focus of ball
Observer 1 Comments		Observer 2 Comments		

Figure 8.5. A criteria sheet in tennis—spin and smash shot (Task description from Fronske, H., p. 231. Permission for adaptation granted by Allyn & Bacon Publishing Co., Boston, MA.)

Current literature emphasizes the use of teaching cues. The term *Teaching Cues* does not refer to "time decisions" as in the Command style, but rather to reminders of the skill's key components (Fronske, 1996). Cues are the rubrics of the skill; rubrics can be used in a variety of ways. Some content cues are words used to trigger the proper form, others are reminders of the skill sequence, while some are phrases that make the skill technique (position) visual. The ability to identify the cues of a skill represents content knowledge. The various books on cues are very helpful when preparing task and criteria sheets.[9]

Comments

1. Initially, preparing criteria sheets for the Reciprocal behavior does take time; however, many tasks in human movement remain fairly constant over the years. In the long run the criteria sheet is a time-saving device for the teacher. Collect and organize your criteria sheets so that you can use them repeatedly.

2. The Reciprocal behavior is particularly useful in review situations, and during the initial practice episodes of tasks following an introduction and/or demonstration. It is more productive for learners to practice new skills under the watchful eye of a partner who is equipped with accurate performance details, than to practice individually, without feedback. Properly designed criteria sheets ensure more accurate initial performances.

3. The observer must be needed in the task. If the task is too simple or if the doer is already proficient in the task, the observer is superfluous. The doer can practice independently.

4. The observers must be given descriptive content information. If the task/criteria sheets are too general or lack precise details about the sequence of movements, the observers cannot perform their roles.

Some Things to Think About

The following sections reflect the particular events, dimensions, and issues that emerge when the Reciprocal style is in operation. Some emerge immediately during the initial episode and disappear once the teacher resolves them; others come up repeatedly because of the new social–emotional nature of this behavior. These issues should be dealt with as they occur, although some are intrinsic to the structure of this behavior. The more familiar teachers become with all these possibilities, the more they will be able to anticipate behaviors, thus skillfully orchestrating the events and carry on for the benefit of everyone.

---

[9] Refer to Chapter 18 for additional information on designing subject matter.

Verbal Behavior   One of the major dimensions of human interaction is verbal behavior. We communicate ideas and feelings through words. In the classroom or the gymnasium, verbal behavior is a major form of communication affecting the teacher, the learner, and the relationship between the two. From a linguistic standpoint, words have meanings and connotations—both meanings and connotations affect the people involved in the interaction. A focus of the teacher observation while circulating among the pairs is to listen to the verbal behavior exchange between the partners. If each teaching–learning style is designed to lead learners to different learning objectives, then it is imperative that the teacher infuse those objectives by reinforcing them. The decision distribution of the Reciprocal style invites learners to develop conversation and interaction skills—focused conversation and guided interaction through the criteria sheet. The criteria and the accompanying content feedback comments serve as models for future interaction. Teachers must respond when they hear abusive, impatient, or crude comments, or when feedback is withheld, extremely picky, obsessive, or when the observers ignore their doers. This teaching–learning style not only reinforces the correct performance, but its primary focus is teaching learners how to socialize and interact.

Asking learners to work together is not an example of the Reciprocal style. The decision distribution that the learners use when asked to work together could represent any teaching–learning style. In some cases it represents the Command Style (one learner makes all the decisions for the other learners); or it could represent the Practice style (learners work individually and them come together to share what they have done); or it could represent a combination of these two behaviors (one learner, because he or she knows the content or has a bullying behavior, directs the actions and provides feedback to the other learners). Working together does not identify specific objectives that the learners are striving to develop.

In the Spectrum's Reciprocal behavior, the objectives drive the interaction and they are the focus of what the teacher is looking for and what the learners are practicing to internalize.[10]

The intentions of the Reciprocal style have been achieved when students can communicate to others exhibiting patience, tolerance, and an understanding of the context of interactions. When negative social interactions occur—always visible as verbal or physical expressions—it is imperative that the appropriate decisions that accompany social interactions and communication be reviewed.

---

[10]In the literature there are other references to "Reciprocal Teaching," however, the decision distributions of those models do not represent or lead to the objectives identified in Mosston's Reciprocal style—C. The decision structure in other models primarily leads learners to the objectives identified in the Practice style.

The decisions of the Reciprocal style emphasize social-communication development and the criteria sheets furnish the initial guidance that learners need when experiencing this type of behavior.

The following are verbal behavior situations that require the teacher to redirect the behavior of the learners.

1. Observer offers inaccurate feedback to the doer. In this case, the teacher refers the observer to the criteria and goes through the criteria step by step to reinforce the expectations of the task as compared to the doer's performance.

2. Verbal abuse is used by the observer ("You're a dummy!"). In this case, the teacher resorts to statements rather than questions. The teacher's role must be to introduce parameters and to protect the integrity of both the doer and the observer. The teacher establishes a class code of ethics, "I can't let you talk to your partner in this manner, just as I will not let him or her talk to you in this way." In initial episodes it is imperative that sample feedback statements be provided. The teacher then redirects the observer: "Your role is to use the criteria and offer the feedback provided on the criteria sheet."

3. At times, observers are silent; they do not offer feedback. The teacher asks questions of the observer about the performance and interjects, "Did you tell your doer? It's your role to let him/her know what is correctly and incorrectly practiced while the doer is practicing."

These examples focus on the spirit of communication and the role of the observer. In instances where the teacher needs to adjust the wording, the essence should be to reinforce appropriate social interaction and to correct feedback observations in reference to the task.

Most learners do not know how to use appropriate verbal behavior while offering feedback. Many shy away from this part of their role because it has not been a part of their past behavior. Offering specific, objective feedback to a peer and using criteria for doing so is a new experience for most people. This new behavior creates a new social–emotional relationship between the two partners, usually a relationship of honesty and mutual trust. People need time to practice it.

Pairing Techniques   There are many ways that the class can be used to organize into pairs.

1. Lining up the class and counting off by twos
2. Alphabetically by first or last names
3. The teacher selects the partners.
4. Students select each other (learner selection).
5. Pairing by height

6. Pairing by weight
7. Pair up with the person next to you.
8. Skill level

Each of these techniques can be used for its own purposes, but to accommodate the purpose of the Reciprocal style (developing communication between the doer and the observer) the most appropriate first technique is learner-selection.[11] Usually people enjoy working with someone they know and like. This initial social comfort permits the learners to focus on the new roles and expectations. Thousands of episodes in this behavior have verified this assumption. Research on the Reciprocal style verifies this assumption (Ernst & Byra, 1998; Byra & Marks, 1993).

Initially, when learners select their partners, the episode begins more swiftly and continues more productively. It is more comfortable to give and receive feedback with a person one likes and trusts. However, social development is the objective of this behavior. Therefore, as soon as possible the learners must begin to work with others—friends and non-friends. Developing tolerance, patience, empathy, etc. while interacting with different people is the primary objective of this teaching–learning behavior. Additional pairing techniques can be designed throughout the year so learners experience the development of social skills while interacting with all learners.

The first objective to reach in the first few episodes is the appropriate behaviors in the roles of the doer and the observer. This is the focus of the initial episodes. Self-selecting partners reach this objective faster and more safely with minimal social–emotional conflicts. If a partnership is selected by any other pairing technique, friction between the partners may delay the initial success of the episode. The teacher will have to deal first with the conflict and then with the new roles—usually it will not work! Partners who begin in conflict often refuse to continue together. If the first experience in this style is negative and unrewarding, learners usually resist participating in it. Often the negative feeling spills over to the activity. For example, students who were introduced to tumbling in the Reciprocal style and had a negative experience will often say, "I don't like tumbling!"

It is imperative to create conditions that are conducive to the successful introduction of this behavior—in this case, be aware of the appropriate pairing technique. After several episodes, when the teacher ascertains that all participants are skilled in both roles, doer and observer, the teacher can announce at the beginning of a subsequent episode, "Now that you know

---

[11]If this technique is the only approach used for all episodes, the objectives of this style will not be developed.

the roles and the decisions of the Reciprocal Practice, for today's episode select a new partner!" The new partnerships can be sustained for one, two, or three episodes; then, again, a new selection of partners takes place, expanding the social dimension. Without this rotation the objectives of this behavior are not accomplished. Learning to adjust to the awkwardness that commonly occurs during initial social interactions with different people is the goal of the Reciprocal style.

Perhaps one of the most significant results of this procedure is the increase in social tolerance and communication among the members of the class. Teachers can actually see the growth of patience and tolerance as learners receive and give feedback. It is, indeed, an extraordinary development for the teacher and the learners to reach this level of social–emotional climate while learning to perform tasks successfully!

Style-Specific Comments

Each time a new teaching–learning behavior is implemented, mishaps will occur. Some are preventable if the teacher knows that such mishaps exist and therefore plans differently. Other deviations are surprises and will evolve as the unique relationship between teacher and learner unfolds. Tangents are a part of the learning process; as they are encountered, examine the verbal behavior used, the design of the task, the criteria sheet, the shift of decisions and the roles, the logistics, and the forms of feedback. Then engage in solving the problem within the spirit and purpose of the designated teaching style. Each behavior contributes to learning and is worth the initial stages of awkwardness that both the teacher and learners will experience.

Because all learners do not enter our gymnasiums skilled in all the decision structures of the various landmark behaviors, deviations and mishaps will occur. Learning is often an awkward process! It takes repeated experiences to learn. The philosophy of the Spectrum framework does not suggest that all learners will implement each style perfectly in the first episode. Learners will vary in their ability to make the different decisions of the various behaviors. The initial purpose of using the different behaviors delineated in the Spectrum is to lead learners to be responsible for making these decisions and to be comfortable in shifting from one set of decision structures to another. Indeed, these skills are necessary in adulthood. Practice in making decisions is a primary focus and intent of the Spectrum. Once learners are able to make the decisions within the different behaviors, the teaching–learning experience can expand in its options, variations, and combinations. New vistas in teaching–learning can be created.

Learners who are unable to make the decisions of any behavior need experiences that can lead them to success. Creating episodes that make adjustments in the task selection, the parameters, the number of decisions, the Developmental Channel emphasis, even the teaching–learning behavior selection, etc. can and must be designed to include learners in the learning process. Excluding learners who—at the moment—cannot, stops and suppresses learning in the subject matter and in behavior. Continually asking learners who fail to perform in the same decision structure, without making adjustments, is inefficient, frustrating for teacher and learner, and emotionally detrimental to the learner when continued for long periods of time.

With-it-ness. The teacher maintains awareness of the learners within the classroom while offering private feedback to one individual. It is imperative that the learners know the teacher is aware of their actions and interactions in the classroom.

If some deviant behavior by a given pair is observed, complete the feedback to the present observer and then deal with the issue at hand. Do not ask, "What's the problem?" You will be flooded with statements and accusations by both partners.

Try not to get involved in this type of manipulative behavior by learners. Do not take the position of an arbitrary or judge; instead, refocus the learners on their roles. If the roles are unclear, ask the learners to identify who's the doer and observer, then proceed by saying, "Let me see the doer perform the task and the observer provide feedback using the information on the criteria card." This will invariably curtail the bickering and conflict. Both are back within their roles. The teacher's role is to stay with the pair and listen to the feedback.

When you move about from pair to pair, do so randomly. Avoid patterns such as clockwise, counterclockwise, pairs closest to you visited first, and so on.

Since learners may ask questions for clarification when needed, establish a procedure or a signal for this occurrence, so it is clear who needs the attention. Without such a procedure, the teacher will sometimes be surrounded by several learners—some doers and some observers—all needing attention about different questions. These learners, knowingly or not, are manipulating the teacher by making decisions for both the teacher and other students. If this "gathering of the eager to learn" happens during the episode, stop all activities to assemble the entire class at a central spot. Then review the different roles: doers ask questions of the observer; the observers use the signal to indicate a question; the teacher circulates to answer observer's questions and initiate interaction with the observers. Then ask the learners to return to their activities. Watch for a while before going to an observer. Again, visit and communicate with all observers, not only with those who indicate that they have some difficulties. It is fascinating to observe the patience learners develop in this behavior with each other and with waiting their turn to receive feedback from the teacher. This patience increases with the security of knowing that the teacher will eventually come to them. This security reduces and eventually eliminates the need to vie for the teacher's attention (particularly in the earlier grades; in later grades, students often try to avoid the teacher's attention). In the Reciprocal style, all learners receive attention in their respective roles as doers and observers. At the end of the episode, offer learners feedback about how they performed in their roles.

Several misconceptions about the Reciprocal style often develop in the minds of teachers.

1. *The smart one working with the dummy.* This behavior is not designed to differentiate levels of "smartness." On the contrary, the major contribution of this behavior is creating a condition where both partners are equal in their roles. Both partners have the opportunity to use their capacities within the social context of this style and to adjust their emotions to accommodate the interaction process.

2. *In the Reciprocal style, the teacher is not working.* On the contrary, the teacher is very much working to teach the learners socialization and communication skills and the new behaviors of being an observer and the receiver of feedback from a peer. Nor is the notion that "the observer is doing my job" accurate. The teacher is constantly engaged in giving feedback, but about a different aspect of the educational process. The teacher is still accountable for the events and the processes in the lesson.

3. *This behavior is not for the learner who has difficulties in comparing and contrasting performance with criteria.* On the contrary, this behavior is excellent for learners who need more time in these cognitive operations. They need practice, and what better opportunity than with a partner who is "equal" in role and supportive in behavior? Learners with "deficits" are often excluded from competitive situations. The cooperative nature of the Reciprocal style invites most learners, sooner or later, to participate.

4. *The observer cannot evaluate the doer.* This behavior is not an evaluating style. The roles are confined to offering feedback by criteria to improve the performance of the task.

With respect to time-on-task, or Academic Learning Time (ALT) in the Reciprocal style each learner practices the task only half the time. However, studies have shown that engaging in the observer's role (by visualizing, observing, reading/seeing the sequence of the movement, and talking about the task parts) provide a different kind of learning that does not hinder performance of the task itself (Goldberger, Gerney, & Chamberlain, 1982.)

Most students appreciate this equality of roles and usually follow through with appropriate behavior and enjoyment. At times, the superior performer who has always been singled out, reinforced, and perhaps unduly praised, demonstrates impatience in the Reciprocal style. (Learners who have been labeled bright, talented, or gifted exhibit a similar behavior in the gymnasium/classroom.) Episodes in this behavior are critical because of the emphasis on social interaction and development.

In general, most problems encountered between partners in this behavior fall into two broad categories: collision and collusion. Events in both categories need to be handled within the boundaries of this behavior without reverting to, say, the Command style.

Trying the following can ease the phase of awkwardness or discomfort that generally accompanies the implementation of a new teaching–learning behavior:

1. Introduce this new behavior to a small group of learners at a time. (The rest of the class can be working in a canopy Practice style at different stations without feedback.) When the groups come to the Reciprocal station, the learners can be introduced to this behavior under the observation of and with feedback from the teacher. After a few short episodes, the entire class will be familiar with the style.

2. For these first few episodes, select a task that is not particularly demanding so the focus will be on the new roles. Keep emphasizing and reinforcing the criteria process of comparing, contrasting, and giving feedback. The internalization of this behavior will pay off in future lessons.

3. It is possible to introduce this behavior to the entire class (or to a small group) by demonstrating the process with only one pair. Ask the learners to gather around. (Select a pair of learners in advance who feel secure enough to learn a new idea in public.) Introduce the behavior step by step while each partner experiences his or her role. All learners, criteria sheets in hand (or projected by a transparency), observe each step and listen to the verbal behavior of the observer. If needed, stop the action. Clarify, emphasize, and reexplain; then the pair continues. When the doer has completed the task, the pair switches roles and the episode goes on. This demonstration serves as a model for the rest of the students.

4. When a new behavior is first used, a period of time is needed to deliver and practice the new behavior/decision expectations. Although the task is always the focus, for these initial episodes, the task needs to be selected carefully so that it does not overwhelm the learners with too

many new points. Once learners internalize the new behavior, a new degree of freedom and trust occurs within the gymnasium/classroom. More challenges and options can then be created.

The Small Group

In physical education classes, one often sees small groups engaged in an activity. These groups are usually formed for one of two reasons: First, there are instances when working in small groups is intrinsic to the task itself. For example, to develop skill and offensive strategy in soccer, sometimes three players are needed to pass the ball among themselves; hence, various drills in threes have been designed. In tumbling, to facilitate a safe, initial performance of the back handspring, two spotters kneel at the performer's side and help the performer using prescribed techniques.

Second, the group is formed to meet organizational needs, such as when there is insufficient equipment for the number of participants. One often hears in the gymnasium, "Group one, work on the balance beam. Group two, on the parallel bars," and so on. This situation is not about working in a group, but is actually a group of people organized around one piece of equipment. (It is, therefore, the Practice style.)

In the context of the Reciprocal style, the term "small group" does not refer to either condition. It refers to the role of the participants in decision making, not to the activity.

When the class has an odd number of students, a small group of three may become necessary. One way to deal with this is to ask the extra person to join one of the pairs. Under such circumstances, there are two options available to the threesome:

1. Two doers and one observer
2. Two observers and one doer

Each of these options has liabilities. In the first option, it is sometimes difficult for the observer to watch two performers at the same time and identify the specific details of the performance. The threesome is not a particularly disturbing situation, but it makes the episode (for those participants) different from Reciprocal behavior practiced in pairs. The second option (two observers and one doer) carries more liabilities because it is more difficult to receive feedback from two observers. In addition, most tasks do not have enough points of criteria to justify two observers. Often, the second observer becomes quite bored because he or she does not have an active role in using the criteria or offering feedback.

Another way of dealing with the odd number is to ask the extra person to do the task in the Practice style and have the teacher offer the feedback.

If the class has a permanent odd number of learners, it is imperative to rotate the extra person in the Reciprocal episodes.

There is one more condition that might necessitate using small groups in this behavior—a given pair may not want to be together due to a social or affective discrepancy. There are, then, two extra people in this episode. Each can join a pair to form two threesomes. Again, it becomes a different condition for the people involved, but these liabilities exist in real classes. The teacher who is aware of these conditions can select the most appropriate option for the situation. The focal point here is the deliberate decision made by the teacher in advance. When this is done and the appropriate explanation is offered to the class, chances are higher for a smooth implementation of the episode.

The Developmental Channels

Design Variations

Although there are many references to design variations that suggest a Reciprocal style affiliation, most are examples of the Practice style with a social developmental focus. Peer teaching, partner learning, cooperative learning, "co-op," "pairs-check," "jigsaw," and tutor–learner are primarily *I Teach You, You Teach Me* models (Metzler, 1990, p. 286). The primary objectives of the Spectrum's Reciprocal behavior are to teach:

1. The process intrinsic to giving feedback (cognitive channel)
2. Feedback skills that enhance social communications (social channel)
3. Tolerance and patience when giving and receiving feedback (emotional channel)
4. Socialization-communication experiences (social channel)
5. Accuracy in performance of the task (physical and cognitive)

Most variations espousing a partner relationship do not include teacher-provided criteria to guide observation, feedback skills, communication skills, or the reciprocal relationship. These behaviors are more akin to the Practice style in their decision distribution and objectives. Without teacher-provided criteria, student feedback is idiosyncratic and unlikely to lead to the objectives of the Reciprocal style. The significance of the Spectrum's Reciprocal behavior is not the designation of one learner as doer or the other as observer. The significance lies in the opportunities the decision distribution (the roles) provides to learners: the opportunity to develop specific socialization and cognitive objectives.

THE RECIPROCAL STYLE—C

The purposes of this style are to work with a partner in a reciprocal relationship and to offer feedback to the partner, based on criteria prepared by the teacher.

Role of the learner

- To select the roles of doer and observer
- As doer, to perform the task (as in Style B)
- As observer, to compare and contrast the doer's work with the criteria, draw conclusions and offer feedback to the doer
- At the completion of the task, to switch roles

Role of the teacher

- To monitor the observers
- To give feedback to the observers
- To answer the observers' questions

Figure 8.6. Style C classroom chart

The period of time learners participate in a behavior is not the criterion that defines a teaching–learning approach. Although there may be units or a series of lessons that rely exclusively on the use of one behavior over others, it is the variety of teaching–learning behaviors (the variety in decision opportunities) that expand learners' content knowledge and attribute development.

The Reciprocal style continues the developmental process for both teacher and learner. This behavior provides the learner with the opportunity to make post-impact decisions, which creates a new reality in the relationships between the learners and the teacher (Figure 8.6). This reality invites the learners to participate in a responsible independence offered by the new decisions shifted to them. It is also a new reality for the teacher who has learned to shift post-impact decisions—a source of power—to the developing learners.

The next teaching–learning behavior requires an additional shift in the decisions so that new objectives and a different emphasis on the Developmental Channels can be identified.

Examples of Criteria Sheets The first example (Figure 8.7) incorporates Fronske's content descriptions and cues into the design of the criteria sheet.

Name _____   Style A B Ⓒ D E
Class _____   Task Sheet # _____
Date _____

Basketball—Dribbling

To the student:
Perform each task as described in the program below, indicate results, and place a check next to the completed task. Follow the role expectations stated.

Task Description	Skill	Cue	Common Error
 Eyes up Fingers spread Range of dribble: knee to waist Absorb ball back into pads of fingers	**Set-Up** *Hand placement—More complex dribble* *Eyes* *Height of dribble* *Range of dribble* *Overall Rules—More complex dribble* *Body protection*	Move hand on different angles of ball "Keep eyes *up*" Below waist Knee to waist Higher dribble for higher speed Lower dribble for lower speeds and tight situations Protect ball with body but see basket Protect/shields ball if guarded	Palming the ball (carrying the ball) Do not watch ball Dribble too high Dribble to hear yourself dribble Not advancing the ball Dribble without purpose Turning back to teammates and basket

Tasks	Quantity	Completed/Feedback	
		Doer 1	Doer 2
A. Shooting 1. Dribble in place without stopping 2. Dribble while walking forward 3. Dribble while walking backward 4. Dribble while trotting 5. One-hand shot—right side of basket 6. One-hand shot—left side of basket	10 consecutive dribbles 1/2 the count 2x 1/2 the count 2x 1/2 the count 2x		
Observers follow doers and offer feedback			

Figure 8.7. Basketball—dribbling (Task description from Fronske, H., p. 47. Permission for adaptation granted by Allyn & Bacon Publishing Co., Boston, MA.)

Name _____	Style A B Ⓒ D E
Class _____	Task Sheet # _____
Date _____	

Heimlich Maneuver

To the student:
Practice the procedures as demonstrated in class for the Heimlich Maneuver in groups of threes. Rotate among the 3 roles: 1) person choking 2) person applying the H M 3) person observing and offering feedback using the criterion below. Practice 3 times- 2 with feedback while performing the task and 1 from memory with feedback after completing all steps.

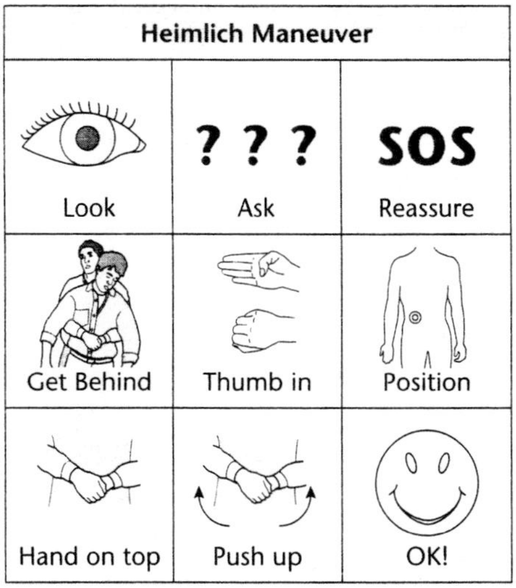

Heimlich Maneuver				Doer 1	Doer 2	Doer 3
Look	Ask	Reassure	Practice			
Get Behind	Thumb in	Position	Completed accurately from memory			
Hand on top	Push up	OK!				

Figure 8.8. Heimlich Maneuver

The criteria design for Figures 8.7 and 8.8 offers observers the information needed to perform their role—an image of the expected task and vital information to be used when comparing, contrasting, and offering feedback.

Figure 8.9 task sheet is appropriate only for skilled performers who *know* the positions, the appropriate body moves, and who can readily identify any deviations from the correct model. For less than skilled performers, pictures are necessary to develop the content proficiency to compare and to contrast against an established model.

Name _____   Style A B ©D E
Class _____   Task Sheet # _____
Date _____

Taekwando—Day 1 Skills

To the doer:
Perform each skill below five times from the right and left sides (where applicable). If you have any questions, ask your observer.

Observer:
Compare the doer's performance with the criteria listed below. Place a check in the space provided when the doer accomplishes the specific criteria. Remember to offer positive feedback to the doer first, then use corrective comments after the skill has been performed five times each from the right and left.

Rotate roles after each skill has been performed five times from the left/right by the doer.

Task/Criteria

Task/Criteria	Left Forward	Right Forward
Attention Stance		
1. Hands at sides	1. _____	1. _____
2. Feet together	2. _____	2. _____
3. Head straight	3. _____	3. _____
4. Eyes looking straight ahead	4. _____	4. _____
5. Remains still	5. _____	5. _____
Bow		
1. Bends at waist 45 degrees	1. _____	1. _____
2. Counts to one-one thousand	2. _____	2. _____
3. Returns to attention stance	3. _____	3. _____
Ready Position	**Left Forward**	**Right Forward**
1. Has chamber hands (in fists, palms facing up, by respective hips	1. _____	1. _____
2. Steps out about 2' with left foot	2. _____	2. _____
3. Punches hands down in front of belt	3. _____	3. _____
4. Looks straight ahead	4. _____	4. _____
Guarding Stance	**Left Forward**	**Right Forward**
1. From ready stance, steps back one shoulder width with right foot	1. _____	1. _____
2. Right hand in fist, comes up under chin, fingers to face	2. _____	2. _____
3. Left hand in fist, comes up in front of right hand by the left shoulder, fingers to face	3. _____	3. _____
4. Both elbows are close to the body	4. _____	4. _____
5. Weight is slightly on front foot	5. _____	5. _____
Double Punch	**Left Forward**	**Right Forward**
1. Starts from guarding stance	1. _____	1. _____
2. Extends left fist out to almost full extension, palm facing down to ground	2. _____	2. _____
3. Retracts left fist to starting position	3. _____	3. _____
4. Extends right fist out with palm facing down and turns right hip and shoulder into punch	4. _____	4. _____
5. Retracts right shoulder, hip, and fist to starting positon	5. _____	5. _____
Front Kick	**Left Forward**	**Right Forward**
1. Starts from guarding stance	1. _____	1. _____
2. Brings back knee up parallel with floor, foot by hip	2. _____	2. _____
3. Snaps foot out and back	3. _____	3. _____
4. Returns foot back to starting position	4. _____	4. _____

Figure 8.9. Taekwondo—For advanced–level students (Task sheet contributed by Dr. Joanne Dusel, Towson University, MD)

CHAPTER 9

The Self-Check Style—D

(T)
(L)
→ *(L)* [1]

The defining characteristics of the Self-Check style are performing a task and engaging in self-assessment. In the anatomy of the Self-Check style, the role of the teacher is to make all subject matter, criteria, and logistical decisions. The role of the learners is to work independently and to check their own performances against the criteria prepared by the teacher. When this behavior is achieved, the following objectives are reached in subject matter and in behavior:

The Objectives

Subject Matter Objectives	Behavior Objectives
To gain independence in performing the task	To become less dependent on the teacher or a partner and to begin relying on oneself for feedback and acquisition of content
To develop kinesthetic awareness in physical performance by individually practicing and assessing performance	To use criteria to verify one's performance
	To maintain honesty about one's performance
To practice the sequence intrinsic to assessment and feedback skills	To cope with one's own limitations
To be able to correct errors in one's task performance	To gain self-awareness about one's proficiency in performance
	To develop independence and personal motivation
To increase active time-on-task	To develop feedback skills to adopt an intrinsic motivation capacity
To master the content leading to automatic performance	To continue the individualizing process by making the decisions shifted to the learner in the impact and post-impact sets

---

[1] This diagram represents the anatomy of the Self-Check style.

The decision distribution (O–T–L–O) of the Self-Check style prompts the learner to reach for new sets of objectives incorporating more responsibility. This landmark behavior emphasizes two dimensions—individual practice and self-assessment.

Many physical education skills, activities, and sports intrinsically provide learners with feedback about their performance. The visibility of performance provides information to learners about the final outcome of their practice. The following list delineates the types of tasks in physical education that represent the Self-Check style.

- Skateboarding
- Surfing
- Juggling
- Shooting baskets
- Jumping rope
- Archery
- Darts
- Bowling
- Performing on a balance beam, high bar
- Serving, catching, or throwing a ball to a designated spot
- Golf
- Climbing a rope
- Performing a "regular" pushup
- Touching the toes with straight legs

The above activities or skills intrinsically provide the learner with feedback about his or her performance results. Either the arrow, the dart, or the ball went where it was supposed to go, or it did not. The distance by which it was off the target is immediately apparent. The skateboarding or surfing move was either completed or it was not. The juggling continued or it stopped. The visibility of the activity announced the final results. The more the learner knows the criterion of the task (knowledge of the performance), the more meaningful and accurate the self-feedback can be (knowledge of results). The self-feedback about the performance guides the next practice, either to replicate or to make adjustments in body positioning or timing.

Many other tasks do not provide the learner with intrinsic feedback. These less visible tasks with undisputed final outcomes need clear criteria of things to look for so the learners can make the new decisions and accomplish the objectives of this behavior. (See section on subject matter).

The decisions of this style emphasize cognitive engagement. They shift to the learners the development of kinesthetic awareness and the assessment of precise body position for the task. An intimacy develops between the learner and the content in the Self-Check style. Independence in practice and the ability to assess and correct one's practice are essential skills necessary in most aspects of adult behavior.

The Anatomy of the Self-Check Style

This landmark behavior evolves from the previous landmark behavior—the Reciprocal style. The decisions intrinsic to using criteria as a basis for feedback to a peer are now shifted to each learner. Hence the name of this behavior: Self-Check. Perhaps the most striking aspect of the Self-Check episode is the carryover from the two previous styles. Ultimately, the learners gain the ability to assess themselves using these techniques. In the Practice style, they learn to do the task. In the Reciprocal style, they learn to use criteria and give feedback to a peer. In Self-Check, the learner uses the same skills for self-assessment.

This landmark behavior relies on the learner's competence in individual practice of the task(s) (making the nine impact decisions of the Practice style) and the Reciprocal style post-impact decisions of comparing, contrasting, and drawing conclusions. The shift in the anatomy of the Self-Check style occurs in the post-impact set because learners check their own performances. In the anatomy of this style, the teacher's role is to make all the decisions in the pre-impact set—the subject matter, criteria, and logistics—and to communicate with the learners during impact. The learners practice in the impact set and assess their own performances in the post-impact.

Schematically, the shift of decisions and the anatomy of this style appear in Figure 9.1.

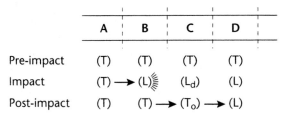

	A	B	C	D
Pre-impact	(T)	(T)	(T)	(T)
Impact	(T) → (L)		(L_d)	(L)
Post-impact	(T)	(T) → (T_o) → (L)		

Figure 9.1. The anatomy of the Self-Check style—The shift from Reciprocal to Self-Check

The Implementation of the Self-Check Style

Each new behavior distributes decisions differently—who makes which decisions, when—to create the new learning focus. Each behavior invites the learners to participate in the subject matter from a different perspective. Consequently, the variety of teaching–learning behaviors expands what learners know about the subject matter.

In this behavior, the teacher provides the opportunity for the learners to develop insights into the content, and to become more self-reliant by shifting both the practice itself and the comparing/contrasting of their performance against the model. This behavior is not for the novice or the learner who does not demonstrate some degree of success in the task—in the specific motor skill, activity, or the content. It is premature to ask inexperienced individuals to make self-assessment decisions when they don't have the basic competence in performing the content (the skill). Even when learners are familiar with the task, it is very difficult to remember kinesthetically where all body parts are when performing physical tasks. Therefore, the task selected and the form in which the criteria are designed are both critical for reaching the objectives of this behavior. (This topic will be expanded in the section on selecting and designing the task.)

Description of an Episode

When the learners disperse in the gymnasium, playing field, court, dance studio, or other venue, they begin performing the task, stop frequently to look at the criteria sheet, compare their own performance with the criteria, and then move on. They either repeat the task to correct or maintain the performance, or go on to a new task. This is the first behavior that allows time for these kinds of decisions. For learners to experience these decisions, they must engage in several subsidiary behaviors. First, they must pause to read and internalize the criteria; then they pause after the performance of a task to think about their performance. At times, they may engage in self-negotiations expressing concern or joy. These behaviors are overt and observable. A great deal more than just performing tasks occurs in Self-Check episodes.

This new behavior is possible because the teacher's role has changed. The verbal behavior that is specific to this style develops and sustains the operation and the spirit of such episodes.

How to Implement the Self-Check Style

The Pre-Impact Set The teacher makes all the pre-impact decisions in this behavior—the decisions about which tasks are appropriate, the criteria sheet, and the logistics. The pre-impact set is a mental rehearsal of the events, sequence, the delivery, and the materials and equipment needed for the face-to-face interaction that follows.

The Impact Set   Notice that in Table 9.1, the order of the subject matter and the behavior presentation has been changed. Order decisions for the three expectations (subject matter, behavior, logistics) vary to accommodate the objectives of the episode. The sequence of events in this episode is as follows.

The Implications of the Self-Check Style

Self-assessment and the opportunity to judge one's performance represent a major step toward self-reliance. If learners are to acquire intrinsic motivation, they must learn to give feedback to themselves. Not only do many of the tasks in life require the ability to engage skillfully in the decisions of this behavior, they also require honesty in participating in the process.

Self-Check implies that:

- The teacher values the learner's independence.
- The teacher values the learner's ability to develop self-monitoring systems.
- The teacher trusts the learner to be honest during this process.
- The teacher has the patience to ask questions focusing on the process of self-check as well as the performance of the task.
- The learner can work privately and engage in the self-checking process.
- The learner can use self-check as feedback for improvement.
- The learner can identify his/her own limits, successes, and failures.

The new classroom reality that evolves in these episodes creates conditions for examining one's self-concept. Learning to be honest with oneself, while learning to recognize and accept one's errors is a moral demand that did not confront the learner in the previous styles.

Selecting and Designing the Subject Matter and the Criteria Sheet

Not all tasks in physical education are conducive to self-examination. The criterion for task selection is that the learners must have some proficiency in performing the task before they can engage in post-impact self-assessment. The short duration of many physical tasks does not allow the performer much time to learn a great deal about the performance. Often, when one asks a novice in tumbling, "What was the position of your left shoulder dur-

Table 9.1 Events—The Self-Check Style

Episode Events		Feedback	Time
Subject-matter presentation	Subject matter: 1. Present the task(s) 2. Present the criteria sheets		

Behavior presentation	3. The teacher states the style's expectations and objectives.
	4. The teacher presents the learner's role (See Figure 9.2.)
	   a. To individually practice the tasks
	   b. To check the performance against the criteria provided
	5. The teacher explains the role of the teacher.		

Logistics presentation	Logistical expectations:
	6. The teacher establishes only those parameters necessary for the episode.
	  • location
	  • time
	  • equipment/material pick up location(s) for task sheets
	  • equipment/material pick up location (s) for criteria sheets
	  • equipment/material return location(s)
	  • interval
	  • posture
	  • attire and appearance		

Questions for clarification	Verify understanding of expectations before action: "Are there any questions for clarification?" Once the questions have been answered, the learners begin.		
Action, task engagement, performance	7. The learners begin to make the designated decisions while practicing the tasks. While the learners perform they will switch between practicing the task (impact) and checking the accuracy (post-impact) in their performance.		

Feedback **(post-impact)**	8. As each learner performs the task, use of the criteria sheet begins. Each learner will decide when to use the criteria sheet for self-feedback, based on individual pace and rhythm.
	9. The teacher's role in the post-impact set is to:
	  a. Observe the learner's performance of the task
	  b. Observe the learner's use of the criteria sheet for self-checking
	  c. Communicate with the individual learner about proficiency and accuracy in the self-check process (see the section on verbal behavior later in this chapter)
	  d. Offer feedback to the learner once the learner's self-assessment statements have been made		

Closure	10. Offer closure about the focus of this new behavior. Address the entire class with statements about their self-checking role.		

THE SELF-CHECK STYLE—D

The purposes of this style are to perform the task and to check your own work.

Role of the learner

- To perform the task
- To make the nine decisions of the Practice style
- To use the criteria to check your own performance

Role of the teacher

- To prepare the subject matter and criteria
- To answer questions by the learner
- To initiate communication with the learner

Figure 9.2. Style D classroom chart

ing the backward roll?" the answer is, "I don't know." This is to be expected because most learners in the early stages of learning are not aware of the details concerning their body's performance. It is difficult, and sometimes impossible, to do an accurate self-assessment when learning a new task. The Reciprocal style will be more appropriate in such situations.

Another hindrance is the lack of accurate recording of the performance. The learner is asked to assess performance against precise criteria using memory as the recording device. This is very difficult for most, and impossible for the novice. When a novice learns a new skill, it is quite unlikely that he or she will remember the detailed conditions of each body part. The same is true for tasks in many sports. (To overcome this hindrance there are two ways to remedy the problem: videotaping, which can establish the knowledge of performance so immediate feedback can result, and mirrors like those used in dance studios.)

These difficulties occur when the focus of the task and the end results are the body itself. When the criteria for excellence focuses on the precise relationships among the parts of the body, the intrinsic problem becomes manifest. This applies to gymnastics, diving, and some branches of dance. All these activities hinge upon kinesthetic sense. Often one hears a gymnast say, "It did not feel right," or "It felt just great." This sense of movement develops with time, experience, and success. Those learning new activities usually cannot use this as an accurate source of information about the performance. The sense of movement may supply a general feeling about the performance, but it does not supply the accurate information needed for improvement. Many tasks in these areas are inappropriate for Self-Check. The Reciprocal style supplies the feedback from an outside source.

Other physical tasks are more applicable to Self-Check. These tasks pursue end results external to the body itself; they are concerned with the results of the movement, rather than the movement itself. Basketball is a prime example of this type of activity. Any basketball shot, despite the technique, is judged by the performance result. It is the distance of the javelin throw that counts in track and field, not the specific form used by the athlete. This relationship between body movements and end results provides the performer with immediate feedback and possibilities for self-check using particular criteria. (These are situations where the feedback is intrinsic to the task.)

In many Self-Check tasks, the implements used are the main source of information. For example, a wiggly flight of the javelin shows the learner that the javelin's release was incorrect. The learner can then refer to the section of the criteria card that highlights the details of the release. During subsequent throws, the learner concentrates on correcting this particular aspect. In soccer, when the task is to practice kicking the ball a relatively short distance through a high arc and the ball does not fly accordingly, the learner knows that something in the kick was incorrect. The learner then refers to the part of the criteria that highlights the details of placing the foot under the lower part of the ball.

The purpose of this analysis is not to offer a classification system for various activities or to interfere with well-established techniques of various sports (these are readily available in kinesiology materials and specific sports books). Rather, the purpose is to invite the teacher to analyze tasks in terms of their applicability to Self-Check. There is no need to use this behavior with a task that can be better accomplished by another style. The role of the teacher is to facilitate efficient learning and reduce frustration.

The criteria supply the answers to the following questions:

1. Where is the error?
2. Why did the error occur?
3. How do I correct the error?

Current publications that sequence physical education skills, provide the cues for correct performance (essential content highlights), and list the common errors are invaluable when preparing criteria sheets for the Self-Check style.[2]

---

[2] Refer to Chapter 18 for additional information on designing subject matter.

Style-Specific Comments

Verbal Behavior

The teacher's verbal behavior must reflect the intent of this behavior and must support the roles of the teacher and learner. Purposes for communication between the teacher and the learner are:

1. To ascertain that the learners can compare and contrast their own performances against criteria

2. To listen to what each learner says about his/her content performance

3. To lead learners to see discrepancies in their assessments (when they exist) by asking questions

4. To identify the discrepancies if the learner cannot see them

Items 3 and 4 require the teacher to be astute, and not to increase the learner's frustration by asking questions that cannot be answered, or by withdrawing feedback. When learners get stuck and assess their performance incorrectly, make an adjustment decision and switch to the Practice style to offer content clarification and feedback to the learner. The learner's feelings are more important than the structure of any single style.

When initiating communication with the learner in this behavior, the teacher asks a general question: "How are you doing?" The learner has several options in answering:

1. "Fine."

2. "I can't do the task, and I'm not sure why."

3. "I can't do the task, but I know how to correct it."

4. "I can do the task and I understand each part on the criteria sheet."

Independent of the learners' responses, the teacher's verbal behavior leads to the focus of this behavior—listening to the learners' comments about their performance and assessments of the tasks. The teacher circulates and watches to see how the learners are interacting with the criteria and how that interaction affects their performances. Communication either reinforces the learner's use of the criteria or redirects the learner's focus. If a learner responds with "Fine," the teacher can ask "What about your performance of the ___ was fine?" Focusing the interaction around the criteria redirects the learner to the content expectations. Acquisition of the task is just one of the objectives of this behavior; of primary importance is the learner's ability to diagnose, according to the prepared criteria, to identify errors, and to correct them. This behavior invites the learners to verbalize what they know about the content and it permits the teacher to watch learners cope with their successes and limitations.

Once learners can verbalize what they are doing, the teacher can verify their observations by acknowledging the performance with a value statement. When errors occur in their observations, the role of the teacher is to point these out to the learner.

It must be acknowledged that people reach a level of comfort in this behavior (or any behavior) at different speeds. There are those who immediately enjoy the demands on individualization and independence implicit in this behavior and then there are those who need more time to appreciate individual responsibility. Self-Check requires cognitive, emotional, ethical, and physical investment; some learners' dispositions and attitudes resist becoming that engaged or involved in the task. A teacher can learn a great deal about students by watching them experience the Self-Check style.

Options in Task Design

Two options are available for task design in this behavior: (1) a single task for all learners and (2) a differentiated task. In the first option, the teacher assigns the same task to all learners; in the second option, the teacher assigns different tasks to different learners. Because the teacher makes content decisions in both, these options remain within the structure of Self-Check. The purpose of each behavior is to include learners in the new decisions. At times, adjustments must be made in content standards for all learners to participate.

Criteria Sheets

The format of the criteria sheet is critical. The more complex the task, the more difficult it is for the learner to engage in self-assessment with only paper and pencil criteria. Videotape is an excellent but time-consuming technique. Tasks that can be broken down (sequenced with each movement delineated) are appropriate for paper. Each learner needs his/her own criteria sheet for tasks that involve multiple parts. Charts are fine for reminders but they are not appropriate for complex tasks. Often the criteria designed for the Reciprocal behavior can also be used in Self-Check. The criteria do not change; only the behavior/decision expectations change.

The Developmental Channels
Design Variations

Personalized System for Instruction (PSI) is an example of the Self-Check style when the task materials include performance criteria, error analyses, and assessment expectations for the individual learner. When PSI descriptions incorporate peer teaching situations, they do not represent the decision distribution (or objectives) of the Self-Check behavior. Independence in learning to practice and assess the task is the hallmark of all Self-Check design variations. Improving performance and developing self-assessment skills are guided by teacher-produced criteria. Initial episodes in Self-Check cannot shift assessment to the learner without prepared criteria. Reliable self-assessment is possible without prepared criteria only when learners demonstrate proficiency in the physical task. Without an understanding of the task expectations and kinesthetic awareness, it is impossible for learners to accurately correct/assess performance.

When learners work in groups or with peers, self-assessment is difficult. Therefore, design variations that incorporate groups, which purport to emphasize the decisions or objectives of Self-Check, need to be examined carefully. Although they are challenging to prepare, Self-Check episodes that emphasize the social Developmental Channel are possible. For example, it is possible to sequence episodes within the lesson using different teaching–learning behaviors to reach a variety of objectives (see lesson plan design in Chapter 11). The cumulative effects of such lesson planning can reinforce the teacher's overall learning focus. The following series of episodes, shown in Table 9.2, includes three teaching–learning behaviors. The cumulative goal is to create a social situation that invites learners to examine their self-assessment decisions.

Table 9.2 Episodes of Teaching–Learning Behaviors

Episode #	Teaching–Learning Behavior
1	Self-Check style: Practice a task individually, privately, and self-check using criteria
2	Reciprocal style in small groups: each learner demonstrates his/her task and the group members offer feedback using the criteria
3	Self-Check style: Individually compare the group's remarks to the original self-assessment comments, then practice the task and self-assess

This design sequence provides a different emphasis to Self-Check. It removes the social isolation by increasing dependence on and interaction with, a group. It reduces the individual time-on-task but increases feedback. It reinforces the decisions and objectives of the Self-Check behavior.

No landmark behavior or variation can involve all learners to the same degree. In each behavior, some learners will enjoy while others will dislike making the designated decisions. Approaching teaching–learning experiences with a variety of design variations and from a non-versus approach, can increase learner involvement in the process.

The decisions of the Self-Check style lead learners to the next behavior—one that shifts even more decisions and responsibility to learners.

Examples of Task Sheets for the Self-Check Style

Name _____   Style A B C Ⓓ E
Class _____   Task Sheet # _____
Date _____

Soccer

To the Student:

There are three stations. Each is designed for you to practice controlled punting. Station One: practice the technique of the punt (ball distance is not the focus). Assess your motor performance against the criteria below. Stations two and three involve punting and accurate ball flight. At these stations assess both technique and record the flight of the ball and its accuracy to the indicated targets.

Punting				
Task Description	Skill	Cue	Alternate cue	Common Error
Like holding a skunk Drop the ball	**Technique** *Hand position*	Like holding a skunk	Hold ball out away	Holding ball too close to chest
	Drop action	Drop the ball		
	Kicking leg	Like an underhand serve in volleyball	Shoelaces flat	
		Like kicking a football	Pull back kicking leg	Swinging leg from standing position does not create momentum
		Swing leg under body making contact with ball below knee		
Pull back kicking leg	*Support leg*	Support leg plants simultaneously with dropping of ball		Ball is met too high on leg with shins or too low on end of toes
Comments/Feedback				

Figure 9.3. Soccer—punting (Task description from Fronske, H., p. 160. Permission for adaptation granted by Allyn & Bacon Publishing Co., Boston, MA.)

Name _____	Style A B C Ⓓ E
Class _____	Task Sheet # _____
Date _____	

Bowling

To the Student:

Practice the 4-step delivery 10 times. Five without the ball, and five with the ball.
Provide performance feedback

Basic Grips and Stance			
Skill	Cue	Alternate Cue	Common Error
Grip			
Conventional	Thumb on top, handshake position	Thumb hole at 12:00, finger holes at 6:00	
	Grip ball with second groove of two middle fingers	Ring finger and middle finger	Squeezing with thumb
Fingertip	Cradle ball in opposite arm		
Stance	Grip ball with first groove of two middle fingers		Thumb in first Squeezing with thumb
	Erect, knees relaxed	Stand tall	Knees locked, shoulders not square to pins
	Ball supported by nondelivery arm	Ball carried on palm of right hand	Ball hanging from thumb and fingers
Left foot slightly advanced then step with right foot	Ball on right side	Ball hides right shirt pocket (good place to start); find your comfort zone	Ball too high or low
	Lower right shoulder	Tilt body slightly to right	
	Feet slightly apart	Three boards between feet	
	Left foot slightly advanced	One-half foot length ahead	
	Eyes focus on aiming spot	Look at second arrow from right	Looking at pins
Completed/Feedback			

Figure 9.4. Bowling—basic grips and stance (Task description from Fronske, H., pp. 56–59.
Permission for adaptation granted by Allyn & Bacon Publishing Co., Boston, MA.)

Approach			
Skill	Cue	Alternate Cue	Common Error
Arm action Pendulum swing, like ball on end of string Step away, push away Arm action (approach)	First step and arm push away together	Step away, push away	Stepping before pushing way
	Extend ball arm straight forward horizontally	Long reach but short step, like handing ball to friend	Pushing ball up or to the right too far
	Use pendulum swing, like ball on end of string	Ball falls downward and backward	Applying too much force changing direction of ball
	Ball swings back, shoulder high	Horizontal in front to horizontal in back	
	Extend left arm outward for balance		Ball goes too high or arcs behind body
	Keep ball swinging, arms relaxed	Gravity and inertia provide main force	Trying to throw ball too fast
	Release ball as arm passes vertical	Ball should land 3 to 4 feet beyond foul line	Dropping ball or setting it down on boards
Leg action Wrist straight and firm Timing Steps: short-medium long-very long Leg action (approach)	First step very short. Second step medium. Third step long. Fourth step longest.	Each step is a little longer and faster	First step too long
	First step and push away together	Keep ball swinging and feet walking	Feet finishing before arm swing
	Second and third steps with down and back swing		
	Fourth step with forward swing and delivery		
Completed/Feedback			

Figure 9.4. Bowling—basic grips and stance (Task description from Fronske, H., pp. 56–59. Permission for adaptation granted by Allyn & Bacon Publishing Co., Boston, MA.)

Delivery			
Skill	Cue	Alternate Cue	Common Error
Straight ball	Wrist straight and firm	Thumb at 12 o'clock position	Arm rotation right or left
	Release ball as arm passes vertical and starts upward	Trajectory like airplane landing 3 to 4 feet beyond foul line	Dropping or setting ball on approach before foul line
			Holding ball too long causes you to loft ball
Leg action (delivery)	Follow-through in straight upward swing	Arm points in direction you want ball to go	Stopping arm action on release of ball
	Shoulders stay square (parallel) to foul line		Body rotates clockwise on ball of left foot
Hook ball	Cup the palm	Thumb at 10:30 position	
	Hand stay behind ball		Hand on side of ball
	Thumb comes out first (ball spins counter-clockwise)	Deliver ball with finger only	Spin like a top
	On release flip the fingers and shake hands	Release with the V form	
	Follow through in straight upward swing		
Leg action	Lower the body during third and fourth steps	Bend knees to smoothly lower body at end of approach	Bouncy up-and-down action
	Decelerate fourth step	Left foot steps and slides to a stop	Loss of balance from too quick a stop
	Keep back foot in contact with floor	Don't spin out	Poor timing results in picking up back foot and clockwise body rotation
	Left knee and foot point toward pins	Keep facing target	Body rotation
Completed/Feedback			

CHAPTER 10

The Inclusion Style—E

(T)
→ *(L)*
→ *(L)*[1]

The defining characteristic of the Inclusion style is that learners with varying degrees of skill participate in the same task by selecting a level of difficulty at which they can perform. In the anatomy of the Inclusion style, the role of the teacher is to make all subject matter decisions, including the possible levels in the tasks, and the logistical decisions. The role of the learners is to survey the available levels in the task, select an entry point, practice the task, if necessary make an adjustment in the task level, and check performance against the criteria. When this behavior is achieved, the following objectives are reached in subject matter and in behavior:

The Objectives

Subject Matter Objectives	Behavior Objectives
To accommodate individual performance differences	To experience making a decision about an entry point into a task by choosing an initial level of performance
To design a range of options that provide varying content entry points for all learners in the same task	To practice self-evaluation skills using a performance criterion
To increase content acquisition by providing opportunities for continued participation	To experience making adjustment decisions that maintain continued content participation
To offer opportunities for content adjustment decisions	To accept the reality of individual differences in performance abilities
To increase the quality of active time-on-task	To learn to deal with congruity or discrepancy between one's aspiration and the reality of one's performance
To reinforce the assessment sequence process	To practice the skills intrinsic to self-reliance
	To practice honesty in appropriate level selection and honesty in self-evaluation

[1]This diagram represents the anatomy of the Inclusion style.

The following statement summarizes the overall objective of the Inclusion style: "Inclusion Ensures Continued Participation."

The Concept of Inclusion[2]

For 30 years Muska Mosston presented the concept of inclusion in hundreds of workshops and presentations. During our 25-year working relationship we frequently presented the following scenario to introduce and illustrate the Inclusion concept.[3]

> *Holding a level rope about one foot above the ground, we asked a group of students to jump over the obstacle one by one (Figure 10.1). When all had cleared the rope, we asked: "What shall we do with the rope now?" Instantly the answer came forth: "Raise it!" We raised the rope by a few inches and asked the students to jump over it again. All the students cleared the rope once more. "And now?" we asked. "Raise it again!" was the answer. We continued raising the rope a few inches each time, and the students continued to jump over it.*
>
> *When the rope reached a given height, the inevitable happened. Some students were unable to clear the rope; they walked a few feet away and sat down. As we continued raising it, more students failed to clear the rope until there was only one student left—and then none. "This experience," we said, "expresses the concept of exclusion—the single standard design of the task."*

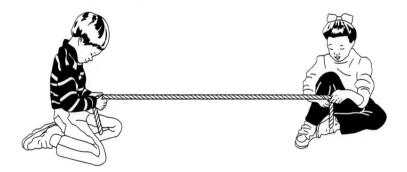

Figure 10.1. Horizontal rope

[2]This section adapted from a forthcoming book on Spectrum Teaching.

[3]This story relates the author's shared experience with her late colleague, Muska Mosston.

We then asked: "What can be done with the rope to create a condition for inclusion—for all learners to be successful in going over the rope?" There was a moment of silence. All the participants were immersed in thought.[4] "I know," announced one student, "I know what we can do—let's slant the rope." We raised one end of the rope to chest level and placed the other end on the ground (Figure 10.2). "Jump over the rope again," we said. Within seconds the students dispersed opposite various heights and began jumping. All the students cleared the rope. "Do it once more," we urged them. Again all students cleared the rope. "This experience," we said, "expresses the concept of inclusion."[5]

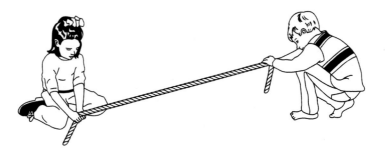

Figure 10.2. Slanted rope[6]

In the many auspicious opportunities we shared, here and abroad, to repeat this experience the results have been identical and the behavior universal. The condition represented by the horizontal rope always excludes people; the condition represented by the slanting rope always includes.

The intent and the action in this episode are congruent because the slanted rope arrangement accomplishes the objectives to create conditions of inclusion (choice of the degree of difficulty within the same task).

---

[4]Although several solutions are possible, the most succinct one, and perhaps the most dramatic, which is always produced by participants, is to slant the rope.

[5]Muska is credited with inventing the "slanted rope concept." He discovered this concept as a teenager in Israel. One day while riding on horseback, he decided to challenge his horse to jump a log that had fallen across a barrel. He told the story that after jumping the log, he suddenly stopped, turned around to examine what had happened. He realized that the diagonal placement of the log had presented "height" options. That event stuck with him, and years later he showed how this concept could be applied to tasks in any field.

[6]Children named this style the "slanty rope" style. This name is often used to designate this behavior.

The Anatomy of the Inclusion Style

Let us now identify the anatomy of the Inclusion teaching–learning behavior and then analyze the functional steps in this process (Figure 10.3).

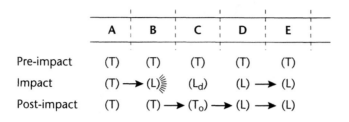

Figure 10.3. The shift from Self-Check to Inclusion

The role of the teacher in this landmark behavior is to make the decisions in the pre-impact set and to anticipate the shift of the learners' roles in the impact set. The learners make the decisions in the impact set, including the decision about the subject matter entry point, where they select the level of task performance. In the post-impact set, learners make assessment decisions about their performance and decide in which of the available levels to continue.

Let us examine more specifically the decisions learners make when offered the multiple-level conditions of the slanted rope. (The sequence is the same for any task.)

1. The learner looks at the options of height made available by the slanted rope.

2. The learner makes a decision of self-assessment and selects the entry point. (The teacher can actually watch the learner going through this selection process; it is almost like a bargaining session within oneself. The teacher will see the learner select a position opposite a given height. This decision might be followed by a hesitation and perhaps another position choice; then the learner is ready to approach the rope.)

3. The learner takes a few running steps and jumps at the selected *height*. Usually it is a height that the learner knows will ensure success (Byra & Jenkins, 1998). The initial choice is always a safe choice![7]

4. The learner knows that he/she was successful in the first choice of height (post-impact decision). Now the learner has three options:

   a. To repeat the same height

---

[7]The only exception to this statement is very young children who have not had enough experiences to assess their previous performances, and make "safe" assessment decisions.

    b. To select a higher (more difficult) spot

    c. To select a lower (less difficult) spot

    Whichever choice the learner makes is acceptable. The important point is that the learner made a choice of where to interact with the task.

5. The learner takes a few steps and jumps over the selected height.

6. The learner assesses the results of this jump against the criteria (post-impact decision) and whether or not the second jump was successful. Again, the learner has three options—to repeat the height, to select a higher (more difficult) spot, or to select a lower (less difficult) spot.

7. The practice and the inclusion process continue.

The principle of inclusion can be grasped by all learners, regardless of age, geographic location, or culture, without any strain or difficulty. In one workshop demonstration with 30 fifth graders as participants, one girl with a cast on her leg asked to be excused and sat on a chair nearby. As we reached the end of the first part, the horizontal rope was raised again and again, and all but one learner were excluded. The learners were asked, "What can we do with this rope so that all can be included?" After a slight pause, one learner offered, "Why don't you dip it in the middle?" In effect, a double slanted rope was designed where the center dipped and touched the floor. All participants were then engaged in the jump and in making all the decisions previously described. Soon the girl with the cast stood up, limped to the rope, and walked over its lowest (least difficult) point where the rope touched the floor. The audience observed that this behavior is, indeed, an inviting one.

The Implementation of the Inclusion Style

Description of an Episode

The Inclusion style can be introduced to physical education classes by demonstrating the concept of the slanted rope. The transfer to other activities will be quite smooth. It is possible, of course, to hold a rope and talk the whole idea, but nothing can match the impact of actually participating in the process and feeling included.

After the demonstration (which emphasizes the concept of choice, so inclusion can occur, with adjustments that can be made) is completed, move on to another task. Ask the students to practice a new task designed for inclusion. (See the sections on tasks designed for inclusion). As in previous behaviors, the learners will disperse, pick up their task sheets, and select their locations. Next, they will survey the levels of performance offered and decide their individual entry points.

While this is occurring, pause for a while and observe the process; give the learners time to start and experience the initial steps (decisions). Now the teacher's role is to circulate and offer each learner individual feedback, as in the previous behavior (Self-Check). Respond to the decision-making role, not to the details of the task performance. The initial contact with the individual learner invites conversation—a chance for the teacher to listen to the learner. The teacher can ask general questions: "What decisions did you make about the task? How are you doing in the level you selected? How are you doing in your role?" The learner's reply will guide the teacher's next comment. The teacher's feedback is to acknowledge the learner's level decision. In the initial practice of this behavior it is important that the teacher accept and not challenge the level decision.

Focus on using neutral feedback; avoid value feedback referring to the selected level. It is not the teacher's role to tell the learner whether or not the level selected was good. The learner's role is to select the appropriate level for him/her, not to please the teacher. It might be a little difficult for the teacher to refrain from commenting on the selected level, but patience is mandatory. And it might be difficult for the learner to refrain from asking the teacher "Which level do you think I should select?" The objective is to teach the learner to make appropriate decisions about which level in the subject matter he/she is most capable of performing. This behavior emphasizes not only the cognitive and physical developmental channel, but also the emotional. This behavior taps the emotions, the self-concept, and the commitment level of the learners as they practice the task.

Errors in performance are not ignored. Regardless of the selected level, ask the learner to refer to the task description and check the performance once more. Either wait to see or return in a few minutes and verify if the learner identified the error; if not, clarify the performance error, then move on to the next learner.

How to Implement the Inclusion Style

The descriptions above provided the idea of an appropriate episode using the Inclusion style. The following table summarizes the sequence of events to use when implementing the Inclusion style in classes. Although it is possible to deliver the sequence of expectations (subject matter, behavior, and logistics) in any order, for the first episode, it is important to set the scene by introducing the concept of inclusion.

The Pre-Impact Set   In the impact set, the delivery of events for the Inclusion style is shown in Table 10.1.

Table 10.1. Inclusion Style

Episode Events		Feedback	Time
Setting-the-scene Introducing the Inclusion Concept	Introduction to the concept of inclusion: The teacher sets-the-scene by introducing the concept of inclusion. One episode of the actual experience with the "slanted rope" will suffice for understanding and internalizing the concept.		

Behavior	The teacher:
	
	1. States the major objective of this practice: *to include learners by providing a range of levels (different degrees of difficulty) within the same task*
	
	2. Describes learner's role expectations:
	
	  a. To survey the choices
	
	  b. To select an initial level as an entry point for performance
	
	  c. To perform the task
	
	  d. To assess performance against criteria
	
	  e. To decide whether or not another level is desired or appropriate
	
	3. Describes teacher's role expectations:
	
	  a. To observe the learners making decisions about level selection and performance
	
	  b. To answer questions from the learners
	
	  c. To initiate communication with the learners
	
	The Classroom Chart is a helpful reminder for the learners of this teaching–learning behavior (Figure 10.4).		

Subject matter presentation	Subject matter:
	
	The teacher presents:
	
	1. The subject matter, the different levels, the factor that determines the "degree of difficulty,"[8] and the criteria sheets are presented. The delivery includes demonstration and the modes of communication when appropriate.
	
	2. The "Individual Program" (tasks sheet)
	
	3. The subject matter logistical decisions about:
	
	  • quality
	
	  • the number of correct responses per level necessary before moving to another level (see comment 1)
	
	  • how to check the "checking procedures"		

[8]See next section on Degree of Difficulty.

Comment 1: Each teaching style is designed to contribute to content acquisition. In the reality of the classroom, it was observed that learners need to meet a performance criterion before moving to a more difficult level. Establishing a performance goal for each level reinforces acquisition of the content (skill) and it prevents learners from haphazardly "doing" the levels, checking answers, and moving on. Inability to replicate with some degree of reliability the physical flow of the movement on any one level indicates a knowledge/cognitive gap that needs attention, particularly where safety is an issue. When multiple errors on one level occur, often the learner must go back a level and reinforce the previous set of skills, or seek content clarification from the teacher.

Table 10.1. Inclusion Style *(continued)*

Episode Events		Feedback	Time
Logistics	Logistical expectations:		
	1. The teacher establishes only the parameters necessary for the episode. Parameter decisions in this style could apply to any or all of the following categories:		
	• material pick up and return of the "individual programs" and criteria sheets		
	• time		
	• location		
	• interval		
	• attire and appearance		
	• posture		
Questions for clarification	Verify understanding of expectations before action:		
	Are there any questions for clarification? When you are asked to begin, what are you going to do first? Next? (The purpose of such questions is to increase initial success in implementation. The learners' age and degree of previous success with implementing new expectations will determine the need to ask questions that seek a review of the beginning behaviors and actions.)		
	Once expectations have been verified, move into action: *You may begin when you are ready.*		
Action, task, engagement, performance	Depending on how the materials are organized, the learners begin by picking up the "Individual Program" (which may include all the levels) or by surveying the various options, and then selecting an initial entry point level.		
	The learners find a location and begin practicing the task. Two behaviors are possible from this point forward: Learners remain engaged, finish their level, and check their performance (post-impact).		

Table 10.1. Inclusion Style *(continued)*

Episode Events		Feedback	Time
Action, task, engagement, performance	Learners will begin working and at a given point some may stop, return to survey the various levels, and make adjustment decisions. These students select either a less difficult or a more difficult level. At times they will stay at the same level. The learners return to their location, continue working, and eventually check their performance (post-impact).		
Post-Impact			
Feedback	The learners:		
	Refer to the criteria sheet to assess their performance, to make continued level decisions, and initiate questions for clarification.		
	The teacher:		
	Waits and observes the learners as they survey their options, gather materials, and begin engagement in the task. If questions arise, the teacher is available; otherwise the teacher waits until the learners have had a chance to engage in the task before circulating privately and individually among the learners. The teacher converses with the learners about their performances and level choices. When a learner demonstrates multiple errors, the teacher suggests that the learner check with the criteria before continuing. (The teacher does not identify the points of error, rather shifts that cognitive process of assessment to the learner.) The teacher moves on to other students, asking questions that invite learners to make content assessment comments.		
Closure	At the end of the episode the teacher offers closure/feedback to the entire class, commenting on the expected roles of making an entry level choice, making adjustments, and engaging in self-checking.		

The gradual, progressively more difficult, content sequence invites learners to remain engaged in the subject matter. Some learners perform at a minimum level while others practice to master performance. Because of the content options and the array of emotional attributes that are triggered in the Inclusion style, broad assumptions about learners' capacities and abilities must be made with caution. A teacher never fully knows which cluster of human attributes an individual learner will embrace or reject when a new behavior is initially introduced. Each behavior contributes differently to the development of human attributes.

THE INCLUSION STYLE—E

The purposes of this style are to participate in a task and learn to select a level of difficulty at which you can perform the task and to check your own work.

Role of the learner

- To make the nine decisions of the Practice Style
- To examine the different levels of the task
- To select the level appropriate for you
- To perform the task
- To check your own work against criteria prepared by the teacher
- To ask the teacher questions for clarification

Role of the teacher

- To prepare the task and the levels within the task
- To prepare the criteria for the task levels
- To answer the learners' questions
- To initiate communication with the learner

Figure 10.4. Inclusion style E classroom chart

The Implications of the Inclusion Style

It is true that each style on the Spectrum has its own beauty and its own effect on the development of the individual learner. This is particularly true when one keeps the non-versus notion in mind.

It is suggested here that this teaching–learning behavior has tremendous implications for the structure and function of physical education. If the goals of physical education include providing developmental programs for large numbers of people, then a wide variety of activities must be offered (which is a programmatic condition for choice) and day-to-day conditions for choice should be considered by increasing the frequency of the Inclusion style episodes in each activity. If inclusion is a true goal of physical education, then what counts is frequent successful participation of every student by creating conditions for multiple entry points! The primary teaching behavior for accomplishing this goal is the Inclusion style.

As in previous styles, the objective analysis of the Inclusion style identifies a cluster of implications:

1. First, when this style is used it implies that teachers philosophically accept the concept of inclusion and participation (on any level of difficulty) rather than exclusion.

2. It implies that teachers can expand their understanding of the non-versus notion by planning some episodes that tend to exclude, while others are specifically designed to include.

3. It implies that conditions have been created for the learners to experience the relationship between aspiration and reality.

4. It implies that learners can learn to accept the discrepancy between aspiration and reality and, at times, learn to reduce the gap between the two.

5. It implies the legitimacy of performing on one's own level; this is not a measurement of what others can do, but rather *what I can do!* The competition during the episodes is against oneself and one's own standards, abilities, and aspirations—not those of others.

6. The last three points are important factors that induce examination of the self-concept. This self-concept includes one's emotional independence from the teacher's decision of where the learner should be in the performance of the task.

It is important to create legitimate entry point options—this can become the hallmark of physical education. Physical education, in particular, must acknowledge the vast differences among people—size, ability, physical attributes, energy levels, and motivation.

Some current research has made conclusions that indicate a contradiction between this style's intent and actual classroom practices. On the surface, these findings appear to be in contradiction to the Spectrum theory. However, it is important to determine the factors that account for these apparent differences. Many factors contribute to the actions (decisions) of learners in the reality of the classroom. Identifying the factors (the reason and the point of deviation) can result in clarification of the theory or in application parameters. For examples, Byra & Jenkins (1998) concluded that the Inclusion style was less effective for exceptional students. Not all exceptional students are incapable of benefiting from the Inclusion style. However, if the exceptional students are inexperienced in making decisions, or making self-related decisions, or unskilled at distinguishing degree of difficulty between task levels as they relate to their performances, or if the students haven't developed in their decision making capacity to realize the relationship between appropriate practice and improvement, then the findings would not be a contradiction to the theory of the style. If a student is not experienced in the decisions of the style in focus, then they cannot be held accountable to successfully obtaining or demonstrating that specific teaching behavior's objectives. Learners' inexperience or lack of development does not nullify the theoretical propositions of a specific teaching style. It only indicates that adjustments of some kind need to be made to lead the learners to the benefits of the intended teaching–learning style.

Likewise, Goldberger, Gerney, Chamberlain (1982) found that, although the Inclusion style was effective in producing improved skill performance, the rate of improvement in the Practice Style was higher. In another study Goldberger and Gerney (1986) observed that some learners consistently selected levels that were too difficult for their skill development and that even after conversation with the teacher they did not change levels. This finding does not nullify the theory, it raises questions: What are the factors that produce this behavior? Was it peer pressure, time constraints, the emphasis the teacher placed on the task/skill? Was the grading system that was used a factor? What was the emphasis or the value placed on decision making as compared to skill accomplishment? What was the task? Did it merit this style? Were the performance details less important (to the learner) than the end result (shooting the ball to the hoop)? What were the stated or implied consequences for learning the skills? When contradictions occur, it is important to continue researching to identify the reason for the deviation. When the same contradiction repeatedly occurs, theoretical questions need to be examined. Researching some of the possible human issues would shed light on just which factors might create learning/developing barriers. If it is found that middle-school age boys are consistently making inappropriate level decisions, then different kinds of tasks may need to be designed. It is exciting to experiment and find the solution(s) that could lead learners to be more accurate in their selection decisions. Perhaps one of the following would help reduce their reported unwanted behavior: reducing the number of levels, creating more *difficulty space* between the levels, sequencing Practice and Inclusion episodes back to back. Perhaps the exceptional students need a style variation (canopy design)[9] where the teacher leads the learner to find the level of difficulty that is appropriate. The teacher's role in this situation would be to ask questions that could lead the learner through the mental and emotional thinking that a person must go through when making the decisions of this style. Deviations generally mean that the learners need adjustments so they can acquire the new set of decisions. The point of the research is not that the learners did not do what the style said, but rather *why*. And, how can conditions be created to lead learners to acquire the landmark decisions and the corresponding objectives of the indicated style?

[9]See section at the end of this chapter on style design variations.

Selecting and Designing the Subject Matter

The first four landmark teaching–learning behaviors have one feature in common—the design of tasks. Each task represents a single standard decided on by the teacher. The learner's task is to perform at that level. The Inclusion style introduces a different concept of task design—multiple levels of performance in the same task. This shifts to the learners a major decision that they could not make in previous styles—at what level of performance does one begin?

Individual Program

Operationally, this behavior extends the periods of independent practice. Individual Programs composed of multiple tasks and levels should be designed for a series of episodes. Single, infrequent episodes in this style are insufficient to reap the full benefits of this behavior. Teaching independence takes time, but the design of individual programs can accommodate this objective. Designing individual programs that incorporate multiple entry-level tasks requires an understanding of the degree of difficulty concept.

The Concept of Degree of Difficulty   Let us look at the slanted rope example again (Figure 10.5). The gradations in height along the rope present the learner with different degrees of difficulty within the same task. The task is to jump over the rope (in a particular way) regardless of the height. The variation occurs in the height, which determines the degree of difficulty.

For any learner, points A, B, and C on the rope represent different levels in the degree of difficulty. More effort is always required to jump over the rope at point C than at points A or B. This is true for all jumpers regardless of their ability. In the example of jumping over the slanted rope, the factor that determines the degree of difficulty is height. Varying the height creates many levels of difficulty within the same task. How, then, can we identify the factors that affect the degree of difficulty in other activities or in other tasks?

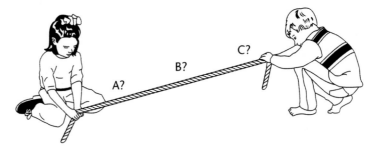

Figure 10.5. A task designed for inclusion

Let us analyze a familiar activity—shooting a ball into a basket (Figure 10.6). The task is not playing the game of basketball; rather, we are taking the particular activity of shooting a ball into a basket to analyze it in terms of factors affecting the degree of difficulty.

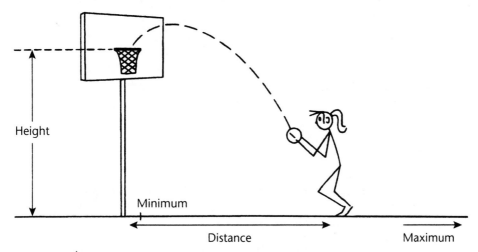

Figure 10.6. Factors affecting the degree of difficulty: Shooting baskets

1. Factor 1—Distance. Distance is intrinsic to the degree of difficulty in getting the ball through the hoop. Difficulty increases or decreases in direct ratio to distance from the basket. (There is also a limit of minimal distance—as we approach the position below the basket, the shot becomes increasingly more difficult.) The range of distance, then, between the point of minimum and maximum distance offers many levels of difficulty to learners who perform the task of shooting the ball into the basket. These different distance options can be marked on the floor to assist learners in making a decision about a concrete entry point.

2. Factor 2—The height of the basket. Varying the height of the basket creates various degrees of difficulty that serve as entry points for different learners.

3. Factor 3—The diameter of the hoop. Varying the diameter of the hoop creates different conditions for successfully shooting the ball into the basket.

4. Factor 4—The size of the ball.

5. Factor 5—The weight of the ball.

6. Factor 6—The angle of the shot. The positions around the basket from which the shot may be taken offer different degrees of difficulty.

7. Factor 7—Add additional factors to the list.

All these factors are part of the experience of shooting the ball through the hoop; during a game some of the factors are standardized (i.e., height, diameter of hoop, etc.) to provide fair competition. The purpose here, however, is to illustrate that changes or adjustments in some factors provide a greater variety for learners who cannot readily participate in standardized episodes developed for exclusion. In this behavior, the focus is on episodes designed for inclusion.

In physical education classes, there are many opportunities to demonstrate the principles of education by incorporating both inclusion and exclusion episodes in units. When students are excluded, they not only feel a sense of failure in that activity but they begin to resent the entire experience of physical education. Offering frequent Inclusion style episodes invites learners to participate at a level of performance where they are capable. The legitimate opportunity to succeed at an entry point and to then progress to subsequent levels of performance ensures continuous participation. No one has ever learned an activity by not doing it! Exclusion breeds rejection; inclusion invites involvement.

Identifying the Factor That Determines the Degree of Difficulty The major question confronting the teacher who wishes to arrange a task for Inclusion is: How do I identify the factors in the selected task?

Here are two procedures to consider.

- Task analysis – Three designs[10]
- The factor grid

All tasks can be categorized as one of three designs.

1. The Classical Design: The classical design reflects the following (Figure 10.7):

   a. The available increments are very small and constitute a continuous range of degree of difficulty. (The slanted rope is an example.)

   b. The range of options emanates from the intrinsic factor inherent in the activity. (In the case of the slanted rope, it is height.)

   c. Successful performance of a task on a given level guarantees success on all levels of lesser degrees of difficulty. (Biomechanical and kinesiological principles guide this type of design.)

Classical designs provide a range of options that are seamlessly connected, thereby avoiding content gaps that could lead to inconsistent content progress.

[10]This section is adapted from a forthcoming book on Spectrum Teaching by Sara Ashworth.

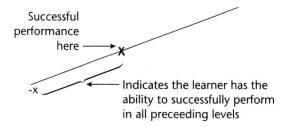

Figure 10.7. Successful performance in Classical design

2. The Semiclassical Design: The semiclassical design reflects the following (Figure 10.8):

a. The increments are progressive but not seamless or continuous; there are occasional gaps between the steps.

b. The factor represented as intrinsic (e.g., striking with a bat) does not always offer a continuous progression of difficulty. Verification of relative difficulty is not always possible.

c. Performance at a given level does not always ensure success in levels with a logically lesser degree of difficulty.

In the reality of doing the exercise, it is possible that some learners might be able to perform a task with a greater difficulty accurately, and yet make errors with tasks of lesser difficulty.

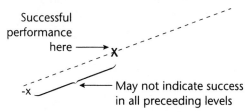

Figure 10.8. Successful performance inSemiclassical design

3. The Cumulative Design. The cumulative design reflects the following (Figure 10.9).

a. The increments are arbitrary.

b. The factor is external.

c. In order to participate in a given level, the learner has to perform all the previous levels in succession.

Suppose, for example, the task is to do push-ups. Clearly, performing 30 push-ups has a high degree of difficulty and it is more difficult than doing 20, 10, or 5. Each level, then, is arbitrarily determined by the number (quantity) of push-ups that the learner chooses at that moment. This factor of "number" is an external factor that is superimposed on the design (see the Factor Grid section). Indeed, it affects the degree of difficulty in strength; it takes more strength to perform 40 push-ups than to perform 10 push-ups. Each level indicates the number of push-ups. To perform the most difficult level, the learner would have to do all the levels in sequence—a cumulative task. In physical education with tasks that incorporate this type of design, it is imperative that students initially indicate the level they think they can perform before practicing. They mark, using a box shape, on the charts their anticipated performance ability. After practicing/performing they indicate, with a circle, the level they actually performed. Without this advance prediction, the learner is in the Practice Style. To reach the objectives of this behavior, self-assessment must guide the entry point into the task.

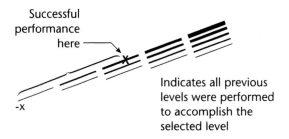

Figure 10.9. Cumulative design successful performance

The Factor Grid

The Factor Grid is the second procedure to consider when asking, "How do I identify the factors in the selected task?" The factor grid reinforces the classical and cumulative designs as they relate to physical education activities. The Factor Grid chart (Figure 10.10) is a tool to guide teachers in identifying the factors in a selected task. It offers a way of thinking about both the intrinsic and external factors affecting the design of physical tasks. (Other disciplines have their own factor grids.)

The following points explain the structure and use of this grid:

1. After selecting the task, the question that must be kept in mind throughout planning is: "Within this task, how do I provide for inclusion?"

2. The grid suggests two kinds of factors: intrinsic and external. The intrinsic factors are a part of the given task's structure. Some tasks may have all of these factors; others, only a few. The external factors are superimposed on the performance of the task. Both kinds of factors affect the

degree of difficulty of the given task; any one of the factors can be manipulated to vary the degree of difficulty.

3. Once the task has been selected, the next step is to decide which intrinsic factor can be manipulated to provide for inclusion in the ensuing episode. (In the example of the slanted rope, the key factor is height.) Sometimes tasks are affected by two or more factors. For example, throwing a ball at a target with an overhead throw suggests "size of the target" and "distance from the target" as possible key factors. Keeping the objective in mind, decide which will serve as the key factor in planning and which will be the supporting factor for the given episode. Rank the factors by writing numbers (1, 2, . . .) to the left of each factor.

Name of the task: • Identify the rank order for the key and the supporting factors(s) • Indicate the range	
External Factors _____ Number of Repetitions: _____ Time:	**Range**
External Factors _____ Distance _____ Height _____ Weight of Implements _____ Size of Implements _____ Size of Targets _____ Speed _____ ? _____ ? _____ Posture	

Figure 10.10. The factor grid

4. Next, identify the range of possibilities in the key factor from which learners will select their entry levels. In the case of size of target, the range may include targets with varying diameters: small, medium, large. Likewise identify the range for supporting factors.

5. If one of the external factors is selected as the key factor (for example: the choices in the number of repetitions of a given task will be 5, 10, 15, 20, etc.), indicate it in the range. If not, indicate a specific quantity next to the external factor.

6. The speed factor. This factor can be placed on a range from slow to fast, controlled by a metronome, the music, or the pitching machine as in tennis or baseball.

7. The posture factor. This factor involves the position(s) of the body required to perform a static and/or a dynamic task. (It is also referred to as "form," "basic skill," or the "technique" of a given sport or dance.) If a learner cannot do the task, then manipulating the factors of distance, time, or size of target will not help. The entry point here is a modified posture such as changing the angle between body parts, adding further extension, and so on. For example, if a learner cannot do the T-scale, you can introduce (on a range) a modification in the angle of the lifted leg or the position of the upper body. This will be the entry point that includes all learners. Later on, factors such as repetition, time, and so on can be added. Knowing what is "less difficult" or "more difficult" in the posture factor is derived from biomechanical analysis of the task.

8. Let us examine the factor grid for the golf chip shot. Note that the two intrinsic factors selected for inclusion by designation of the range in size of target and distance. The external factor involves the number of repetitions. From this grid (Figure 10.11), the teacher designs the individual program for practicing the chip shot (Figure 10.12).

External Factors	Range
_____ Number of Repetitions: 10	
_____ Time:	
External Factors	
_2_ Distance	Lines A, B, C (3 yards, 5 yards, 7 yards)
_____ Height	
_____ Weight of Implements	
_____ Size of Implements	
_1_ Size of Targets	Small target 10'; Large target 30'
_____ Speed	
_____ ?	
_____ ?	
_____ Posture	

Figure 10.11. Factors affecting the degree of difficulty: Golf

Name _____   Style A B C D (E)
Class _____   Individual Program # _____
Date _____

Golf Chip Shot

To the student:
1. Select an initial level and circle the number you expect to do.
2. Practice the task and place an X over the number actually performed.
3. Compare your execution of the task with the performance criteria.
4. Decide whether to repeat the test at the same level or at a different level.

Chip shot Criteria:

1. Stand with your feet close together.
2. Bend your knees slightly, as though starting to sit.
3. Contact the ball off your left heel.
4. Follow through along the path of the ball, keeping the left wrist firm at contact.
5. Refrain from letting the club head pass the left hand.
6. Keep the flight of the ball low.
7. Hit to a predetermined spot and have the ball roll to the cup.

The task: choose a distance (line A, B, or C) and a target area (either the large or the small). Take 10 chip shots and record the number of times you hit the target area.

Line A _____
Line B _____
Line C _____

Small target
Large target

Distance	Large Target									
A	1	2	3	4	5	6	7	8	9	10
B	1	2	3	4	5	6	7	8	9	10
C	1	2	3	4	5	6	7	8	9	10

Distance	Small Target									
A	1	2	3	4	5	6	7	8	9	10
B	1	2	3	4	5	6	7	8	9	10
C	1	2	3	4	5	6	7	8	9	10

Figure 10.12. An individual program for the golf chip shot

Let us now examine the part of the factor grid dealing with the manipulation of the posture factor. If, for example, the objective of the episode is to develop strength in the shoulders and arms by using the push-up movement, then different positions of the body (such as starting positions or positions to be maintained during the movement of the push-up) offer a range in the levels of difficulty (Figure 10.13).

In Figure 10.14, position B, in which the hands are placed forward in front of the shoulders, is more difficult to assume and maintain than position A. Performing the push-up movement from this position is also more difficult than performing the movement from position A. The same is true for position C, in which the arms are extended further. The push-up movement from position C is more difficult than either A or B (for a fuller kinesiological analysis concerning this issue, see Mosston, 1965).

In the individual program (Figure 10.15), a cluster of developmental movements are designed to strengthen various regions of the body. The task itself is the same for any learner using this program. The differentiation for each movement occurs by identifying the different levels. In each level, the task is to be performed from a different starting position, each more diffi-

The Factor Grid will look like this:

Name of the task: Push-Up

External factors   **Range**

_____ Number of repetitions: 3
_____ Time:

Intrinsic factors

_____ Distance
_____ Height
_____ Weight of implements
_____ Size of target
_____ Speed
__1__ Posture-angle between
       the arms and the body.

From   to

Figure 10.13. The factor grid—Push-up

cult than the previous. The degree of difficulty was determined by the appropriate factor for each task.

The same factor, then, can serve several tasks (as in the case of hitting the target), or a different factor can be identified for each task in the program (as in the last example).[11]

The kinesiological analysis does not only apply to developmental movements or exercises. In many sports, it may be useful to reduce the degree of difficulty in the starting position, the swing, the lift, the stretch, the arc, the spin, the bend, or whatever else is involved in the sport. This is only a temporary compromise to provide an entry point. Don't let the desire for purity of form cause exclusion. A person who is excluded will never participate in the activity; a teacher must always be ready to offer the learner an opportunity to participate using another entry point.

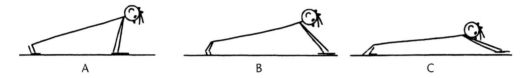

A   B   C

Figure 10.14. Position of the body: A factor in the degree of difficulty

Name _____		Style A B C D Ⓔ		
Class _____		Individual Program # _____		
Date _____				

Task Description	Factor	Level 1	Level 2	Level 3
1. Perform the push-up from the described starting position. Practice it 3 times.	Angle between the arms and the body			
2. Perform the push-up from the described starting position. Practice it 3 times.	Width of the base			

Figure 10.15. Individual program developmental movement

[11]Refer to Chapter 18 for additional information on designing subject matter.

3. Perform the scale and hold for 10 counts. Repeat 3 times. – Stand on right leg. – Lift left leg. – Extend arms to the sides. – Arch back. – Keep head up.	– Right leg bent – Bent left leg raised hip high	– Right leg bent – Straight left leg raised hip high	– Right leg straight – left leg straight, hip high	– Right leg straight – left leg straight, above the hip level
4. In the described position, hold the upper body for 20 counts. Repeat 5 times, with 10 count intervals.	Length of lever			
5. Other				

Style-Specific Comments

Since one of the goals of Inclusion teaching is continuous participation and development, pay particular attention to learners who stay at their initially chosen level. Be aware that while trying to reduce the gap between aspiration and reality, at times the aspiration may be high when the reality is low. Sometimes it is the reverse—the aspiration is low but the reality (the ability to perform) is high. Often this gap is emotionally based rather than physically based. It is the teacher's role to lead the learner toward understanding this gap and working to close it. This is a delicate issue and requires appropriate verbal behavior. Usually commands will not accomplish your purpose. Allow time to develop dialogues with the student so that he/she will understand the gap and be willing to reduce it.

The Inclusion style produces an interesting phenomenon that did not surface in the Command–Self-Check styles. Good performers sometimes have difficulty with Inclusion episodes. They seem to function well in conditions where they are told what to do and where they know the pecking order. Their emotional structure requires feedback that frequently singles them out as being the best. Shifting to Inclusion episodes sometimes disturbs them, because each learner is OK in his or her level. Accepting that all learners are equal in such episodes can be quite difficult for the skilled learner. Learning to be independent and make all the decisions of this behavior is demanding, as is breaking the emotional dependency on the teacher. This can often be a painful and delicate process.

Students who have frequently been excluded often enjoy this behavior. It is often the first time they have been included over a longer period of time. These students identify with this behavior because:

- It provides an entry point that allows them to participate and succeed in the task.
- They see a chance for continuous progress and development.

Although this teaching–learning behavior is inviting to most learners, it is perhaps mandatory for students in special education. Students experiencing worthwhile Inclusion episodes learn that all students are valued and worthy of learning opportunities. Once students feel secure in the learning process, other styles can then be used. All students need to experience the non-versus realities.

In the Inclusion style, the entry decision is highly private. The right to survey and select must be respected. In gymnasiums where peer pressure is strong, some students may be coerced into choosing the same level as their peers, even when failure is likely. The research of Goldberger, Gerney, and Chamberlain (1982) found that peer pressure is a strong variable that affects entry decisions. These researchers found that peer pressure influenced fifth-grade children to practice tasks at a much higher level than they could successfully perform. These situations are opportunities for the teacher to deal with the social issue of peer pressure and the right of individuals to make decisions that are appropriate for them.

Verbal behavior that emphasizes "do your best" is inappropriate in this behavior. The seemingly positive instruction "do your best" has consequences. This phrase is rooted in a competitive principle that inculcates in the young that "doing your best" is always the best thing to do. This may be true some of the time, but it can create unbearable pressure always to perform at unattainable levels. This, in turn, results in exclusion with all its emotional and psychological consequences.

The appropriate initial verbal behavior is, "In this practice you make the decision where to enter the activity. You decide on which level to begin…." The focus is on the learners' decisions, not the teacher. The Inclusion style does not eliminate the essence of competition; it only presents it in a different form. Instead of competing with others against a single standard, multiple standards (levels) of competition can be designed so that more learners with varying performance skills can have an opportunity to compete.

Perhaps the single most important comment that can be made about this style is its power of inclusion. The stigma caused by exclusion in physical education classes can be reduced by different arrangements in the gymnasium and by different teaching behaviors. The invitation to participate offered by the slanted rope is so powerful that sooner or later all learners who had previously been excluded (regardless of reason) join in. It is as if the learner says, "I have a place, too. I belong!"

The Developmental Channels

There are many examples of, and opportunities for, design variations and style combinations using the Inclusion concept. Design variations in the Inclusion style emphasize different attributes and channels while providing a range of difficulty in the task. Like other styles, the concept of Inclusion is present in varying forms in many existing activities.

Let's examine three physical education examples.

Virtual reality (simulated) sports gyms are opening throughout the USA. At gyms for snow skiing, 12 different programs, each more difficult than the last, are offered to customers. The skier stands on a moveable platform, wearing snow skis and a safety harness holding on to a bar while watching a huge screen that projects a virtual reality snow course matching the selected degree of difficulty. The comfortable indoor experience is designed to permit the skier to practice the sport's skills with few of the "on the hill in the cold" liabilities. The snow course scenes provide the reality and thrill of the ski slope in accordance to the selected degree of difficulty. By reducing the "inconveniences and tangents" of their consequences, skiers (both novice and expert) are permitted to focus on skill development. Indeed, this virtual reality or simulated experience is compatible with the decision distribution of style E.

Likewise, there are indoor climbing walls that provide safe and challenging practice experiences with varying degrees of difficulty. Climbers choose the level, wear safety harness and protective equipment, and enjoy the benefits and challenge of the climbing practice.

Amateur golf is one of the few social sports that uses the concept of the Inclusion style (under the canopy, not the landmark style). The design of golf permits players at different levels of proficiency to play against each other in a common game. Individual "handicaps" balance the playing field so that all players can perform from their particular level of proficiency and yet compete against others who may be either more or less skilled. The legitimacy of the handicap even makes it possible for a less skilled player to win and for the other members of the group to accept this victory as fair play.

Combining Styles[12]

Design variations expand the learning objectives within the primary decision structure of each style, while combining styles merge the primary objectives of two (or more) styles to create a specific learning experience. Combining styles applies the inclusion idea—designing tasks with different levels of difficulty—to different styles.

Both design variations and combining styles add diversity and creativity to classroom teaching and learning.

The possibilities are infinite for inventing new design variations that emphasize different attributes, developmental channels, and different teaching style combinations. The freedom to create and combine styles does not suggest that anything goes. All design variations must adhere to the decision analysis and contribute to the overall quality of the educational experience and answer the questions: "What are the overall learning objectives? What are the learners expected to learn?"

Command/Inclusion Style (A/E Episode)   For example, it is possible to design a teaching–learning episode that combines the Command and Inclusion styles (A/E episode). Note that the first style name (or letter designation) represents the primary learning focus and the second teaching style name (or letter designation) indicates that only particular aspects of that style are incorporated into the design variation. In an A/E episode, the dominant objective is precision performance. However, the task is arranged on the "slanted rope principle" and each learner selects his/her entry point. Aerobic directors use this combination—they provide movement options (different degrees of difficulty) for the participants. Although this example incorporates concepts of both the Command and Inclusion styles, the decision structure does not represent either of the two landmark behaviors. This learning experience combines the objectives of both the Command and Inclusion styles (A/E) to create an experience in precision performance that accommodates individual differences in ability.

Reciprocal/Inclusion Styles (C/E Episodes)   This combination combines the Reciprocal style's partners and assessment of skills using prepared criteria, with the Inclusion style's range of content difficulty and learner's selection of content entry points. This C/E design variation must deal with several logistical possibilities.

It is more likely in physical education, than in other fields, that observers can use the prepared criteria to give feedback to doers who perform at a more difficult level. Consequently, selecting partners does not

---

[12]This section is adapted from a forthcoming book on the Spectrum.

carry many restrictions. The doers select their entry levels and the observers use the corresponding criteria to offer feedback. When learners switch roles, the new doers select their entry levels and receive feedback according to the level choice. In physical movement tasks, if both doers and observers choose the same level it is not an issue; however, in other tasks, where "correct answers" appear on the criteria parameters, restrictions may be needed.

Combining two styles leads to opportunities beyond those of each individual behavior. Before teachers implement episodes that combine styles, it is necessary for learners to have experience in, be successful in demonstrating the attributes of, and making the decisions of each style.

Practice/Inclusion Styles (B/E Episodes) In the Practice style the teacher identifies the task for the learners to practice and in the Inclusion style the teacher designs multiple levels of difficulty within the same task and the learners make their own entry level decisions. In the B/E episode, the teacher designs the multiple levels of difficulty within a task but assigns the learners, according to the teacher's assessment of the learner's ability, to practice on specific levels of difficulty within the task. In this combination the teacher values the idea of differentiated degrees of difficulty for performance inclusion within tasks but does not want to shift to the learners entry decisions in this teaching–learning episode. Because learners do not make their own entry-level decisions, the learning objectives that are emphasized in this design variation are more akin to the Practice style than to the Inclusion.

Currently the term "differentiating instruction" has been promoted urging teachers to adapt instruction to student differences (Gregory and Chapman, 2001). This approach encourages teachers to design different tasks for individual learners or groups of learners to accommodate the diversity that exists in the classroom. Initially, the overall intent of this approach might be associated with the Inclusion behavior; however, on examination of who is making the decisions, it is the teacher who indicates which tasks the learners will perform. Additionally, the tasks are not arranged using the concept of degree of difficulty within the same task. Tasks, though the same topic, are not related. Therefore, the objectives highlighted by the actions of the teacher and learners in differentiating instruction are more akin to the Practice style.

Self-Check/Inclusion (D/E Episodes) If the teacher altered the above Practice/Inclusion (B/E episode) design so that the learners made their own assessment decisions in their assigned group, then the combined styles' decision structure would represent D/E (Self-Check/Inclusion). In this style combination, the teacher assigns each group a different task, based on the group's content proficiency, and provides prepared criteria for self-checking opportunities. The overriding objectives then become those of a Self-Check practice. Although the decisions and objectives of the landmark Inclusion style are not the primary learning focus, they serve as a guide for the teacher in planning the content.

All teaching–learning styles have many combination possibilities. Since no single teaching–learning approach offers exposure to all objectives, learning to combine styles is crucial for active, interesting, and motivating lessons.

Examples of Individual Programs   All examples (see Figures 10.16 and 10.17) in the Inclusion style share several characteristics.

1. They adhere to the theoretical structure (decision distribution) of the style.
2. They contain general logistical information.
3. They identify the activity and the task(s).
4. They may identify the key factor that is manipulated to create the different levels.
5. They offer samples of levels designed by the principle of the slanted rope.
6. They offer flexibility in design although the general format is similar.

Styles A–E represent the cluster of teaching–learning behaviors that emphasize reproductive (memory) cognitive processes. The next cluster of teaching–learning behaviors highlights production—the learners discover and produce the content. Each behavior in this cluster emphasizes different aspects of discovery. At this point the reader has a choice: to skip to Chapter 12 and continue with the discovery cluster of behaviors or to read Chapter 11, which examines a variety of implementation and miscellaneous issues that are common to all teaching–learning styles.

Name _____   Style A B C D Ⓔ
Class _____   Task Sheet # _____
Date _____

Weightlifting

To the Student:
Follow the decisions of Style E and complete all of the five tasks below.

Task	factor	1	2	3	4
1. To perform the deadlift, stand with feet II, shoulder width; mixed grip, shoulder width; back straight; head up; hips and knees bent; feet flat under bar; arms remain straight. Pick up bar from a bent to a straight body position, with bar always in front. Perform 5 repetitions using any weight.	1. Weight increments: 8 barbells are arranged in a series of progressive resistances from 20 lbs. (bar) to 400 lbs.	0–100 lbs. wt.	105–200 lbs. wt.	205–300 lbs. wt.	305–400 lbs. wt.
2. To perform the squat, stand with feet II, slightly wider than shoulder width; support barbell across back of shoulders wide grip; back straight; bend knees and hips until thighs are parallel to floor; return to standing position.	2. Weight increments: 2 barbells, may be adjusted to any resistance the lifter desires from bar weight (30 lbs.) to 100 lbs. over body weight.	30-1/2 BWT wt. ____	3/4 BWT – BWT wt.____	BTW + 20-BWT + 50 wt.____	BTW + 60-BWT + 100 wt.____
3. To perform the Big Four exercise, assume a deadlift position; grasp handles; pull to a standing position (a); pull handle up to chin, elbows up (b); press handle full arm extension over head (c); raise up on toes (d.)	3. Resistance levels; lifter may adjust resistance level on apparatus from 0 to 89 lbs. by rotating dial clockwise.	1 rep. 1–10lbs	2 reps. 11–29lbs	3 reps. 30–59lbs	4 reps. 61–89lbs
4. To perform 25 incline situps, assume bent knee position, feet supported; grasp hands in back of head; curl trunk and head until elbows extend beyond knees; return to position.	4. Angle of incline board can be adjusted by the performer from 5°–45°.	5°	15°	25°	45°
5. To perform the bench press, lie in supine position on bench, with feet on floor; support barbell in straight arm position using wider than shoulder width grip. Lower barbell to chest, push straight up to extended arm position. Return barbell to support.	5. Weight increments; may be adjusted by lifter from barbell weight (30 lbs.) to resistance level exceeding body weight of lifter.	Bar Wt.	1/2 BWT	3/4 BWT	BWT

Figure 10.16. Individual program—Weightlifting

Name _____   Style A B C D Ⓔ
Class _____   Task Sheet # _____
Date _____

To the student:
These lacrosse tasks are designed for your practice and improvement of performance. Your role is to:
1. Decide which task to do first.
2. Select an initial level and circle the number you expect to do.
3. Do the task and draw a square over the actual performance.
4. Compare the actual performance of the task with the criteria.
5. Decide either to repeat the task at the same level, a different level, or to move on to another task.

1. Lacrosse Overhand Pass (criteria):   acc.   n.t.
a. Place bottom hand on the butt (lower part) of the stick, top hand
   8–10 inches above.
b. Slant stick 45 degrees over the shoulder.
c. Point stick in the direction of the target.
d. Step forward with the leg on the same side as the hand
   that is on the butt of the stick. Flex knees and begin to move stick.
e. Push with the top hand and pull with the bottom hand,
   while always keeping your eyes on the target.
f. During the following-through point the stick in the direction of the target.

The task: Decide to which target you are going to throw (large or small), and from which distance
   to pass the overhand throw. Take 10 shots from the distance you decide and record the results.

	Small target										
Distance											
1	0	1	2	3	4	5	6	7	8	9	10
2	0	1	2	3	4	5	6	7	8	9	10

	Large target										
Distance											
1	0	1	2	3	4	5	6	7	8	9	10
2	0	1	2	3	4	5	6	7	8	9	10

Distance 1 is 20 feet
Distance 2 is 30 feet

                                                                                 acc.   n.t.
2. Sidearm Shot (criteria):
a. Hold the stick in the same position as in the overhand pass.
b. Sweep stick back and step forward.
c. Slant stick 90 degrees from the body.
d. Whip the left arm forward and pull back on the right arm (left hand shot).

Figure 10.17. Individual program—Lacrosse

The task: Follow the same procedure as in the overhand pass. Choose a distance and target size. Use the sidearm shot. Record your results after taking 10 shots.

Distance	Small Target										
1	0	1	2	3	4	5	6	7	8	9	10
2	0	1	2	3	4	5	6	7	8	9	10

Distance	Large Target										
1	0	1	2	3	4	5	6	7	8	9	10
2	0	1	2	3	4	5	6	7	8	9	10

3. Underhand Shot (criteria):

a. Sweep stick back in a large circle over the shoulder.
b. When the stick is almost at the floor, bring it forward rapidly.
c. Use both arms, as it is a difficult shot to control.

acc.   n.t.

The task: Follow the same procedure as in the underhand shot. Record your results after taking 10 shots.

Distance	Small Target										
1	0	1	2	3	4	5	6	7	8	9	10
2	0	1	2	3	4	5	6	7	8	9	10

Distance	Large Target										
1	0	1	2	3	4	5	6	7	8	9	10
2	0	1	2	3	4	5	6	7	8	9	10

4. Shuttle Run-Pick-Ups and Stick Handling (criteria):

a. Pick up the ball using either the trap and scoop pick-up (the stick is placed on top of the ball to stop any movement and the pulled back over the ball causing it to roll into the pocket) or the Indian pick-up (the stick is first inverted, putting the pocket downwards, and then with a quick motion the ball is hit with the wood of the stick causing it to bounce; then the stick is twisted with a half circular movement to capture the ball in the pocket).
b. Cradle the ball back and forth in the pocket while running by moving the stick from side to side.
c. Use the top hand to bring about the cradling action while using the bottom hand as a pivot point for the stick.
d. Cradle the stick close to the body.

acc.   n.t.

The task: Decide on task 1 or task 2. You have the choice of pick-up technique for either task.

Task 1

Start at a line 30' from the goal. Have a series of balls on this line. Pick up a ball using whichever technique you prefer, run straight to the goal and place the ball in the goal. Then, run around the net, return to the line to pick up another ball, and repeat. Repeat this action for 60 seconds and record the number of balls that you can place in the net.

Task 2:
a. Use the above criteria.
b. Handle the stick through a maze before you place the ball in the goal.

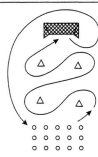

Task 1					Results											
0	1	2	3	4	5	6	7	8	9	10	11	12	13	14	15	More

Task 2					Results											
0	1	2	3	4	5	6	7	8	9	10	11	12	13	14	15	More

5. **Standing and running accuracy shooting (criteria):**
   (Shots are described for a shooter shooting over the left shoulder. Right-shouldered shooters, do the reverse.)
   a. Start with both hands on the stick several inches apart—the right hand at the bottom of the stick handle, the left hand higher.
   b. Start with the stick on an angle over the left shoulder and with the pocket above and behind the shoulder.
   c. Aim the face of the stick at the target. To shoot, push the left hand forward, and, at the same time, pull the right hand back towards the body. Shoot the ball straight over the shoulder.
   d. Step forward with the right foot and bend the body forwards as the shot is being made.
   e. Follow through by extending the left arm fully and pointing the stick directly at the target as the ball leaves the stick.

acc.   n.t.

The task: Decide on task 1 or task 2 and decide on whether to shoot from distance 1 or distance 2.
Task #1: From a standing position, take 10 shots at the goal. Record the number of times that you put the lacrosse ball into the goal. Shoot from either distance 1–20 feet or distance 2–40 feet.
Task #2 From a run take 10 shots at the goal. Record the number of times that you put the lacrosse ball into the goal. Shoot from either distance 1–20 feet—or distance 2–40 feet.

↑ Distance 1 _____

↑ Distance 2 _____

Distance	From standing position										
1	0	1	2	3	4	5	6	7	8	9	10
2	0	1	2	3	4	5	6	7	8	9	10

Distance	From a run										
1	0	1	2	3	4	5	6	7	8	9	10
2	0	1	2	3	4	5	6	7	8	9	10

CHAPTER 11

Issues Common to All Teaching Styles

This chapter examines a variety of implementation and miscellaneous issues that are common to all teaching–learning styles. Although each individual teaching behavior is unique in its objectives and implications, there are certain concepts, issues, and characteristics that apply to all teaching behaviors.

Task Teaching, Learning Centers, and Station Teaching

Task teaching, learning centers, and station teaching are terms currently used to indicate a type of teaching. These terms share the meaning that "different students practice different tasks at the same time." They differ, however, in that some arrangements:

- provide task sheets, task card, posters that explain the tasks; others do not
- provide multiple tasks at one station; others provide only one task
- provide choice among the tasks; others do not
- require students to maintain a progress record; others do not
- require students to rotate from station to station; others permit students to select *x* number of stations
- are used because of limited equipment; others do not use equipment
- focus the tasks on the same topic; others use unrelated tasks
- use a signal to indicate change or movement from station to station; others use time; others require accomplishment of performance criteria before rotating
- are totally independent of the teacher; others are not

- design tasks that consider different ability levels; others do not
- require students to work alone; others require groups or partners

The logistical variables affect the work at each station. The most important issue teachers must consider when designing station or task teaching is "What are the primary learning objectives to be accomplished at each station/center? Which teaching–learning behavior will be used to accomplish the intended task objectives at each station?"

Station/task teaching is not a distinct, separate, or unique teaching behavior. It is simply a logistical arrangement. The exciting aspect of station/task/center arrangements is the possibility of exposing learners to multiple experiences through the use of alternative teaching–learning behaviors. When the tasks at the various stations/centers represent different decision structures, they result in varied educational experiences. This reinforces decision making and provides diverse involvement in the content for each learner.

Some ideas that could guide the planning for each station/center/task activity are:

- Different teaching–learning behaviors
- Different physical attributes—strength, balance, agility, flexibility, accuracy
- Developmental Channels
- Cognitive operations—replication station; designing station; comparing station
- Social interaction—small groups; 1:1 partners; individual activities
- Content topics—sequenced or random content
- Multiple intelligences focus—physical engagement focusing on language, musical, artistic, aesthetic, mathematical, and logical activities
- Perception practices—physical engagement delivered through auditory, visual, or kinesthetic activities
- Combinations of any of the above

When designing the logistics for station/center/task teaching, it is imperative that teachers be aware of the teaching–learning behaviors that are involved. The term station/center/task teaching does not define the learning experience; rather, it is the teaching–learning behaviors used while engaging in the task at each station/center that create the learning experiences.

Organizational Options

Before implementing task/station/center teaching it is helpful to understand the concept of the organizational options.

One of the problems in physical education is that of efficient learning, which depend on an appropriate ratio between the quantity of an activity and the unit of time. To learn any physical task and reach a reasonable level of performance, the learner must repeat the task. The learner must perform, receive frequent feedback, and perform additional tasks. How, then, can the teacher organize the class to use time efficiently?

The issue of time-on-task, or academic learning time, has become prominent as a focal point in educational research for improving teaching. In physical education, the issue is to organize the learners, equipment, space, and available time in particular relationships to create conditions for efficient learning.

Because any style should operate within organizational conditions that promote efficient learning, the following suggestions apply to all teaching–learning behaviors.

The Issue of Efficiency

The following pages include charts depicting inefficient organizational patterns that still exist in schools; other charts suggest options for improvement. The organization of space, equipment, and people shown in Figure 11.1 is common in many schools. In particular note the considerable unused space and the number of learners per basket. This inappropriate logistical arrangement—of people, space, and equipment—infringes on the time each learner has for practice.

Examine the alternative organization suggested in Figure 11.2. This arrangement provides frequent opportunities for all learners to practice specific skills within the same activity, in this case, basketball. The nine assigned tasks represent various aspects of shooting and the small groups rotate from task to task at designated time intervals. The ratio of participation per learner per unit of time increases considerably with this arrangement. Learning and development increases for each learner.

To play basketball well, one must learn to shoot, dribble, pass the ball in various ways, and evade the opponent, etc. Each skill constitutes a particular task to practice. Figure 11.3 offers an example of space organization that accommodates all these tasks simultaneously, increasing the efficiency of learning. This procedure and organization are successfully used in "circuit training," conducting physical fitness tests, and during coaching sessions. Using them during physical education classes allows more people to benefit from the activity. These arrangements can be adapted for baseball, soccer, hockey, or other ball games.

Before an organizational analysis and alternatives are offered for gymnastics, it is necessary to identify the physical prerequisites of gymnasts for

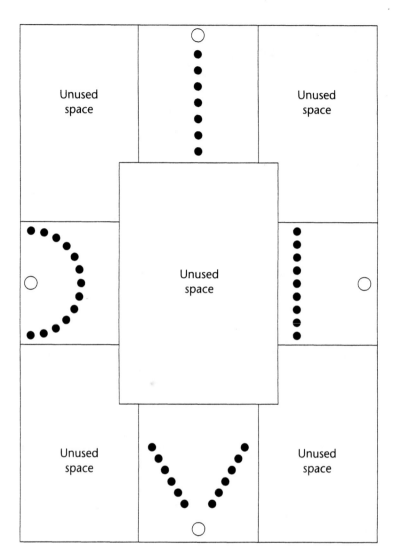

Figure 11.1. Inappropriate use of space: Basketball—common equipment and space organization (four baskets in the gymnasium)

working on the apparatus. They need agility, balance, flexibility, and strength, before and during the work on the apparatus. This certainly applies to novice gymnasts. Instead of sitting and waiting for their turns on an apparatus, students can and should be learning developmental movements that will help them progress in areas that need improvement.

Gymnastics class is an excellent opportunity for the teacher to develop multiple tasks. For example, some students may need extensive work in

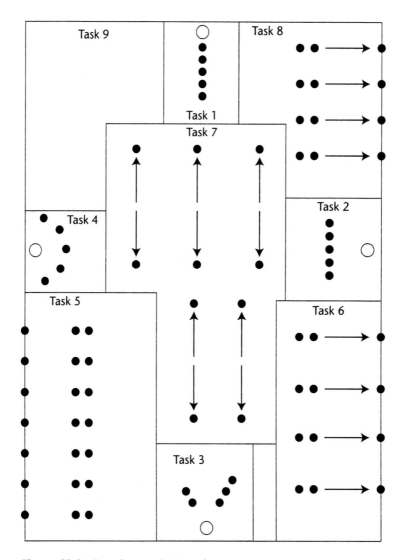

Figure 11.2. Sample organization of space

upper body exercises to develop the necessary strength to support the body in a simple parallel bar sequence. These students should be involved in this development instead of sitting near the parallel bars doing nothing.

It might be revealing for the teacher to measure actual time wasted during the traditional large-class gymnastics unit. Follow two or three students through the lesson, recording the actual time spent both passively and actively using the apparatus. You will discover that most of a student's time is spent waiting for his/her turn. Obviously, this calls for a more desirable and productive alternative arrangement.

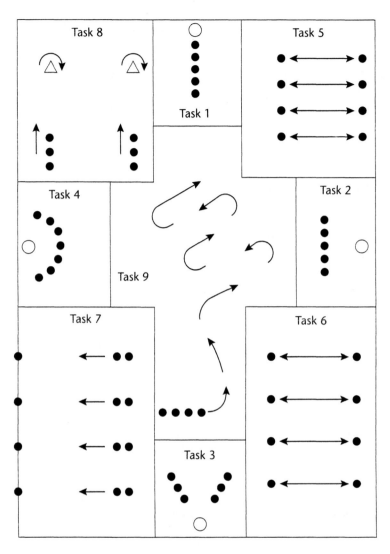

Figure 11.3. Basketball: Space organization for multiple tasks.

Tasks 1-4: Shooting tasks, either different shots or different tasks within the same shop

Tasks 5-6: Passing tasks (with a partner)

Task 7: Passing practice against a wall (and use of targets)

Task 8: Dribbling practice

Task 9: A dribbling course (changing direction)

In many schools with large classes, you will find unused spaces in the gymnasium, such as those in Figure 11.4, because students are grouped according to the pieces of gymnastics equipment. With large numbers of students and few pieces of equipment, the frequency of experience is low; the

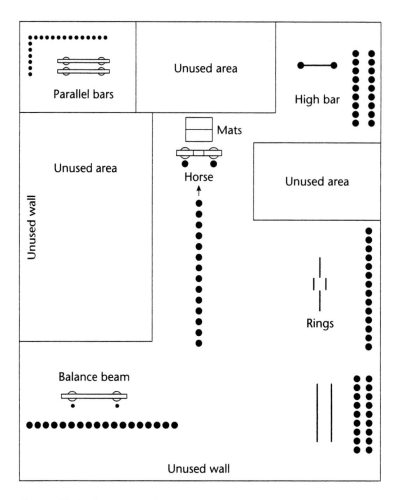

Figure 11.4. Gymnastics: Common equipment-space organization showing unused space

development of agility, balance, strength, and so on are correspondingly low. Because students rarely get to use the apparatus, many students are not only poor performers in gymnastics techniques, but they also lack the physical abilities necessary to pursue a successful gymnastics program. When physical development is negligible and learning does not take place, the student's attitude toward the activity may be negative, or at best, neutral.

By using the empty floor and wall spaces, you actually add equipment to your program. Present activities to the class that are relevant to the gymnastics unit and the students will develop the required qualities and techniques for gymnastics. It is important, moreover, to explain to students the connection between the variety of floor tasks, the development of the body, and the application to better performance on the apparatus. It is helpful for students to realize that, through strength-building activities, they develop shoulder, arm, and chest muscles.

Explain that this development is vital in parallel bars performance because most movements and sequences of movement are performed while the body is constantly supported by the arms. (The bulk of the body weight is usually above the base of support in parallel bars sequences.) However, the rings and high bar shift the center of gravity below and above the base of support; therefore, the muscles involved in hanging must be developed for the performer to hang in comfort and without effort for some time.

These supplementary activities can be carried out in any regular gym class by using an alternative floor plan and time–activity sequence. Such an arrangement has impressive advantages, because even the weakest student can make significant progress.

Figure 11.5 shows a sample alternative arrangement of an equipment-space relationship. In some classes, it may be necessary to photocopy the floor plan with the tasks written in the various spaces. This enables each student to have a guide for the tasks. This practice saves a great deal of time and eliminates the need for repeated explanations. The teacher is thus free to move about, observe, and offer feedback.

The unused space in Figure 11.4 is reorganized in Figure 11.5 to show relevant gymnastic activities. The principle of maximum activity per student per unit of time is observed here. More frequent experiences for each student increases learning, development, and enjoyment.

Let's examine the use of time in the arrangement shown in Figure 11.4. If 15 students gather around the parallel bars for a 30-minute lesson and each is allowed 30 seconds for a short sequence, it will take 7.5 minutes to conclude one "inning." During the entire lesson, each member of the group will be on the parallel bars four times for a total of 2 minutes. For each student, therefore, there will be 28 minutes of inactivity. Suppose we cut the time on the parallel bars in half (15 seconds); each participant will then be on the bar eight times—a rather unconvincing argument for the contribution of gymnastics to the development of each individual. This calculation applies to any activity or unit that employs this kind of equipment-space-time relationship. Learners can use those lost 28 minutes more efficiently in other activities.

Four Organizational Options

The analysis of the relationship between number of learners, time, and space results in four organizational options:

1. Single station-single task (S.S./S.T.)

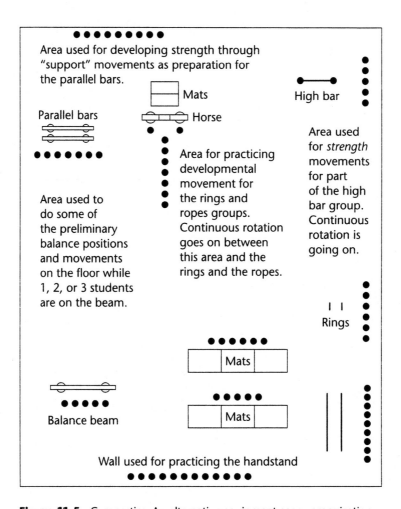

Figure 11.5. Gymnastics: An alternative equipment-space organization

2. Single station-multiple tasks (S.S./M.T.)
3. Multiple stations-single task (M.S./S.T.)
4. Multiple stations-multiple tasks (M.S./M.T.)

Single Station–Single Task This arrangement allows learners to make a decision about their location (one station) and perform one task at that location. After the teacher demonstrates and explains a particular task to the gathered learners, they go to their locations in the gymnasium and perform the task the number of times designated by the teacher (quantity decision).

Single Station–Multiple Tasks This arrangement calls for more than one task to be performed in succession at the same location (station). The teacher demonstrates and explains two or more tasks, and the learners perform these tasks one after the other.

For example:

Task 1. Dribble the ball in one spot, as demonstrated, 50 times with the right hand.

Task 2. Dribble the ball in one spot, as demonstrated, 50 times with the left hand.

Task 3. Dribble the ball in one spot, as demonstrated, 60 times; change hands every 10 dribbles.

In this case, each learner will have the opportunity to practice and develop the skill of dribbling in three consecutive tasks using one location (if there are not enough basketballs, use volleyballs or any other type of ball—the purpose is to dribble!)

Multiple Stations–Single Task This arrangement provides each learner the opportunity to perform a task at a given location (station) and, when that task is done, to move to another station and perform one task at the new location. This rotation can continue, depending on the number of stations and tasks designated.

This arrangement is very efficient when there is not enough equipment for everyone. (See the examples for basketball in Figure 11.3 and gymnastics in Figure 11.5.) It is a popular arrangement in weight-training sessions. Different weights and other pieces of equipment are distributed in different stations and the learner performs a task at each station and then moves to the next one.

Multiple Stations–Multiple Tasks This is the same as the previous arrangement, except that at each station the learner performs more than one task.

Note: These examples do not include the teaching behavior to be used at each station. The points presented are to clarify the different organizational formats.

At Station No. 1

Task 1. Twenty set shots

Task 2. Twenty hook shots

At Station No. 2

Task 1. Twenty-five consecutive chest passes to a target on the wall

Task 2. Twenty-five consecutive bounce passes against the wall

At Station No. 3

Task 1. Dribbling the ball forward along the designated distance on the blue line

Task 2. Dribbling the ball backward along the designated distance on the blue line

Task 3. Dribbling as above, sideways

There can be as many stations as the area permits; no square foot remains unused. Several clusters of variations in these three stations bring about impressive results (Figure 11.6).

These four organizational arrangements accommodate all teaching–learning behaviors. They provide each learner with the time, equipment, and space to practice the task. While the learners are engaged in the tasks, using the indicated teaching behaviors, the teacher has time to move from station to station and offer the appropriate feedback according to the teaching style at a given station.

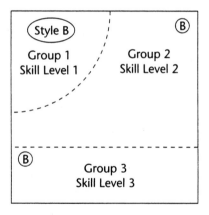

Figure 11.6. Different levels of a task within the same style

Using stations permit the concept of *concurrent styles*—using more than one teaching–learning style at the same time (Figure 11.7). Different stations could employ a different behavior or leaning emphasis. For example, the class is divided into three stations, each practices different tasks in the same subject matter (volleyball), but each group engages in a different teaching–learning behavior. Both the task and the objectives in each style are different. Lessons designed to use stations can increase the quantity of content covered, the quality of the active time-on-task, and the variety of educational objectives experienced.

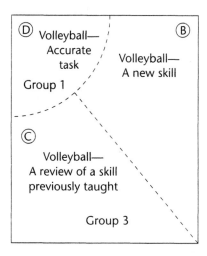

Figure 11.7. Concurrent styles

The Demonstration[1]

The demonstration merits a special discussion because of its importance in teaching physical activities in the reproductive styles. Understanding the power of demonstration helps us to understand why it is inappropriate in the productive styles.

Demonstrations provide the model, the image of the content; therefore, content replication and clarification are the primary reasons for conducting demonstrations. A demonstration can be brief or lengthy. In physical education all reproductive teaching–learning styles rely on demonstrations during the subject matter expectations to convey the desired physical positions, movements, sequences, etc. The behavior expectations, describing *how* the learners will practice, determine the specific teaching–learning style. When demonstrations are lengthy, it is possible to conduct an episode with the sole purpose of delivering content. In such situations the demonstration would be similar to a formal lecture in the classroom. The role of the learners in such situations is to observe and listen for content information. However, once the lecture and/or demonstration is completed, another episode begins where the learners are told how to practice the information or demonstrated content.

A demonstration of a physical activity executed by a skilled performer can have an enormous impact on an observer, which has psychological

---

[1] This section on demonstration is adapted from the first edition of Mosston, M. (1966), *Teaching Physical Education.*Columbus, OH: Charles E. Merrill Pub. Co.

implications for learners. A good demonstration has the following strengths:

1. It presents a holistic image of the activity.

2. It presents a visual image of the various parts of the activity and the integrative process of movement.

3. It creates a sense of admiration and can serve as strong motivation for learning.

4. It fortifies the position of the performer as an expert, leader, and authority.

5. It can inspire a sense of the beauty of human motion.

6. It can draw the learner's attention to details that are important in the activity (the finger position on the grip of a tennis racket; the position of the feet against the starting blocks; the curve of the lower back—or lack of it—in a handstand).

7. It establishes a model for successful performance.

8. It saves time. Explanations are often too long, tedious, or unclear. A neat demonstration tells the whole story quickly.

9. It is efficient. All that is needed is to "show and tell," and then it is left to the learner to emulate the demonstrator.

10. A demonstration can illustrate the ideal initial movement toward a desired purpose: the first step after the start in the dash, the movement of the arm in serving a volleyball, the forward lunge in fencing, etc.

11. It can show the series or sequences of movements employed in a given activity.

12. It can focus on the results of precise execution (as in the performance of an accomplished dart, pool, or archery player).

13. It can affect the learner's awareness of skills sequence and motor skills.

14. It presents the standard of what the teacher considers correct or good.

Providing the correct standard via a demonstration is a vital element of teaching and evaluation of achievement. It is an appropriate technique for presenting subject matter in the reproduction styles. The Command style relies on demonstration to the highest degree, and the Inclusion style relies on it the least. In the Command style, the teaching obligation begins with the act of demonstration. While the teacher is illustrating, the student must observe. The manner in which the learners repeat the demonstrated data depends on which reproductive teaching–learning style is used.

The demonstration is not unique to the field of physical education. When demonstrations in any field are conducted, they are designed to achieve specific, limited goals.

When the demonstration is used well, learning can be achieved—learning what is prescribed. Demonstration is a particular kind of learning, which has been discussed in many physical education method books. Practically all use this famous *quadrivium:*

- Step 1: Demonstration
- Step 2: Explanation
- Step 3: Execution
- Step 4: Evaluation

The manner in which learners execute (practice) and receive feedback about the demonstration (Steps 3 and 4) determine the specific teaching style. The behavior expectations for executing the demonstrated task can be conducted in any of the reproduction teaching styles—from Command to Inclusion.

Implementing the Spectrum Theory[2]

Perhaps the most frequently asked question about the implementation of the Spectrum is: Should you tell the students the decisions of each style? This depends on the intent: What objectives do you want to accomplish in subject matter and behavior?

In this text, each landmark style is presented in its most complete and detailed image. During the behavior expectations, in the classroom the decisions of each style are named and defined. Naming each decision is only one way to implement a teaching–learning style. There are four possible options that can be used when implementing the theory of the Spectrum. It is essential that teachers be skilled in all four options, and use each of them in the classroom. Since teaching is a chain of decision making, all teaching events fall into one of these four implementation options:

1. Focusing on content
2. Shifting only some landmark style decisions
3. Shifting all landmark style decisions
4. Using style name or letter to indicate expectations

Focusing on Content

In this option, content is the exclusive focus, and only the minimum behavior expectations need to be expressed. Behavior expectations (how learners are to participate) are embedded within the content delivery. Learners perceive behavior as it relates to completing or accomplishing the content. In

---

[2] This section is adapted from the forthcoming book on Spectrum Teaching by Sara Ashworth.

Table 11.1 Minimum Teaching Style Behavior Expectations

Teaching Style	Minimum Behavior Expectations	Inappropriate Behavior
Command	All together with the signal. Do as I do (or the video, or the recorder...). Follow exactly with me ... etc.	Don't do anything unless I tell you exactly when and how to do it.
Practice	Practice this task by yourself. Complete this task individually and privately.	Don't ask anybody for help on this task. Do it alone.
Reciprocal	Work with a partner. One learner does the task and asks questions to the partner. The other learner, using the prepared criteria sheet, lets the partner know how they are performing. When finished with task one, switch roles and complete task two.	Work with a partner. One partner has the answers and will evaluate your work.
Self-Check	Individually practice the task and check your performance against the criteria provided.	Do this task, then check to see how many you got wrong.
Inclusion	Look at the different options in the task. Select the one where you can. If needed, you can make an adjustment in the level choice.	Practice any option, it doesn't matter.

these situations, stating behavior expectations to the learners would only detract from the content focus, and would be redundant.

Aerobics classes are an example. Immediately "getting into the content" is the primary intent, not the participants' decision awareness or development of attributes beyond those necessary for performing the specific task.

In the events per episode chart, the behavior expectations are minimal. The table above presents the *minimum* directions that can produce the essence of the five reproductive teaching styles. Although the following verbal behavior comments reflect the essence of the style's intentions, it will not lead learners to all the landmark objectives.

All of the teaching–learning behaviors can be implemented using similarly concise verbal behavior.

Shifting Only Some Landmark Style Decisions

The primary reason for shifting only some, and not all, landmark decisions is to maintain a productive learning environment: a learning environment that supports developing decision-making skills, while offering meaningful engagement in content. This option is useful in three possible circumstances.

When Learners Are Inexperienced in Making Decisions Some learners are too young or too inexperienced to move from one landmark style to another. Shifting the cluster of decisions in each landmark style is too big a step for them. These students may need episodes that shift (define and/or practice) one or two decisions at a time, until they understand and develop behavior competence in each decision.

Maintaining a Safe Learning Experience Some learners have developmental limitations or they are unable (emotionally, physically, cognitively, socially, and ethically) to handle all the landmark decisions of some styles. Such limitations do not warrant their exclusion from alternative teaching–learning experiences, but they do require careful planning about which decisions to shift to create a safe and positive environment. For example, physical outbursts, even fights, can result when location decision and individual material pick-up are shifted in styles B, C, D, and E. Prematurely and inappropriately shifting location decisions can result in a total loss of classroom control. In the process of teaching personal responsibility, it is sometimes necessary to specify tight parameters for certain decisions, before shifting them to students.

Limiting Conditions Time, space, and material limitations often prevent the shifting of all the landmark decisions.

Shifting All Landmark Style Decisions

This option is used when teachers perceive their roles as leading students to develop individual and social responsibility. Developing individual and social responsibility requires awareness of specific decisions, objectives, and the notion of developmental factors. The primary reason for shifting decisions is to deliberately expand individual capacities to demonstrate *mobility ability* in making decisions and experience a variety of educational objectives.

Using Style Name or Letter to Indicate Expectations

Once learners can execute the decisions of a teaching style, it is useful to refer to the landmark expectations using the style name or letter. This shorthand reference reduces the teacher's air-time during the delivery of behavior expectations, moves the learners into the content expectations more swiftly, and establishes a trusting relationship between teacher and learner. Constant use of the style name or letter only should be avoided; once learners get into the routine of the style, they often forget the purposes and specific decision of the individual styles, if they are not reinforced. Occasional reviews and making references to the teaching styles' specific decisions, implications, and contributions are necessary.

Although fidelity to the theory during implementation is the heartbeat of any theoretical system, there are options when implementing teaching behaviors. When the decision-making theory is understood, the infinite variety of teaching–learning options becomes apparent.

The Lesson Plan

Lesson plans indicate the intended learning expectations and the process for attaining them. Each distinct objective within the lesson constitutes an episode. The term "episode" is defined as a unit of time within which the teacher and learner are engaged in the same teaching–learning style (behavior), heading toward the same set of objectives (O–T–L–O) (Figure 11.8). A lesson can be composed of one objective; however, most lessons require several episodes, each with its specific objective and its particular task (activity), representing a particular teaching style (O–T–L–O) (Figure 11.9). When the series of episodes representing different objectives are well connected and sequenced, they directly contribute to the *overall objective* of the lesson.

Time

O - T - L - O

Figure 11.8. An episode

| Time | Time | Time | Time |

| O - T - L - O | O - T - L - O | O - T - L - O | O - T - L - O |
| Episode 1 | Episode 2 | Episode 3 | Episode 4 |

Figure 11.9. A series of consecutive episodes

A successful lesson is one in which intent is congruent with action. A thoroughly worked-out lesson plan accomplishes the following:

1. It specifies the intent of each episode, answering the questions: What are the learning outcomes? What are the learners expected to learn?

2. It provides guidelines for checking the lesson's progress and answering the question: Am I on the right track? Adjustments can be made as needed.

3. The lesson plan makes it possible to determine at the end of the lesson whether or not the objectives were reached. Was the action congruent with the intent? Did the learners accomplish what was expected?

Planning is a rational activity based on a particular sequence of decisions that is related to the teacher's subject matter knowledge and to the teacher's conception of teaching and learning. The action during the face-to-face interaction corresponds to the lesson plan.

The most visible features of the following lesson plan chart (Figure 11.10) are the steps (the episodes) and their sequence throughout the planning. The starting point is deciding which aspect of the content to present in the lesson: What is the overall learning intent of the lesson? To reach this overall intent, learners must participate in a series of episodes, each with specific tasks and objectives: What aspects of the content are most important for this episode? In what sequence should the content be presented to reach the objectives?[3] Which attributes and developmental channels need to be emphasized to lead learners to the overall objective?

Subject matter _____ Date _____

The overall intent of the lesson _____

Episode Numbers	Subject Matter Topics	Objectives	T–L Behavior	Logistics and Parameters	Time	Comments
	"What" is the specific content sequence?	"Why" are you doing what you are doing?	"How" will the teacher and learner "look" while engaged in the task?	Organization of learners, equipment, papers, materials etc.		Assessment; reflection
1						
2						
3						
4						
5						
6						
Closure						

Figure 11.10. Lesson plan chart[4]

The next decision involves selecting a teaching style. This decision determines the behaviors the teacher and the learner will use to reach the objectives (O–T–L–O, see Chapter 2). Then comes logistical considerations involving decisions about organization of learners, equipment, materials,

[3] Content knowledge is critical in this step. Teachers must know the subject matter's logical and structural content if they are to make decisions about the sequence of the episodes and the corresponding objectives to be accomplished in each episode.

[4] The order of the categories can be altered; however, none can be omitted.

task sheets, content props and supplies, etc., all of which are aspects of class management.

The next step in lesson planning deals with setting time parameters for each episode, and results in guidelines for time distribution during the lesson. Teachers can use the assessment/comment column to reflect/assess the episode, the learners, the subject matter design or the teaching–learning approach used. These notes can guide the next lesson's preparation or emphasis. Subsequent lessons can be planned in the same manner and, when appropriate, several lessons can be linked in a sequence that constitutes a unit, a topic, a theme, or a project.

The order of the lesson plan categories can be changed. Some teachers prefer to indicate the objectives as the first column. The order of the categories that appear in the lesson plan can be altered; however, none can be omitted. All episodes must account for each category.

Each lesson plan is part of a continuous sequence that connects the various elements represented in Figure 11.11. Awareness of the continuous sequence that exists among these elements can ensure that the flow of planning is seamless and logical.

Objectives
(What do I want to accomplish?
What are the learners expected to learn?) ⟶

   Specific Tasks
   (What is to be done?) ⟶

      Teaching Style
      (How will the teacher
      and learner behave?) ⟶

         Logistics and Parameters
         (What managerial accommodations
         are needed?)

Figure 11.11. Continuous flow of the plan

Episodic Teaching

To reach the intended objectives of a lesson, options and variety are necessary to accommodate the complexities and specifics of each subject matter presentation. All lessons can be conceived, planned, and executed as a series of episodes. Teaching that incorporates a series of planned episodes is termed *episodic teaching*.

The notion of planning and teaching in "episodes" accommodates the diversity in educational objectives and legitimizes the non-versus approach to implementing alternative teaching–learning styles. Although designing lessons as a series of episodes is desirable, not all planned episodes accomplishes the intended focus of the Spectrum. There are two approaches to designing consecutive episodes.

In the first approach, each episode represents the same teaching style (decision distributions) and reinforces a similar set of objectives. Throughout the day different episodes occur because the subject matter tasks vary. The tasks in the various episodes may even emphasize different attributes and Developmental Channels. However, the learners experience a common set of educational objectives from episode to episode because all the teaching–learning experiences represent a similar decision structure in spite of the developmental emphasis or the changed content topic. In this first approach the educational objectives in subject matter and behavior are more similar than different (Figure 11.12).

Episodic Teaching

Figure 11.12. Episodic teaching—same objective design

In the second approach, episodes represent different teaching styles (decision distributions) and therefore reinforce different sets of objectives in subject matter and behavior. Throughout the day, activities designed to follow this approach deliberately provide learners with a variety of decision-making opportunities, cognitive experiences, attribute exposure, and development emphasis. The set of educational objectives that are the focus of the learning experience in each episode is different (Figure 11.13).

Episodic Teaching

Figure 11.13. Episodic teaching—multiple objective design

Episodic teaching encourages the teacher to scrutinize the content to determine the supporting objectives (experiences) that are necessary and the logical sequence that would lead the learner to the lesson's overall outcomes. Episodic planning (Figure 11.14) and teaching places an indispensable value

Subject matter _Volleyball_____

The overall intent of the lesson _To develop initial competence in the techniques of setting and serving_

	Subject Matter	Objectives	Behavior	Logistics	Time	Comments
Episode number	Specific tasks	Subject matter and/or role	Teaching–learning style	Organization of learners, equipment, papers, materials etc.		Feedback/reflection
1	Warm-up—individual practice before class time begins	Warm-up—to initiate self-starting	Self-Check practice style D			
2	Deliver short history	To deliver new content	Canopy practice style B	Designate area for LS to sit	5 minutes	
3	Demonstrate skills-setting and new vocabulary understanding Explain criteria sheet	To demo the exact model and form for the set	Canopy practice style B	Ball Windows Wall	5 minutes	
4	Practice set shot Use criteria for correct posture/position	To receive immediate feedback of set position To provide socialization experience To reinforce feedback skills	Reciprocal style C	Practice markers by window and wall Balls	15 minutes	
5	Practice underhand serve Use criteria	Same as 4	Reciprocal style C	Same as 4	15 minutes	
6	Reinforce skills Q-action practice	Closure Review–individual/group performance	Practice		2–3 minutes	

Figure 11.14. Example of a PE lesson plan

on each episode in the lesson. In episodic lessons the learners not only experience a variety of educational opportunities, but they are also exposed to lessons deliberately designed to maximize acquisition of content (Baoler, 1999).

Terminology

Perhaps the most pressing issue confronting theory and practice is the ambiguity of pedagogical terminology. To be beneficial, terms must be consistent and reliable. New ideas have the tendency to generate terms; however, when terms with inconsistent and imprecise meanings clutter a field, it becomes increasingly unlikely that progress on a significant scale will occur. Teachers and students are underserved when terms do not provide consistent theoretical guidelines for classroom practices. Theory on teaching–learning is too vast for anyone to suggest that a single idea prevails; however, there are ways of thinking about teaching and learning that can guide investigations and discoveries. If it is true that teaching is a chain of decision making, then each teacher needs to be well-versed and skilled in understanding the theory about decisions as they relate to classroom teaching and learning.

The most widely used terms in pedagogy, including those listed below, do not share consistent definitions. Each author has a slightly different slant, a unique way of elaborating or emphasizing the same term. Each wishes to contribute to the theory and practice of teaching; however, this definition ambiguity makes it impossible for the educational community—teachers, supervisors, researchers—to dialogue or replicate accurately, with uniform rationale, and mutual understanding of ideas. This definition ambiguity causes teachers to idiosyncratically define and interpret the classroom behavior of the teacher and learner that would represent new ideas and terms in education. The following terms are examples of educational ideas that have inconsistent definitions and classroom expectations:

Direct instruction	Centers
Guided practice	Active teaching
Interactive teaching	Independent practice
Task teaching	Mastery learning
Individualized	Learning packages exploration
Unlimited (Free Exploration)	Limited exploration
Cooperative learning	Child-designed
Peer teaching	Convergent
Inquiry	Teaching through questions
Inquiry learning	Guided discovery
Problem solving	Pairs-checking
Jigsaw	Station teaching

Definitions of terms are important since they have an impact on the actual classroom behavior image of the teacher and learner, which determines the learning objectives. Although there are many terms within the physical education arena, let's review the term "direct instruction" for definition consistency (Table 11.2), keeping in mind the implied decision expectations that determine the teaching style and objectives.[5]

Table 11.2 Direct Instruction

Definitions	Implied Teaching Style
"In direct instruction the teacher directs the responses of the students: by telling them what to do, showing them how to practice, and then directing their practice. The students usually work in a whole class or in a small group." (Graham et al., 1998, p. 163)	Styles A,B,C
"Strongly direct teaching places the teacher at the center of control in class.... As the managerial authority, the teacher makes and oversees nearly all decisions about how students are organized, when practice segments start and stop, when learning tasks change, and what class rules are to be in effect." (Metzler, 2000, p. 142)	Style A
"The direct style is the most teacher-controlled approach. The teacher prepares all facets of the lesson, is wholly responsible for instruction, and monitors lesson progress by direct methods. Basically, the direct style includes explanation, demonstration, and practice. The amount of time devoted to each is determined by the instructor. Evaluation is usually accomplished by the instructor, who has certain preset standards for student performance. Children are guided along almost identical paths towards similar goals." (Pangrazi, 1998, p. 41)	Styles A,B
"In active teaching, teachers provide direct instruction, either to a whole class or small groups followed by guided practice in which major errors are corrected, followed by independent practice in which student work is actively supervised, all within a supportive climate in which high, realistic expectations are set for student work and students are held accountable for performance." (Siedentop, 1991, p 228)	Styles A,B,C

Each author implies different decisions and classroom interactions among teacher, learner, and content. Since the definitions are ambiguous, classroom teachers must interpret the classroom behavior image for this term. This latitude to interpret the classroom image reduces the educational effectiveness of this, or any, idea.

Since all specific teaching–learning behaviors indicate a decision distribution that leads to distinct learning objectives, the term "direct instruction" is not a single, specific teaching–learning behavior; rather, it is a philosophical or categorical term that encompasses characteristics shared by

[5]Ambiguity of terms is an issue that confronts all fields in education, not just physical education.

many behaviors. For example, direct teaching could apply to all behaviors that reinforce memory cognitive operations (reproduction tasks), whereas all indirect teaching could be used to indicate all behaviors that reinforce discovery cognitive operations—production tasks. Presently, neither of these two terms is used consistently in theory or practice.

Development in any field relies on new ideas. Each of the above ideas contributes to teaching; however, none of them represent the total perspective of teaching–learning. Connecting ideas to a unifying framework allows the merits of ideas to be more readily understood and reliably used. Ideas that contribute to the logic of a framework not only expand the framework, but they also establish the value of the ideas. Ideas that are random, scattered, in isolation, or ideas that are presented from a versus position restrict the growth of a profession. The issue is not which should be used, either direct or indirect instruction; but rather when to use direct and when to use indirect instruction. When, for what content, with which students, for how many lessons, etc., should the various ideas in education be used?

The Discovery Teaching Styles

Now that we have examined the cluster of memory teaching–learning styles from Command to Inclusion (A–E), let's move to discovery teaching. What would the first discovery teaching style look like? How could the next teaching style be designed to gradually shift learners from memory to a discovery experience?

CHAPTER 12

The Guided Discovery Style—F

Pre-impact   (T)
Impact   → (T/L)
Post-impact → (T/L)[1]

The defining characteristic of the Guided Discovery style is the logical and sequential design of questions that lead a person to discover a predetermined response. In the Anatomy of the Guided Discovery Style, the role of the teacher is to make all subject matter decisions, including the target concept to be discovered and the sequential design of the questions for the learner. The role of the learner is to discover the answers. This implies that the learner makes decisions about segments of the subject matter within the topic selected by the teacher. When this behavior is achieved, the following objectives are reached in subject matter and in behavior:

The Objectives

Subject Matter Objectives	Behavior Objectives
To discover the interconnection of steps within a given task	To cross the discovery threshold
To discover the "target"—the concept, the principle, the idea	To engage the learner in the discovery of concepts and principles representing convergent thinking
To experience a step-by-step discovery process—develop sequential discovery skills that logically lead to broader concepts	To engage the learner in a precise cognitive relationship between the stimulus (given by the teacher or surrogate) and discovered response
	To teach both teacher and learner about cognitive economy—i.e., using minimal, accurate, and logical steps to get to a target
	To develop an effective and affective climate conducive to engagement in the act of discovery
	To provide the learner with the moment of "Eureka"

[1]This diagram represents the anatomy of the Guided Discovery style.

The first behavior that engages the learner in discovery is called *Guided Discovery* (Katone, 1949). The essence of this behavior is a particular teacher–learner relationship in which the teacher's sequence of questions brings about a corresponding set of responses by the learner. Each question posed by the teacher elicits a single correct response discovered by the learner. The cumulative effect of this sequence—a converging process—leads the learner to discover the sought-after concept, principle, or idea. (For a review of convergent thinking see Chapter 5). If the learners already know the target concept, the objectives of this behavior are nullified and the question and answer experience reverts to a design variation of the Practice style (a review).

The Anatomy of the Guided Discovery Style

Who makes which decisions about what, when is the defining analysis that determines the O–T–L–O. In this behavior, the teacher makes all the decisions in the pre-impact set (Figure 12.1). They include decisions about the objectives, the subject matter concept target, the design of the logical sequence of questions that will guide learners to discovery of the target, and all the logistical decisions.

More decisions than in previous styles are shifted to the learner in the impact set. The act of discovering the answer means that the learner makes decisions about elements of the subject matter within the topic selected by the teacher. The impact set is a sequence of corresponding decisions made by the teacher and the learner.

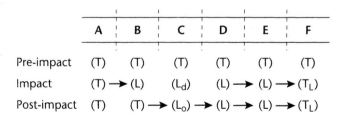

Figure 12.1. The shift from inclusion to Guided Discovery

In the post-impact set, the teacher (or surrogate) verifies the learner's response to each question (or clue). In some tasks, the learner can verify the responses for him/herself. The role of continuous, corresponding decisions in the impact and post-impact sets are unique to this style.

The Implementation of the Guided Discovery Style

Although episodes in Guided Discovery are generally very short, they require more than one question. Episodes consist of a series of questions that logically guide the learner to discover the predetermined target. Asking random questions, review questions, divergent questions, questions that seek exploration, creative movements, or multiple designs are not examples of this teaching–learning structure. Often teachers say, "We usually use guided discovery; we often ask questions." Merely asking questions does not imply the use of Guided Discovery. Questions are asked in all teaching–learning behaviors and the kind of questions asked corresponds to the selected teaching-learning objectives. Questions in Guided Discovery use a convergent process that leads the learner to discover a predetermined target. Although Guided Discovery can succeed when used with groups, theoretically, it produces the best results in one-on-one situations.

Description of an Episode

The planning (pre-impact) set is all about content. After determining the subject matter, the next, and most important, step in guided discovery is to determine the sequence of steps (questions or clues) that will gradually and securely lead the student to discover the end result (i.e., a concept, a particular movement, etc.). Figure 12.2 describes the relationship between each stimulus (the question) and its corresponding response. Each step is based on the response given in the previous step

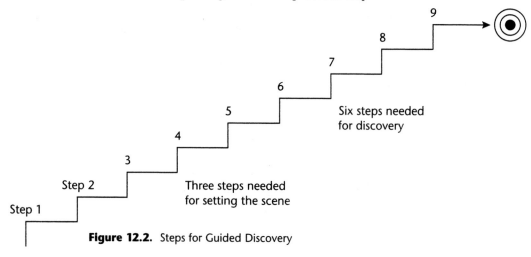

Figure 12.2. Steps for Guided Discovery

Each step, then, must be carefully weighed, judged, tested, and then established at each particular point in the sequence. There will also be an internal connection between steps that is related to the structure of the subject matter. To design related steps, the teacher needs to anticipate possible student responses to a given stimulus (step). If these possible responses seem too diverse or tangential, then the teacher needs to design another step. The new step needs to be perhaps smaller and closer to the previous step, thus reducing the number of diverse responses. In fact, the ideal form of Guided Discovery is structured to elicit only one response per clue. Figure 12.3 represents the size of the step and the need to design steps within the grasp of most (if not all) learners.

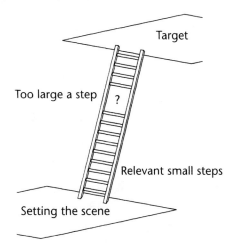

Figure 12.3. The ladder of Guided Discovery

The process of Guided Discovery embodies the $S \rightarrow D \rightarrow M \rightarrow R$ relationship at every step. The first stimulus (S_1) is designed to move the learner to dissonance (D) and mediation (M) in which the learner searches for the answer; when the learner is ready, he/she will produce the response (R). The teacher continues by presenting the second stimulus (S_2), which again moves the learner to mediation, resulting in the production of the second discovered response (R_2), and so on until the last stimulus (S_n) elicits the anticipated response (R) which is the actual discovery of the target. This last response can be expressed by stating the discovered concept or by showing it through movement.

The impact set tests the sequence design. Any failure by the student to respond indicates inadequate design of the individual step or the sequence as a whole. When learners fail to discover the target concept, avoid judging or making assumptions about the learner. Examine the questions, retest them with another student, and check the sequence for reliability in producing the anticipated response.

In addition to a flawlessly designed sequence, the teacher must follow several "rules" for this process:

1. Never tell the answer.
2. Always wait for the learner's response.
3. Offer frequent feedback.
4. Maintain a climate of acceptance and patience.

While these behaviors can be demanding, they are necessary for a successful episode in this style. The first rule is mandatory—if you tell the answer, you will abort the entire process of connecting one small discovery to another. The second rule, to wait for the answer, is necessary to provide the learner time to engage in mediation. The teacher must demonstrate wait-time and acknowledge the learner's mediation pace.[2]

The third rule calls for frequent feedback to the learner. A short "Yes," a nod, or "Correct!" are sufficient after responses in the initial experiences in this style. In tasks where the feedback is built in, the learner will already know the results of some responses. The teacher's role is to continue the questions, which indicates to the learner that he/she is on the correct path.

The fourth rule calls for an affective awareness. The teacher must exhibit patience and acceptance. These maintain the flow of the process. Reprimands and impatience will trigger frustration and discomfort in the learner that will eventually stop the process. The emotional and cognitive streams are visibly intertwined during the learning process by guided discovery.

The impact phase in Guided Discovery is a delicate interplay of cognitive and emotional dimensions between teacher and student. Both teacher and learner are bound intimately to the subject matter. The tension and anticipation that develop at each step are relieved only when the final discovery has occurred. The student, without being given the answer, has accomplished the purpose, has found the unknown, has learned!

In the impact set, then, the teacher must be aware of the following factors:

- The objective or the target
- The direction of the sequence of steps
- The size of each step
- The interrelationship of the steps
- The speed of the sequence
- The emotions of the learner

---

[2]Note: Waiting is a part of all the styles that engage the learner in discovery. In the styles that deal with memory, waiting beyond a reasonable amount of time will not produce the answer. Instead, it will produce frustration.

The nature of feedback in Guided Discovery is unique. The reinforcing behavior that indicates the student's success at each step is positive feedback about his/her learning and accomplishments. The very fact that the process is completed, the purpose achieved, and the subject matter learned is a form of total evaluation.

An approving response at each step constitutes an immediate, precise, and personal evaluation. In turn, the immediacy of positive reinforcement serves as a continuous motivating force to seek solutions, and to learn more.

How to Implement the Guided Discovery Style

The Pre-Impact Set   The role of the teacher in the pre-impact set is to make decisions about:

1. The specific target of the episode—the concept to be discovered by the learner.
2. The sequence of steps (questions) that will evoke a chain of discoveries by the learner.
3. The size of each step.
4. Setting the scene so that the learner is invited to participate in the process of Guided Discovery

In making decisions 2 and 3, the teacher should keep in mind that each step is based on the response given to the previous step. This means that each step must be carefully weighed, judged, and tested, to establish its efficiency in the sequence. The process also requires an internal connection between steps that is related to the structure of the subject matter. In order to design related steps, the teacher must anticipate possible learner responses to a given question or clue. (See the section below, "Selecting and Designing the Subject Matter.")

As in previous styles, the learners do not make decisions in the pre-impact set.

Impact Set   Once the teacher sets the subject matter scene, the interplay between the learner and teacher (or surrogate) begins (Table 12.1). Notice that in this behavior the teacher does not state the behavior or logistic expectations. Since this behavior leads to discovery, the teacher does not say, "You are going to discover a concept today." This verbal behavior frequently shifts learners into a state of cognitive dissonance before they have been led into the content process.

The eureka moment is exhilarating for both learner and teacher. This behavior is especially rewarding to teachers as they watch learners make connections guided by the sequenced questions that logically lead them to discover new content.

Table 12.1 Events—The Guided Discovery Style

Episode Events	Sequence of Events	Feedback	Time
Subject matter presentation	"We will be learning about..." (state content's general topic: balance, strategies, pressure on the lungs, three classes of levers, etc....)		
Behavior logistics questions for clarification	(Behavior expectations are not stated in this style.) (Logistics support the task and process of discovering.) (Questions in this style are generally considered tangents. The more "clean" the design, the less questions are asked.)		
Action, task engagement, performance	The subject matter: The teacher or the surrogate teacher: 1. Sets the scene 2. Begins the questioning sequence, leading the learner to the point of discovering the anticipated content target 3. Weaves the logistics into the delivery to support the logical linking and sequencing of the content. The learner: 1. Answers each question 2. Eventually discovers and states the "content target"		
Feedback (Post-impact)	The teacher : 1. Frequently acknowledges the learner's responses 2. Makes adjustment decisions when tangent responses occur The learner: 1. Receives the teacher's feedback 2. Engages in verification when feedback is built into the task sequence		
Closure	The teacher acknowledges the learner's achievement in discovering the content target.		

The Implications of the Guided Discovery Style

The use of style F implies that:

1. The teacher is willing and able to cross the discovery threshold.
2. The teacher values logic and convergent discovery as a part of his/her education goals.
3. The teacher is willing to study the structure of the subject matter and to design an appropriate sequence of questions.
4. The teacher is willing to risk experimenting with the unknown. In styles A–E, the onus of performance is on the learner. In guided discovery,

however, the onus is on the teacher. The teacher is responsible for the precise design of questions that will elicit the correct responses. The learner's performance is directly related to the preparation by the teacher.

5. The teacher trusts the cognitive capacity of the student to discover the appropriate aspects of the subject matter.

6. The teacher is willing to make the changes necessary to accommodate this teaching–learning behavior.

Selecting and Designing the Subject Matter

Selecting the Task

As in all styles, the selection and the design of the task must be congruent with the objectives of the episode. In the Guided Discovery style, the teacher must consider these five points before selecting the task for a particular episode:

1. Learners can discover ideas in the following categories.

   a. Concepts

   b. Principles (governing rules)

   c. Relationships among entities

   d. Orders or systems

   e. Cause and effect relationships

   f. Limits

2. The topic or the target to be discovered must be unknown to the learner. One cannot discover what one already knows.

3. The target to be discovered must not be a fact, date, specific word, name, or technical term. These categories of information cannot be discovered.

4. Some subject matter topics may not be appropriate for this style. The fact that this elegant and powerful style, when properly designed, always produces results does create a potential danger. When guided discovery is used in universal subject areas such as math, physics, chemistry, and anatomy there is no problem. Students learn to engage in a process of logical sequences to discover universal scientific truths. But caution is required when this style is used in areas such as social studies, religious issues, sex education, political science, etc. By their nature these topics are dependent on personal opinion or cultural mores related to particular beliefs and value systems. Since the process of style F guides the learner toward a predetermined target, a teacher can induce the learner to utter statements, principles, or ideas that are contrary to his/her beliefs and convictions.

5. The target must be discoverable.

In physical education Guided Discovery episodes most often lead learners to understand the mechanics of movement, the principles in science that guide performance, or the relationships of one movement position to another. Episodes in Guided Discovery can deliver the rationale for a particular body position or a positioning requirement in an activity. For example, in scuba diving it is possible to construct a series of questions that lead learners to discover that it is essential to breathe out when ascending or in dance/movement activities the importance of center of gravity for maintaining balance. In physical education, Guided Discovery episodes can deliver the underlying principles that govern movement. Once the principles, concepts, or relationships are discovered, the learners move to a different teaching–learning style to apply the principles discovered.

Refining the guided steps requires multiple trails with different learners; initially, this behavior is difficult to master. However, once a guided sequence is valid, it is a rewarding experience watching learners discover.[3]

Style-Specific Comments

Cognitive Economy. Guided Discovery is designed for cognitive economy. The particular structure of guided discovery does not invite deviation or cognitive wandering. This structure gets the learner to the target with maximum efficiency using the dominant cognitive operation. By "maximum efficiency" we do not mean that Guided Discovery is the "best" style. Like all styles, this behavior has its boundaries and limitations. It is the "best" style only for those objectives it can reach effectively.[4]

Guided Discovery has a considerable influence on memory. When one discovers something for oneself, the chances of remembering it are greater (Bruner 1961). The act of discovery seems to serve as strong motivation for some, if not most, learners. Because Guided Discovery gradually and seemingly effortlessly leads the learner to discover the subject matter, the learner experiences a reduction of fear, especially fear of failure. With the sense of success Guided Discovery can induce confidence and motivation to continue learning.

Group or Individual Implementation of Guided Discovery. Although Guided Discovery can succeed when used with groups, it produces the best results in one-to-one situations. Although many learners within a group setting can benefit from this process, the liability is that learners discover at different speeds. When one learner has discovered the answer (anywhere in the

---

[3] Refer to Chapter 18 for additional information on designing subject matter.

[4] Note that the Command style is the most cognitively efficient style on the reproductive side of the Spectrum.

sequence) and utters it aloud, the other learners who hear (or see) the response become the receivers. They can no longer discover it. For these students, the discovery process has been aborted. At best, different learners offer their discoveries at different points in the sequence, and thus the discovery experience "belongs" to the group. However, the full benefit of this process is realized when each individual learner moves through the sequence and is engaged in discovery at every step.

Logistics are obviously a factor. It is difficult to create conditions for a one-on-one process except (1) when the teacher spends time with one learner while others are engaged in other styles, or (2) when the learner uses a computer programmed for this task, or (3) during private and individual feedback time in other styles (except the Command style). The teacher can temporarily shift to Guided Discovery to clarify a concept. To do this, in what seems to be a spontaneous behavior, the teacher must be very skilled in the content and the structure of Guided Discovery.

Guided Discovery is very useful in the introduction of a new topic. The learner is quickly engaged and becomes curious about the specifics.

In time, the classroom chart can be displayed so that learners become aware of the structure of this teaching–learning relationship (Figure 12.4).

THE GUIDED DISCOVERY STYLE—F

The purpose of this style is to discover a predetermined concept by answering a sequence of logically designed questions.

Role of the learner

- To listen to the questions, or clues
- To discover the answer for each question in the sequence
- To discover the final answer that constitutes the *targeted* concept

Role of the teacher

- To design the sequence of questions, each resulting in a small discovery by the learner
- To provide periodic feedback to the learner
- To acknowledge the discovery of the concept by the learner

Figure 12.4. Guided Discovery classroom chart

The Developmental Channels

All design variations and canopies under Guided Discovery center on the manipulation of the following characteristics:

1. The quantity of content (including the number of clues provided) that the teacher provides, compared to content the learner provides.
2. The ratio of memory questions to discovery questions.
3. The social interaction compared to independent production.

The more the design variations include teacher talk, memory questions, and peer interaction, the less the design indicates Guided Discovery and the more it represents the Practice style.

As in all teaching behaviors, there are educational ideas and variations that suggest a liaison to one teaching–learning approach over another. As stated in previous chapters, names of programs can be misleading in that they do not accurately represent the decision structure for accomplishing the intended objectives. The programs' intent must be compared to the decisions (stated or implied) to determine which teaching behavior and set of objectives are in focus. Inquiry teaching has been called a specific teaching–learning behavior. However, this pedagogical term is inconsistently used in the literature and in the classroom. Some examples of inquiry teaching (based on the decisions and content design) represent the Practice style (guided practice), while others are examples of a divergent process representing either the Practice style or the next style—Divergent Production. Since the general term *inquiry* does not indicate a specific cognitive operation, it could apply to many different teaching–learning behaviors.

Design variations in Guided Discovery can expand the theoretical limits of this style; however, they must correspond to the decision premise of guiding the learner to discover a predetermined concept.

Guided Discovery can transform and delight the most insecure of learners, by encouraging them to go beyond memory and to trust the process of discovery.

Examples in Physical Education and Related Areas

Example 1—Soccer

Specific purpose   To discover the use of the toe-kick in long and high-flying kicks.

Q-1: What distance kick is needed when you want to pass the ball to a player who is far from you?

Anticipated Response and teacher feedback-1: A long kick! (Correct!)

Q-2: Suppose there is a player from the opposing team between you and your teammate and that there are no other teammates near by. How can you safely kick the ball to your teammate?

AR-2: Kick the ball so that it flies high! (Correct!)

Q-3: To raise the ball off the ground, where should the force be applied on the ball?

AR-3: As low as possible! (Yes!)

Q-4: While you are running, which part of the foot can comfortably get to the lowest part of the ball?

AR-4: The toes! (Very good conclusion. Let's try it!)

Let us analyze this short process of interaction between the questions and the inevitable responses produced. This process will always work because there is an intrinsic, logical relationship between the question and the answer in terms of the stated purpose—the high toe-kick. Sometimes it might be necessary to inject an additional question depending on the learner's age, the level of word comprehension, and similar variables. The basic sequence, however, remains the same.

The example illustrates how the two behavioral adjustments proposed at the beginning of this chapter work to achieve this cognition-motion bond. The same physical objective of using the toes for the high flying kick could have been accomplished by showing or telling. The student would have learned the high kick by observing the teacher's demonstration and repeating the action. But in that case, the comprehension of relationships, the understanding of "why," which is essential to learning, would be missing from the whole experience.

Let us examine the technical aspect of the sequence design. How do you decide which question comes first? Second? As a practical guide, proceed from the general to the specific, relating each question to the specific purpose of the movement. The purpose of the long high kick is to get the ball to a distant player. When the learner perceives that two players are far apart, the need for a long kick becomes obvious. Since there are two kinds of long kicks—one rolling on the ground and the other high flying—the teacher introduces the condition of an opponent in question 2, which suggests the need to raise the ball into the air. Now move to simple mechanics that are within the realm of every child's experience. If you want to raise the ball into the air, you must, in most cases, apply force to the bottom of the ball in an upward direction. Question 3 leads to this inevitable answer. The next question practically follows by itself; you need to use a particular part of the foot to meet the conditions established in the previous response.

The following benefits are derived from this process:

1. The student has learned the physical response for the soccer lesson planned by the teacher.

2. The student has learned the relationship between the flight of the ball and the foot—both the rudimentary mechanics involved and the role of this kick in soccer tactics.

3. The student has learned that he/she can discover these things by him/herself.

4. Psychologists believe that when this process is employed frequently and purposefully, the learner will begin to ask the questions by him/herself whenever a new situation arises; the learner will be able to transfer this thinking and discovery process.

The beauty of Guided Discovery is most evident when teaching novices, those who know nothing about the subject matter in focus. They respond almost uninterruptedly to the sequence of clues and are not pulled astray by partial knowledge or dim memories of some movement detail. Learning is fresh, clear, and flowing.

Example 2—Scuba Diving [5]

Specific purpose   To discover the principle of Boyle's law and the importance of blowing air out when surfacing.

Q-1: Bob, when you were surfacing, I noticed you weren't blowing bubbles out. What did I tell you about blowing bubbles when you are surfacing?

Anticipated Response and teacher feedback-1: I should do it all the time. I should always blow out when coming up to the surface.

Q-2: OK, do you know why that's important?

AR-2: No, only that you told me to do it.

Q-3: Imagine if you would … I had a balloon in my hands and I took the balloon and blew it up to its capacity. If I blew it up anymore, what would happen to it?

AR-3: It would burst.

Q-4: OK, and I tied it off. Now, I take the balloon and place it in my hands

[5]Dr. Michael Goldberger, professor, School of Kinesiology and Recreation Studies, James Madison University, VA, designed the sequence of this Guided Discovery episode.

completely around it and start to squeeze on it. What happens to the size of the balloon, the external size of the balloon as you squeeze in?

AR-4: OK, it gets smaller.

Q-5: OK, what about the pressure inside the balloon, the air pressure inside the balloon forcing out, what happens to it as I squeeze in?

AR-5: I think that it has to get greater.

Q-6: What about the volume or amount of air trapped inside the balloon?

AR-6: We haven't lost any of it. It's all in there.

Q-7: It's all in there. Yes. Assume this time that I took that balloon we just talked about and I brought it down, let's say, 30 feet underneath the water. What would happen to the size of the balloon as the water pressure came in on it?

AR-7: OK, it's gonna get smaller.

Q-8: What about the pressure inside the balloon forcing out? What would happen to the pressure?

AR-8: That's like before. It's gonna get greater.

Q-9: Right, and the volume?

AR-9: It's both the same.

Q-10: I bring the balloon back up to the surface and when I reach the surface, how would the balloon now compare in size to the original size?

AR-10: It's gonna have to be the same size.

Q-11: Exactly the same size. Very good! OK, we're gonna change a little bit this time. This time, we're gonna take an air tank at the bottom of the pool and we're gonna fill our balloon up to its capacity while at 30 feet. If I blew it up anymore, what would happen to it?

AR-11: It would burst like we said.

Q-12: Now I'm going to tie the balloon off and start taking it to the surface of the water, what happens to the external size of the balloon as I start taking it up?

AR-12: It's gonna start stretching and then it'll break. It'll blow open.

Q-13: Somewhere before it reaches the surface, it'll break?

AR-13: Right.

Q-14: Our lungs are similar in respect to balloons. In our lungs there are little air sacks called alveoli.

AR-14: (The learner engages in action and practices.)

Q-15: A diver fills his lungs up to capacity while at 30 feet underwater. He can't take in more air. He holds his breath … and starts to surface. What will happen to the size of those tiny air sacks in his lungs as he rises?

AR-15: They will expand; increase in size.

Q-16: But we said he filled his lungs to capacity. What will happen?

AR-16 He's gonna blow his lungs out.

Q-17: What do you think a good principle or rule in diving should be?

AR-17: Whenever he comes up, he's got to breathe out all the time.

This episode leads the learner to understand the principle that underlies the task request to "breathe out when surfacing." Simply warning a student that safety is the reason for this request does not illustrate the principle as vividly or as convincingly as leading the student through this series of questions. In addition, the student is learning about Boyles' law, which explains the relationship between pressure and volume in gases; i.e., as volume decreases, pressure increases. When the interaction between the questions and the inevitable responses is flawlessly produced, the learners discover the logical connections, principles, relationships, etc. of the content.

Example 3—Shot put

Specific purpose   To discover the stance for putting the shot.

Q-1: Recall the three main purposes of putting the shot in competition.

Anticipated Response and feedback-1: To put it as far as possible.

Q-2: To achieve a far distance, what does the body need?

AR-2: Strength, power! (Correct!)

Q-3: What else?

AR-3: Speed! (Good)

Q-4: In the total motion of putting the shot (starting point, middle release), where should the power and speed reach their maximum?

AR-4: At the point of release! (Correct!)

Q-5: Where is the point of minimum strength and speed?

AR-5: At the stationary starting position! (Very good.)

Q-6: To achieve the maximum strength and speed at the point of release, how far from this point should the starting position be?

AR-6: As far as possible! (Correct!)

This is the rationale behind the starting position used by top shot putters. If the answer to question 6 is not readily given, an additional step must be taken: "To gain maximum momentum, should the body and the shot travel a short or a long distance?" Then ask, "How long?" From this point on, physical responses are called for.

Q-7: If the point of release is at this line in front of your body, figure out your starting position that fulfills the requirements of response 6.

AR-7: Here some students might stand in a wide stance with the shot resting someplace on the shoulder. (The balance requirement becomes clear immediately, and some sort of straddle position is usually offered. If this is not apparent you may ask, "Are you well-balanced?" and wait for the new physical response.) However, others may take the concept of "maximum distance from the point of release" quite literally and attempt to stretch out the arm holding the shot; here you intervene with another question.

Q-8: Since the shot is quite heavy, can the arm do the job alone, or could the body help?

AR-8: The body could help! (The student has already felt the weight of the shot and the awkwardness of holding it in the outstretched hand.)

Q-9: Find the location where you can place the shot to get maximum push from the body.

AR-9: On the shoulder! (Correct!)

Q-10: To gain maximum momentum, do you place your body weight equally on both legs?

AR-10: No. On the rear leg! (Correct!)

Q-11: To gain maximum thrust from the ground, determine the position of this leg.

AR-11: Slightly bent! (Yes!)

Q-12: Now, indicate the position of the trunk to fulfill the conditions we've just discovered.

AR-12: Slightly bent and twisted toward the rear leg! (True!)

Teacher: Good! Does this position seem to be the starting one we were looking for?

This procedure may seem too painstaking at first, but one gets used to it. The learning accomplishments far outweigh the initial difficulties and apprehension, and teachers are usually motivated to try this style whenever the situation merits. The sequence developed here follows the same principles as the previous example. As always, the biggest obstacle is deciding which question to ask first. Once the purpose of putting the shot becomes clear, the interrelated steps toward accomplishing this purpose become clearer. In fact, the intrinsic structure of the shot put becomes clearer to the student and teacher alike. We have progressed in the teaching–learning process by moving backwards, by retracing the movements and positions from the end result (the put) to the starting position (the stance). It is the same technique used to discover the road between point A and point B in a maze. Often one starts from point B and traces the road back to point A.

Together we have discovered the technique of structuring the Guided Discovery process. Polya (1957) sums it up in the following way:

There is certainly something in the method that is not superficial. There is a certain psychological difficulty in turning around, in going away from the goal, in working backwards, in not following the direct path to the desired end. When we discover the sequence of appropriate operations, our mind has to proceed in an order which is exactly the reverse of the actual performance. There is a sort of psychological repugnance to this reverse order which may prevent a quite able student from understanding the method if it is not presented carefully.

Yet it does not take a genius to solve a concrete problem working backward; anybody can do it with a little common sense. We concentrate upon the desired end, we visualize the final position in which we would like to be. From what foregoing position could we get there? It is natural to ask this question, and in so asking we work backwards.[6]

Example 4—Developmental Movement, Dance, Gymnastics

Specific purpose To discover the effect of the base of support and center of gravity on balance. (This lesson has been taught to third and fifth graders many times.)

Q-1: Do you know what balance is?

Anticipated Response and feedback-1: Answer is given in motion; there is no need here for a verbal response. Some children will place themselves in a variety of balance positions, and some will move sideways, which requires a degree of balance other than "normal." Chances are that all children will have a response that illustrates balance.

Q-2: Place yourself in maximum balance. (Sometimes it is necessary to use the word most instead of maximum.)

AR-2: Usually the responses here vary. Some will assume a variety of erect positions, and some will assume lower positions they have seen in football, wrestling, or various gymnastics stunts. It may be necessary to repeat this question.

Q-3: Let's check to see if this is your most balanced position. (Check the solutions by pushing each child slightly and, thus, upsetting the position of balance.)

AR-3: Within a short period of time, several children will get close to the ground in very low balance positions. Some may even lie flat on the floor. (These will be the hardest positions to upset by a slight push.)

[6] Polya, Gyorgy. *How to Solve It*. Garden City, NY: Doubleday & Company, Inc., 1957.

Q-4: Now, arrange yourself in a position that is a little bit less balanced.

AR-4: Most or all children will assume a new position by reducing the size of the base. This is often accomplished by removing a supporting hand, raising the head in supine position, or rolling over to one side from a supine position.

Q-5: Now, could you move to a new position that is still less balanced.

AR-5: Now the process is in motion. All children will assume a position that has less area of contact between the body and the floor. Some will start rising off the floor. Within two or three more steps to reduce the balance, most of the class will be in rather high positions with close to the minimum point of contact between the body and the floor (questions 6, 7, and 8).

Q-6: Could you be now in the least balanced position?

AR-6: Most children stand on the toes of one foot; some raise their arms. Occasionally somebody will suggest standing on one hand or even on one finger.

By use of motion the students offered the correct answers and discovered some factors affecting balance. They discovered that a low, wide-based position is more balanced, more stable than a high, small-based position.

This is sufficient—the concept is understood through the use of motion. Verbalizing the principles is unnecessary. However, if the teacher feels that a verbal summation is needed, he or she can ask, "State the difference between the most balanced and least balanced position and what made it so." The correct answers will be readily available to the children. Children can learn to discover not only new movements, but also the principles that organize them into a concept.

Example 5—The Three Classes of Levers

A classic lesson in Guided Discovery is teaching students to discover the three classes of levers, and the roles of the axis (fulcrum), the force arm, and the resistance arm in the operation of the lever in each class.

This lesson has been used many times in kinesiology classes. To understand the relationship between the three classes of levers and muscular action, the student must see clearly the components of each lever class and their integration into a system of levers. The rote method and sheer memory rarely produce insight into new examples, or the ability to apply the principles, or the skill to analyze situations to determine the appropriate level. The use of Guided Discovery has proven successful with most students gaining the information and being able to accurately apply the three principles.

The equipment for this lesson is the standard meter stick and a balancing stand used in physics classes. Two equal weights (50–100 grams), two weight hangers, and a string will complete the set.

Step 1:	Place the meter stick on the balancing stand in a balanced position.
Step 2:	How can we upset the equilibrium?
AR-2:	Push one side down or up! (Correct!)
Step 3:	Can we do the same by using weight?
AR-3:	One of the students usually places one of the weights on one side of the meter stick. (Yes. Good.)
Step 4:	Balance the seesaw now.
AR-4:	Another student will place the other weight on the other side of the meter stick, moving it around until it balances.

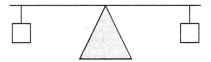

Step 5:	Identify the factors that are involved in the maintenance of equilibrium.
AR-5:	Equal weights at equal distances from axis A.

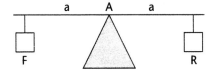

Step 6:	Which factor can we change now to upset the balance?
AR-6:	The distance of either weight from the axis. (One of the students is asked to do this by moving one of the weights.)
Step 7:	How far can you move it?
AR-7:	To the end of the meter stick.

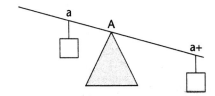

Step 8:   Verify to see if this is the maximum distance possible
AR-8:   between the weight on the end of the stick and axis A.

               No. It is possible to move the axis farther.

Step 9:   Do this, please.
AR-9:   Action:

Step 10:   Now, do anything, using the present equipment, to
               balance the stick.

AR-10:   More often than not students discover the following
               solution: Put the string around the stick between the
               weight (F) and the axis (A) and slowly pull the stick up
               until it is balanced in the horizontal position.

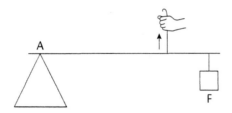

Step 11:   In terms of A, F, and R, what kind of balanced
               arrangement have we had thus far?

AR-11:

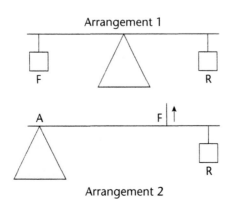

Step 12:   Look at the second arrangement. Now, determine if it is possible to change any factors and have a new balanced arrangement.

AR-12:   After a possible short pause the following will be offered:

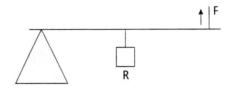

Step 13:   Yes, these are the only three possible arrangements of the levers (Figure 12.5). They are called:

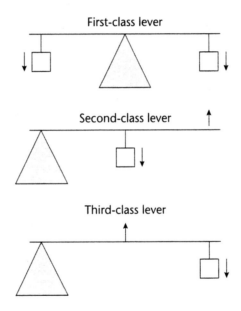

Figure 12.5. Three classes of levels

The next step is to relate this to muscular action by identifying the skeletal joint as the axis (A), the weight of the limb as the resistance (R), and the pulling muscle as the force (F). This makes it relatively easy for the student to relate the lever principle to a particular part of the body that is involved in a particular movement. This concept, too, is taught by Guided Discovery.

Bruner, in analyzing the assets of the discovery process, proposes that memory is greatly enhanced when the student discovers things by himself or herself.[7] Learning the lever principles by Guided Discovery commits this phenomenon to memory for a long period of time.

Because of the scientific nature of physical education—the relationships, principles, laws, rules of biomechanics, kinesiology, physics, etc.—it is rich with content that is appropriate for Guided Discovery. The following is a list of topics or phases in various activities that can be taught using the Guided Discovery style. Select one topic at a time and develop a lesson in Guided Discovery. Episodes can be short. When comprehension is crucial for successfully learning a physical concept, 15 minutes of Guided Discovery (if done with some frequency) will develop a new learning climate in the class—a cognitive climate!

As suggested earlier in the chapter, to invoke full learning participation the teacher must move the student from the state of cognitive acquiescence to the state of cognitive dissonance in order to cross the discovery threshold. This shift triggers the process of inquiry and leads to discovery.

After each episode, identify and isolate the obstacles that came up during the lesson. Then go back to these awkward moments in the sequence and adjust the clues or questions. Check to see whether each step is relevant to the development of the subject matter at hand. Analyze the responses to particular clues and try to discover why the students did not produce the anticipated responses. Was the step unclear? Did the clue lead to two or more choices besides the correct one? Was the step too large? Were too many additional clues needed?

After analyzing and refining the sequence, try the process again with another individual or small group of learners.

If teachers are not knowledgeable or have only a rudimentary grasp of the content, this teaching–learning behavior will be impossible to implement. The teacher must first understand the content, its logical connections and sequence before selecting this behavior. Teachers can become quite proficient using Guided Discovery when they understanding the intimate relationship between sequencing content and designing questions that lead learners to discover.

Suggested Topics to Be Taught by Guided Discovery

Gymnastics

1. The role of the center of gravity in performing turns on the balance beam
2. The role of momentum in maintaining balance on the balance beam

[7] Bruner, Jerome S. "The Act of Discovery," *Harvard Educational Review* 31 (1961): 21–32.

3. The relationship between the trunk and the appendages in developing balance

4. The factors affecting stability in positions on the balance beam

5. The factors affecting stability in motion on the balance beam

6. The factors affecting the smoothness of connecting elements in a continuous sequence of movements on the balance beam

7. Suggest a phase related to the mounts on the balance beam that you would like to teach by Guided Discovery

8. Suggest a phase concerning the dismounts

9. Suggest any topic in any phase of teaching balance that could be taught by Guided Discovery

All these topics involve more than just learning a particular movement; they involve principles and concepts that are the building blocks of any activity. When learners themselves discover these principles and concepts, they gain a more complete understanding of the activity, and this understanding provides them with the tools and motivation for further search, for broader learning, and for better performance.

This level of insight and comprehension can be reached only through cognitive involvement, and this can be invoked only by styles of teaching that, by their structure and operational procedures, evoke the heuristic process. Do not allow the learner's cognitive faculties to take even a small nap during an episode!

Let us continue with more examples in gymnastics:

10. The categories that exist in the variety of rolls in tumbling

11. The principles that relate the variety of rolls to one another as a resource

12. The relationship between directions and postures in tumbling movements

13. The relationship between the length of the lever produced by the legs and success in performing the kip

14. The relationship between the kip principle learned on the mat and the kip used for various mounts on the parallel bars

15. The role of the lever (the whole body) in producing various degrees of momentum when swinging on the parallel bars

16. Can your suggestions for the parallel bars lead to discovering the application to other apparatus?

17. In vaulting, the various phases involved in a vault

18. The assets and liabilities in each phase of a vault, and discovery of a generalization

19. Application of the generalization to a specific vault

20. The variables affecting changes in the form of a given vault

21. Suggest two consecutive aspects to be taught by Guided Discovery

The teacher who is new to Guided Discovery and other discovery styles will be amazed at the wealth of subject matter materials suggested by the students as the discovery process develops and blooms.

Developmental Movement

An area in physical education that is most adaptable to Guided Discovery is developmental movement. Examples for specific episodes include:

1. The physical attributes that exist as prerequisites for movement (agility, balance, flexibility, strength, endurance—see Chapter 18)

2. The kinds of movements that contribute to developing a specific attribute

3. Specific movements that contribute to developing a specific attribute

4. Movement that overlaps two physical attributes

5. Movements that develop a particular attribute by using a specific part or region of the body

6. The involvement of a particular part or region of the body in a specific movement

7. The limits of involvement of a particular part or region of the body in a specific movement

8. The variables affecting the degree of difficulty in exercises of strength development (i.e., amount of resistance, duration of resistance, repetition of resistance, intervals of resistance)

9. Specific movements and patterns that cause the change in degree of difficulty in strength development when one or more of the mentioned variables are manipulated

10. The relationship between a particular physical attribute, a phase of a given sport, and a specific developmental movement

11. The relationship between the need for flexibility of the shoulder for a javelin thrower and specific developmental movements

12. The relationship between the need for flexibility at the hip joint for a hurdler and specific developmental movements

13. The relationship between the need for leg strength in the shot put and specific developmental movements

14. The relationship between the need for abdominal strength in a performer on the uneven parallel bars and specific developmental movements

Basketball

1. The need for a variety of passes
2. The relationship between various game situations and the variety of passes available
3. The possible connection between two consecutive passes, three passes, a series of passes
4. The logic (or reason) behind a particular arrangement of players on the court
5. The feasibility of this arrangement in a variety of situations
6. The best positioning in zone defense against a given strategy of offense
7. The efficiency factors of a given offense strategy against a particular defense arrangement
8. Can you teach by Guided Discovery all the techniques of basketball? Some? In which ones would you prefer not to use Guided Discovery? Why?

Swimming

1. The buoyancy principles
2. Specific postures for specific purposes (i.e., dead man's posture for best floating)
3. The principle of propulsion in the water
4. The role of breathing during propulsion
5. The role of each specific part of the body in propulsion
6. The role of each specific part of the body in propulsion in a specific direction
7. The relationship between a particular phase in a stroke and the physical attribute needed

Other Sports

All sports and activities in physical education—from football, soccer, hockey, volleyball, archery, wrestling, to synchronized swimming, modern dance, and track and field—rely on scientific principles, phases, strategies or techniques that lend themselves to the Guided Discovery approach.

Crossing the discovery threshold is a eureka moment for both teacher and learners. Once students have experienced the logical and sequential progression of questions leading to content discoveries, they are ready for the next discovery style. The next behavior shifts an even greater share of the discovery process to the learners.

CHAPTER 13

The Convergent Discovery Style—G

(T)
→ *(L)*
→ *(L/T)*[1]

The defining characteristic of the Convergent Discovery style is to discover the correct (predetermined) response using the convergent process. In the anatomy of the Convergent Discovery style, the role of the teacher is to make subject matter decisions, including the target concept to be discovered, and to design the single question delivered to the learner. The role of the learner is to engage in reasoning, questioning, and logic to sequentially make connections about the content to discover the answers. When this behavior is achieved, the following objectives are reached in subject matter and in behavior:

The Objectives

Subject Matter Objectives	Behavior Objectives
To discover the single correct answer to a question or the single correct solution to a problem	To engage in convergent discovery—the production of the one correct response
	To activate logic, reasoning, and sequenced problem solving skills
To discover the content sequence that, when logically linked, leads to the final response	To construct a specific sequence and search for the cognitive operations that produce the temporary hierarchy that will solve the problem
To discover a pattern for thinking about the content	To experience the cognitive and emotional exhilaration that accompanies the eureka experience

In the previous behavior (Guided Discovery), the teacher prepared the questions and arranged the tightly woven sequence that led to the anticipated response. But now, in Convergent Discovery, the learner produces the questions and arranges the logical sequence that ultimately leads to dis-

[1]This diagram represents the anatomy of the Convergent Discovery style.

covery of the anticipated response. Although learners may use different approaches to solve the problem, they will each converge on the same response using rules of logic and reasoning. The specific cognitive operations used depend on the structure of the task.

The Anatomy of the Convergent Discovery Style

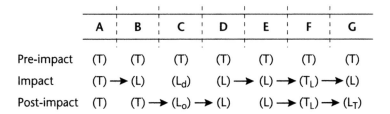

Figure 13.1. The shift from Guided to Convergent Discovery

The shift of decisions in Convergent Discovery occurs in the impact set (Figure 13.1). The learners make decisions about:

1. The steps to take for discovering the one correct answer to a question, or the one solution to a problem.
2. The series and sequence of questions to ask (this aspect distinguishes Convergent from Guided Discovery, in which the teacher makes the decision about each step.)
3. The selection of cognitive operations (the temporary hierarchy) to recruit to converge on the discovered answer. The learners are autonomous during the search for the solution and in the construction of the solution itself.

In the post-impact set, learners verify the solutions/responses by rechecking the reasoning process, the trial and error, and at times simply by seeing that the solution did indeed solve the problem. Depending on the task, criteria sheets prepared by the teacher could be available for learners to use in verifying their solutions.

The role of the teacher is to make all of the pre-impact decisions, focusing on the design of the problem(s) that will lead to the expected cognitive/physical discovery. In the impact set, after presenting the problem(s) to the learner(s), the role of the teacher is to observe the learners as they move through the discovery process (Table 13.1). This role requires patience, because there is a tendency for the teacher to jump in and intervene. It is imperative for the teacher to wait. Discovery thinking takes time.

Table 13.1 Events—The Convergent Discovery Style

Episode Events		Feedback	Time
Behavior	The teacher:		
	1. States the major objective of this episode: *To discover the solution to a problem (or to clarify an issue, or to arrive at a conclusion) by employing logical, converging, and reasoning cognitive skills*		
	2. Describes learner's role expectations…		
	3. Describes teacher's role expectations…		
Subject matter presentation	Subject matter:		
	The teacher sets-the-scene and presents the question, situation, or problem.		
Logistics	Logistical expectations:		
	1. The teacher establishes only the parameters necessary for the episode. Parameter decisions in this style could apply to any or all of the following categories:		
	• material pick up and return		
	• time • location		
	• interval • attire and appearance		
	• posture		
Questions for clarification	Verify understanding of expectations before action:		
	Are there any questions for clarification before the question/situation is presented?		
Action, task engagement, performance	The learner:		
	1. Begins to cognitively approach the problem and logically converge on the discovered answer		
	2. Eventually states the "discovered target"		
Feedback	The teacher…		
	The learner…		
Closure	The teacher acknowledges the learner's achievement in converging on the discovered content target.		

The learners need time to evolve ideas, examine them, sift through ideas, and decide on the appropriate solution. This process is a very private one—don't intervene!

In the post-impact set, the teacher may participate by asking questions to verify the solution, after the learner has spent time in inquiry, in trial and error, and in examining the solution.

The Implementation of the Convergent Discovery Style

How to Implement Convergent Discovery— The Planning Sequence

Unlike the landmark Guided Discovery style, behavior expectations are stated in Convergent Discovery. Because the subject matter is "produced" by the learners, the teacher's content presentation time is relatively short. The teacher may engage in setting-the-scene, but the learners are engaged in "producing" the subject matter answers.

Because of the captivating nature of the stimulus, it is appropriate (especially in the beginning episodes) to present behavior expectations before introducing subject matter. The more relevant and challenging the stimulus, the more quickly learners are stimulated to become *irritated to know* (state of cognitive dissonance). Stopping the thinking process to deliver expectations is an interruption and distraction. The reader may ask, "If the question automatically elicits the desired thinking process, why give a behavior introduction/expectation at all?" The reason for an introduction to the behavior is to focus learners on the cognitive capacities they exercised. Just arriving at the discovered correct solution provides the learners with one level of accomplishment. However, when learners realize that they are capable of complex thinking processes, a greater sense of pride and self-awareness occurs. The goal of this teaching–learning behavior is for the learners to realize that they are capable of:

- producing questions
- seeking out and sequencing information
- linking and connecting content
- converging data and
- discovering the correct response

Selecting and Designing the Subject Matter

Physical education has numerous scientific concepts (biomechanics, anatomy and physiology, principles in physics, etc.) that are conducive to Convergent Discovery. As a general guideline for selecting tasks in Convergent Discovery, use the following criteria:

1. Does the question or situation to be solved have a single correct response? (The response can be in a form of an answer, a movement, a solution, a construction of real objects. etc.)
2. Does the task invite convergent thinking?

3. Is the discovery process by the learner visible?
4. Does the task represent mechanical analysis of the movement?
5. Does the task invite the discovery of a specific sequence of movements?
6. Does the task require the learner to discover his/her limits in performing the task?

All tasks selected or designed for this style must adhere to the criteria stated above. Note that not every question, problem, or issue in academia or in daily life, fits these criteria. Many problems that require reasoning are resolved by the opposite process—the process of divergent thinking (see Chapter 14).[2]

Subject Matter Examples

Task 1: Effect of Posture and Speed of Movement on Heart Rate Perform each of the activities in Figure 13.2 on page 242, and immediately on finishing the exercise, measure (record) your pulse rate. Rest 2–3 minutes in a prone position between exercises. Work with a partner on question number three.

Task 2: The Rule That Governs Balance Positions The teacher initiates this episode by asking the class to "design movements that are close to the floor. Balance in each position for a few seconds, noticing what happens to your ability to balance:

1. With six points of contact between the body and the floor
2. With four points of contact with the floor
3. With two points of contact

Now, place yourself in as high as possible vertical balance position with two points of contact.

Next, place yourself with one point of contact, in a non-vertical position.

Ask the learners to state a rule: "Using the information about your balance in each design, state the rule that governs balance positions.

This rule consists of three interacting principles that always govern the ability to maintain a balance position. To solve this problem, the learner must engage in trial and error (actually trying these balance positions). These experiences provide the learner with information needed to discover the solution. The discovery process involves the activation of several cognitive operations: (1) comparing the data derived from "doing" these balance positions, (2) organizing the compared data into categories, (3) drawing conclusions about each category, and (4) identifying the relationship among the

---

[2]Refer to Chapter 18 for additional information on designing subject matter.

Activity	Heart Rate
1. Lie down for 2 minutes (no talking, relax)	
2. Sit up for 1 minute	
3. Stand at attention for 2 minutes	
4. Slow walk 1 time around the gym	
5. Fast walk 1 time around the gym	
6. Slow jog once around the gym	
7. Medium run once around the gym	
8. Fast sprint once around the gym	
9. Jump rope for 1 minute	
10. Consecutively perform jumping jacks, sit-ups, and push-ups, 20 seconds each	

Questions:

1. As you varied your body positions, how did your heart rate results change?
2. How did your heart rate change as you moved from #3 (standing at attention) to #4 (walking slowly)?
3. Based on this information, draw a conclusion about the relationship between heart rate and exercise patterns.

Figure 13.2. Convergent Discovery style example (Dr. Joanne Dusel, Department of Kinesiology, Towson University, MD, contributed this subject matter task.)

three (and only three) principles involved in the sought, single rule.

Since this problem has only one solution—one rule that governs balance—the road traveled by the learner illustrates the process of Convergent Discovery. (Note: Since this universal rule is based on the laws of physics, all participants will arrive at the same conclusion.)

The Implications of the Convergent Discovery Style

The successful use of Convergent Discovery implies that:

1. The teacher is willing to move with the students another step beyond the discovery threshold.

2. The teacher is willing to shift from delivering the content details to letting the learners construct them.

3. The teacher trusts the learners to participate in convergent thinking and to discover on their own.

4. The teacher believes that all learners can improve their performances in cognitive operations and in using the temporary hierarchies.

5. Each student can engage in the discovery process and develop the skill of convergent thinking (Figure 13.3 and Table 13.1.).

6. The teacher believes that the discovery process of convergence teaches students how to solve problems.

Style-Specific Comments

Although many examples of Convergent Discovery exist in society, this style is infrequently used in the classroom.

Standardized tests. Most standardized tests are composed of Practice style and Convergent Discovery questions because scoring methods require a single correct answer. Practice style questions measure what learners can recall, while Convergent Discovery style questions assess how well learners can sequence and apply known information to answer a test question. Both behaviors cover a number of diverse cognitive operations; both kinds of questions assess what learners know and their ability to apply knowledge to new situations.

The decisions of the reproduction styles. In the discovery styles, the decisions emphasized in the reproduction styles (A–E) are not mentioned. When the discovery styles are introduced, it would be inappropriate to discuss location decisions or interval decisions. The focus of each style centers on its new set of decisions and objectives, not those of the previous behavior. In this respect, the Spectrum is both sequential and cumulative. Whenever the previous style's decisions are incompatible with the implementation of another style, the teacher will need to backtrack, review, and/or practice those decisions that presented problems.

Many Convergent Discovery episodes are short; the time allotted for these episodes is minimal. Review the example provided in this chapter on

Convergent Discovery. This episode represents only one within the class lesson plan. There are additional tasks that must occur after this short Convergent Discovery episode to reinforce the discovered target. One possibility is to design a series of Practice style tasks that deepen the learners' understanding of heart rate. For example:[3]

1. The method for establishing your personal target zone is given below. Calculate your own target zone.

    a. Maximum heart rate x 70% = target heart rate zone.

    b. Maximum heart rate = 220 – your age.

    c. 220 – your age _____ = _____ (your maximum heart rate)

    d. Maximum heart rate _____ x.7 + _____ (your target heart rate zone)

2. Calculate the target heart rate zone for a 45-year-old. Show your work and circle your answer.

3. Compare your target heart rate with the average of 140. Is your threshold higher, lower, or about the same?

4. Is the target heart rate for a 45-year-old higher, lower or about the same?

5. Make a concluding comment that explains the relationship between target heart rate and age.

(The next several questions ask the learners to make opinion statements according to what is best for them.)

6. If you looked only at heart rate, which of the activities listed above would help you develop cardiovascular endurance?

7. Which activity listed above could you perform for at least 15 minutes continuously?

8. Therefore, which activities do you think would develop cardiovascular endurance *for you*?

9. List three or more sports or activities not mentioned that you think will develop cardiovascular endurance.

Designing lessons that employ episodic teaching is a primary intent of the Spectrum. Content is conveyed by using a series of episodes that represent different teaching–learning behaviors. This exposes learners to a variety of learning objectives in both subject matter and behavior. The series of episodes and the design variations are infinite.

The order in which teaching–learning styles appear in the Spectrum framework is deliberate. The evolution of the Spectrum is created by logically and gradually shifting specific decisions in forming a relationship that

[3]Dr. Joanne Dusel, Department of Kinesiology, Towson University, MD, contributed this subject matter task.

is related to the previous style, yet also one that produces a significantly different set of objectives. This is not to suggest that the Spectrum must be implemented in sequence from Command to Discovery, although awareness of the decisions inherent in each teaching style is essential. Knowing the prerequisite decisions and the learners' proficiency in making these decisions can avert unnecessary confusion when alternative teaching styles are introduced.

The classroom chart (Figure 13.3) can be used as a reminder.

THE CONVERGENT DISCOVERY STYLE—G

The purpose of this style is to discover the solution to a problem by employing logic and reasoning skills and by constructing and linking questions, which lead to the anticipated response.

Role of the learner

- To examine the problem or issue
- To evolve a procedure, which recruits the cognitive operations, that will lead to the question's solution/target response
- To verify the process and the solution by checking them against appropriate content criteria

Role of the teacher

- To present the problem or issue
- To follow the learner's process of thinking
- To offer feedback or clues (if necessary), without providing the solution

---

Figure 13.3. Convergent Discovery style classroom chart

The Developmental Channels

All design variations in this behavior focus on two variables:

1. The number of clues
2. The opportunity for assistance—to work with another person or in a group

While no clues are offered in the landmark style, they are given in design variations. Properly used, clues reinforce logic and suggest how to think about the content, but leave the learner to make connections and produce the next question. However, when too many clues are offered, the content is revealed rather than discovered. At this point the design reverts to the Practice style.

The intent of social design variations is to offer students a chance to share their thinking process and receive feedback. A drawback for social variations is that feedback could be unreliable.

Combining Styles

Two possible style combinations are Convergent/Inclusion (G/E episode) and Convergent/Command (G/A episode). The expectations of the first combination are that convergent discovery is the primary objective, that the task is designed with varying degrees of difficulty, that learners make the decisions about their task entry points, and that the learners assess their own performances. Convergent questions/situations can be designed according to the "slanted rope" principle and this design variation can lead learners to the primary objectives of Convergent Discovery.

Convergent/Command (G/A episode) is another possible combination. The primary objective of style G/A episodes is timed convergent discovery. Limited time parameters force the convergent discovery to be flawless, in that it represents precision performance in recruiting logic, reasoning, and linking cognitive operations. Many competitive situations rely on this combination of styles.

Convergent/Inclusion/Command (G/E/A episode). The primary objectives are those of the convergent discovery style; however, the subject matter is arranged in multiple levels with varying degrees of difficulty, and the experience requires timed performance. The possible design variations are infinite. They can be fun; they can challenge; they can emphasize multiple attributes and Developmental Channels.

The Convergent Discovery style engages learners to initiate the thought processes that ultimately converge on a single correct solution. The next discovery style invites divergent discovery.

CHAPTER 14

The Divergent Discovery Style—H

(T)
→ *(L)*
→ *(L/T)*[1]

The defining characteristic of the Divergent Discovery style is to discover divergent (multiple) responses to a single question/situation, within a specific cognitive operation. In the Anatomy of the Divergent Discovery Style, the role of the teacher is to make decisions about the subject matter topic and the specific questions and logistics to be delivered to the learner. The role of the learner is to discover multiple designs/solutions/responses to a specific question. When this behavior is achieved, the following objectives are reached in subject matter and in behavior:

The Objectives

Subject Matter Objectives	Behavior Objectives
To discover and produce multiple responses or solutions to a question or problem	To engage in divergent discovery—the production of multiple responses that can satisfy a stimulus
To experience divergent production in specific cognitive operations	To activate divergent thinking in the cognitive operations designated by the stimulus
To expand content boundaries—to discover that alternative possibilities can exist in any content	To become sufficiently emotionally, cognitively, and socially secure to move beyond memory to risk producing alternative ideas
	To accept that an individual can approach problems or issues in different ways
To view some aspects within content as developing and evolving, rather than static	To tolerate others' ideas
	To feel the emotional and cognitive energy that the production of ideas can generate
To develop the ability to verify solutions and organize them for specific purposes	When appropriate, to engage in the Reduction Process (the P–F–D process: Possible → Feasible → Desirable process to examine solutions)

In this landmark Divergent Production style, the decision shift in who makes which decisions about what, when creates a new O–T–L–O relation-

---

[1]This diagram represents the Anatomy of the Divergent Discovery Style.

ship that immerses learners in the subject matter more than any previous teaching–learning behavior has done.

The Concept of Divergent Discovery

The Divergent Production style occupies a unique place on the Spectrum. For the first time the learners are engaged in discovering and producing options within the subject matter. Until now, the teacher has made the decisions about the specific tasks in the subject matter—the role of the learners has been either to replicate and perform or to discover the specific target. In Divergent Discovery, within certain parameters, the learners make the decisions about the specific production/configuration of the chosen subject matter. This behavior involves learners in the production of subject matter. It invites learners to go beyond the known and to expand their boundaries of the subject matter.

The fields of physical education, sports, and dance are rich in opportunities to discover, design, and invent. There is always another possible movement or another combination of movements, another way of passing the ball, another strategy, another dance choreography, or an additional piece of equipment. The variety of human movement is infinite—the possibilities for episodes in Divergent Discovery are endless. Equally unlimited are the possibilities of combining the concept of divergent production with other teaching–learning styles.

Although questions in this style can activate any of the discovery cognitive operations (see Chapter 5), the dominant cognitive operation in many Divergent Discovery episodes in physical education is designing. Physical movement lends itself to designing routines, strategies, or uses of equipment with movement. Designing movements in all physical activities is not only possible but desirable because it expands the limits and boundaries of what is possible. The discovery of new movements can modernize many traditional activities/sports; it can innovate new activities/sports; it can provide opportunities for more people with different levels of physical proficiency to become increasingly more involved in activities/sports; it can emphasize the cognitive adeptness that is needed to perform many physical activities/sports; it can offer learners a personalized experience to initiate physical content. Episodes in Divergent Discovery are essential for expanding the imagination of learners in physical performance. Without experiences in Divergent Discovery, learners' experiences are limited to replication of the known movements, basic skills, and fundamental strategies in the different activities and sports.

In this behavior the stimulus(S), which includes a discovery cognitive focus, moves the learners into a state of cognitive dissonance(D) (a need to know). This need leads the learner to search (the mediation phase—M) for a variety of solutions that will solve the problem. The search results in the discovery and thus the production of multiple responses(R) (movements, strategies, designs, etc.).

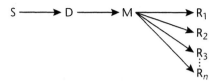

Figure 14.1. A model for Divergent Discovery

The Anatomy of the Divergent Discovery Style

The shift in this behavior occurs in the impact and the post-impact sets (Figure 14.1). As in previous styles, the teacher makes all the decisions in the pre-impact set, emphasizing the importance of the question(s) that will trigger the discovered responses and the logistical considerations. In the impact set the question is stated, and when appropriate to the specific subject matter question, the criteria for the reduction process are provided (see later section). In the post-impact set, the learners receive neutral feedback about the multiple responses, or value feedback about their engagement in the divergent process.

In the impact set, the learners make the decisions about the multiple discovered movement designs/solutions/ideas. In the post-impact set, learners make assessment decisions appropriate to the task selected and its criteria (Figure 14.2).

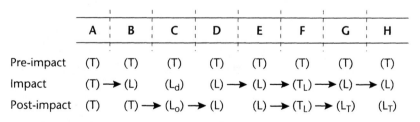

	A	B	C	D	E	F	G	H
Pre-impact	(T)	(T)	(T)	(T)	(T)	(T)	(T)	(T)
Impact	(T) →	(L)	(L_d)	(L) →	(L) →	(T_L) →	(L) →	(L)
Post-impact	(T)	(T) →	(L_o) →	(L)	(L) →	(T_L) →	(L_T)	(L_T)

Figure 14.2. The shift from Convergent to Divergent Discovery

The Implementation of the Divergent Discovery Style

As with previous styles, an introduction to the new expectations is required. Because learners are more accustomed to producing convergent correct responses than discovering divergent responses, it is important in this style to emphasize:

- The meaning and implications of divergent discovery
- The fact that no single correct answer is being sought
- The new roles of the teacher and the learner: both of whom must accept the multiple responses elicited by the posed question

Description of an Episode

The teacher sets the scene by describing divergent production, including the legitimacy of seeking and producing alternative solutions. The teacher introduces the learners to their new role and reassures them that their ideas and their solutions to problems will be accepted within the parameters of the situation.

Next, the teacher presents the subject matter focus and the question/problem/issue. The question(s) is designed to focus on a specific learning intent that engages the learner in a particular dominant discovery cognitive operation. The question can be presented orally or in written form, using any of the organizational formats (see Chapter 11).

Then, the relevant logistical parameters are delivered. At this point, the learners disperse within the gymnasium to begin producing multiple solutions to the problem. Time must be provided for the learners to inquire, explore, move, and assess the alternative designs, and the teacher must wait for the learners' responses to emerge. As the responses begin to appear, the teacher circulates and offers neutral feedback. This acknowledgement signals to the learners that their responses are acceptable; it encourages them to continue the process of divergent discovery. The role of the teacher at this stage of the episode is to maintain a nonthreatening climate by accepting and inviting more responses—more divergent production—when communicating and circulating among the learners. In this kind of class climate many designs/solutions/ideas are produced; some are exciting, others are not. The teacher maintains the flow of ideas by avoiding corrective and/or value feedback to the individual responses. The only time corrective feedback is given when responses do not conform to the original question. The corrective verbal behavior used reinforces the cognitive process. For example: "That design develops flexibility; this question seeks designs that develop strength"; or "That response is not within the game parameters; refocus on the criteria for the game design." Divergent Discovery is not the anything goes style; when digressions occur, correct them. Responses must fit within the parameters of the question. The feedback (which can be value statements) is directed toward the process of production itself: "Great job producing alternative designs"; "You are doing an excelling job providing many different ideas"; "You've produced many divergent responses."

Some topics require that the multiple responses be treated (P–F–D process). The randomly produced responses are organized systematically using criteria that further clarify the content. Treatment of responses can include verification, neutral acknowledgment, or engaging in a selection process that reduces (using specific criteria) the initial number of responses. The decision about which treatment to use is discussed below in the section on "The P–F–D Process."

At the end of the episode, the teacher assembles the group for closure. The closure offers feedback to the learners about their participation in the process of divergent production.

When both teacher and learners become skilled in the process of divergent discovery (and when they develop mutual trust), the flow of ideas becomes rich, varied, and valuable. The resulting climate of discovery generally motivates learners to reach for further discovery.

How to Implement Divergent Discovery
The Pre-Impact Set

As in all previous behaviors, the teacher makes the pre-impact decisions, giving special attention to the task design. The teacher must have sufficient insight to select the specific elements, sequence, and structure of the activity, and to identify tasks that are conducive for divergent production. Subject matter decisions include:

1. The general subject matter topic (i.e., tumbling, golf, modern dance, etc.)

2. The specific focus within the topic (i.e., back handspring, the putt, spinning, etc.)

3. The design of the single or series of problems/situations/questions that will invite the learner to produce multiple and divergent solutions.

The Impact Set   In the impact set the teacher delivers the pre-impact decisions (see Table 14.1).

Because of the implications and subject matter demands of this style, there is variability in the manner in which this style can be implemented. Some tasks using this style merit a single episode, while others require time for a series of tasks or themes to be explored. Some subject matter topics may require the insertion of episodes in reproduction styles before learners can meaningfully continue to explore content in the Divergent Discovery style. All configurations of this style invite the learners to discover alternative designs within the content (Figure 14.3).

Table 14.1 Events—Divergent Discovery Style

Episode Events		Feedback	Time
Set the scene	The teacher conducts a separate episode or demonstration that clarifies the terms and implications of divergent discovery.		
Behavior	The teacher: 1. States the major objective of this episode: "To discover possible divergent responses to a question" 2. Describes learner's role expectations 3. Describes teacher's role expectations (Posting the classroom chart serves as reminders. Figure 14.3)		
Subject matter presentation	The teacher 1. Sets the scene 2. Explains the cognitive operation (this sometimes occurs after #3) 3. Presents the question, situation, issue, or problem (this sometimes occurs after #1)		
Logistics	Logistical expectations: The teacher establishes only the parameters necessary for the episode. Parameter decisions in this style could apply to any or all of the following categories: • equipment and material pick up and return • time • location • interval • attire and appearance • posture		
Questions for clarification	Verify understanding of expectations before action: "Are there any questions for clarification before the question/situation is presented?"		
Action, task engagement, performance	The learner: engages in the task by producing multiple discovered answers or solutions. The teacher: when necessary, provides the criteria for the P-F-D reduction process. (This process is introduced after the learners have produced their initial responses on the possible level.)		
Feedback **(Post-impact)**	The teacher: accepts the responses, uses neutral feedback, and offers value feedback about the divergent discovery process. The learner: verifies the responses against the criteria, with the teacher, or by self-assessment.		
Closure	The teacher acknowledges the learners' accomplishment in discovering divergent responses for the content.		

DIVERGENT DISCOVERY STYLE—H

The purpose of this teaching–learning behavior is to discover multiple (divergent) responses in a specific cognitive operation.

Role of the learner

- To make the nine impact decisions of the Practice style
- To produce divergent responses (multiple responses to the same questions)
- To ascertain the validity of the responses
- To verify/assess responses in particular subject matter tasks

Role of the teacher

- To make the decision about the question to be asked
- To accept the responses
- To serve as a source of verification in particular subject matter tasks

---

Figure 14.3. Divergent Discovery style classroom chart

The Implications of the Divergent Discovery Style

The consequences of behaviors that incorporate Divergent Discovery expectations are:

1. The teacher is willing to move with the students another step beyond the discovery threshold.

2. The teacher accepts the possibility of new designs within subject matter that in previous styles was conceived as fixed.

3. The teacher is willing to risk encountering new responses and ideas without judging them.

4. The teacher accepts the notion that each cognitive operation is a skill that can be cultivated by practice.

5. The teacher believes that students can improve their performances by activating discovery cognitive operations.

6. The teacher is agreeable to providing students with adequate time for the process of discovery.

7. The students can learn the relationship between cognitive production and physical performance.

8. The students are capable of producing novel ideas that expand the horizons of the subject matter.

9. The students are willing to take the risk of producing divergent responses.

10. The students understand that certain problems and issues have more than one solution or point of view.

11. The students trust the teacher not to embarrass them during the production of ideas.

12. The students learn to tolerate solutions and ideas presented by peers.

As the behaviors are used more in the classrooms, additional style-specific implications are being identified. The research of Goldberger et al., (1995) found that when the Divergent Production style was used with fifth graders who were working in groups,

> *The first step in the process had nothing to do with solving the problem at hand. The first step had to do with issues involving leadership and power. It had to do with which students got "air time" and whose ideas the group would follow. This phase of the process had little to do with cognitive strategies and everything to do with social strategies.*

Their research revealed that when girls and boys were in the same group, the boys did not always listen to the *girls'* responses; however, after trying the *boys'* solutions, the boys would then consider the response(s) made by the girl(s). This research observation influences the classroom introduction and the teacher's decision about what to emphasize when delivering the behavior expectations. Goldberger et al. (1995) suggested that teachers be aware of this social issue and "spend time discussing the importance of listening to everyone and selecting a strategy based on merit." The theoretical framework of each style allows the human dimension to be more readily observed. Teachers may see the need to place parameters on certain issues, as to discuss certain behaviors, before students can experience the objectives of the selected teaching style.

Selecting and Designing the Subject Matter

When designing episodes in this behavior, one must consider whether the experience is relevant, worthwhile, and appropriate for divergent discovery. Some sports are fixed (nonvariable) in their movement design. Their movements or techniques have been determined by experience and biomechanical principles; therefore, exercises in divergent production would be quite futile. In crew, the rowing movements are dictated by the design of the shell and by the goals of the sport. Designing problems to elicit alternatives in crew are not productive nor useful for the performance of the sport. (This discussion refers only to the appropriateness of using Divergent Discovery for those learning to row, not for research into improved rowing techniques.)

In contrast, there are activities in many disciplines and sports that do allow for variability and alternatives. In fact, variety is the essence of these activities and disciplines. Examples abound where designing multiple movement combinations, patterns, exercises, routines, dances, tactics, and strategies are most useful, desirable, and relevant.

Although all the discovery cognitive operations can be used to good effect in physical education, one cognitive operation dominates. When the Divergent Discovery style is used in physical education, the most prevalent discovery cognitive operation is designing. This operation is conducive to many activities in movement and sports.[2] Episodes in designing can be simple or complex. They can be used as a single question/situation, as a series of questions/situations, or as a program design that spans several episodes. They can be used in an introduction to a lesson or as the primary learning focus. The opportunities to design alternative movement patterns are infinite.

The crux in designing is that the learners are triggered to produce alternative responses. Let's examine the process using the familiar area of tumbling, with a focus on rolling.[3] Theoretically, there are endless possibilities in rolling, involving variations in direction, posture, rhythm, and movement combinations. In the initial stage, single questions/situations trigger the divergent process: "Design four possibilities for rolling the body." Each learner will produce four different rolls. Some learners will perform each roll in rapid succession; others will need more time between rolls. The operative aspect is that this request invites the learner to decide which four rolls to perform.

Chances are high that many of the performed rolls will replicate what the learners already know. Learners feel safe relying on what they have seen in the initial phase of this style. The teacher should accept this and move on with the episode. Acknowledging feedback is given to the entire group, followed by the added expectation, "Your task is to design and per-

---

[2]In previous editions, the term "problem solving" was used to denote the prevalent cognitive operation in physical education. The term problem solving is cognitively ambiguous; therefore, it has been changed to designing, which more accurately captures the cognitive function.

[3]If tumbling is not a performed activity in the readers' gymnasium, make a substitution. Select any activity that is frequently used in the gym. For example, use Skateboard with turns as the focal task.

form five more rolls that are different from the ones you just designed and performed." At this point, it may be appropriate to remind the learners of the objectives: to discover new designs. Encouraging the learners to design and perform rolls they have not seen before will move them closer to the discovery threshold. The intent is for the learners to perform unfamiliar rolls that represent divergent production in the cognitive operation of designing. The teacher may actually observe some learners pause (the state of cognitive dissonance), search for a new roll, and then try it out. As this process continues, the purposes of this episode are realized.

When first introduced to this behavior, most learners will produce memory responses. At a given point they will pause, as though they have run out of memory responses; then most learners cross the discovery threshold and begin producing unfamiliar responses. Schematically, the process looks like this:

R1—memory

R2—memory

R3—memory

Rx—memory

Pause point before crossing the discovery threshold

R4—discovery design

R5—discovery design

R6—discovery design

Rx—discovery design

Some learners reach the pause point and stop. They freeze at the prospect of producing a new idea, and are reluctant to risk going beyond the known. These learners need time, encouragement, and multiple experiences in this behavior. They appear to be cognitively stuck and have embraced the divergent Practice style—recalling previously learned rolls.

Since it is predictable that the first set of responses in Divergent Discovery represents memory, the following technique is useful for reaching the pause point quickly. Elicit the first cluster of predominately memory responses from the whole group. This action reinforces the meaning of divergence, the acceptability of responses, and it leads the group as a whole toward the pause point. Once a hesitation occurs, the teacher can stop the group action and restate the objective of producing unfamiliar, new responses. Then shift the learners to working individually or in small groups to continue producing responses without repeating those already stated by the group. The sooner the learners reach the pause point, the sooner Divergent Discovery begins.

The purpose of this behavior is not anything goes; the teacher's verbal behavior must not include the phrase do whatever you like. Two issues surface when this behavior is inappropriately used.

1. When responses are not relevant to the task or acknowledged in any meaningful way, learners often feel that they are doing busy work; that there is a lack of direction to the experience; that trying to think and produce ideas is a waste of time.

2. When undirected experiences are repeated, learners often develop the inaccurate perception that they are competent in the content. Repeatedly giving learners autonomy to explore, to do as they wish, to create, without guidelines, content follow-up, or use of other teaching–learning styles allows learners to define the learning experience.

Continuing to add parameters to the original single question/situation expands the learner's involvement in the subject matter. For example, "Your task is to design and perform six different rolls in a forward direction." This parameter requires the learners to produce designs, rather than replicate them. When Divergent Discovery is used, learners have an opportunity to experience more possibilities in movement. The following is an example of what this process could look like.

Once success occurs, the teacher can assign tasks involving a series of related questions/situations. For example, within the concept of rolling, it is possible to focus on discovering alternatives in rolling forward, backward, and then sideways. The tasks can be presented to learners one at a time or announced as a cluster of consecutive tasks for the ensuing episode. The learners can pursue the alternative solutions for each task at their own cognitive and physical pace. Solving these related tasks consecutively allows the learner to be engaged in discovery for relatively long periods of time, and to see the relationships among various aspects of rolling.

Anyone who has experienced Divergent Discovery knows that movement designs may extend beyond the teacher's movement vocabulary. The teacher must develop an attitude of acceptance, welcoming these new possibilities; any projection of judgment will quickly abort the divergent production. If a teacher's view of the subject matter is fixed, if content is judged according to its correctness, if only the known responses are sought, then a teacher will not use this Divergent Discovery Style but rather only the reproduction styles A–E.

The teacher may select one of the learners' divergent designs to frame the next task (this is called branching off). The teacher might say, "Within the forward direction, design additional possibilities of rolling." This task focuses the learner on one variable (forward direction), but within this variable the learner discovers and performs multiple solutions.

The branching off can continue. The teacher presents an additional task: "In a forward direction, design several possibilities in rolling with different leg positions." The learners, staying within the general area of rolling and the one variable of forward direction, will now discover and examine the next variable—posture during rolling.

This process can continue for several episodes. The teacher continues to present tasks that focus on additional variables, all related to the previous ones. As a result each learner will discover and perform multiple movements within the particular subject matter and will begin to see the connections that exist among the variables in a given subject matter.

When designing programs within a subject matter topic, the learners are engaged in intense scrutiny of a topic for the purpose of discovering new possibilities within it. Such designs take time and span several episodes. (See Chapter 18, Developmental Movement.)

The content focus and format of the question/situation are critical if learners are to experience the objectives of this style and adequate time is needed for some learners to cross the discovery threshold. It is not comfortable for some learners to produce ideas. The Command to Inclusion styles (A–E) demands an almost immediate response from learners—a response that is provided/known. Guided and Convergent Discovery styles (F–G) provide for some thinking time with a delayed response—still a predetermined correct response. Now, in Divergent Discovery, time for discovering each solution depends solely on the individual learner's capacity to think beyond known responses. Individuals will proceed at different pace and rhythms—first, in the affective domain, second, in the cognitive process, and third, in the physical performance. With time and practice, the learner's divergent production increases in quantity and quality.

Wording of the Question/Issue

Each of the discovery styles requires precision in the wording of the question(s). The following are examples of Divergent Discovery because they indicate the general subject matter topic, a specific focus within the topic, and a specific question/situation for the learners to investigate. Each example specifies a specific divergent cognitive operation and a distinct learning focus.

Examples   The first example describes the task, and provides possible responses that different learners could produce. Notice the task sheet includes parameters that guide the thinking of the learners (Figure 14.4). This prevents Divergent Discovery from being an anything goes experience. It also allows learners time to engage in the process of discovering solutions. Learners approach the same criteria from their points of reference. The sec-

Task: Design 3 different sequences in balance— change the order and movements.

Requirements (any order of elements)
1. High position on one foot
2. Low position on two feet, on toes
3. A front scale
4. A jump turn, land on one foot, with bending at all joints
5. Upside-down posture

Possible Solution No. 1

Possible Solution No. 2

Possible Solution No. 3

Figure 14.4. Possible designs for a sequence in balance (Task and drawings from Mosston, *Developmental Movement*, 1965, pp. 312–313)

ond and third designs invite the learners to think divergently beyond what they already know.

The following tasks can be adapted for dance, gymnastics, movement exploration, or aerobic experiences.[4]

1. As a "wrap up" to a unit on folk dances, the learners are asked to produce dance sequences that maintain the qualities and characteristics of a particular region. Identify the movements and cultural characteristics of a region's dance and design four sequences that could be connected, using music from that region. (Parameters may include the number of learners working together, length/time of the sequences, music selection, attire to accentuate the cultural traditions, etc.)

2. This activity reinforces production of divergent movements using action words that are provided by the teacher. Example: float, melt, collapse, hide, hop, stretch, hang, shrink, explode, climb, squeeze, creep, spin, wave, spread, grasp, sail, soar, etc.

   Survey the list of words, then pick one and produce five different movements representing that word. (Repeat several times, choosing different words.)

   Variations or extensions of this task could include:[5]

- Select a word, then produce five different movements but each must represent a different elevation (or any attribute or characteristic could be used).
- Add to each of the above "elevation" designs a variation within a particular physical attribute—agility, strength, flexibility, or speed, etc. (or the learners could select different attributes).
- Connect three of the action movements together. (Repeat with different words.)
- Connect three movements that include.... (state parameters for different physical attribute—flexibility, strength, agility, etc.)
- Add a complete turn between two designs...

The number of extended tasks or variation possibilities is infinite. The teacher selects these tasks to fulfill the intended subject matter objectives.

Many companies that produce physical education equipment and materials now design equipment for different teaching–learning styles.

---

[4]Dance examples contributed by Dr. Elizabeth Gibbons, East Stroudburg University, PA.

[5]J.Rink uses the term *extensions* or *extending the task* to denote a continuation in the task. Extending the task can occur in any teaching–learning behavior. At times this term also refers to increasing the degree of difficulty for a learner.

Sportime® has been a leader in designing equipment for Inclusion and Divergent Production styles. Mosston, in the last few years of his life, had a working relationship with Sportime.® He had the pleasure of seeing some of his many designs produced. Other Spectrum colleagues, notably Dr. Phil Gerney, have had their own Spectrum-related ideas produced. Gerney infused into many of his physical education units discovery teaching–learning episodes. He also designed a two-week unit in only discovery activities for his elementary classrooms. By the time he retired, he had designed or collected for his students a hundred discovery activities, representing both convergent and divergent processes. For the two-week unit, he would set equipment and tasks in different stations around the gymnasium and learners would rotate from station to station. He had one rule—students could not tell others the answers to the convergent discovery tasks.

Many of Gerney's designs have spread throughout the field of physical education. Teachers frequently share suggestions and ideas on chat lines, and invariably, a design of Gerney's is described.

Gerney's imagination embellished the descriptions of his tasks. Let's look at two examples that introduce the same task in Divergent Production.

Example 1:

The teacher asks the learners to move from point A to point B in the gym with the task parameter that all the learners in the group must not touch the floor. The group must use the equipment provided to design a way of traveling from one point to the other.

Example 2:

The teacher, in this example Dr. Gerney, named the activity and set-the-scene for the divergent problem using a period in history. For this activity he coined the name The Pharaoh's Stones™ and he set-the-scene by saying the pyramid required one last stone and must be completed before the Pharaoh dies tonight. The challenge is for each "building team" to move the stone across the desert in broad daylight. The stone is quite heavy, so will require the entire team to set it in place. Even worse, the sand is so hot during the day, that the only way to cross is by sitting on the stone. At times the challenge requires moving one builder at a time; sometimes two. The "team builders" must design a solution to solve the problem (Sportime, *2000 Spring Edition*).[6]

Both examples represent the Divergent Production style, however, the second example used imagination (a discovery cognitive operation) to invite the learners to participate in Divergent Discovery thinking. In this example, the teacher demonstrated divergent thinking even in the wording

---

[6]Permission granted by Sportime® www.sportime.com, 1-800-444-5700.

of the problem. Dr. Gerney's students had many previous experiences in the Divergent Production style, they knew the expectations for their behavior in the subject matter; consequently, they could sustain two weeks of cognitive–physical production.

Some of the names for Gerney's designs are: *The Pharaoh's Stone*™, *Nuclear Waste Transfer*™, *Yogurt Pit*™, *Quicksand Crossing* (climbing ropes and tires problem), *High Rise Disaster* (wood to wood), *The Glasnost Peristroika Problem, The Poles and Rope Lift Problem, Radioactive Isotope Transfer, Acid River,* etc. His designs teach divergent thinking, physical movement, cooperation, and awareness of history and social issues. It is rare to see such sustained episodes in this style. Such episodes are pure joy for both the students and the teacher. Watching students produce ideas, within a variety of subject matter topics and within the parameters of the problem, is thrilling. This statement is not an endorsement for the "constant" use of this particular behavior—remember the Spectrum is a non-versus theory. It is equally thrilling to watch learners as they give and receive feedback in the Reciprocal style, or perform with precision and uniformity in the Command style, or accurately Self-Check in style D, or self-assess to find an entry level that invites participation in the Inclusion style. Each style produces its unique joy in the process of learning and teaching.

Mosston's *QuadBall*™, *Spider Web*™, and *Agility Web*™ are just a few of the thinking and moving equipment designs that Sportime® produced. The different styles lend themselves to the design of equipment that deliberately engages learners in the relevant decisions.

Non-Examples of Divergent Discovery   The following are non-examples of Divergent Discovery. Some do not indicate a specific discovery cognitive operation (therefore, the distinct learning focus is unclear). Others seek a single response, rather than divergent production. All the examples contain flaws.

The following do not indicate a specific discovery cognitive operation. The underlines indicate the ambiguous words that are incapable of triggering discovery. In most cases, learners will revert to memory responses when asked to make up, find, do. The questions/situations also fail to specify the learning focus.

Make up your own activities today.

Find ways to solve this situation...

Do your own movements...

Select a piece of equipment and see what you can do with it.

Get a hula-hoop and try any activity.

Try to kick the ball to the wall using the side of your foot. See how you can do this.

Non-examples in the next set seek one (a) response. Because divergent production is not requested, the learners will produce *a* response that is exactly, or closely aligned with, memory. If learners are not engaged in divergent solutions, the pause point is not reached, and learners do not have an opportunity to cross the discovery threshold. Although a few children in each class may produce unique responses, the majority of learners will play it safe, they will conserve their cognitive energies and rely on what they can quickly recall. Notice that although divergent responses will come from the class as a group, each learner is not engaged in producing divergent designs within the task parameter.

Design *a* sequence including....

Create *a* twist-shaped balance movement.

Design your own game. (This implies *one* game.)

Explore this concept... (The learners could stop after one "exploration.")

The non-examples in both sets above represent the Practice style—they trigger divergent memory to seek a response. The intent of the Divergent Discovery style is to engage the learner in divergent discovery (eliciting more than one response) within a specific cognitive operation.

When identifying tasks in Divergent Discovery:

1. Indicate the cognitive operation—avoid permitting learners to choose the cognitive focus (either reproduction or production).
2. Indicate the subject matter parameters so the developmental focus and intent are clear—avoid large questions/situation (design a game; take time now to explore the concept, try some movements).
3. Indicate a specific quantity that seeks divergent responses—avoid using *a* in the initial question/situation.

Each learner experiences the following in Divergent Discovery episodes. He/she:

1. Cognitively produces responses beyond the known
2. Experiences divergent production within the same question/situation
3. Assesses his/her responses according to the task parameters
4. When appropriate, examines the responses using the P–F–D process

The P–F–D Process

The Treatment of Solutions

The essence of this teaching–learning behavior is to experience the discovery of multiple solutions; however, at times there is a need to reduce by

selecting certain responses and discarding others to reach a specific meaning or closure in the subject matter.

In physical education, the treatment of discovered responses or solutions is guided by subject matter objectives. Are the discovered responses
leading to a performance or a routine? Are the multiple responses to be categorized or clustered according to variables or principles in movement? Are
the responses to be examined such that the learners can discover which
responses support a specific relationship or connection? Do all or some of
the discovered responses illustrate or conform to specific standards of an
activity or competitive event?

There can be several stages (levels) of the reduction process. The initial
question/solution seeks responses that are free of restrictions (other than
the parameters of the task). These responses represent the possible level (a
procedure known as brainstorming). Learners cognitively explore the subject matter asking what designs are possible in this task? Their role in this
style is to go beyond the known, beyond designs they have seen, and discover new boundaries (Figure 14.5).

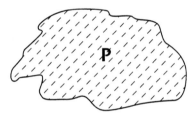

Figure 14.5. P (possible solutions)

Theoretically all the possible responses could be applicable; however,
for many tasks, the subject matter calls for a reduction process. Once the
possible ideas have been produced, the process of reducing or filtering can
begin. In this next stage (Feasible level) the possible ideas are examined
using a specific criterion (in the initial experiences of this behavior, the
teacher selects this criterion). The criterion serves as the standard by which
the responses are measured—accepted or rejected; included or discarded.
This reduction process by criteria is a critical learning experience in that it
teaches learners the importance of establishing criteria when selecting or
rejecting ideas. Students learn that the criterion determines the selection
process. When the possible responses are evaluated according to different
criteria, students can see differences in the final results. This convergent
process is not "pick the one you like" or "now, do whatever you want."[7]

[7]The term "convergent" in this case refers to cognitive process of convergence, which is different from the cognitive expectations/process in the Convergent style.

The process of selecting is the result of an examination process—a reduction process by criterion. This second level reduces the possible responses to a feasible level (Figure 14.6).

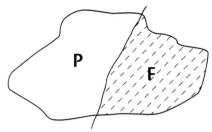

Figure 14.6.   F (feasible solutions)

This step of going from the possible to the feasible is called the "reduction" or filtering process. It can be represented schematically as follows:

Feasiblility criterian   P
                            F
Desirablility criterion   D

The process of reduction according to a criterion leads to a rational selection of feasible designs from the possible ones presented.

The next step involves further selection—a reduction from the *feasible* to the *desirable* level by applying another criterion. Each of the feasible designs are examined against specific criteria to determine which one or ones are *desirable* (Figure 14.7).

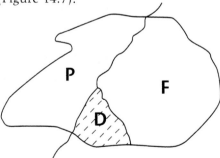

Figure 14.7.   D (desirable solutions)

Schematically, the reduction process now looks like this:

Feasiblility criterian   P
                            F
Desirablility criterion   D

This process ensured two factors: a variety of designs were presented and examined and the designs finally selected for use were the best in terms of the two indicated criteria.

Solutions to other issues (economic, social, physical, or moral) can be treated in the same manner. Possible solutions are offered first. Then a feasibility criterion for reduction is established. Each idea is examined against this criterion and the non-feasible solutions are eliminated. The P–F–D process leads to a rational selection of "best" solutions and—because agreed-on criteria are used—reduces the potential for emotional or competitive reactions when selecting ideas.

Using the P–F–D in the Classroom

When using the reduction process, it is important to maintain the theoretical intent of this behavior—divergent discovery. The criteria must not be provided until after the learners have produced their possible responses. When learners are told at the beginning that their answers will be reduced, they will resist divergent thinking. Engagement in the question from the desirable level bypasses the divergent path, and moves the learners to think in a convergent path, thus aborting the intended objectives of this behavior. Therefore, to develop the discovery divergent process, it is imperative to initially confront questions without conditional factors. Only after learners have produced a set of possible ideas should the teacher provide the criteria for selecting the feasible ideas. The verbal behavior could be: "Using the criterion of **X**, which of these possible solutions are feasible?" Ascertain that the criterion applies—that it will, indeed, reduce the possible to the feasible. Then establish the desirable criterion and ascertain that it applies. In some content, personal opinion can serve as the criterion for this last reduction process. When this occurs, divergence will occur as each student selects his/her desirable solution. This process reinforces the value that even though some issues have desirable solutions, it is important to examine all possibilities. By scrutinizing all suggested possibilities within the content against criteria, learners develop patience and tolerance in dealing with other people's ideas.[8]

Divergent Discovery and the Reproduction Styles— Episodic Teaching

The Divergent Discovery style embodies moments of inspiration, creation, production; it does not represent the practice time needed to refine, apply, or perfect the performance of the discovered ideas. Applying or replicating

[8]Refer to Chapter 18 for additional information on designing subject matter.

the discovered ideas shifts the focus of the teaching–learning episode to the reproduction side of the Spectrum. Dancers, gymnasts, ice skaters, etc., who design novel routines spend countless hours in the reproduction Styles (B, E, D, and A) refining the movements for precision performances of the unique routine that was designed in Divergent Discovery.

There is a complimentary relationship, not an adversarial one, between the discovery styles and the reproduction styles. Both are necessary in the educational process.

Verbal Behavior

Feedback in this style requires appropriate verbal behavior that encourages and supports the divergent discovery process. Analysis of verbal behavior used in the classroom shows that the following phrases frequently precede many problem designs in physical education:

- *Can you ...?*
- *How many ways can you ...?*
- *Produce all the different ways ...*
- *Okay, but what else ...*
- *You can do better than that.*
- *I like that one, that's a terrific design ...*
- *Hold it everyone! Let's all look at Jane's solution.*

These phrases deliver implications that hinder the divergent discovery process. The first three comments affect the number of responses.

- "Can you...?" gives learners permission to say, "No, I cannot!" It permits learners to stop without getting cognitively engaged.

- "How many ways can you...?" can also limit production and give permission to stop after producing only a single response. One may be all the learner believes he/she can produce, and the teacher's verbal behavior has legitimized this feeling. The issue of magnitude of responses also applies to this and the next phrase.

- "Produce all the different ways ..." suggests that learners are to produce *all* conceivable ways. For many learners, regardless of age, the implications of this phrase are cognitively inhibiting; learners are so overwhelmed thinking how many is all? that they freeze and can't produce ideas.... Affective discomfort results in cognitive inhibition. This inappropriate verbal behavior by the teacher creates an affective discomfort that leads to cognitive inhibition which, in turn, leads to the learner's stating "I can't!" or to the termination of responses.

Alternative Verbal Behavior   "Design three possible ways to...." First, this verbal behavior eliminates the potential hazard of the word *can*. Second, it eliminates the pronoun *you*.[9] The burden is off the individual. The focus is on the divergent cognitive production—the possible designs. Third, the introduction of a limited number of solutions creates a manageable condition for the learner. Seeking three or four initial solutions feels manageable. When the solutions are produced, the teacher must display an attitude of neutral acceptance. This will indicate to learners that all their responses were correct. This initial sense of acceptance creates a reality of inclusion of one's cognitive production. When the learner is asked to produce three more solutions, there will be less hesitation; the learner will be motivated to continue and to produce even more.

The next three verbal comments judge the responses.

- "Okay, but what else...." and "You can do better than that" are phrases that reject responses. These phrases tell learners that their solutions are not really valued by the teacher. It may also indicate to the learner that the teacher has particular solutions in mind and therefore does not accept the learner's solutions. This kind of climate is not only contrary to the process and spirit of Divergent Discovery, it will abort the entire process. Learners will stop their involvement in divergent production.

- "I like that one, that's a terrific design..." since it is difficult to top a terrific response, this feedback stops production. It also dismisses previous responses, establishes the teacher as the source of feedback, suggests that there is a correct response, implies completion of the task, and it invalidates the objectives of this behavior.

Alternative Verbal Behavior   Verbal behavior that encourages the process of divergence and multiple solutions: "Yes, now produce another possible response. You are doing great at producing divergent responses."

- "Hold it everyone! Let's all look at Connie's solution." When the demonstration is over, one often hears, "Excellent, Connie!" This seemingly positive comment erroneously establishes a standard for the class to aspire to. Many teachers believe this behavior illustrates a good solution and motivates the class, but it usually has the opposite effect. This singling out of a solution tells the learners what the teacher prefers. In this style, the teacher's preferences should not be apparent. If they are the very process the style is designed to develop will be aborted. Usually, after such a phrase, the learners will narrow their responses to conform to the demonstrated and rewarded solutions; eventually they will abandon divergent production.

[9]Refer to Chapter 5 for a review of cognition.

The teacher's role is to observe and accept the solutions offered by each learner (provided the solutions are relevant to the problem). When they are not, the teacher acknowledges the area of the solution that does not fit the design parameters. For example, "That response develops flexibility—this question seeks designs that develop strength"; "That response is not within the game parameters—refocus on the criteria for the game design"; "This solution is not valid because it does not solve the problem at hand—continue with your search for solutions."

The more we study teaching behavior, the more we see the importance of verbal behavior. The teacher's verbal behavior affects the design of the problems, the inclusion of the learners, the feedback offered to learners, and their continual engagement in discovery.

Style-Specific Comments

The Skilled Performers

Skilled performers, especially those with a single sport expertise, generally do well in the reproductive styles and especially in the Command and Practice styles. Because these students' successes occur within the known boundaries of activities/sports, they are often reluctant to step outside the boundaries of the rules when experiencing Divergent Discovery. Therefore, the initial experiences in this new behavior will need to expand the adept performers' content and performance competence. This entry point provides relevant experiences to their goals as performers

The Affective Domain

Each style imposes demands on the learner in the various developmental domains. Divergent Discovery creates unique conditions in the affective domain. Every learner must learn to deal with either the joy or the stress experienced in the process of discovery.

The expression of joy results from participating in the evolution of new ideas—one's own ideas. A sense of ownership pervades the climate of episodes in this behavior, as a particular sense of connection develops between the learner and subject matter. Every style produces some degree of connection with the subject matter, but in the previous styles, the learner develops a relationship with subject matter in episodes designed and presented by another. In this behavior, the subject matter belongs to the learner.

Stress results whenever learners face the demands of divergent production. Although the stress varies in intensity and frequency, it exists for most learners. Delving into the unknown involves risk-taking—which produces stress. While some learners perform well under stress, others may fear failure, being incorrect, or revealing their cognitive limitations. All of these feelings may stop the process of divergent production. The teacher must be constantly aware of these conditions and manifestations while developing the necessary insight to distinguish among the capacities of different learners.

Cognitive Production and Physical Performance

The process described thus far deals with the theoretical and operational relationships between cognitive production and physical responses. The reality of the gymnasium and the playing field impose limitations on this process, and affect episodes in this behavior.

Physical Limitations   A learner sometimes designs alternative solutions to a problem yet is not capable of performing them. In such a situation, the cognitive processes are functioning productively, but the performance is limited by physical capacities. This is a reality that must be accepted by both the learner and teacher.

One way of handling this dilemma is to ask the learner to identify two sets of solutions: one set that includes all the products of the learner's cognitive capacities, and a second set with only those solutions the learner can actually perform.

As a variation, the learner can ask a skilled peer to perform and verify the solutions that he/she could not execute. This is identified as the reduction process. It reduces the possible cognitive solutions to acceptable performance solutions.

Cultural Limitations   Cultural limitations are those imposed by agreement among people. They are often called the rules of the game. Rules always define the "dos" and the "don'ts"; they define the limits for conduct within a particular activity. In physical education, then, it is necessary to distinguish between two conditions:

1. The condition in which the structure of the activity occurs within the agreed-on rules. Any game played according to national or international rules, any track and field event in national or international competition, or any dance performance that reflects a particular "school" represents this category.

   Any problems designed in this set of activities must accommodate the rules that govern the activity. This means that although many alternatives are possible, only some are acceptable. This represents the reduction process from the possible cognitive solutions to acceptable performance solutions.

2. The condition in which the purpose of the activity is not to compete against others within a set of rules, but to challenge the present limits of

knowledge. The purpose of discovery is to develop beyond the known, to push beyond established boundaries. This sense of inquiry and expansion can be the domain of every learner in physical education.

Keeping within the notion of the non-versus, the physical education teacher should plan activities in both conditions—the behavior to practice and perfect the known, and the behavior to discover and experience the unknown.

The Group

Divergent Discovery offers a unique opportunity for group interaction. When a group unites to solve a common problem, incredible dimensions and forces are recruited to produce a solution. Group participation in this style calls for the social, emotional, and cognitive domains to interact with great intensity and balance. The interactive process involves balancing the following components:

- Opportunity for everyone to suggest a solution
- Opportunity to try anyone's solution
- Negotiating and modifying solutions
- Group reinforcement of the valid solution
- Group tolerance of the invalid solution
- A climate of inclusion
- Other?

When these components interact in physical education, a social basis is created for producing a solution that will be manifested through physical responses. These physical responses will, in turn, move the group toward achieving its common goal. Developing group cohesion is not restricted to outdoor education and wilderness courses where risk and danger unite the group emotionally. These components are recruited, in varying degrees of intensity, whenever a group is engaged in problem-solving activities.

The Developmental Channels
Design Variations and Style Combinations

The design variations in this behavior offer learners opportunities to divergently discover different attributes along each of the Developmental Channels. Although the objectives of the landmark style seek individual production, social interaction in Divergent Discovery is essential if learners are to accept others' ideas, tolerate differences, and examine others' opinions and values. If learners are to develop the objectives of this style, experiences on each of the Developmental Channels is necessary. Learning to accept and tolerate differences in attributes on one Developmental Channel does not necessarily guarantee that learners will transfer these skills to other attributes on different Developmental Channels. Cognitive tolerance does not ensure physical tolerance; emotional patience does not guarantee social patience. Because each of us has emotional preferences and experiences that direct our behavior socially, physically, and ethically, learning to exercise patience and tolerance in the attributes of the different Developmental Channels is a lifelong task.

Perhaps the most frequently used combination in physical education, dance, and drama is Divergent Discover/Command (H/A). This combination emphasizes the uniqueness of a production (routine, play, cheerleading sequence, marching band pattern, etc.) and the perfection of implementation. In physical performances, novel ideas (divergent production) are most often replicated in the Command style. This combination of teaching–learning styles can be inspiring, awesome, and breathtaking. It can represent outstanding moments in creativity.

Divergent Discovery/Command (H/A) can be a combination where the speed of producing alternative designs drives the experience, such as in competitive situations where a problem is presented to an individual or group of learners who must design, under the pressure of time, a desirable solution. Each group produces a divergent design that solves the problem. Before a response is produced, the group/individual produce multiple responses before selecting the desirable solution to construct within the time/equipment parameters. The time factor moves this experience; therefore it is under the canopy of the Command style and not the Practice style. The learners are not shifted time to practice; they are striving for a precision divergent response. This H/A combination expands the set of objectives that are being developed in just style H episodes.

This style could also be combined with the Inclusion style (H/E). The complexity of the task (the parameters, risk factor, use of equipment, etc.) would govern the levels of difficulty.

It may take time to learn to combine Divergent Discovery with other teaching–learning situations, but the results are worth it. It can be exhilarating to watch learners of any age discover and produce subject matter. Expanded learning opportunities are possible when teachers design new teaching–learning combinations that go beyond conventional boundaries.

Closure

The Divergent Discovery process creates a level of endurance that is self-motivated. Knowing that, there is still another way to keep the cognitive process kindled, one that leads to inquiry that in turn brings about discovery.

Divergent Discovery is an open-ended process in two avenues. First, the subject matter itself is open-ended because there is always the possibility of another solution, movement, way to pass the ball, or way to break through the opponent's defense. Thus, the subject matter becomes dynamic; it is constantly renewed. Second, the process of discovery is self-perpetuating. The act of finding a new solution validates the process of discovery. The joy of discovery is so powerful that the act of discovery itself becomes the reinforcing, motivating agent that propels the student to seek more solutions, alternatives, and ideas.

All previous styles on the Spectrum have the dimension of *finality*—finality in the subject matter content and in the learning process. The divergent production process proposes to develop greater independence in both cognition and in physical responses. This teaching–learning behavior is the first thus far on the Spectrum that actually promotes differences among the learners in their cognitive and physical dimensions.

The next landmark style shifts to the learners even more independence in cognitive and physical development.

CHAPTER 15

The Learner-Designed
Individual Program Style—I

(T)
→ *(L)*
→ *(L)*[1]

T he defining characteristic of the Learner-Designed Individual Program (I.P.) style is the independence to discover a structure that resolves an issue or problem. In the anatomy of the Learner-Designed I. P. style, the role of the teacher is to make general subject matter logistical decisions for the learners. The role of the learner is to make decisions about how to investigate the general subject matter topic: to produce questions that lead to a specific focus within the general topic, to produce the questions that result in identifying the process and procedures, to discover the solutions/movements, and to designate the performance criteria. When this behavior is achieved, the following objectives are reached in subject matter and in behavior:

The Objectives

Subject Matter Objectives	Behavior Objectives
To discover, create, and organize ideas on one's own	To accommodate individual differences in thinking and performance
To develop subject matter that deals with a complex issue over an extended period of time	To provide an opportunity for the learner to experience increased independence over a relatively long period of time
	To exercise perseverance and tenacity
To engage in a systematic process to explore and examine an issue	To provide opportunities for individuals to be self-directed
To set standards of performance and evaluation on one's own	

Learner-Designed I.P. style shifts more responsibility to the learners and represents another step beyond the discovery threshold. In the Guided Dis-

---

[1]This diagram represents the Learner-Designed Individual Program style.

covery style—F, the specific response at each step of the process was discovered by the learner, but the learner's responses depended on the careful sequence of stimuli (questions, clues) presented by the teacher. Convergent Discovery style—G called for greater independence on the part of the learner in the process of discovering the one correct answer. Dependency on the teacher (or surrogate source) decreased because the learner did not require a separate stimulus from the teacher at each step. The structure and the reality of convergent discovery still maintained a powerful bond between learners and the teacher, because the teacher designed the question or problem. In Divergent Production style—H, the teacher continued to make the decisions about the design of the specific problems, while each learner produced multiple solutions/movements/responses to the problem.

In the Learner-Designed I.P. style, the learner's independence becomes even more pronounced because the teacher designates only the subject matter area (a particular activity, sport, developmental attribute, game, or equipment restriction, such as skateboard, skiing, balance beam, etc.). Within that subject matter area, the learner discovers and designs the questions or problems *and* seeks the solutions. Unlike all previous styles/behaviors (A–H), the objectives of the Learner-Designed I.P. style, and the remaining styles, cannot be accomplished in one episode or one classroom period. A series of episodes over a period of time, including both reproductive and productive experiences, structured by the individual learners, are necessary to accomplish the objectives of the Learner-Designed I.P. style. In this style, learners begin designing episodic teaching–learning experiences that support their individual subject matter expectations. Since each learner in this teaching–learning experience is working toward his/her individual program, each is responsible for designing, sequencing, and linking the episodes.

It is imperative to understand that Learner-Designed I.P. is not an anything goes or a do whatever you want or do a project style. On the contrary, this behavior is a highly disciplined approach intended to evoke and develop the cognitive and creative capacities of the individual learner. It is a model for a systematic way to explore and examine an issue in order to discover its components, the relationships among the components, and a possible order or sequence for these components. The Learner-Designed I.P. style enables the learner to discover the structure of the issue at hand. The learner must know some facts, be able to identify categories, engage in analysis, and then construct a schema. It requires an integration of all the skills learned in all previous styles. Although the structure of Learner-Designed I.P. style requires a highly disciplined and focused approach, it does not exclude the possibility of spontaneous ideas and random discoveries. These can always be integrated into the remainder of the structure and placed in juxtaposition to appropriate ideas.

This behavior is most productive with students who have successfully experienced the decision responsibilities of the previous behaviors. It works well for the student who is ready for this expanded discovery, the one who has mastered the previous decisions and the processes. Without the background of the previous styles, students may face difficulties in organizing both the questions and the answers into a rational and workable structure. Learner-Designed I.P. style provides the learner with the opportunity to practice all previous skills and find ways of interrelating them over an extended period of time; consequently, this behavior requires time.

The Anatomy of the Learner-Designed Individual Program Style

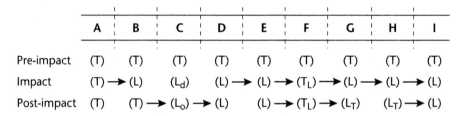

	A	B	C	D	E	F	G	H	I
Pre-impact	(T)	(T)	(T)	(T)	(T)	(T)	(T)	(T)	(T)
Impact	(T) → (L)	(L$_d$)	(L) →	(L) →	(T$_L$) →	(L) →	(L) →	(L)	
Post-impact	(T)	(T) → (L$_o$) →	(L)		(L) →	(T$_L$) →	(L$_T$)	(L$_T$) →	(L)

Figure 15.1. The shift from Divergent Discovery to Learner-Designed Individual Program

As was true in all previous behaviors, the Anatomy of the Learner-Designed I.P. Style calls for the teacher to make the decisions in the pre-impact set (Figure 15.1). The teacher's planning focuses on two decision categories: selecting the general subject-matter area and preparing the introduction for the new expectations (new degree of independence and subject matter involvement). In the impact set, the teacher delivers these two sets of expectations and is available to interact with the learners as they request. In the post-impact set, the teacher is available, listening, asking and answering questions, and offering feedback to the learner about their content involvement and decision-making process.

The learners' new role in the impact set is to make all the behavior and logistical decisions relative to their subject matter choices: selecting the topic focus, the questions and procedures for investigating and designing their individual program, deciding the evaluation criteria, and the process for keeping the teacher informed.

The learners' role in the post-impact set is to verify their solutions according to the criteria they designated, to make adjustments, to interact and communicate results to the teacher, and to assess the final experience.

The Implementation of Learner-Designed Individual Program Style

How to Implement the Learner-Designed I.P. Style

The Pre-Impact Set   Notice that the teacher continues to make the decisions in the pre-impact set with a focus on:

1. Making the decision to allocate time for some (or all) students to engage in this experience.

2. Making decisions about how to introduce this style's expectations and how to invite the learners to participate in a new degree of independence.

3. Making decisions about the general subject matter area within which the learner will evolve the questions and the answers. For example, the historical period to be investigated, the general area of literature (poetry; short story) or an activity in physical education (ball games, water environment, aerial apparatus, etc.), a general law or a cluster of laws in physics, or a general topic in teaching (a teaching unit).

The Impact Set   The events in the impact set are shown in Table 15.1.

Table 15.1   Events—Learner-Designed Individual Program Style

Episode Events		Feedback	Time
Set the scene	Optional.		
Behavior	The teacher:		
	1. Delivers the objectives of this episode: "To design, develop, and perform a series of tasks organized into a personal program."		
	2. Delivers the learner's role expectations.		
	3. Delivers the teacher's role expectations.		
Subject matter presentation	The teacher:		
	1. Presents the general subject matter area for the individual learner-designed individual program.		
Logistics	Logistical expectations:		
	1. The teacher establishes only the parameters necessary for this experience. Parameter decisions could apply to any or all of the following categories:		
	• material pick up and return • posture		
	• time • location		
	• interval • attire and appearance		

continues

Table 15.1 Events—Learner-Designed Individual Program *(continued)*

Episode Events		Feedback	Time
Questions for clarification	Verify understanding of expectations before action: "Are there any questions for clarification?"		
Action, task engagement, performance	The learners begin the process of engaging in the specific topic. A variety of individual approaches will be used by the learners as they begin to: • Identify a topic and the series of questions that will guide the investigation • Explore, experiment, examine alternatives • Design their personal programs • Practice their ideas • Make adjustments, begin new investigations, linkages, alternatives • Select the criteria for assessing the experience The teacher is available for the requests and questions of the learners: 1. To observe the learner's performance/solutions as they are developing 2. To observe the process being used by the learner 3. To offer answers only when directly asked by the learner 4. To alert the learner to any discrepancies between the stated intent and action		
Feedback	The learners are engaged in assessment: • Each time they verify their ideas or solutions against their own criteria • When they compile or record ideas or solutions • When they make adjustments • When they communicate these processes and procedures with the teacher The teacher listens, asks questions, and offers feedback to the learners with reference to the their planning, execution, and evaluation programs.		
Closure	The teacher acknowledges the learners' accomplishments in designing and producing individual programs.		

Successful and challenging experiences in Learner-Designed I.P. style give learners a feeling of accomplishment, pride, and self-worth. A eureka feeling generally delights learners when they realize they have endured and sustained the cognitive and emotional challenges of designing an individual program.

Subject Matter Considerations

Areas that deal with basic information and entry-level data are not conducive to this behavior. Most preliminary knowledge and elementary courses (in any subject area) are anchored in factual data and, therefore, require the use of the Command–Inclusion styles (A–E). Subject matter appropriate for this behavior needs to be complex enough to be manipulated and examined for new connections, links, and comparisons among its components. Although it is possible to design content for all age groups, learners who are inexperienced in both the content area and with the discovery process cannot participate productively in this behavior.

The Learner-Designed I.P. style can only be implemented effectively when time is allotted for a series of episodes. Learners need time to immerse themselves in the process of discovering, creating, and organizing ideas.

In this behavior the teacher must wait. This does not mean the teacher is passive, removed, or absent from the experience. Rather, it implies that the teacher does not impose comments or directions on students, nor capriciously or randomly give feedback. Questions, rather than statements, are the primary forms of communicating with the learner when the teacher observes discrepancies or has insights to share. Value (or corrective) feedback comments are appropriate once learners have made their own assessment. Theoretically, this behavior shifts the decisions to the learners who must communicate with the teacher about their process, product, and final design. Learners do not work in isolation, nor are they detached from the teacher. A communication bond is strong; a learner expectation is to keep the teacher informed. The teacher expectation is to observe how the learners are thinking and making decisions; the role of the teacher is to be a source of reassurance and guidance in the individual-design process.[2]

The Implications of the Learner-Designed Individual Program Style

If autonomy of the learner is, indeed, one of the goals of education, then the process of becoming an autonomous learner must be manifested in this teaching–learning process. Both the teacher and the learner need to know and accept this goal. Both must be engaged in the process of deliberately shifting decisions. Both must accept the consequences of learner autonomy.

---

[2]Refer to Chapter 18 for additional information on designing subject matter.

Style-Specific Comments

Complexity of the Content and the Time Allocation

As in previous styles, the content expectations for Learner-Designed I.P. style can be either simple or complex. As with any style, a gradual entry into the new expectations is more beneficial (cognitively, emotionally, and ethically) than abrupt immersion. Complex content expectations should be avoided in beginning episodes. All individual program designs are not time-consuming creative masterpieces. Some content topics can be confined to a short investigation with minimal time parameters. Each experience in this behavior must emphasize the degree of investigation, the attributes, and the Developmental Channels that the students are expected to assume. Students are more likely to develop the investigation skills, tenacity, and motivation needed to engage in this behavior when they know the expectations. When students do not have the prerequisite skills for a new style, sudden immersion has the tendency to paralyze them. Time is wasted, anxiety heightens, and cognitive frustration sets in when learners enter new experiences without the appropriate entry-level development. For certain styles, especially this behavior and the next (styles I and J), this preparation is more critical than for others.

Episodic Planning   Learner-Designed I.P. style requires learners to think, plan, and design in a variety of episodes representing an array of different teaching–learning styles. If they have not previously experienced such deliberately planned episodes in different teaching–learning styles, they will be inadequately prepared for this experience. There will be exceptions and some learners will perform giftedly. However, if the Practice style is the primary teaching–learning behavior to the learners, their investigation and final product in the Learner-Designed I.P. style will more closely resemble the expectations and objectives of the Practice style.

Only when teachers have provided deliberate and sustained opportunities for the learner to develop a variety of objectives and behaviors can they accurately assess individual learners in the context of educational objectives or behaviors.

Two Drawbacks of the Learner-Designed I.P. Style

Time   Perhaps the greatest liability of this experience is the time needed to communicate with, and to acknowledge, the individual program of each learner. Finding the time to give proper support and feedback to each student's product is a logistical issue that must be resolved.

Cognitive Differences and Assessment   The concern most frequently voiced by teachers and learners is, "How are the individual programs REALLY going to be assessed?" Theoretically, in the Learner-Designed I.P. style the individual students determine the criteria for assessment and evaluation. Perhaps at some point in the learning process, this set of feedback decisions can be totally shifted to the learners without any parameters from the teacher. However, in the beginning episodes, learners may need some parameters, some specific decision categories, and some logistical expectations to guide their assessment planning. Caution must be taken to prevent the feedback from reverting to the Practice style; this occurs when the teacher's feedback criteria are fixed and overly specific. Learning to shift and to trust learners' self-assessment decisions are new realities for both the teacher and the learners. Communication about each decision during the impact set is critical to the success of the overall experience (Figure 15.2).

The Learner-Designed Individual Program Style—I

The purpose of this style is for the learner to design, develop, and present a series of tasks that are organized into a personal program.

Role of the learner

- To select the topic that will be the focus of the study
- To identify questions and issues appropriate for the topic
- To organize the questions, to sequence the tasks, and to design a personal program—a course of action
- To collect data about the topic, to answer the questions, and organize the answers into a reasonable framework
- To verify the procedures and solutions based on criteria intrinsic to the subject matter at hand

Role of the teacher

- To select the general subject matter area from which the learners will select their topics
- To observe the learner's progress
- To listen to the learner's periodic presentation of questions and answers

---

Figure 15.2. Learner-Designed I.P. style classroom chart

The Developmental Channels

Design Variations

It is possible to emphasize the social Developmental Channels in this behavior. Although working with a partner or in groups alters the landmark objectives and implications, a social dimension provides additional attributes and adds new assets and liabilities to the experience. Although socialization in this behavior is worthwhile at times, it is important for learners to experience the responsibilities, content, and behavior complexity of designing an individual program.

All design variations in this behavior focus on the quantity of parameters established by the teacher. The more parameters, the more the experience reverts to Practice style. Establishing tight parameters in beginning episodes can reinforce the steps and sequence that are intrinsic to designing an individual program. However, moving the teaching–learning episode to a landmark experience requires that teachers relinquish the restrictions and also shift the decisions to the learners.

The next teaching style shifts even more decisions—resulting in more independence—to the learners. The Learner-Initiated style—J is the first style we encounter in which the learner is engaged in the pre-impact set of decisions.

CHAPTER 16

The Learner-Initiated Style—J

→ *(L)*
→ *( )*
→ *(L)*[1]

The defining characteristic of the Learner-Initiated style is the *learner's initiation* of, and responsibility for designing, the learning experience. In the anatomy of the Learner-Initiated style, the role of the learner is to independently initiate this behavior and make all the decisions in the pre-impact, including which teaching–learning behaviors will be used in the impact, and create the criteria decisions for the post-impact. Provided the teacher is qualified in the subject matter, the teacher's role is now to accept the learner's readiness to make maximum decisions in the learning experience, to be supportive, and to participate according to the learner's requests. When this behavior is achieved, the following objectives are reached in subject matter and in behavior:

The Objectives

Subject Matter Objectives	Behavior Objectives
To honor the individual who:	To honor the individual who:
• Chooses to initiate a learning experience to discover, create, and develop ideas in an area of his/her choice.	• Chooses to be independent.
	• Chooses to challenge him/herself by assuming the responsibilities for creating his/her learning experience.
• Chooses to initiate a multifaceted learning experience.	• Has a need to go beyond the boundaries of the activities presented to the rest of the class.

The primary objective of this behavior emphasizes honoring a learner's need to be independent.

---

[1]This diagram represents the anatomy of Learner-Initiated style.

The Anatomy of the Learner-Initiated Style

This style occurs only when an individual approaches the teacher (authority figure) and initiates a request to design his/her own learning experiences (Figure 16.1). The essence of this behavior's image is the learner's intent, not only to initiate, but also to assume the responsibilities, of the learning experience.

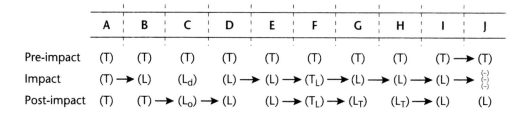

Figure 16.1. The shift from Learner-Designed I.P. style to Learner-Initiated style

The teacher and learner have traveled a long way since the Command style. In the Learner-Initiated style, we have reached the point where the individual learner is ready to make maximum decisions during teaching–learning episodes.

This behavior, although quite similar to the Learner-Designed I.P. style in its structure and proceedings, represents a significant change. It is the first time that the individual learner initiates the behavior itself. The individual learner recognizes his/her readiness to move on, to inquire, to discover, to design a program and perform it for self-development.

The learner comes to the teacher and states the willingness to conduct a series of episodes in this decision structure. The readiness and ability to initiate create a different reality for the learner and for the teacher—a reality in which the learner takes maximum responsibility for initiating and conducting the teaching–learning episodes.

The learner expresses the request to identify an area of investigation: to develop a plan of action, to identify issues and questions, to search for information, to construct knowledge, and to organize all these elements into a meaningful framework—to make all decisions within the anatomy.

The impact role of the teacher, which is quite subtle, is to accept the reality that the learner is, in fact, ready to make all the decisions in the ensuing series of episodes. The teacher, then, assumes the role of a stand-by resource—a guide or advisor who is available to the learner.

This does not mean the teacher is left dangling, not knowing what to expect, or when he/she will be summoned. Once the learner initiates this style, he/she is obligated to delineate the expectations. At a given point, the learner will specifically indicate when and how the teacher's involvement will be requested.

The teacher does have the obligation to initiate questions when discrepancies develop between the learner's intent and actions. The teacher can certainly acknowledge the learner's successful implementation of his/her plans, and can ask questions about perceived inconsistencies or discrepancies.

The Implementation of the Learner-Initiated Style

The intent of this teacher–learner relationship is to honor those individuals who have the ideas and motivation necessary to engage in independent and creative learning experiences. In this behavior the learners initiate; therefore, when teachers ask learners to "do a project" it cannot be construed to be an example of this style. Nor is this behavior one that permits a learner to "do whatever you want." The learners need to be aware that this teaching–learning option is available. The teacher can introduce its existence at a given point and a chart (Figure 16.2) can be posted so that learners can be reminded of this learning possibility.

This experience is appropriate for students who are well versed in the decisions and processes presented in the other behaviors. In addition to personal motivation and intellectual curiosity, this behavior requires emotional endurance to follow through with the plan, to grapple with and overcome obstacles, and to wait for the final product to emerge. This behavior takes a considerable amount of time; the series of episodes necessary for this experience may last for weeks or even longer.

How to Implement the Learner-Initiated Style

In this experience the learner will be working in a variety of teaching–learning episodes and each episode will include the decision sequence that follows.

The Pre-Impact Set   The learner's role in the preimpact set is as follows:

1. To initiate both general and specific sets of intentions—in subject matter and behavior.

2. To make decisions about the general subject matter area, the specific focus within the selected area, the questions to guide the investigation, and the detailed plan of study.

3. To select the teaching styles that will best accomplish the intents and plan of study.

4. To sequence the series of episodes.
5. To make the logistical decisions.
6. To make all the remaining pre-impact decisions.
7. To make the decision of how and when to use the teacher as a resource.

The teacher, for the first time on the Spectrum, is not involved in the pre-impact decisions. These planning decisions are shifted to the learner.

The Impact Set   The learner's role in this set is:

1. To make all the impact decisions in every episode. This includes implementing the decisions made in the pre-impact phase and decisions about how to involve the teacher. The learner thus decides in which style(s) the teacher will be invited to conduct an episode. For example, the learner can say to the teacher "Teach me the skill ___ using the Command style—A" or "I need to understand the particular concept of ___; teach me using the Guided Discovery style—F." The learner's independence to select the teaching style reflected in the schematic designation

$$(-)$$
$$(-)$$
$$(-)$$

in Figure 16.1. It shows that during the impact set (indicated by the outer parentheses) the learner can request from the teacher any style for a given episode (the inner brackets). It is clear that style J can be used to its fullest only when both the learner and the teacher are thoroughly familiar with the variety of decision-making skills.

2. To decide the duration of the impact phase and how it will be divided over the particular time into a series of learner-initiated episodes.

The teacher's role in the impact set is:

1. To accept the decisions initiated by the learner and to provide general conditions appropriate for the learner's plans.
2. To ascertain the broadest possible parameters for the learner's plans. If the plans call for activities and conditions that are beyond the capabilities—in terms of time, money, administrative, or judicial factors—the obvious conclusion is that this plan cannot currently be pursued.
3. To redirect the learner to other sources within or outside the school, if the teacher does not know the subject matter area in which the learner wants to work.
4. To comply with the requests of the learner.

The Post-Impact Set   The learner's role is:

1. To make all post-impact decisions concerning his/her performance in the selected subject matter. These evaluation decisions are made using the criteria previously selected by the learner.
2. To make post-impact decisions about his/her learning behavior.
3. To make the postimpact decisions about the attainment of the objectives of all the episodes—O–T–L–O.

   (Since the learner makes all the evaluation decisions in the post-impact phase, it is the learner who evaluates the O–T–L–O relationships. This means that when the learner invites the teacher to conduct episodes in particular styles, the teacher is subject to the evaluation done by the learner for these episodes.)

The teacher's role in the post-impact set is:

1. To receive and accept the decisions made by the learner.
2. To alert the learner to any discrepancies between the learner's intent and action.

Subject Matter Considerations

The teacher's involvement in the subject matter occurs only when the learner requests input. In this behavior, the teacher decides whether he/she is capable of supporting the learner's proposed subject matter learning experience. Because the learner initiates the content focus in this teaching–learning experience, no subject matter examples can be offered.

The Implications of the Learner-Initiated Style

Learners who can function in the Learner-Initiated style for a period of time must, by definition, have the ability to make many decisions about and for themselves along all the developmental channels. If we accept the notion that the Spectrum is cumulative, then a person who can function in the Learner-Initiated style demonstrates the ability to move along the Spectrum in both directions and to benefit from the contributions of all of the styles.

The Learner-Initiated Style

The purpose of this style is to provide the learner with the opportunity to initiate his/her learning experience.

Role of the learner

- To initiate the style
- To design the program for him/herself
- To perform it
- To evaluate it
- To decide how to involve the teacher

Role of the teacher

- To accept the learner's decision to initiate his/her own learning experience
- To provide the general conditions required for the learner's plan
- To accept the learner's procedures and products.
- To alert the learner to any discrepancies between intent and action

---

Figure 16.2. Learner-Initiated style classroom chart

Style-Specific Comments

Success in implementing this behavior hinges on the learner's ability to persevere. Getting sidetracked, expanding the investigation beyond desirable content or time parameters, or getting stuck are all possible obstacles for the learner.

Resisting the urge to offer direction or judgment is generally the teacher's primary challenge. Honoring the Learner-Initiated process can prove frustrating for the teacher who wants to make decisions for learners and give feedback. However, this behavior can be both exhilarating and humbling when teachers see what learners are able to initiate.

The Developmental Channels

Design Variations and Combining Styles

The most frequent design variation is the emphasis on the social channel. Two or more students may come to the teacher to initiate a joint learning experience. When this occurs, the teacher may need to ask clarification questions of the students about how they perceive their individual roles. Generally, when students initiate a Style J experience, they have already thought about their individual roles and contributions.

Style combinations are not relevant to this experience. Participation in the Learner-Designed I.P. and Learner-Initiated styles is structurally dependent on the learner's ability to make the decisions of the previous styles. The more the student has experienced the previous landmark teaching styles and combinations of styles, the better equipped the learner will be to use these same structures in his/her investigation.

The Self-Teaching style is the last landmark style on the Spectrum. Let's see how it differs from the Learner-Initiated style.

CHAPTER 17

The Self-Teaching Style—K[1]

$$\rightarrow (T)$$
$$\rightarrow (T)$$
$$\rightarrow (T)^2$$

Note: This teaching-learning style does not exist in the classroom.

The defining characteristic of the Self-Teaching style is individual tenacity and the desire to learn. In the anatomy of the Self-Teaching style, the individual participates in the roles of both teacher and learner and makes all the decisions—in the pre-impact, impact, and post-impact sets. When this behavior is achieved, the objectives that the individual has established in subject matter and in behavior are achieved. This behavior does not have a precise designated set of objectives: the individual selects objectives.

The internal logic of the Spectrum leads to the realization that it is, indeed, possible for a person to make all the decisions—in the anatomy—for him/herself. This behavior cannot be initiated or assigned by a teacher in the classroom, it does not exist in the classroom. However, it does exist in situations when an individual is engaged in teaching him/herself.

Who is the self-teaching individual? It could be any person who fathoms the intricacies of a complex hobby, an individual who is fascinated by and driven to know something, or the scientist who is propelled to understand the unknown. It could be the student, amateur or professional writer, architect, composer, painter, choreographer, sculptor, or explorer who is bold enough to push back boundaries, tenacious enough to endure obstacles, and romantic enough to march to a different drummer.

Leonardo da Vinci is a well-known example of an individual who lived most of his life anchored in the Self-Teaching style. Not all individuals who are involved in self-teaching are "da Vincis," but they do, in varying degrees,

[1]This chapter adapted from the forthcoming book on Spectrum Teaching by Sara Ashworth.

[2]This diagram represents the anatomy of the Self-Teaching style.

share the characteristics of curiosity, wonder, and the tenacity to endure a process of discovering.

The Anatomy of Self-Teaching Style

In this Self-Teaching style, all decisions in each of the three sets of decisions have been shifted from the teacher to the learner. In Figure 17.1, which shows the shift in decisions from Learner-Initiated to Self-Teaching, the self-teaching individual is still designated as L, the learner, since his/her teaching role is a function of the primary learning role.

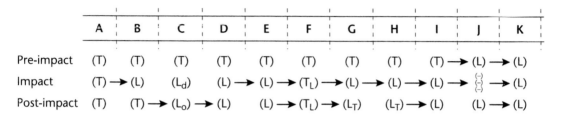

Figure 17.1. The shift from Learner-Initiated to Self-Teaching style

The interplay of roles usually occurs in the privacy of an individual's mind and experiences; it does not require an audience, an outside receiver, or appreciator. Feedback from outside sources occurs when the individual chooses to take his/her ideas to others; the individual chooses to shift from Self-Teaching to another decision relationship. There are many examples of independent thinkers who have had to endure criticism of their ideas by others. Some withstood the attacks, while others surrendered to the negative judgments. Still others reverted to the privacy of Self-Teaching.

The Implications of the Self-Teaching Style

The ability to engage in Self-Teaching may seem to be the ultimate in human development. Certainly, in education, it has been perceived at times as the apex of development, the stage where one becomes a truly free person. But our study of the Spectrum has led us to a somewhat different view of freedom in respect to educational goals. As we saw at the beginning of the Spectrum, when style A is used exclusively, there is a limit to the goals that can be met. With all its assets, the decision structure of the Command style represents only a portion of human behavior. Similarly, the Self-Teaching style, despite its assets, has limitations when it stands alone. A person who makes all of the decisions about everything all of the time may function well in Self-Teaching, but not be able to adapt to conditions that bring him/her into contact with other people, social mores, and traditions.

Thus the Self-Teaching style, like any of the styles on the Spectrum, represents only a portion of the human experience. Therefore, a unified theory of teaching must take into account the relationships among, and the integration of, all the styles. It is the full Spectrum of Teaching styles—not a particular style used in isolation—that will serve as a cornerstone for an expanded pedagogy. Such a pedagogy involves a different vision of human development: a vision of an independent person who can function in all of the styles' expectations and be mobile in both directions along the entire Spectrum.

CHAPTER 18

Designing Subject Matter[1]

This chapter has three objectives:

1. To examine some issues related to content and pedagogy
2. To summarize Mosston's first book, *Developmental Movement*[2]
3. To offer several approaches for designing subject matter

Teaching requires knowledge of both content and pedagogy. How the teacher selects, designs, and sequences classroom tasks demonstrates the teacher's ability to produce worthwhile learning experiences. During classroom implementation, pedagogy and content are inextricably connected.

Content and Pedagogy

This bond between content and pedagogy is frequently misunderstood. Research on classroom teaching–learning behaviors indicates that, although teachers believe they use a wide variety of alternative behaviors in the classroom, they are, in fact, significantly uniform in their teaching behavior. The decisions and objectives most frequently experienced by students are almost always aligned with those of the Practice style (Goldberger & Gerney, 1990). This uniformity of school experiences means that students are not exposed to the vast number of objectives that educators have identified as being critical to the learning process. The research indicates that this discrepancy may be caused by teachers' inability to accurately identify the pedagogical events in their classroom (Good & Brophy, 1997).

---

[1] This chapter is adapted from a forthcoming book on Spectrum Teaching by Sara Ashworth.

[2] In 1965, Muska Mosston wrote *Developmental Movement*, which presents an integrated concept of movements designed to achieve total physical development. Sections of this chapter are reproduced from *Developmental Movement* (1965), Charles E. Merrill Books, Inc. Columbus, Ohio.

This misunderstanding can be traced to three issues. First, teacher training programs generally present pedagogy and content in separate classes. Although many classes are titled "Methods of...," they focus primarily on content. Content classes focus on presenting and experiencing skills, safety issues, proper body position, sequence, common errors, rules, cues, common strategies, etc. Pedagogy classes present details and ideas about how to teach with minimal practice lessons or scant connection to content. Classes rarely emphasize the link between content and pedagogy and most lesson plans do not even request identification of a specific teaching behavior for the content. None seek an episodic design where content and pedagogy are sequenced and linked. When teaching behavior is addressed, the topic is general and applies to the entire agenda within the lesson, rather than to specific episodes. Many lesson plans require that overall objectives be stated, but none require pre-service teachers to identify the individual episodes (and their objectives) that contribute to the overall objectives of the lesson.

Current lesson plan designs reinforce and perpetuate the classroom research so that students experience only one teaching–learning behavior in classrooms. Many current pedagogical ideas are abstract, terminology is inconsistent, and examples are too often only theoretical. This results in lesson plans that do not focus on inextricable connections among O–T–L–O. The importance of constructing episodes within the lesson that incorporate different behaviors is not reinforced in undergraduate teacher training programs. A consequence of this approach is that teachers erroneously believe they use a variety of teaching behaviors when, in fact, they do not. When teachers identify one teaching–learning behavior and one set of objectives for each lesson, they are overlooking the reality that episodes occur in the classroom and that different teaching–learning experiences can be designed within a lesson. This lack of connection contributes to the misconceptions teachers have about alternative teaching behaviors.

Second, standards and curriculum ideas are designed to improve classroom teaching and learning experiences; however, they frequently pit ideas against each other and often promote a particular content focus for physical education classes. Standards often change as the ideas and content that are in the spotlight shift. Over the last several decades, this shift in content focus has moved from: fitness vs. games; sports vs. recreation; skills vs. play; traditional (such as gymnastics, etc.) vs. new activities (skateboard, etc.), lifelong skills vs. motor skills, etc. At times elective programs were recommended—weight training, outdoor experiences, cooperative games, international games, outdoor adventure, obstacle courses. At other times, themes or units were encouraged: circus arts, bowling, throwing, catching, and striking skills, manipulative skills, teamwork activities. Some programs never strayed from the standards that promoted the sports/activity model, such as basketball, football, volleyball, soccer, etc., while others tried to incorporate all standards by providing eclectic experiences.

This versus approach to standards and curriculum is confusing and restrictive. The line between pedagogy and content was often blurred by the new content focus as a new way to teach. Teachers often say, "I teach differently this year," when in fact they mean, "I teach different content this year."

Physical education is so rich in its content options and opportunities that it is counterproductive to support one focus over all others. Although standards are important for establishing boundaries and expectations for professional quality, they must accurately embrace the essence of physical education. The content in all programs should be held accountable for demonstrating physical developmental opportunities. Selecting a few valid content standards, which significantly establish the worthwhile contributions of physical education to individuals and ultimately to the society, is the strongest rationale for recommending physical education experiences.

Standards, including the current National Association for Sport and Physical Education's (NASPE) standards, aim to influence classroom activities by suggesting criteria that guide what is emphasized in physical education classes. Curriculum texts frequently provide content ideas (actual lesson plans) that teachers replicate in the classroom. These standards and curriculum texts, like teacher training programs, often blur the distinction between pedagogy and content. Although standards and curriculum ideas attempt to be neutral about content focus or teaching approaches, they do concurrently identify guidelines, goals, and examples that focus on two dimensions: subject matter considerations (content) and the manner in which the teacher and learners are to interact (pedagogy/teaching–learning approach). Seldom do these standards and curriculum ideas differentiate these two distinct categories. Therefore, teachers are left to interpret these standards from their own perspectives, using knowledge they have about content and teaching and learning.

For example, NASPE content guidelines (the subject matter in physical education), do not suggest that each student must demonstrate competence in basketball, or gymnastics, or archery, etc., but rather they state that each learner should experience and be competent in the qualities that comprise physical movement. Specifically,

> identify fundamental movement patterns; use basic offensive and defensive strategies in noncomplex settings; or apply advanced movement-specific information (NASPE, 1995).

Such guidelines require teachers to understand the fundamentals (the universal attributes[3]) of physical education apart from the elements that comprise any specific sport or activity.

Other NASPE standards delineate how the teacher and learner are to interact. Although the term "alternative teaching–learning behavior" is not used, the standards can only be accomplished when teachers vary their teaching–learning behaviors. These guidelines/objectives are not intrinsic to the content knowledge of physical education, rather they are intrinsic to pedagogy. For example, the objectives—"work cooperatively and productively with a partner or small group, try new movements, associate positive feeling with participation, produce interpretations, know scientific principles, demonstrate independent learning"—can only be accomplished when teachers consciously employ a variety of teaching styles—from Command to Discovery (NASPE, 1995).

Without both conceptual and practical pedagogical knowledge, teachers interpret standards according to their personal viewpoints of teaching. Consequently, establishing and issuing standards does not change the fundamental manner in which teachers teach; it only affects the emphasis of the lesson or procedures. Thus, as the classroom research indicates, the majority of teachers have a uniform teaching approach.

The structure of pedagogy—the fact that decisions create alternative teaching–learning options with different objectives in subject matter and behavior—is not well understood. When teachers are skilled in pedagogical knowledge, standards become less threatening and more useful. Standards are not new expectations imposed on the teaching–learning process; rather standards represent elements that have been isolated for shifting social or professional reasons. Teachers who are competent in a comprehensive pedagogical structure, which embraces alternatives from Command to Discovery, will be well equipped to handle any of the pedagogical standards, rules, and regulations that may be emphasized during their teaching careers.

Third, although most curriculum textbooks offer a section delineating alternative teaching approaches, the numerous lesson content examples provided represent only one primary teaching–learning behavior. The language used to describe the tasks (how the learners are to perform in the task) reflects expectations more aligned to the Practice style than any other behavior. The examples do offer teachers a variety and sequence of tasks that can be used in the classroom; however, alternative teaching styles are not used or described. Consequently, the link and the distinction between content design and alternative teaching–learning behaviors remain unclear.

---

[3]See later section on Mosston's *Developmental Movement*.

The following examples are comparable to those included in most curriculum texts—they all intrinsically reinforce behavior expectations that are similar to the Practice style:

Walk on the equipment without falling off; now walk backwards; now sideways.

Play a half-court game.

Conduct a skills competition (i.e., free throw).

With a partner, volley the ball in the areas indicated.

Practice tossing and catching the ball yourself. Then volley against the wall.

Books are filled with hundreds of task examples, like the ones above, that inherently trigger the decisions of the same teaching style—Practice style—B.[4] The design of these curriculum tasks always imply, or directly state, that the teacher delivers the tasks, the order, sets the time for practice, gives feedback, and expects the learners to follow the directions and immediately perform. The learners move from one task to the next as the teacher delivers the directives.[5]

In the previously stated examples, learners are dependent on the teacher for each task and the emphasis of these tasks for the learners is to follow the directions of the teacher. All behavior expectations reinforce one primary teaching–learning relationship and set of objectives. In the future, classroom teaching practices will be influenced by textbook curriculum examples that make a distinction between content and pedagogical options.

Before presenting different approaches that make a distinction between content and pedagogy, it is necessary to recognize the contribution of Muska Mosston's first book, *Developmental Movement*.[6] In this book Mosston describes a framework designed to use an integrated concept of movement to achieve physical development.

---

[4]Generally these examples do not reinforce the landmark Practice style.

[5]Indeed, for preschool, primary age, or special needs children this behavior may be necessary. However, even these children can experience alternative teaching–learning behaviors. They can even successfully participate in behaviors that do not require the teacher to be the source for each task. Very young children can make the decisions along the Spectrum. Initially, they need minimal directions, clear tasks, coaching, and lots of immediate feedback to reinforce the new behaviors. The youngest children to ever travel along the Spectrum from Command to Discovery were three-year-olds.

[6]In 1965, Muska Mosston wrote *Developmental Movement*, which presents an integrated concept of movements designed to achieve total physical development. Sections of this chapter are reproduced from *Developmental Movement* (1965), Charles E. Merrill Books, Inc. Columbus, Ohio.

Mosston's Developmental Movement Concept

The focal points of this concept are:

1. That all physical experiences rely on shared physical attributes (agility, balance, flexibility, strength, endurance, accuracy, etc.)
2. That these attributes can be developed.

These points are governed by:

1. The universal principles of physiology and kinesiology
2. The concept of degree of difficulty (which is the foundation of the Inclusion style—E.)[7]

Mosston merged the concept's focal points with the governing (universal) principles to create developmental movement.

Mosston observed, in the early 1960s, that redundancy of content, isolation of skills, rule-oriented experiences, exclusion of participants, etc., resulted when activity units were the primary approach for lessons in physical education gymnasiums. In contrast, he observed that lessons that incorporated the concepts of physical attributes and degree of difficulty created:

- A broad, yet connected, view of the intrinsic content within physical education
- A link among different activities because of the common variables
- A developmental skills carryover effect from one content area to another
- A common movement approach that reinforced all activities/sports
- An inclusion experience for the participants.

The primary focus in *Developmental Movement* is total physical development. This does not mean that each learner will be maximally physically fit but that individuals will have opportunities to develop from the broadest perspective of physical development. Before teachers can design subject matter using the concepts in *Developmental Movement*, they must understand the point of view from which Mosston developed his ideas.

Developing a Point of View[8]

Human Movement Categorized Throughout the history of physical education, various *values* have been attached to human movements. Mosston

---

[7] Refer to the Inclusion style for clarification of this principle.

[8] Some portions of this section are reproduced verbatim, while other are adapted from Mosston's 1965 book.

observed that the values placed on movement fell into three distinct categories: *assigned, functional,* and *intrinsic* value.

Assigned Value

Assigned value belongs to movement experiences that are judged by standards of "beauty" and "good form." The assigned value belongs to the domain of the dancers and choreographers who attribute a feeling, an idea, or a mood to a performed movement. These values are determined (assigned) by the decisions and imagination of individual dancers and by the culture of a given society (as in interpretation of social or folk dancing). Other examples of assigned value are the competitive gymnast, ice skater, or diver who adhere to an assigned code of "beauty" and "good form" determined by their restricted group. (Pointed toes in performance becomes almost second nature to gymnasts, classical ballet dancers, and divers.) The performance is judged not only by the detailed accuracy of the movement but also the "beauty" or "good form" ascribed to the execution. Assigned movements are valued for their elegant replication of the standard.

Functional Value

The functional value belongs to movements that are under the jurisdiction of the rules. This value belongs to the domain of the coach. The player, coach, and game are under the jurisdiction of a set of strict rules and a specific measurable purpose/outcome. The rules and purpose determine the value (efficacy) of a given movement. Although certain details in the movements must be adhered to, "beauty" and "good form" do not determine the value of the movement action. Track and field events, basketball, volleyball, soccer, skate- or snowboard competition, dirt-buggy races, etc. are all governed by the rules of the activity and are not subject to subjective (assigned) standards. Functional movements are valued for satisfying or accomplishing the outcome.

Intrinsic Value

The intrinsic value belongs to movements that are intentionally designed for physical development. Examples of the intrinsic value are consonant with a developmental concept that movement contributes to the intentional development of physical attributes such as strength, agility, balance, flexibility, accuracy, etc. These values are designated as intrinsic since they are not related to a culture, individual mood or personality, or to a limited set of rules that determine what is performed. A set of push-ups will help develop the shoulder girdle and arms of an American fifth grader or a French adult, a basketball player, or a swimmer. Rope skipping with high knee raising will promote the agility of any individual who does it. Intrinsic movements are valued for their developmental contributions.

The Developmental Concept

Intrinsic value movements are universal because they rely on the principles of physiology and kinesiology. This developmental concept treats content in a step-by-step progression that helps learners internalize the developmental nature of their activities. A jump can be viewed in many ways. It can be a competitive movement (high jump) which sooner or later excludes the less skilled student and the beginner, and becomes the mark of the topnotch competitive athlete. Or the jump can be recreational, as it is in various games or in random play. Both of these jumps represent the functional value. In the developmental concept, the jump is treated as a tool for gradual and intentional development. There are simple jumps and more complicated ones, easy and more difficult leaps. Through presentation of the variety of jumps, learners develop agility and strength in a systematic way. The students will be able to identify specific objectives they can attain on their individual levels. It is not proposed that this developmental subject matter replace the traditional sports, fitness, recreational, games, etc. approaches. On the contrary, these activities must be combined with games for the all-around development of individuals. Like the Spectrum of Teaching styles, this developmental concept embraces a non-versus framework.

The structure of the developmental concept is presented in the Inclusion style—E (Chapter 10). It proposes that the problem confronting teachers is whether they can present individual students, each starting from his/her initial level of achievement, with materials arranged so that each step represents a success.[9] Using the concept of degree of difficulty ($X+a$, $X+b$, $X+c$) requires knowledge of factor analysis, anatomy and physiology, and an appreciation for the inclusion principles presented in Chapter 10. Incorporating the developmental concept in episodes within lessons ensures participation (inclusion). When learners are excluded, because tasks are designed at developmental levels that are either too difficult or not difficult enough, acquisition of skill and the learner's physical development are delayed.

Participation in movement is fundamental to physical development. Recently attention has been given to providing a fair and equitable education to students who have disabilities. These curriculum programs promote special content materials and special teaching methods for students with disabilities. When these programs isolate groups of students and offer special teaching methodologies for each group, they do a disservice to education, to teachers, to students, and to parents. Although additional and specific information, content, and procedural adjustments are necessary when working with many special groups, the comprehensive structure of peda-

---

[9] For a discussion on success and motivation in learning, see Jerome S. Bruner, *The Process of Education* (New York: Random House, 1960).

gogy applies to all teaching and learning situations. Teaching–learning behaviors are universal; there are not unique teaching methodologies for each special group of students or adults.

Designing worthwhile curricula for students with disabilities relies on the teacher's knowledge about the limitations of the specific disability and about the universal principles in physical movement, the factor analysis, the inclusion (developmental) concept, and a comprehensive approach to teaching and learning, with all its variations from Command to Discovery. All students, regardless of their circumstances, deserve movement experiences and a variety of decision-making experiences within their physical and mental capabilities.

Three-Dimensional View of Movement Classification

Mosston's conception of a universal structure of movement includes three dimensions of movement classifications. One dimension is the matrix of *physical attributes* (strength, agility, flexibility, balance, rhythm, endurance, accuracy, etc.).

The second dimension is the *anatomical divisions* of the body. It focuses on the part of the body or regions that are being developed by a given movement (the shoulder girdle, the lower leg, et.).

The third dimension is the *kind of movement* used to develop the desired attributes in a particular part (or region) of the body (bending, leaping, turning, throwing, etc.). (See Figure 18.1.)

The relationship of the three dimensions is inherent in the very nature of movement. Obviously, every movement involves a part of the body or the whole body. Repetition of the movement due to life needs or performance aspiration results in the development of some particular physical attribute, from the finger dexterity of a violinist to the combination of qualities required for a ski jumper.

Any movement can be analyzed and classified in this three-dimensional view of movement. This awareness can help the teacher, coach, and student select the movement or series of movements to accomplish a stated objective. "He needs more strength in his leg to improve his take-off"; "she needs to improve her coordination in order to be more graceful"; "his inflexible pelvic region curtails the accuracy of the dive." Movements can be designed to overcome deficiencies. Rather than designing lessons that focus on a specific list of sports skills, the developmental concept allows teachers to insert episodes within the lesson in motor learning that can enhance all performance.

Let us examine the three-dimensional diagram. Let point X represent a one-foot-high hop (Figure 18.1). The anatomy involved is the leg; the kind of movement is a hop or jump; this relates to the development of strength (in the leg). Suppose point X represents alternate arm swings and circles. The diagram shows the relationships of the shoulder, the swing, and the development of flexibility (at the shoulder joint).

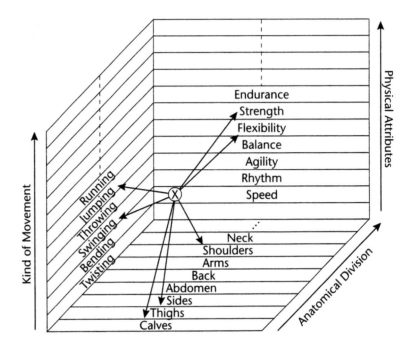

Figure 18.1. Three-dimensional view of movement classification

A child can understand the questions: "How fast can you run?" "Are you strong enough to pull this rope?" "Can you stand on your head?" The child does not need to think, "Now I am developing strength in my abdomen by raising my leg high during the climb." He just enjoys the presence of strength and agility by accomplishing his objective. However, the teacher must be aware of the contribution of the movement to this particular child's development, its place on the degree of difficulty scale for the child, and its role in the child's growth pattern.

Mosston's three-dimensional model classifies movement for developmental purposes—the intentional development of physical attributes that would otherwise remain undeveloped or, at best, be left to chance. In *Developmental Movement* Mosston presents the physical attributes of agility, balance, flexibility, strength, and endurance. He treats rhythm as an integral and necessary part of all movements in any attribute development. He then offers four approaches for the performance of these movements:

1. Movement designed for the individual student using the body as an instrument
2. Use of simple (inexpensive) apparatus
3. Use of a partner
4. Related simple games

His designs focus on the one excellent apparatus that we all possess—the human body.[10]

Recognizing the developmental concept will aid teachers in preparing a program of instruction that takes the following steps:

Step 1   Determine objectives, based on the knowledge of the students' needs.

Step 2   Determine each student's present level of performance in a specific physical attribute, through observation, trial and error, or by taking measurements. This step can be done by the students themselves once they learn the concept of development.

Step 3   Select the movements which are intended to develop the attribute.

Step 4   Program the movements for the class, the smaller group, or the individual.

The three-dimensional view of movement can be used to achieve developmental success, to increase participation, and to provide challenging opportunities in all three dimensions. Teachers can use the three-dimensional model to guide content selection so all anatomical divisions, kinds of movement, and physical attributes are experienced. Regardless of the focus of the physical education program (fitness, games, sports, etc.) the three-dimensional model can be applied as a guide for content selection. This model can also help teachers assess the developmental opportunities of specific programs.

Designing Subject Matter

Any approach for designing subject matter must consider the first two objectives of this chapter: Lessons designed for the public school gymnasiums/classrooms must make distinctions between content and pedagogy and

---

[10]Mosston was very knowledgeable in the history of physical education. In *Developmental Movement* he presented "A Short Historical Survey of Movement Classifications" (pp. 10–13). While studying the history of physical education he discovered that different kinds of systems were emphasized by a German, Guts Muths (1759–1839), a Swede, Pier Henrik Ling (1776–1839), and by two Danes, Johannes Lindhart (1870–1927) and Niels Bukh (1880–1950). This knowledge led to the integrated concept of developmental movement.

they must offer episodes that support the intrinsic value of movement—the developmental concept. Physical education gymnasiums must be places where learners physically develop in the attributes, in the anatomical divisions, and in the various kinds of movements while they are experiencing fitness, sports, games, outdoor experiences, themes, etc.

Teachers who are knowledgeable in pedagogy and the universal attributes approach physical movement experiences from a learning perspective. They focus on the specific skills of the activity or sport from a developmental perspective. This means that, while teachers are introducing specific skills or activities, they are also able to assess the learners' physical developmental needs. Rather than the task becoming the end-all final product, developing the learner's ability to acquire the skills becomes a priority. When skills are not reached within minimal episodes, the teacher can make adjustments to accommodate the learners' developmental needs by using the concepts within Mosston's 3-D model. The 3-D model provides teachers with knowledge and options that can lead learners to more active, rather than passive, learning experiences.

Although there are many approaches for designing subject matter, all eventually must answer similar questions. The first example for designing subject matter uses the lesson plan as the guide to determine the content tasks.

Independent of the manner in which content is designed, there are broad questions that must be addressed before approaching individual lesson plans. These issues are:

1. Overall curricular selection (sports, games, fitness, outdoor experiences, recreation, etc.)
2. Overall objectives for the learners in the physical education program
3. Others

The answers to these questions may be determined by school policy, social influences, professional guidelines, teacher or learner choice, etc. It is not the intent in this chapter to discuss these broad issues; rather the focus is the actual design of the classroom lesson plan.

Independent of specific curriculum decisions, all subject matter designs must consider the categories in the continuous flow of the lesson plan (presented in Chapter 11). Once the subject matter is selected, the relationship among objectives, specific task, teaching–learning behavior, logistics, and parameters must be identified.

Questions can be asked within each category. (The following are only samples of the many questions that can be asked in each category.)

Task selection—objectives:

1. The overall objective for the selected subject matter?
2. Which overall value (assigned, functional, intrinsic) is the content focus?
3. Others?

Specific task:

1. Select or identify the specific topics within the subject matter (the rubrics).[11]
2. Identify the sequence for the topics.
3. Others?

Teaching style

1. Does the task have a model that is to be replicated, copied, imitated?

   If so, what do the learners need, per topic, for successful participation in reproducing the model? (Immediate stimulus-response practice, individual and private practice, 1:1 immediate feedback; self-check, inclusion practice with a range of entry levels or do they need a design variation or combination of the previous mentioned behaviors)?

2. Can the task use a discovery process?

   If so, what do the learners need for successful participation in discovery? (guided questions, convergent question, divergent question, individual program)?

3. Others?

Logistics and parameters

1. What materials and procedures are needed to accommodate the selected task and teaching style?
2. What time and interval materials are necessary for each topic?
3. What safety issues must be considered for each topic?
4. Others?

Let's plan a lesson.

Task selection: fencing[12]

Objectives:

1. The overall objective for the selected subject matter?

   To develop the skills to participate in mini-game experiences

---

[11]The rubrics represent the teacher's knowledge about the specific topic.

[12]This content information was contributed by Dr. Phil Gerney of Newtown, PA.

2. Which overall value (assigned, functional, intrinsic) is the content focus?
   Assigned
3. Other?

To recall information about the sport's history, recall meaning and position of fencing terms, and to be able to participate in a minimatch game.

Specific task:

Select or identify the specific topics within the subject matter (the rubrics).[13] (The more inexperienced the teacher the more detailed this listing needs to be. This section literally lists the details of the content: the terms, the positions, the individual parts that lead to the ultimate goals in the content. When information is omitted in this section, it demonstrates gaps in the teacher's content knowledge.)

- History and facts about the sport
- Video of a match
- Terms:

Equipment	Fencing Vocabulary	
Foil	- grip	position one (ballet)
Epee	- on guard	salute (in two counts)
Saber	- advance	retreat
Mask	- lunge	recovery of the lunge
Gloves	- target area	parries two
Jacket: half & full, plastron	- balestra	reposte
Fencing strip	- touch	right of way
	- pass	remise

- Safety issues and procedures
- Strategies:
simple attacks	compound attacks
straight thrust	the beat
disengage—under the blade	the press
cut over or coupe—over the blade	the glide
- Practice basic skills (with and without weapons)
- Bouts

At this point, information about sequence, teaching style per episode, and logistics and parameters can be placed directly into the daily lesson plan.

Special comment about the primary teaching style: This subject matter relies on the replication of the model; therefore, each movement in this beginning introduction is to be replicated, copied, imitated. Only the repro-

---

[13] The rubrics represent the teacher's knowledge about the specific topic.

duction teaching styles are used. Once the details are identified, the time estimations are included.

Designing a lesson plan for the introduction to fencing techniques.*

Sequence of Episodes	Objective Purpose	Subject Matter Content	Teaching–learning Behavior	Logistics and Parameters	Time (min)
1.	Gain attention; enjoyment	Short video—demo from a popular action movie. Ask divergent recall question: "Recall what you think you know about fencing." (Record comments, without offering feedback. Use this data later to confirm, clarify, or to correct what they think they know.)	Canopy of the Practice style—B Watch video	- video equipment - movie—ready at the point to be shown - identify space for all learners to sit and be able to see the video screen	2
2.	Safety Deliver new content	Intro safety issues. The teacher delivers important safety expectations—issues and procedures. Ask review questions at the end.	Canopy of Practice style—B Listen for info Recalls safety points	Design poster with images of key safety procedures—examples and nonexamples	5
3.	Present new content	Present historical facts. The teacher presents a timeline (with pictures) of the history of fencing, (include combat, dueling—as a badge of honor, entertainment in movies, etc.). If any of the learners, comments refer to history, confirm, clarify, or correct their ideas.	Canopy of the Practice style—B	Design timeline chart Provide some key pictures illustrating historical settings and styles of fencing.	10
4.	Provide example of a real match Deliver terminology Name equipment	Show a video of a professional match—lead into terminology—equipment and vocabulary. Use a show and stop technique to deliver and clarify terms and to reinforce the objective of the game. Ask the learners to focus on the terms (movements) because they will practice them in the next episode.	Canopy of Practice style	- Select video and have ready at the point to show. - Make vocabulary cards of key terms (those constantly repeated). - Have equipment organized and ready to show.	10

continues

Sequence of Episodes	Purpose	Subject Matter Content	Teaching–learning Behavior	Logistics and Parameters	Time (min)
5.		Practice, without weapons, the terms identified in episode #4	Reciprocal style—C		20
			Each student will be a doer and an observer. Let the learners know that in the next episode they will be asked to recall from memory the positions of the vocabulary term.		
		Design a task sheet with drawings that illustrate the vocabulary terms. Learners will review and practice content, following teacher-made criteria.			
6.	Application and recall of content	Review the terms	Command style—A	Identify:	7
		All learners will assume a stance indicated by the teacher and on the cue (command word determined by the teacher), the students will immediately assume the position of the fencing term. In this episode the teacher will reinforce or correct posture. Each position will be practiced several times leading the learners to reproduce the position immediately and accurately.	Immediate recall of the movement position when the name is called	- *stance* - *cue* word - order of the positions Have word cards available for use as needed	
7.	Closure	Provide feedback about the lessons expectations.			2

* The content for this lesson design was contributed by Dr. Phil Gerney of Newtown, PA.

In the beginning, content topics must be scrutinized and constantly revised to be sure the sequential flow from one task to the next is logical, safe, and eventually leads to the desired content objective.

Another approach for designing subject matter focuses on identifying the variety of alternative teaching–learning behaviors that could be used for a content. In this approach, teachers must be aware of the characteristics of each behavior on the Spectrum and be able to adjust content expectations to correspond with the different decision expectations. Generally content is not confined to one teaching style. It can be adapted and delivered in a variety of teaching–learning styles. However, the teacher's decision about the focus of the content does reinforce a set of characteristics that highlight one side of the Spectrum rather than the other—reproduction or production (see Figure 18.2). The teacher's intention to implement specific objectives determines the specific teaching–learning experience.

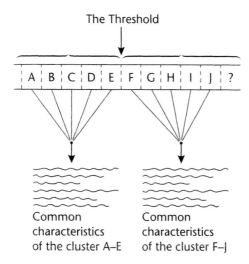

Figure 18.2. The non-versus reality

The teaching–learning behaviors in each cluster share common characteristics (or general objectives) that are the hallmark of the particular cluster. Figure 18.3 presents some of these characteristics. The greater the teacher's awareness of these characteristics, the easier it becomes to determine the cluster of teaching styles that is best suited for designing the subject matter. The Spectrum supports a non-versus approach in classroom teaching where deliberate mobility ability along the Spectrum is a daily occurrence.

Common Characteristics Objectives of Styles A–E	Common Characteristics Objectives of Styles F–J
1. Reproduction of knowledge and skills known to the teacher and/or the learner.	1. Production of knowledge and skills new to the learner and/or the teacher.
2. The subject matter is concrete, mainly containing facts, rules, and specific skills. (Basic knowledge, fixed knowledge).	2. The subject matter is variable, mainly consisting of concepts, strategies, and principles.
3. There is a correct image (either convergent or divergent path) to perform the task—by emulation of the presented model.	3. Alternatives in design and performance are called for. There is no single model to emulate.
4. Time is needed for practicing and learning to adhere to the model.	4. Time is needed for the cognitive processes involved.
5. Memory and recall are the main cognitive operations.	5. Time is needed to evolve an affective class climate conducive to producing and accepting alternatives and options.

Common Characteristics Objectives of Styles A–E	Common Characteristics Objectives of Styles F–J
6. Feedback is specific and refers to the performance of the task and its adherence to the model.	6. The cognitive operations engaged are comparing, contrasting, categorizing, problem solving, and inventing.
7. Individual differences are accepted only within the learner's physical and emotional boundaries.	7. Discovery and creativity are manifested through these cognitive operations.
8. The class climate (the spirit of the learning environment) is one of performing the model, repetition, and reduction of errors.	8. Discovery by the learner is developed through convergent and divergent processes or a combination of both.
	9. Feedback refers to producing alternatives, not a single solution. Individual differences in the quantity, rate, and kind of production are essential to maintaining and continuing these styles.
	10. The class climate (the spirit of the learning environment) is one of searching, examining the validity of alternatives, and going beyond the known.

Figure 18.3. Characteristics of the clusters of teaching styles

Using the ideas of the clusters, let's identify a content and see how it could be used in a variety of teaching–learning styles. The following content example was found on the Sportime, *pe-talk*® discussion group (www.sportime.com) and was offered as a rainy day or out-of-the–gym day fun task. It was stated in the Web site that the task—sports and clues— expands Sue Friener's ideas, which appeared in an article in *Great Activities*. The question here is: To which teaching–learning behaviors could this content be adapted? The task includes a list of clues and a list of sport names. The learner's task is to match the specific sport with the clue. For examples, the sport clues are:

I have a key in my name.
A structure that you could walk under is in my name.
Something you wear on your feet is in my name (but spelled differently).
A noisy insect is the name of my sport.
I am a vegetable.
I'm 3 sports in one. All require you to endure while racing, like a person made of "iron."
Etc.

List of Sports

Triathalon
Surfing
Cricket
Squash
Steeplechase
Hockey
etc...

Now, this task could be designed for a variety of teaching–learning behaviors, starting with the familiar behavior in which the teacher reads the clues and the learners raise their hands to answer the questions. However, neither a shift of decisions, nor individual active participation, nor involvement in the attributes along the developmental channels are emphasized.

It is also possible to place the learners in groups while the teacher reads the clues; however, that behavior arrangement shifts neither decisions nor content involvement. Each of these behaviors represents a canopy of the Practice style—B. Let's identify some possibilities.

Landmark Practice Style—B   It is possible for learners to match the list of clues and sport names on a task sheet individually and privately. The teacher would circulate and offer feedback. But since the overall task expectation is to have fun, this design is not particularly desirable.

Landmark Reciprocal Style—C   Because of the quantity of clues and sport names offered on the Web site, it clearly is possible to design two task sheets, one with clues designed for doer 1, and a different set of clues for doer 2. Separate criteria sheets could be made with the correct answers. This task design actively involves all learners in all content, while reinforcing social interaction.

Landmark Self-Check Style—D   The learners could be asked to individually and privately practice the task using an answer sheet to check their performance. Although each learner has high active time-on-task, individual practice of this task in a classroom setting limits the number of attributes and Developmental Channels the learners could experience.

This style and content could also be presented as a bulletin board display. Individual clues on cards with the answers on the back could be randomly placed on a bulletin board. Learners could check their knowledge when they have free time, or when entering or exiting the gymnasium. In this situation the content becomes an interval activity (in the Self-Check style) rather than the primary classroom task.

Landmark Inclusion Style—E Because some of the clues are more obviously identify the sport name than others (my name has a key in it—hockey), it is possible to arrange the clues according to degree of difficulty. The factor determining difficulty would be how obvious to make the hint. The range could be from obvious hints to clues that make only general associations. The learners could work individually and check their answers against a prepared criteria sheet.

Canopy of the Command Style—A Several arrangements could be designed using this behavior and content. Speed-on-cue responding is the essence of design in the Command style. Clues could be given and several competing learners or groups of learners could respond. Two points could be awarded to the individual or group who responded first and one point could be given to all other groups who had the correct answer (this point procedure includes more learners while acknowledging the one who recalls the quickest).

Landmark Divergent Production Style—H This task could seek divergent discovery. The learners could to be invited to produce additional clues that name sports. A variety of parameters could be given to guide their production, such as to identify clues related to elementary school children and the sports and games they play. Or they could be given the parameter to design clues for the activities they play at their school. They could even be asked to design clues that have a range in difficulty and correspond to the Inclusion style concept.

The learners' expectations for this subject matter task can be designed to relate to a variety of landmark and canopy teaching–learning behaviors.

The next approach focuses on the 3-D model and the infusion of the intrinsic value of movement when designing subject matter. Awareness of total physical development and tasks designed to support the specific sport/activity are the hallmark of this approach.

Specific movements define each sport/activity. Baseball players are fundamentally aware of batting, throwing, catching, fielding, pitching, and sliding movements. They know a variety of techniques in each of these movement categories, and they spend time primarily practicing and playing the game according to the functional value of movement. This third approach to designing subject matter invites the teacher to view movements associated with the functional or assigned value with the 3-D model to increase the learner's total physical development. This approach compliments the development of specific skills for any sport or activity.

Identifying skills within a sport or activity according to their physical attributes can reveal which parts of the body are overused and which are underused. The 3-D model can be used to design skills that compliment the anatomical or "kind" of movement that are needed for development in the specific sport or activity.

Three different task sheet forms are provided. Each supports a different teaching style—the Practice, Inclusion, and the Divergent Production styles. Most sports/activities that are viewed for their functional value will use the Practice style—B and the Inclusion style—E 3-D task sheets. The Divergent Production task sheet is more appropriate for students who are designing intrinsic value movements. These designs could be used to support a specific sport/activity. The reasons for designing divergent production movements are infinite.

Designing Practice Style Skills Task*

1) Select a sport/activity and list the skills needed to successfully participate in that sport/activity. 2) Determine the "focus" of the skills according to the 3-D model. 3) Design tasks that provide the learner with developmental movement opportunities that lead to the acquisition of the skills in the specific Sport/Activity: _____

Skills	Attribute	Anatomical Division	"Kind" of Movement		
	Agility • •				
	Balance • •				
	Flexibility • •				
	Strength • •				
	Accuracy • •				
	Endurance • •				
	Rhythm • •				
	Others				

*These task designs could be used in styles B, C, or D and as one level in style E.

Designing Inclusion Style—E Tasks

The Inclusion style is based on the notion that inclusion ensures continued development.

Select a sport/activity and list the skills needed for successful participation. Then, draw/present those skills in level 3. For each skill, design alternative levels of difficulty by identifying the factor(s) that change the task's degree of difficulty (by manipulating the attribute position, anatomical division, or "kind" of movement). Design tasks for total physical development rather than selecting tasks that highlight just one attribute or one "kind" of movement. Sport/Activity: _____

Attribute	Anatomical Division	"Kind" of Movement	Factor to Manipulate for Range of Degree of Difficulty
Agility • •			
Balance • •			
Flexibility • •			
Strength • •			
Endurance • •			
Rhythm • •			
Others			

(chart continues)

The 3-D model can be used to guide or to analyze movement designs. Designing movement routines is a Divergent Discovery behavior. The next task sheet invites learners to consider the 3-D model when producing movement routines.

Rather than telling students to "Go design a new movement sequence," this Divergent Discovery task sheet reminds students to first consider the "possible movement options." The 3-D model can provide learners with a point of reference from which they begin to explore possible movement designs.

This task sheet form is useful for choreographers, aerobic trainers, and physical therapists who wish to assess the movement variations and physical development use in their designs. Students can use this form to discover new movements that challenge their total development.

Level 1	Level 2	Level 3 Skill Attainment	Level 4	Level 5 (more difficult)

Designing Divergent Production Style—H and Style—I Tasks

Subject Matter: _____   **Specific Content Focus:** _____

Content: (Indicate the reference point from which the learner is to examine the problem)[*]

_____

Logistics: (Indicate which of the following are to be included) __ equipment, __ props, __ working with others, __ others?

Parameters: __ time, __ quantity, __ duration of positions, __ others?

Attribute	Anatomical Division	"Kind" of Movement	Divergent Production Designs
Agility • •			
Balance • •			
Flexibility • •			
Strength • •			
Accuracy • •			
Endurance • •			
Rhythm • •			
Others			

[*]An example of Divergent Production style—H point of reference is: Design three separate movement sequences that differently incorporate two movements for each attribute, four anatomical divisions, and five "kinds" of movement. In style I the learners indicate their chosen point of reference, which defines their investigation.

This section presented just three of the many possible approaches to designing subject matter. The aim of this section is to invite teachers to think in a variety of approaches when designing content, and to reinforce the importance of connecting content with teaching–learning behaviors when designing subject matter. Awareness of, and the ability to prepare, lessons using episodic teaching can transform classroom teaching and learning experiences. When episodic teaching focuses on different sets of objectives, it embraces a non-versus approach to teaching. This approach honors learners' needs and their diversity and it supports the variety of objectives that subject matter requires.

Content knowledge guides what teachers teach. Pedagogical knowledge guides how teachers teach content.

The next chapter reviews the Spectrum research.

CHAPTER 19

A Review of Spectrum Research

MARK BYRA

Readers frequently ask for research on the Spectrum. Mark Byra,[1] who has thoroughly examined the Spectrum research, produced a comprehensive review and insightful analysis of Spectrum research. That article is adapted, by permission, for this chapter (Quest, 2000).

Review of Spectrum Research: The Contributions of Two Eras

It has been 33 years since Muska Mosston introduced the Spectrum of Teaching Styles in his book, *Teaching Physical Education* (1966). Many in the field of physical education and education alike from around the world have embraced the Spectrum of Teaching Styles as a framework for delivering instruction in schools (Gerney & Dort, 1992; Greenspan, 1992; Mellor, 1992), designing undergraduate teacher preparation programs (Byra, in press; Ashworth, 1992; Mueller & Mueller, 1992), and conducting research (Byra & Jenkins, 1998; Goldberger & Gerney, 1986, 1990; Telama, 1992). In marking the silver anniversary of the Spectrum, the *Journal of Physical Education, Recreation, and Dance* (Franks, 1992) featured a collection of articles to reflect the importance the Spectrum has had on physical educators, teacher educators, and researchers in the arena of physical education. The impact of the Spectrum on research in physical education is the focus of this paper.

In the early 1970s scholars in physical education believed that the Spectrum represented a plausible theoretical framework for conducting research on teaching in physical education. Nixon and Locke (1973) claimed that the Spectrum of Teaching Styles (Mosston, 1966) was "the most significant

---

[1]Mark Byra teaches at the University of Wyoming, Laramie, WY 82071 in the division of Kinesiology and Health.

advance in the theory of physical education pedagogy in recent history" (Nixon & Locke, p. 1227), even though it had "yet to undergo full experimental testing" (p. 1227). Based on the results from two early studies (Dougherty, 1970; Mariani, 1970), Nixon and Locke deemed that the Spectrum could predict both teacher behavior and student outcomes. However, to meet its full potential, they confirmed that much more research involving the Spectrum was required.

Approximately 20 years later Goldberger (1991; 1992) describes the Spectrum as an inclusive, yet discriminating framework that has specific definitions and parameters from which to systematically explore teaching in physical education. Given 25 years of research and reflection Goldberger (1992) concludes that, "although the theory [Spectrum] has not yet completed the full program of testing Nixon and Locke called for, results to date confirm the theory's power to both describe teaching events and predict learning outcomes" (p. 45). Mosston's (1966; 1981) and subsequently Mosston and Ashworth's (1986; 1994) Spectrum of Teaching Styles has provided researchers with a framework to systematically study teaching and learning within the context of physical education.

The research that has been conducted over the past 30 years on the Spectrum has been closely linked with the development and refinement of the Spectrum of Teaching Styles. During the initial development of the Spectrum, Mosston (1966) conceptualized the command style of teaching as having the "least amount of value" and teaching styles that involved problem solving or creativity as having the "greatest amount of value." Mosston perceived value to be associated with learner decision making and independence. In the Command style of teaching, learner decision making is minimal (to adhere or not to adhere to the teacher presented model), which forces the learner to be wholly dependent on the teacher. In contrast in the problem-solving teaching style learners are intimately involved in the decision making that transpires during the lesson. This leads the learner toward independent learning. This early conception of the teaching styles, as stated by Mosston (1981), was "based on the VERSUS—one style vs. the others" (p. viii).

In the second edition of *Teaching Physical Education*, Mosston (1981) emphasized the Spectrum from a "non-versus" perspective. A decade or more of experimentation resulted in the understanding that each style of teaching was not inherently better or more effective than the others, but rather that each style met a specific set of unique objectives or goals. For example, in the Reciprocal style immediate feedback and cooperative behavior are the essence of the style and learners are given an opportunity to practice a given task under the direct observation of a peer. Theoretically, this provides the learner with high practice time and frequent, immediate feedback. In comparison, the goal of the Command style is to learn to do a rote task accurately in a short period of time. The teacher provides the stimulus, or model, and the learner replicates that model on command. Rather than focusing on the disparity among the teaching styles, Mosston "highlighted the relationships among the styles" (Mosston, 1981, p. 4) in his second edition of *Teaching Physical Education*. This change had a monumental effect on the advancement of Spectrum research.

Other changes to the Spectrum from its inception in 1966 include the refinement of the decision categories, the addition and elimination of several teaching styles, the expansion of the individual teaching styles, and the clarification of all styles. These changes appear to have strengthened the philosophical basis and structure of the Spectrum. However, the effect that these changes have had on the advancement of Spectrum research is minimal in comparison to the "versus" issue.

Spectrum research that has been completed over the past 30 years is examined in the remainder of this paper. Dissertation studies and data-based studies published in journals and conference proceedings (written in the English language) are reviewed. The studies have been organized around two time periods, 1970 to 1980, and 1980 to the present. These time periods are titled the "early era" and the "recent era." Grouping the studies as "early" and "recent" helps to describe the relationship that existed between the emergence of Spectrum research and the evolution of the Spectrum of Teaching Styles. This paper is written with the expectation that the reader has a basic understanding of the landmark teaching styles associated with the Spectrum.

Early Era of Spectrum Research

During the 1970s and early 1980s numerous dissertation studies (Ashworth, 1983; Johnson, 1982; Gerney, 1980; Chamberlain, 1979; Virgilio, 1979; Jacoby, 1975; Bryant, 1974; Boschee, 1972; Dougherty, 1970) and one published study (Mariana, 1970) were completed specific to the Spectrum of Teaching Styles. In each study two or more teaching styles from the reproductive cluster were examined in light of learner skill, social, and/or cognitive development. These researchers attempted to investigate Mosston's (1966) proposal that the greater the decision making afforded the learner, the greater the advantage for change in learner growth on the physical, social, emotional, and intellectual dimensions (the "versus" issue). An underlying research question for these researchers was, which style(s) produces the best results (e.g., the greatest amount of learning).

The results from these studies were characterized by no significant differences. For example, Dougherty (1970) reported no significant differences between the Command, Task, and Individual Program styles of teaching on learner fitness and motor skill performance ($N=115$). In a study involving these same three teaching styles, Boschee (1972) found no significant differences between the teaching styles on learner physical, social, emotional, and intellectual development. And in a study of the Reciprocal and Practice (task) styles of teaching, Gerney (1980) reported no significant differences between the two styles on the skill acquisition of a hockey task ($N=32$).

When a significant difference was revealed, few of which were, the findings were mixed. For example, for the backhand tennis stroke Mariani (1970) found that male college students receiving instruction in the task style posted higher scores on a post-test than learners receiving instruction in the more traditional Command style of teaching. On the other hand, for the forehand tennis stroke no group differences were revealed on post-test skill scores; learners ($N=15$) instructed in the Command style performed just as well as learners ($N=15$) instructed in the Task style.

The premise on which the studies were conducted during the early era is no longer supported by Mosston (1981) and Mosston and Ashworth (1986; 1994). In the three most recent editions of the text, *Teaching Physical Education*, the authors espouse the "non-versus" notion. Mosston (1981) explains that

> *the conceptual basis of the Spectrum rests on the "non-versus" notion. That is, each style has its place in reaching a specific set of objectives; hence, no style, by itself, is better or best. . . . Each style is equally important (p. viii).*

Asking the question, which style is better, is deemed unproductive within the definition of the concept of "non-versus."

In addition to violating the concept of "non-versus," several scholars in the field of physical education voiced concerns about the methodological procedures employed in Spectrum research conducted during this early era. Griffey (1983), Locke (1977), and Metzler (1983) raised issues about the (a) inadequate definition of experimental treatment, (b) inadequate control over treatment applications, (c) adoption of abbreviated treatment periods, often too short to promote any change in student learning, (d) the use of college students as study participants rather than elementary and secondary school students, and (e) research being conducted by graduate students rather than experienced university researchers. It was suggested that these issues in combination likely contributed to the numerous methodological problems that plagued the early Spectrum research. Metzler (1983) submits that the frequent absence of significant differences between teaching styles for skill acquisition is "attributable to the nearly complete vacuum of information about process variables" (p. 151) in the studies. Level of learner skill performance prior to the application of treatment (teaching style) was not factored into the statistical procedures used in Mariani's (1970) study or Dougherty's (1970). Nor were any process measures for teacher and student behaviors systematically collected to verify the application of the different teaching styles. These examples of methodological deficiencies, as well as others, raise doubts about the findings in Dougherty's (1970) and Mariani 's studies (1970) as well as in other studies conducted during this era.

More recently, the issues identified by Griffey (1983), Locke (1977), and Metzler (1983) have also been raised by Michael Goldberger, the foremost scholar in Spectrum research and advisor to many of the graduate students who completed the early Spectrum studies (1992). In his review of early Spectrum research, Goldberger found that the investigators (a) failed to systematically verify style implementation, (b) lacked knowledge of Spectrum theory, (c) made claims that were illogical according to the style-specific learning conditions being studied, and (d) failed to provide treatment periods sufficiently long enough to produce learning outcomes. Although researchers were attempting to find the answer to an unanswerable question (which style is better?) during this time period, and the methods employed to study this question were at best problematic, the research conducted during the early era seems to have served an important function in the overall evolution of Spectrum research. It has served current researchers to better identify important and appropriate research questions about the Spectrum and to use appropriate research methods.

Recent Era of Spectrum Research

The recent era of Spectrum research emerged during the early 1980s following the publication of the Griffey (1983), Locke (1977), and Metzler (1983) articles. The issues raised by these three scholars, and later by Goldberger (1992), about the employment of inadequate research methodologies were addressed by investigators from the onset of the recent era of Spectrum research. The research presented in this section is categorized according to the cluster of teaching style it belongs, reproductive or productive. During the early era, research was restricted to the reproduction cluster of teaching styles. Research conducted during the recent era spans both the reproduction and production clusters of teaching styles.

The Spectrum of Teaching Styles is divided into two genres or clusters, reproductive and productive. The reproductive cluster includes the Command, Practice, Reciprocal, Self-Check, and Inclusion teaching styles. In this cluster the learner is called on to reproduce known material or knowledge. The focus is on replication of a specific model. Often the subject matter involves concrete facts, rules, or specific skills. Therefore, the learner must be provided a correct model to emulate, adequate time to practice the model, and congruent feedback related to the original model.

The production cluster is dependent on the learner producing new knowledge to self or teacher. In a production teaching style the teacher invites learners to engage in cognitive operations like problem solving, creating, inventing, or critically thinking to discover new movements. The subject matter is variable and often contains concepts, strategies, and principles. The teacher must provide the student time for cognitive processing, a class climate focused on searching and examining, and feedback for producing alternative solutions rather than a single solution.

Six teaching styles are identified in the production cluster: (a) Guided Discovery and (b) Convergent Discovery, two styles that require convergent thinking from learners; and (c) Divergent Production, (d) Individual program-learner design, (e) Learner-Initiated, and (f) Self-Teaching, four styles that require divergent thinking from learners. Based on informal discussions with teachers and observations of teachers in physical education classes, the Guided Discovery, Convergent Discovery, and Divergent Production seem to be the teaching styles most frequently used from the production cluster in school settings.

Reproduction Teaching Styles

The research reviewed in this section involves the Command, Practice, Reciprocal, and Inclusion styles of teaching. No research involving the Self-Check style has been conducted to date.

Griffey (1983) was one of the first investigators to conduct a Spectrum study for the purpose of addressing some of the methodological shortcomings of the earlier research. Specifically, in his study Griffey systematically verified the application of treatments and considered students' initial ability level. Student skill learning of the volleyball forearm pass and serve within the Command and Task styles was examined ($N=145$). The findings of this study showed that higher ability high school-aged learners performed better when instructed in the task style. Griffey suggests that the higher ability learners had sufficient knowledge of the skill to make informed decisions about appropriate use of practice time, while lower ability students lacked this knowledge.

The Task style as presented by Mosston (1966) is best described as a combination of Mosston and Ashworth's (1994) Practice and Inclusion styles of teaching. Given that the Task style (Mosston, 1966) doesn't match any one of the more recent Spectrum styles (Mosston, 1981; Mosston & Ashworth, 1986; 1994), it is difficult to compare the results of Griffey's study to those conducted more recently.

Goldberger, Gerney, and Chamberlain completed several studies of the Practice, Reciprocal, and Inclusion styles of teaching during the first half of the 1980s. In two of these studies middle school children (N=328; N=96) learned a hockey accuracy task while receiving instruction within their regular intact physical education classes (Goldberger & Gerney, 1986; Goldberger, Gerney, & Chamberlain, 1982). The goal of these studies was not to determine which style was better, but rather to see if different formats produced different levels of learning. The methodological problems associated with the early research were addressed by Goldberger and his colleagues in this series of studies. Specifically, treatment conditions (teaching styles) were well defined, the length of treatment time was sufficiently long, the implementation of each style was systematically verified, the statistical procedures used were appropriate, and the research team leader was an investigator who was knowledgeable in the Spectrum and an experienced researcher.

The results showed learner skill gains to be associated with all three styles. Although not significantly different from the other two styles, students who received instruction under practice conditions consistently produced the highest rates of change. In the Practice style the learners work at their own pace and complete teacher-designed tasks in the order they choose. Often the class is organized around stations; while a small group of students completes the task(s) at a given station, the teacher provides individual feedback to the learners.

The results from other Practice style studies grounded in sound methodology reflect the findings revealed in the Goldberger et al. research (Goldberger & Gerney, 1986; Goldberger, et al., 1982). The Practice style of teaching was found to be effective in fostering skill changes in college-aged students as they performed soccer-ball-juggling (N=120) (Beckett, 1991) and rifle shooting (N=135) (Boyce, 1992), and in school-aged children (N=119) as they performed striking with a racquet (Jenkins & Byra, 1997). These researchers ascertained that the instructional approach employed in the Practice style was effective in promoting motor skill changes in school-aged and college-aged learners.

In a more recent study Goldberger and Gerney (1990) examined the effect of two different organizational "formats" as presented within the instructional framework of the Practice style of teaching. Under one format (teacher-rotate) the participants, fifth grade boys and girls (N=165), rotated from station to station, in a specific order, every few minutes on the command of the teacher. Under the second format (learner-rotate) the fifth graders decided the order in which to rotate (from station to station), the amount of time to spend at each station, and when to rotate (from station to station). Both formats were found to be effective in fostering student learning. In addition the learner-rotate format was found to be more effective for the low-ability students than the high-ability students.

The Reciprocal style was also examined by Goldberger, Gerney, and Chamberlain (Goldberger & Gerney, 1986; Goldberger, et al., 1982). In this style learners form partners, and as one learner (doer) performs, the other (observer) gives specific feedback to the doer based on information provided by the teacher (criteria sheet). When the doer completes the task(s), the doer and observer switch roles. The extent of peer teaching in the reciprocal style is specifically the provision of feedback from one learner to another. In addition to improved skill performance, Goldberger, Gerney, and Chamberlain found that learners in the reciprocal style "provided more feedback, expressed more empathy, offered more praise and encouragement to each other, and requested more feedback from each other when compared to the control group" (Goldberger, 1992, p. 43). The results from Goldberger, Gerney, and Chamberlain's studies support Mosston and Ashworth's (1994) contention that feedback is provided at a much higher rate when the instructional strategy requires learners to provide task-related information to a partner.

Byra and Marks (1993) examined the effects different learner pairings had on elementary-aged students (*N*=32) while engaged in the Reciprocal style of teaching. The results showed that the elementary-aged learners gave more specific feedback to partners who were identified as friends, and felt more comfortable receiving feedback from friends than non-acquaintances. The authors also found that grouping by ability had no effect on amount of feedback given or received, or the comfort level of either the observer or the doer. This study provides evidence to support Mosston and Ashworth's (1994) claim that the most appropriate pairing technique for peer teaching is self-selection.

In an attempt to examine how student learning (physical, cognitive, and social) is best facilitated in the Reciprocal style of teaching, Ernst and Byra (1998) paired junior high school learners (*N*=60) by skill ability during an eight-lesson unit on juggling. All learners improved their juggling scores from pretest to post-test (except those in the control group). The greatest amount of skill achievement was accomplished by low-ability learners regardless with whom they were paired. In terms of knowledge gains (ability to identify skill elements of the movement), all learners (except those in the control group) improved their score from pretest to post-test. Once again, with whom a student was paired was of no significance. Level of comfort working with a partner was perceived to be high by all students. All of the students, regardless of the pairing, reported that giving feedback to and receiving feedback from a partner was a positive experience.

In a comparative study that involved elementary-aged gymnasts (N=10), Cox (1986) examined four types of student behavior in the Reciprocal, Practice, and Command styles of teaching. The purpose of this study was to demonstrate liabilities and assets of different teaching styles as they pertain to gymnastics instruction. The number of attempts made at prescribed movements, feedback statements offered, nature of feedback statements, and antisocial behaviors were recorded as the gymnasts received instruction in the three different teaching styles. The results revealed that the number of skill movements attempted was very similar across the three styles. On the one hand, this was surprising in that in the Reciprocal style each learner assesses a partner half of the time, a condition that is not associated with either the Command or the Practice styles. On the other hand, the finding is not surprising in that this study was conducted in an environment that necessitated some queuing in all of the teaching episodes because of a lack of space and equipment.

Differences were found in the number and type of feedback statements provided and antisocial comments made (Cox, 1986). Three times the number of feedback statements were offered to performers in the Reciprocal style and 10 times more positive feedback compared to the Command and Practice styles. Antisocial behaviors were frequently recorded in the Command and Practice styles; in the Reciprocal style they were almost nonexistent. For those teachers who value the development of social relationships between pairs and the conditions for immediate feedback, the results of this study, as well as the others (Byra & Marks, 1993; Goldberger & Gerney, 1986; Goldberger, et al., 1982) support the contention that skill and knowledge gains can transpire while engaging in the socializing process unique to the Reciprocal style.

Goldberger, Gerney, and Chamberlain (Goldberger & Gerney, 1986; Goldberger, et al., 1982), as well as Beckett (1991), Goudas, Biddle, Fox, and Underwood (1995), Byra and Jenkins (1998), and Jenkins and Byra (1997) have investigated learner performance and decision making related to the Inclusion style, the last of the five reproductive styles. Within the Inclusion style of teaching, learners choose level of difficulty within a task and assess their own skill performance (self-referenced evaluation). The primary goal of the Inclusion style of teaching is to provide students opportunity to engage in activity at an appropriate skill level. In choosing level of difficulty, learners are given the opportunity to compare their aspirations to reality of performance. In assessing their own skill performance, the learners compare and contrast skill execution against the model and then conclude what is correct and incorrect. As reflected in the preceding statements, thinking and reflecting are critical to the role of the learner in the Inclusion style of teaching.

Goldberger, Gerney, and Chamberlain (1982) and Goldberger and Gerney (1986) found the Inclusion style of teaching effective in producing improvement in learner skill performance, but not at the same rate as found with the Practice style. In addition, the authors found the Inclusion style to be less effective for exceptional learners. This finding is inconsistent with Spectrum theory. Spectrum theory suggests that the conditions provided by the Inclusion style should promote success for all learners.

So why these results? Goldberger, Gerney, and Chamberlain (1982) and Goldberger and Gerney (1986) observed numerous learners making inappropriate decisions for their skill level in the Inclusion style episodes. The learners chose levels that appeared too difficult for them to reach success, and even with encouragement or prompting from the teacher would not change levels. Perhaps self-concept or peer pressure influenced the student's decision making. In combination this may have contributed to the inconsistency between Spectrum theory and the findings reported.

In a study of college-aged students ($N=120$), Beckett (1991) found the Inclusion style to be as effective as the Practice style for learner skill performance, and as suitable for learners of average and exceptional aptitude for learning motor skills. These findings do not support the conclusions of Goldberger, Gerney, and Chamberlain (1982; 1986). Beckett suggests that differences in students' ages (college students versus fifth graders), motor tasks learned (soccer juggling versus floor hockey accuracy task), and settings (natural versus laboratory) may help to explain why the findings from his research support Mosston and Ashworth's (1994) contentions specific to the Inclusion style, and why Goldberger, Gerney, and Chamberlain's do not.

Goudas et al. (1995) examined the motivational effects of the Inclusion style of teaching in the sport of track and field. An intact class of 24 12- and 13-year old girls received track and field instruction in the Practice and Inclusion styles of teaching for a 10-week period of time. Based on this experience, the girls reported a preference for the Inclusion style of teaching for reasons associated with intrinsic motivation. The girls specifically expressed that they perceived to have greater control over what they did and the amount of effort they put forth, and less anxiety as a result of being able to select level of task difficulty, in the Inclusion style of teaching. Individualizing instruction to permit greater student success is the underlying premise of the Inclusion style of teaching (Mosston & Ashworth, 1994). These findings support this premise.

Byra and Jenkins (1998) examined learner decision making in the Inclusion style of teaching. Fifth-grade students ($N=42$) from one school received instruction in striking with a bat for two 30-minute lessons. The learners performed three sets of 10 trials of a batting task each lesson and made decisions about level of task difficulty. Data sources were the lesson task sheets and transcribed post-lesson interviews. The results indicated that the fifth graders did select different levels of task difficulty when provided the opportunity, and made task decisions regarding level of difficulty according to their perceptions of success, challenge, and curiosity. These findings support Mosston and Ashworth's (1994) notion that when given the opportunity learners will engage in an activity at an appropriate skill level.

Beckett (1991) and Jenkins and Byra (1997) examined gains in learner knowledge in the Inclusion style of teaching. Beckett found that college-age learners who received instruction on soccer-juggling under the conditions of the Inclusion style scored significantly higher on a written knowledge test than learners who received instruction under the conditions of the Practice style. Jenkins and Byra (1997) found that elementary-age learners in both the Inclusion and Practice styles made significant gains in the number of skill elements reported from pretest to post-test, and learners in the Inclusion style reported a significantly greater number of skill elements during post-test than learners in the Practice style. These findings support Mosston and Ashworth's (1994) contention that learners should understand and recall elements of task performance better when taught in a style that requires the learners to assess their own skill performance.

So what have researchers uncovered about the reproductive cluster of teaching styles during the most recent era of Spectrum research? A summary of the findings is presented below.

1. The Practice style has been studied most frequently, followed by the Reciprocal and Inclusion styles.

2. The Self-Check style has not been researched.

3. The Command, Practice, Reciprocal, and Inclusion styles of teaching are effective in promoting motor skill acquisition in school-age and college-age students (Jenkins & Byra, 1997; Byra & Marks, 1993; Boyce, 1992; Beckett, 1991; Goldberger & Gerney, 1990; Goldberger & Gerney, 1986; Goldberger, et al., 1982).

4. Low ability fifth-grade students perform better in the Practice style when given the opportunity to allocate practice time differentially, and spend more time practicing tasks yet mastered (Goldberger & Gerney, 1990).

5. More feedback is given to the performer in the Reciprocal style than in the Command, Practice, or Inclusion styles (Cox, 1986; Goldberger, et al., 1982).

6. In the Reciprocal style of teaching elementary-age learners give the greatest amount of feedback to a partner who is selected on the basis of being an acquaintance (Byra & Marks, 1993).

7. In the Reciprocal style of teaching, pairing by ability level (same or mixed) seems to have little effect on the amount of feedback a partner provides (Byra & Marks, 1993) or student learning (Ernst & Byra, 1998).

8. Elementary and junior high learners are most comfortable giving and receiving feedback (Reciprocal style) from partners who are friends (Ernst & Byra, 1998; Byra & Marks, 1993).

9. Elementary-age students emit fewer antisocial behaviors in a physical education setting where equipment and facilities are limited when instruction is provided within the Reciprocal style compared to the Command and Practice styles (Cox, 1986).

10. Research findings related to skill acquisition are mixed for exceptional learners (high and low) in the Inclusion style of teaching. Goldberger, Gerney, and Chamberlain (1982), and Goldberger and Gerney (1986) found the Inclusion style to be less effective for exceptional learners in the fifth grade. Beckett (1991) found the inclusion style to be as effective for exceptional ability college-age learners as average ability college-age learners.

11. When given the opportunity to engage in activity at an appropriate level (Inclusion style), fifth graders consistently selected different levels of task difficulty (Byra & Jenkins, 1998).

12. Fifth graders reported success and challenge most frequently as reasons for making a task less or more difficult in the Inclusion style (Byra & Jenkins, 1998).

13. Greater knowledge gains were reported by college-age and elementary-age learners in the Inclusion style of teaching compared to the Practice style (Beckett, 1991; Jenkins & Byra, 1997).

14. Adolescent girls reported a preference to the Inclusion style (over the Practice) for reasons associated with intrinsic motivation (greater autonomy and effort, and less anxiety) (Goudas et al., 1995).

Production Teaching Styles

Until recently little research has been conducted within the "production" cluster of Mosston and Ashworth's (1994) Spectrum of teaching styles. A search of the literature in physical education revealed a total of five published papers involving teaching styles from the production cluster. Four of these research studies have been published in the 1990s and have as the lead author Fran Cleland. One study was published in 1995 and it included an examination of both production and reproduction teaching styles.

McBride's (1992) scholarly writing on critical thinking seems to have been as much of a stimulus for the development of Cleland's research focus as has the Spectrum itself. Of the six production styles, Cleland and her colleagues have examined Divergent Production, Convergent Discovery, and Guided Discovery. In her first study Cleland studied the divergent movement patterns of children aged 4, 6, and 8 to establish baseline information about children's divergent movement patterns, and to examine different factors that might contribute to a child's production of divergent movement (Cleland & Gallahue, 1993). While being tested individually, the participants (*N*=40) were given the following instructions: "try to move in as many ways possible using all of the equipment [at the locomotor task, stability task, or ball-handling task]" (p. 538). When asked to engage in the discovery process, the young children demonstrated that they could modify, adapt, or combine fundamental movement patterns to produce divergent movement. Experience and age were found to be factors that contributed to a child's ability to produce divergent movement. Although Mosston and Ashworth (1994) were not referenced in this paper, it was clear from the description provided that what the children did to produce divergent movements matched what they would have been required to do within the framework of Mosston and Ashworth's Divergent Production style. The participants were given a problem to solve, and through their actions demonstrated the divergent thinking process.

In a second study of children's divergent movement ability, Cleland (1994) randomly assigned second- and third-grade children (*N*=50) to one of three different instructional groups: (a) Divergent Production—content based on skill themes and movement concepts; (b) Command/Practice—content based on low-organized games; and (c) Control, no instruction. The purpose of this study was to examine the effect of content and specific teaching styles on learner ability to produce divergent movement. The findings were favorable for the learners receiving treatment under conditions of Divergent Production. These students generated a significantly greater number of divergent movement patterns than those who received treatment under conditions of direct instruction or no instruction (control group). Cleland concluded that employing critical thinking strategies in the form of Divergent Production positively affects learner's ability to generate divergent movement patterns. It would be interesting to conduct a follow-up study of children's divergent movement production where content for both treatment groups is constant, based on skill themes and movement concepts (Graham, Holt/Hale, & Parker, 1998), and conditions of instruction are different (Divergent Production style, Command/Practice style, control). Cleland's findings may be attributable to the difference in content delivered (skill themes/movement concepts vs. low-organized games), not the teaching styles employed.

In a yearlong study of fifth graders' critical thinking in physical education, Cleland and Pearse (1995) examined how the physical education specialist can structure the learning environment to promote critical thinking. Critical thinking, as defined by McBride (1992), is "reflective thinking that is used to make reasonable and defensible decisions about movement tasks or challenges" (p. 115). Children's divergent movement ability is one aspect of critical thinking. Cleland and Pearse found that critical thinking in children (*N*=27) could be fostered via the employment of two of Mosston and Ashworth's (1994) productive teaching styles, specifically, Divergent Production and Convergent Discovery. The teachers in this study employed the Practice style of teaching to deliver domain-specific knowledge to the learners relative to lesson content prior to having them engage in problem-solving activities. Conditions of the Reciprocal and Self-Check styles were used to guide the learners in tasks that involved working individually, or working in pairs or small groups. Based on systematic analysis of videotapes, the investigators concluded that a student's ability to think critically (to produce divergent movement) "depends on the movement task and the teacher's ability to effectively use indirect [Divergent Production and Convergent Discovery] teaching styles" (Cleland & Pearse, 1995, p. 36). According to the student interviews, the learners reported that they enjoyed the critical thinking activities employed in the lessons, that they preferred to engage in tasks that involved small groups, and that written movement problems were more difficult to solve.

The research of Cleland and her colleagues (Cleland & Pearse, 1995; Cleland, 1994; Cleland & Gallahue, 1993) serves to affirm that critical thinking in children, specifically as it applies to the production of divergent movement, can be fostered through Mosston and Ashworth's (1994) Guided Discovery, Convergent Discovery, and Divergent Production teaching styles. Based on this knowledge, Cleland's most recent research effort focused on how teachers could promote critical thinking in children in the physical education setting (Cleland, Donnelly, Helion, & Fry, 1999). A group of four experienced physical education teachers participated in a comprehensive workshop that included: (a) instruction on how to use specific teaching styles (Guided Discovery, Convergent Discovery, and Divergent Production) and McBride's (1992) schema of the critical thinking process to promote an atmosphere of inquiry in class; (b) opportunity to implement lesson plans aimed at promoting critical thinking that were designed by the participants and workshop instructors in collaboration; and (c) opportunity to discuss and analyze the practice lessons taught. Three lessons of each participant's teaching was videotaped prior to participating in the workshop. After participating in the workshop, the teachers were videotaped while teaching a unit of instruction in which critical thinking strategies were employed.

The intervention employed in this study enabled the four teachers to structure the environment and frame learning tasks to promote critical thinking in physical education classes. All four participants were able to use conditions of the Guided Discovery, Convergent Discovery, and Divergent Production teaching styles to ascertain specific process and product variables identified within McBride's (1992) schema on critical thinking.

In the fifth study reviewed involving the productive teaching styles, Salter and Graham (1985) examined the effect of three disparate instructional approaches on four product variables in a single–lesson experimental teaching unit (ETU). The four product variables were skill learning, cognitive learning, skill attempts, and rating of self-efficacy. Instruction was delivered to the elementary-age students ($N=244$) under conditions of Guided Discovery, the Command, and a no-instruction (learners performed the same task without verbal instruction/feedback).

The results of this study showed that significant skill learning occurred in all three treatment groups. However, no significant between-group differences were found for skill learning. Significant cognitive learning also occurred for all three groups. However, in contrast to skill learning, the students in the Guided Discovery and Command styles recorded significantly better scores on the cognitive criterion than the participants in the no-instruction group. No differences were found on the measure of self-efficacy. For skill attempts learners in the no-instruction group made significantly more attempts at the task than learners in both the Guided Discovery and Command styles.

Salter and Graham (1985) attribute the lack of between-group difference for skill learning to the limitations imposed by the ETU (single, 20-minute lesson) and the higher number of skill attempts performed by the learners in the no-instruction group. Practice time was higher for the no-instruction group because no skill information was given to the learners during the lesson. Under the Guided Discovery and Command instructional conditions, where skill information was offered, learners demonstrated a higher level of cognitive understanding.

So what have researchers uncovered about the productive cluster of teaching styles during the most recent era of Spectrum research? Following is a summary of the findings.

1. When instructed within the Divergent Production style, children can modify, adapt, or combine fundamental movement patterns to produce divergent movement (Cleland & Gallahue, 1993).

2. Experience and age are factors that contribute to a child's ability to produce divergent movement while engaged in the Divergent Production teaching style (Cleland & Gallahue, 1993).

3. Children who receive instruction in the Divergent Production style are more capable of generating divergent movement patterns than children

who receive instruction in a combination of the Command and Practice styles (Cleland, 1994).

4. Children's ability to produce divergent movement in a physical education setting is dependent on the teacher's ability to effectively use the Divergent Production and Convergent Discovery teaching styles (Cleland et al., 1999; Cleland & Pearse, 1995).

5. Opportunity for elementary-age learners to attempt skill trials in the Guided Discovery and Command styles is similar (Salter & Graham, 1985).

6. The Guided Discovery style is as effective in fostering student skill and cognitive learning in an elementary population as the Command style (Salter & Graham, 1985).

Summary

Between 1982 and 1999, the lower and upper years defining the recent era of Spectrum research, 17 data-based research studies were published in physical education journals specific to the Spectrum teaching styles. Reproduction teaching styles were examined in 12 of the 17 studies, and production teaching styles in 5. Approximately 20 different researchers have contributed to this data-based research.

Researchers who have conducted Spectrum studies during this recent era have paid close attention to the comments made by Goldberger (1992), Locke (1977), and Metzler (1983) regarding the early Spectrum research. For example, the recent research is no longer being driven by the question, Which style is better? It is being conducted within the non-versus premise, that is, no single style is superior in itself to any other style; rather, each style has its own set of objectives, assets, and liabilities. Nor is the research being criticized for having methodological deficiencies. Researchers are systematically verifying style implementation, basing the conclusions of studies within the framework of each style, conducting studies for long enough periods of time to allow for student learning, and proceeding to do research only after having gained substantial knowledge of the Spectrum. Goldberger (1992) seems to have hit the nail on the head when suggesting that the "early work was necessary for us to learn how to better conduct Spectrum research" (p. 42). The research that has been completed during the recent era reflects Goldberger's thoughts.

Are we moving forward with Spectrum research? One of the major problems identified with the Spectrum in the early 1980s was the lack of research conducted to verify the assumptions of Spectrum theory (Metzler, 1983). To that point in time, few well-designed Spectrum studies had been completed. A decade later, some 10 studies later, Goldberger (1992) concludes, "although the theory has not yet completed the full program of testing Nixon and Locke called for, results to date confirm the theory's power to both describe teaching events and predict learning outcomes" (p. 45). Now, almost 20 Spectrum studies have been completed. Is Spectrum research moving forward? The answer is unequivocally yes. We have made strides in understanding Spectrum theory, however, much work remains to be done. For each question answered, three to five new questions have been raised. It seems that we have just exposed the tip of the iceberg of possible Spectrum research.

So where do we go now with Spectrum research? We need to continue to investigate the theoretical assumptions associated with Mosston and Ashworth's (1994) teaching styles. Some assumptions have been confirmed. For example, the reciprocal style does facilitate the provision of feedback, more so than in other styles, and having learners self-select partners based on who they like does foster partner interaction (Byra & Marks, 1993; Cox, 1986; Goldberger, et al., 1982). Other assumptions, like the Self-Check and Inclusion styles, move a learner further along the cognitive Developmental Channel, and the Inclusion style equally fosters participation of low, medium, and high ability learners still need to be examined.

We need to examine Spectrum teaching styles through the eyes of the learner. Mosston and Ashworth (1994) indicate that the role of the learner changes from one teaching style to the next according to the decisions they are afforded. What do we know about their role in the various teaching styles? The results from one study suggest that learners associated success and challenge with the Inclusion style of teaching (Byra & Jenkins, 1998). Would learners report as many successes in a setting where every task represented a single standard? By asking the learner, Lee (1997) suggests that "we will learn things we never knew we did not know" (p. 274).

We need to conduct replication studies to confirm what we already know about the Spectrum. For example, will the Reciprocal style of teaching facilitate student learning in junior high school students in different schools and school districts in the same way as it did the junior high participants in Ernst and Byra's study (1998)? In a replication study of the Practice, Reciprocal, and Inclusion styles, Goldberger and Gerney (1986) confirmed the student skill acquisition findings of an earlier study of same-age participants (Goldberger, et al., 1982). More of these types of studies are needed.

We need to complete similar studies to those already conducted but in different contexts to extend what we have learned about the Spectrum. For example, will elementary learners make skill performance selections in the Inclusion style of teaching for the same reasons as secondary-school students? Will fifth graders receiving instruction in the Reciprocal style of teaching interact with a partner in the same way when performing a volleyball skill as a tennis skill? These types of studies will hopefully provide evidence that allows researchers to make greater generalizations about the Spectrum findings.

Another area critically important to the future of the Spectrum is how Mosston and Ashworth's (1994) teaching styles compare with other spectra and styles like Joyce, Weil, and Showers' (1992) models of teaching, and Johnson, Johnson, and Johnson-Hulebec's (1994) cooperative learning model. An underlying premise of both Mosston and Ashworth's, and Joyce, Weil, and Showers' models of teaching is that students learn differently and need to grow in all areas including the personal, the motor, the cognitive, and the social. A single style or approach cannot in itself accommodate the individual differences that exist among students. Joyce, Weil, and Showers' models of teaching are structured around four families of teaching styles—each family having a shared orientation toward humans and how they learn. Mosston and Ashworth's teaching styles focus on the decision making relationship that exists between the student and the teacher in each style, which invariably impacts who is at the center, teacher or learner, of the instructional environment. In future research we must examine how Mosston and Ashworth's teaching styles are similar and different from other models of teaching and in doing so determine the limitations of the Spectrum and the possibilities for future enhancement.

These are but a few directions that we can pursue in our quest to better understand Spectrum theory. Over the next decade we need to continue to employ the Spectrum of teaching styles as a framework to study teaching and learning in physical education.

CHAPTER 20

The Spectrum[1]

This chapter addresses some thoughts about the Spectrum's implications and relationships to a variety of educational aspects and issues. The Spectrum goes beyond the structure and function of each style. It shows the connections and links among the variety of educational issues toward a unifying theory of teaching.

Implications Network

Current issues affecting physical educators include: outcomes-based teaching, standards, time-on-task,[2] social and personal responsibility teaching, ESOL awareness, inclusion, discipline, class management, motivation, feedback, self-efficacy, etc. Ways have been devised for treating these variables by proposing techniques to improve all teaching experiences.

However, the Spectrum approaches these educational variables and information from a different point of view. An assumption inherent in the Spectrum is that in face-to-face relationships, the behavior of the teacher affects the behavior of the learners; therefore, each of these educational variables must be examined in light of each style. These issues cannot be resolved with a single solution, but rather from the expectations of each teaching–learning behavior. When we approach educational issues from the O–T–L–O of each style, we derive different meanings, solutions, and implications to these variables.

Since the Spectrum framework differentiates teaching–learning behaviors according to their intrinsic O–T–L–O, the implications for the educa-

---

[1]This chapter is adapted from the forthcoming book, *A Comprehensive Approach to Teaching and Learning: A Spectrum from Command to Discovery*.

[2]Time-on-task is also referred to as academic learning time-PE or ALT-PE.

tional variables must correspond with the behaviors' intents. Therefore, when making implications about these educational issues, a distinction must be made about the specific behavior that is in focus. What is appropriate in one behavior may not be appropriate in another. What occurs with high frequency in one may occur only infrequently, or not at all, in another style.

For example, feedback behavior in the Practice style—B *must* be different from feedback in the Self-Check style—D, and again different in Inclusion style—E from that in Divergent Production style—H, etc. Although there is a general body of knowledge concerning feedback, implications for feedback practices must relate to the particular teaching–learning behavior in use at that particular time.

In the same fashion, a discipline approach cannot be generalized to all educational events. Discipline requirements and expectations vary from teaching behavior to teaching behavior. Although a general body of knowledge about discipline is applicable to all deviations, the definitions and treatments of discipline problems vary and are always related to the particular behavior in use in a given episode. What is appropriate in the Command style is not acceptable in the Practice style. The desired behaviors of the Divergent Production style are out of line in the Command style. This manner of thinking about discipline requires both teachers and learners to be aware of the intended expectations and to maintain consistency and respect for those expectations in focus. Application of educational issues to actual teaching events must take into consideration the specific teaching–learning expectations.

Likewise, behavior that is motivating in the Reciprocal style would not be effective in the Divergent Discovery style. The techniques for motivating learners vary; each design must correspond with the overall objectives and learning focus of the specific teaching behavior.

The issues of social and personal responsibility are not developed by only one teaching–learning approach or solution. Social and personal responsibility is developed when learners become skilled at making decisions and interacting with others in a variety of decision-making situations from Command to Discovery. Social responsibility, ethics, sportsmanship, and many other human attributes cannot be developed fully when learners are denied a variety of teaching–learning experiences. A larger educational network is established when teachers are able to see the relationship among issues to a repertoire of possible teaching–learning behaviors.

Indeed the educational network will expand when variables, which have an impact on learning, are examined for each teaching style. Examples of these variables include ESOL awareness, inclusion, outcomes-based teaching; ALT-PE, classroom management and procedures, self-efficacy, etc. Determining the implications of educational issues to teaching practices must stem from the particular behavior used at a given time. Figure 20.1 represents the network of implications that are intrinsic and unique to each style. All teaching styles view these same issues from different perspectives. Indeed style C views these issues differently from styles H or A, or E, etc. Each style shades the various educational events according to its distinct set of objectives.

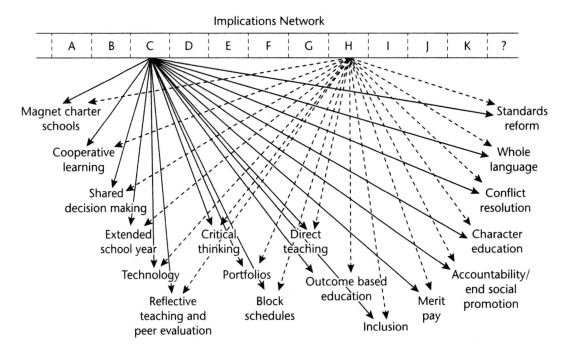

Figure 20.1. Implications network for each style, focusing on programs and, policies affecting education

Implementing the Spectrum

Perhaps the first step in implementing the Spectrum is to *learn to see* the variety of universal behaviors that occur in school and in society. *Learn to see* the different expectations that exist for behaving and interacting with subject matter and other people. *See* the aerobics class, as students perform exactly to the timed model, or the cheerleaders, or the Simon Says game, or the choral performances as examples of the Command style. *Learn to see* the three expectations—subject matter, behavior, and logistics—that shape this behavior. While looking at the arts sections of any large city's Sunday paper, *see* the advertisements that promote uniform performances. *See* the beauty that is intrinsic to these experiences—even if these experiences are not your personal preference. *See* the Divergent Discovery situations—from the choreographer's design to the science fair topics; the modern architectural structures; the content of the comedians' routines; the teenagers' clothing combinations! *See* the divergence that exists in society; examine your reactions, your patience and your tolerance for these divergent situations. *Learn to see* the cognitive operations that drive the divergent production. *Learn to see* the three expectations that are inherent and the common outcomes that they all produce—products that are different from the norm, from the establishment.

See the Convergent Discovery process that is required when solving word puzzles, or mazes, or problems that must be solved by one solution—a solution that must be discovered. *See* the Self-Check decisions surface as a teenager practices driving when an adult is in the car! Or when a person is experimenting with a new recipe, or learning a new hobby by him/herself. *See* the decisions of the Practice style when a teenager is taking music lessons, completing a requested task, or filling out an application form.

Learning to see the variety of behaviors and the three expectations of each behavior is the first step in being able to implement the Spectrum. Seeing the variety of behaviors not only establishes the legitimacy and necessity of the different behaviors, it also provides the models. A repertoire of teaching patterns permits a tremendous, wonderful variety of learning experiences. The Spectrum offers the blueprint, the road map, for implementing a full range of educational experiences. The manner in which we teach always represents a specific model of learning.

Review Your Teaching Patterns   Bring your analysis to your gymnasium. Teach as you always do, but with attention to the patterns inherent within your teaching. Look for the delivery of the three expectations, listen to your feedback choices, observe the variety, or the lack of it, in the options you provide your learners. Notice the time spent on, and the relationship between, reproductive and productive tasks. Become more aware of your deliberate decision making patterns. Identify which decisions you always consider and those that you tend to ignore when preparing lessons and sequencing events. Determine the variety of educational objectives you use while presenting physical education content. Become familiar with your teaching–learning patterns.

Design Short Episodes   After reviewing your teaching patterns, select a teaching style that would complement, clarify, and enhance what you already do. Try planning the three expectations to deliberately lead learners to the objectives of the specific style selected. Select a specific teaching–learning behavior and plan an episode using the events per episode form. Select the desired order for the three expectations—subject matter, behavior, logistics. Keep your learning focus in mind and teach with the intent of accomplishing the objectives of the selected behavior. Watch your learners participate in the decisions and in the subject matter. Plans seldom go perfectly; expect to make adjustments. Look for the decision(s) that caused the deviation; make adjustments, if possible, and continue, or end the episode and implement another episode later. The goal for both teacher and learner is to change the teaching and learning patterns with dignity. In these initial experiences, all teachers feel awkward—perhaps even embarrassed if events don't go perfectly! It takes time and practice to expand one's repertoire of teaching options.

Assess and Reflect   After the episode, review the intent of the teaching style and your actual teaching. Identify what was congruent and also what was incongruent between your intent and action (INTENT $\cong$ ACTION). Use the events per episode form to compare what went well and what didn't. Recall the feedback used, the cognitive intent, the questions asked, the time-on-task. Evaluate how you included the learners in the task and the quality of your attention to the learners (eye-contact, feedback, content reinforcement), etc.

Initially, it is difficult to recall events from memory. Far more reliable is the use of videotaping. Try taping your short episodes, learn to see yourself and your teaching–learning behavior. In the beginning it is difficult for many teachers to watch themselves teach. This process is necessary if teachers are to develop awareness of what they do and to make judgments about the effects of their behavior. Learning to see oneself moves teachers to the Self-Check style. The more accurate teachers are at comparing their performances against the intended objectives, the more professionally equipped they become to make decisions that result in worthwhile teaching–learning experiences. The more adept they become at implementing alternative teaching–learning options, the more skilled they are at leading learners to a variety of educational objectives.

Design Additional Episodes in the Same Style and in Different Styles
First, plan additional episodes in the same style to reinforce what you did well and to correct areas that needed attention. Practice until you feel as though you own the behavior.[3] Practice in different situations and with different classes. After each practice, review and assess the results against the intended learning expectations. The cycle of practicing—planning, implementing, assessing, and reflecting by criteria—is the only way to become skilled in new teaching–learning behaviors.

---

[3]A student once stated, "I'm still renting—I don't own the behavior of style *X* just yet!"

Teachers who use the Spectrum are not necessarily more skilled than other teachers—but they become more skilled when they use the ideas with authenticity and fidelity. Labels do not validate processes. Many teachers *say* they use a variety of educational ideas; however, their implementation procedures often invalidate the programs they are trying to replicate.

The Spectrum, like all other worthwhile ideas, requires a learning process, practice, introspection, and feedback. It requires reorganization of procedures. It requires courage to change and expand what one naturally or ordinarily does. It requires a reexamination and expansion of preferences. It requires strength to withstand the cynical comments of others. It requires a commitment to the ultimate goal of education—learning. Learning—the hallmark of education—requires that both teacher and learners participate in the process. Although the Spectrum proposes a shift in the way we look at teaching and learning, it is an open structure that invites new alternatives, combinations, creative examples, and uses. Mosston's formulation of the structure inherent within all teaching and learning is a discovery. It offers educators an all-encompassing framework in which they can explore the teaching–learning process.

The Spectrum of teaching styles is defined by its emphasis on deliberate teaching–teaching that demonstrates mobility-ability; teaching that emphasizes the attributes along the Developmental Channels; and teaching that values a non-versus approach in making decisions and recognizing differences. The Spectrum celebrates and maintains the integrity of human differences from Command to Discovery.

BIBLIOGRAPHY

Anderson, R. C. (1959). Learning in discussion: A résumé of authoritarian democratic studies. *Harvard Educational Review, 29,* 201–215.

Anderson, R. C., & Anderson, R. M. (1963). Transfer of originality training. *Journal of Educational Psychology, 54*(6), 300–304.

Anderson, R. C., & Ausubel, D. P. (eds.). (1965). *Readings in the Psychology of Cognition.* New York: Holt, Rinehart & Winston, Inc.

Anderson, W. G. (1980). *Analysis of Teaching Physical Education.* St. Louis: C.V. Mosby.

Ashworth, S. (1983). "Effects of training in Mosston's spectrum of teaching styles on feedback of teachers." Unpublished doctoral dissertation, Temple University, Philadelphia.

Ashworth, S. (1992). The Spectrum and teacher education. *Journal of Physical Education, Recreation, and Dance, 63*(1), 32–35, 53.

Atkin, M. J., & Karplus, R. (1962). Discovery or invention? *The Science Teacher, 29,* 45–69.

Baoler, J. (1999). Mathematics for the moment, or the millennium? What a British study has to say about teaching methods. Educational Week, XVIII 29, 30–34.

Beckett, K. (1991). The effects of two teaching styles on college students' achievement of selected physical education outcomes. *Journal of Teaching in Physical Education, 10*(2), 153–169.

Bellon, J. J., Bellon, E.C., & Blank, M.A. (1992). *Teaching From a Research Knowledge Base: A Developmental and Renewal Process.* New York: Macmillan Publishing Company.

Beyer, B. K. (1987). *Practical Strategies for the Teaching of Thinking.* Boston: Allyn & Bacon.

Bloom, B. S. (ed.). (1956). *Taxonomy of Educational Objectives (Handbook 1: Cognitive Domain).* New York: David McKay Co., Inc.

Bloom, B. S. (1976). *Human Characteristics and School Learning.* New York: McGraw-Hill Book Co.

Boschee, F. A. (1972). A comparison of the effects of command, task, and individual program styles of teaching on four developmental channels. *Dissertation Abstracts International, 33,* 2066A.

Boyce, B. A. (1992). The effects of three styles of teaching on university student's motor performance. *Journal of Teaching in Physical Education, 11*(4), 389–401.

Brophy, J. E. (1981). Teacher praise: A functional analysis. *Review of Educational Research, 51,* 5–32.

Bruner, J. S. (1961). The act of discovery. *Harvard Educational Review, 31,* 21–32.

Bruner, J. S. (1962). *On Knowing: Essays for the Left Hand.* Cambridge, MA: Harvard University Press.

Bruner, J. S. (1963). Needed: A theory of instruction. *Educational Leadership 20,* 523–532.

Bruner, J. S. (1963). *The Process of Education.* New York: Random House, Inc.

Bryant, W. (1974). "Comparison of the practice and reciprocal styles of teaching." Unpublished manuscript, Temple University, Philadelphia.

Byra, M. (in press). A coherent PETE program: Spectrum style. *Journal of Physical Education, Recreation, and Dance.*

Byra, M. (2000). A review of spectrum research: the contributions of two eras. *Quest, 52*(3), 229–245.

Byra, M., & Jenkins, J. (1998). The thoughts and behaviors of learners in the inclusion style of teaching. *Journal of Teaching in Physical Education, 18*(1), 26–42.

Byra, M., & Marks, M. (1993). The effect of two pairing techniques on specific feedback and comfort levels of learners in the reciprocal style of teaching. *Journal of Teaching in Physical Education, 12*(3), 286–300.

Chamberlain, J. (1979). "The effects of Mosston's practice style and individual program teacher design on motor skill acquisition and self-concept of fifth grade learners." Unpublished doctoral dissertation, Temple University, Philadelphia.

Chinn, C.A., & Anderson, R.C. (1998). "Pattern of participation during literature discussions." Pre-publication article review.

Cleland, F.E. (1994). Young children's divergent movement ability: Study II. *Journal of Teaching in Physical Education, 13*(3), 228–241.

Cleland. F.E., Donnelly, F., Helion, J., & Fry, F. (1999). Modifying teacher behaviors to promote critical thinking in K–12 physical education. *Journal of Teaching in Physical Education, 18*(2), 199–215.

Cleland, F.E., & Gallahue, D.L. (1993). Young children's divergent movement ability. *Perceptual and Motor Skills, 77,* 535–544.

Cleland, F., & Pearse, C. (1995). Critical thinking in elementary physical education: Reflections on a yearlong study. *Journal of Physical Education, Recreation, and Dance, 66*(6), 31–38.

Cox, R.L. (1986). A systematic approach to teaching sport. In M. Pieron & G. Graham (eds.), *Sport Pedagogy* (pp. 109–116). Champaign, IL: Human Kinetics.

DeBono, E. (1985). *Six Thinking Hats.* Boston: Little, Brown, and Company.

Dewey, J. (1916). *Democracy and Education.* New York: The Macmillan Company.

Dewey, J. (1933). *How We Think.* Boston: D. C. Heath & Company.

Dewey, J. (1963). *Experience and Education.* New York: Collier Books.

Diem, L. (1957). *Who Can?* (H. Steinhous, Trans.). Frankfort am Main, Germany: W. Limpert.

Docheff, D. (1990). The feedback sandwich. *Journal of Physical Education, Recreation, and Dance,* 17–18.

Dougherty, M. (1970). A comparison of the effects of command, task, and individual program styles of teaching in the development of physical fitness and motor skills. *Dissertation Abstracts International, 31,* 5821A–5822A. (University Microfilms No. 71-10, 813)

Ernst, M., & Byra, M. (1998). What does the reciprocal style of teaching hold for junior high school learners? *The Physical Educator, 55*(1), 24–37.

Farson, R. (1997). *Management of the Absurd Paradoxes in Leadership.* York, PA: Touchstone Books.

Festinger, L. (1957). *The Theory of Cognitive Dissonance.* Evanston, IL: Row, Peterson.

Flanders, N. A.(1961). Analyzing teacher behavior. *Educational Leadership, 19,* 173–180.

Flanders, N.A. (1970). *Analyzing Teaching Behavior.* Reading, MA: Addison-Wesley Publishing Co.

Franks, D. (ed.). (1992). The Spectrum of teaching styles: A silver anniversary in physical education [Special feature]. *Journal of Physical Education, Recreation, and Dance, 63*(1), 25–56.

Fronske, H.A. (1996). *Teaching Cues for Sport Skills.* Needham Heights, MA: Allyn and Bacon.

Gage, N. L. (1964). Toward a cognitive theory of teaching. *Teachers College Record, 65,* 408–412.

Gage, N.L. (1972). *Teacher Effectiveness and Teacher Education: The Search for a Scientific Basis.* Palo Alto, CA: Pacific Books, Publishers.

Gagne, R. M. (1965). *The Conditions of Learning.* New York: Holt, Rinehart, & Winston, Inc.

Gagne, R. M., & Brown, L. T. (1961). Some factors in the programming of conceptual learning. *Journal of Experimental Psychology, 62,* 313–321.

Gerney, P. (1980). The effects of Mosston's "practice style" and "reciprocal style" on psychomotor skill acquisition and social development of fifth grade students. *Dissertation Abstracts International, 41,* 154A–155A. (University Microfilms No. 80–14, 535)

Gerney, P., & Dort, A. (1992). The Spectrum applied: Letters from the trenches. *Journal of Physical Education, Recreation, and Dance, 63*(1), 36–39.

Goldberger, M. (1991). Research on teaching physical education: A commentary on Silverman's review. *Research Quarterly for Exercise and Sport, 52*(4), 369–373.

Goldberger, M. (1992). The spectrum of teaching styles: A perspective for research on teaching physical education. *Journal of Physical Education, Recreation, and Dance, 63*(1), 42–46.

Goldberger, M. (1995). Research on the Spectrum of teaching styles. Proceedings AIESEP World Congress, Natanya, Isreal, 429–435.

Goldberger, M., & Gerney, P. (1986). The effects of direct teaching styles on motor skill acquisition of fifth grade children. *Research Quarterly for Exercise and Sport, 57*(3), 215–219.

Goldberger, M., & Gerney, P. (1990). Effects of learner use of practice time on skill acquisition of fifth grade children. *Journal of Teaching in Physical Education, 10*(1), 84–95.

Goldberger, M., Gerney, P., & Chamberlain, J. (1982). The effects of three styles of teaching on the psychomotor performance of fifth grade children. *Research Quarterly for Exercise and Sport, 53*(2), 116–124.

Goldberger, M., Vedelli, J., & Pitts, C. (1995). "The effects of the divergent production style of teaching on children's problem-solving ability." Paper presented at the Southern District Convention AAHPERD, Orlando, FL.

Good, T.L., & Brophy, J.E. (1997). *Looking in Classrooms,* 7th ed. New York: Longman.

Goudas, M., Biddle, S., Fox, K., & Underwood, M. (1995). It ain't what you do, it's the way that you do it! Teaching style affects children's motivation in track and field. *The Sport Psychologist, 9,* 254–264.

Graham, G., Holt/Hale, S.A., & Parker, M. (1998). *Children Moving: A Reflective Approach to Teaching Physical Education* (4th ed.). Mountain View, CA: Mayfield.

Greenspan, M.R. (1992). The Spectrum introduced: A first year teacher's project. *Journal of Physical Education, Recreation, and Dance, 63*(1), 40–41.

Gregory, G. H., and Chapman, C. (2001). *Differentiated Instructional Strategies.* Thousand Oaks, CA: Corwin Press.

Griffey, D. C. (1981). What is the best way to teach? *Journal of Teaching in Physical Education, 1,* 18–24.

Griffey, D.C. (1983). Aptitude X treatment interactions associated with student decision-making. *Journal of Teaching in Physical Education, 3*(2), 15–32.

Guilford, J.P. (1959). Three faces of intellect. *The American Psychologist, 14,* 469–479.

Hayakawa, S.I. (1939). *Language in Thought and Action.* New York: Harcourt, Brace and Co.

Hellison, D.R. (1995) *Goals and Strategies for Teaching Physical Education.* Illinois: Human Kinetics Publishers.

Hetherington, C. W. (1922). *School Program in Physical Education.* New York: World Book Company.

Jacoby, D. (1975). A comparison of the effects of command, reciprocal and individual styles of teaching on the development of selected sport skills. *Dissertation Abstracts International, 36,* 7272A–7273A.

Jenkins, J., & Byra, M. (1997). An exploration of theoretical constructs associated with the Spectrum of Teaching Styles. In F. Carreiro da Costa (ed.), *Research on Teaching and Research on Teacher Education: What Do We Know About the Past and What Kind of Future Do We Expect?* Lisbon, Portugal: AIESEP.

Johnson, P.W. (1982). "A comparison of the effects of two teaching styles on tumbling skill acquisition of college students." Unpublished doctoral dissertation, Virginia Polytechnic Institute and State University, Blacksburg, VA.

Johnson, D., Johnson, R, & Johnson-Hulebec, E. (1994). *Cooperative Learning in the Classroom.* Alexandria, VA: ASCD.

Joyce, B., & Weil, M. (1972). *Models of Teaching.* Englewood Cliffs, NJ: Prentice Hall, Inc.

Joyce, B., Weil, M., & Showers, B. (1992). *Models of Teaching,* 4th ed. Needham Heights, MA: Allyn and Bacon.

Katone, G. (1949). *Organizing and Memorizing.* New York: Columbia University Press.

Kounin, J.S. (1970). *Discipline and Group Management in Classrooms.* New York: Holt, Rinehart and Winston.

Lee, A.M. (1997). Contributions of research on student thinking in physical education. *Journal of Teaching in Physical Education, 16*(3), 262–277.

Lindhard, J. (1939). *The Theory of Gymnastics,* 2nd ed. London: Methuen & Co., Ltd.

Locke, L. (1977). Research on teaching physical education: New hope for a dismal science. *Quest, 28,* 2–16.

Louisell, R. D., & Descamps, J. (1992). *Developing a Teaching Style: Methods for Elementary School Teachers.* Prospect Heights, IL: Waveland Press, Inc.(Ch. 5, p.12)

Mariani, T. (1970). A comparison of the effectiveness of the command method and the task method of teaching the forehand and backhand tennis strokes. *Research Quarterly, 41,* 171–174.

McBride, R.E. (1992). Critical thinking—An overview with implications for physical education. *Journal of Teaching in Physical Education, 11*(2), 112–125.

McIntyre & O'Hair (1996). *The Reflective Roles of the Classroom Teacher.* Belmont, CA: Wadsworth.

Mechling, H. (1990). "Anticipation and automatization in teaching and learning motor skills." In R. Telama (ed.), *Physical Education and Life-Long Physical Activity.* Jyvaskyla, Finland: AIESEP.

Mellor, W. (1992). The Spectrum in Canada and Great Britain. *Journal of Physical Education, Recreation, and Dance, 63*(1), 47.

Metzler, M. (1983). On styles. *Quest, 35,* 145–154.

Metzler, M. W. (1990). *Instructional Supervision for Physical Education.* Champaign, IL: Human Kinetics Books.

Metzler, M. W. (2000). *Instructional Models for Physical Education.* Needham Heights, MA: Allyn & Bacon.

Mosston, M. (1965). *Developmental Movement.* Columbus, OH: Charles E. Merrill Publishing Co.

Mosston, M. (1966a). *Teaching Physical Education.* Columbus, OH: Charles E. Merrill Publishing Co.

Mosston, M. (1966b). "The integration of a style of teaching with the structure of the subject matter." Paper presented to the National College of Physical Education Association of Men, San Diego, CA.

Mosston, M. (1968a). "Problem solving—A problem for physical educators." Paper presented to the annual meeting of the New York City Association of Physical Education Teachers, New York City, NY.

Mosston, M. (1968b). "Physical education—No more." Paper presented to the Forum in Physical Education, New Brunswick, NJ.

Mosston, M. (1969a). Inclusion and exclusion in education—II. In *Innovations in curricular design for physical education*. Symposium sponsored by Department of Educational Psychology; Falk Lab. School; Department of Physical Education; Learning Research & Developmental Center; Department of Special Education & Rehabilitation, Pittsburgh, PA.

Mosston, M. (1969b). "Notes on the Spectrum of teaching styles." Paper presented to the Second and Third General Sessions of the 1969 S.A.P.E.C.W. Conference, Memphis, TN.

Mosston, M. (1969c). "New models in physical education: Developmental movement and the Spectrum of styles." Paper presented to the Differential Education Project, Madison Heights, MI.

Mosston, M. (1981). *Teaching Physical Education*, 2nd ed. Columbus, OH: Merrill.

Mosston, M. (1990). The 3 R's for teachers: Reflect, refine, revitalize. NJASCD *Focus on Education Journal*, 11–17.

Mosston, M. (1992). Tug-o-war no more. *Journal of Physical Education, Recreation, and Dance*, 63, 27–31, 56.

Mosston, M. & Ashworth, S. (1990). *The Spectrum of Teaching Styles*. NY: Longman.

Mosston, M., & Ashworth, S. (1986). *Teaching Physical Education*, 3rd ed. Columbus, OH: Merrill.

Mosston, M., & Ashworth, S. (1994). *Teaching Physical Education*, 4th ed. New York: Macmillan.

Mosston, M., & Mueller, R. (1969, December). "Mission, omission and submission in physical education." Paper presented to the NCPEAM National Conference, Chicago, IL.

Mueller, R., & Mueller, S. (1992). The Spectrum of teaching styles and its role in conscious and deliberate teaching. *Journal of Physical Education, Recreation, and Dance*, 63(1), 48–53.

National Association for Sport and Physical Education, Developer (1995). *Moving into the Future: National Standards for Physical Education*. Boston: WCB MCGraw-Hill.

Nissen, H. (1892). *A B C of the Swedish System of Educational Gymnastics*. New York: Educational Publishing Company.

Nixon, J.E., & Locke, L.F. (1973). "Research on teaching physical education." In R.M.W. Travers (ed.), *Second Handbook of Research on Teaching* (1210–1242). Chicago: Rand McNally and Company.

Ornstein, A.C. (1988). Questioning: The essence of good teaching. *NASSP Bulletin*, 72 (505), 72–78.

Oxman, W.G., & Michelli, N.M. (1979). *The Center on Teaching: A Title IV-C Project*. Glen Ridge, NJ: Gemini Educational Services, Inc.

Oxman, W.G., & Michelli, N.M. (1979). "Analysis of student achievement data: A research report." For Center on Teaching, unpublished paper, Trenton, NJ.

Pangrazi, R.P. (1998). *Dynamic Physical Education for Elementary School Children*. Boston: Allyn & Bacon.

Pichert, J. W., Anderson, R. C., Armbruster, B. V., Surber, J. R., & Shirley, L. L. (1976). *Final Report: An Evaluation of the Spectrum of Teaching Styles*. Urbana, IL: Laboratory for Cognitive Studies in Education.

Polvi, S., & Telama, R. (2000). The use of cooperative learning as a social enhancer in physical education. *Scandinavian Journal of Educational Research*, 44(1), 105–115.

Polya, G. (1957). *How to Solve It*. Garden City, NY: Doubleday & Company, Inc.

Random House Dictionary of the English Language, Unabridged, 2nd ed. (1987). New York: Random House.

Rink, J. E. (1993). *Teaching Physical Education for Learning*, 2nd ed. St. Louis, MO.

Safire, W. (1979, May 13). On language. *The Sunday New York Times Magazine*, Section 6, pp. 9–10.

Salter, W.B., & Graham, G. (1985). The effect of three disparate instructional approaches on skill attempts and student learning in an experimental teaching unit. *Journal of Teaching in Physical Education, 4*(3), 212–218.

Siedentop, D. (1991). *Developing Teaching Skills in Physical Education,* 3rd ed. Palo Alto, CA: Mayfield Publishing Co.

Siedentop, D. (1983). *Developing Teaching Skills in Physical Education,* 2nd ed. Palo Alto, CA: Mayfield Publishing Co.

Simri, U. (ed.). (1995). *Muska: A Biography of Dr. Muska Mosston.* Tel Aviv, Israel: The Friends of Muska Mosston.

Skinner, B.F. (1954). The science of learning and the art of teaching. *Harvard Educational Review, 24,* 86–97.

Smith, F. (1990). *To Think.* New York: Teachers College Press.

Taba, H., & Elzey, F.F. (1964). Teaching strategies and thought processes. *Teachers College Record, 65,* 524–534.

Telama, R., et al. (eds.). (1983). *Research in School Physical Education.* Jyraskyla, Finland: The Foundation for Promotion of Physical Culture and Health.

Telama, R. (1992). The Spectrum in Finland. *Journal of Physical Education, Recreation, and Dance, 63*(1), 54–56.

Thulin, J.G. (1947). *Gymnastic Handbook.* Lund, Sweden: Sydsvenska Gymnastick Institutet.

Veciana-Suarez, A. (1989, November 26). Undivided attention is a dying art. *The Palm Beach Post,* pp. F1, F13.

Vickers, J. N. (1990). *Instructional Design for Teaching Physical Activities.* Champaign, IL: Human Kinetics Books.

Virgilio, S. (1979). The effects of direct and reciprocal teaching strategies on the cognitive, affective, and psychomotor behavior of fifth grade pupils in beginning archery. *Dissertation Abstracts International, 40,* 5367A. (University Microfilms No. 80–08, 631)

Weston, A. (1962). *The Making of American Physical Education.* New York: Appleton-Century.

Wilen, W., Ishler, M., Hutchison, J., & Kindsvatter, R. (2000). *Dynamics of Effective Teaching,* 4th ed. New York: Longman.

Willis, S. (ed.). (2000, Winter). Differentiating instruction. *Curriculum Update,* 1–3.

Yerg, B. J. (1981). The impact of selected presage and process behaviors on the refinement of a motor skill. *Journal of Teaching in Physical Education, I,* 38–46.

Yerg, B. J. (1981). Reflections on the use of the RTE model in physical education. *Research Quarterly for Exercise and Sport, 52,* 38–47.

INDEX

Note: A page number followed by *f* indicates a figure (e.g., 338*f*) , by *t* indicates a table (e.g., 30*t*), and by n (e.g., 31n) indicates a footnote.